THE UNITED STATES AND

THE MAKING OF MODERN

GREECE

THE UNITED STATES AND THE MAKING OF MODERN Greece

HISTORY AND POWER, 1950–1974

JAMES EDWARD MILLER

THE UNIVERSITY OF NORTH CAROLINA PRESS   CHAPEL HILL

© 2009 The University of North Carolina Press
All rights reserved
Set in Scala and Scala Sans
by Tseng Information Systems, Inc.
Manufactured in the United States of America

The paper in this book meets the guidelines for permanence and durability of the Committee on Production Guidelines for Book Longevity of the Council on Library Resources.

The University of North Carolina Press has been a member of the Green Press Initiative since 2003.

Library of Congress Cataloging-in-Publication Data
Miller, James Edward.
The United States and the making of modern Greece : history and power, 1950–1974 / James Edward Miller.
p. cm.
Includes bibliographical references and index.
ISBN 978-0-8078-3247-9 (cloth : alk. paper)
1. United States—Foreign relations—Greece. 2. Greece—Foreign relations—United States. 3. Greece—Politics and government—1935–1967. 4. Greece—Politics and government—1967–1974. 5. Greece—Foreign relations—Cyprus. 6. Cyprus—Foreign relations—Greece. I. Title.
E183.8.G8M55 2009
327.73049509'04—dc22

2008031981

13 12 11 10 09   5 4 3 2 1

THIS BOOK WAS DIGITALLY PRINTED.

CONTENTS

Preface *vii*

Abbreviations in the Text *xv*

Introduction: Manifest Destiny Meets the Megali Idea 1

1 The Greek Tar Baby, 1950–1953 23
2 No Report from Cyprus Is Ever Cheerful, 1950–1959 44
3 The Right, 1953–1963 66
4 Black Mak: Cyprus, 1960–1964 84
5 Coup d'État, 1964–1967 111
6 The Andreas Version, 1967–1973 136
7 Dancing with the Dictators, 1969–1974 157
8 A Perfect Storm: Cyprus, 1967–1974 176

Epilogue: The Andreas Era 201

Notes 213

Bibliography 281

Index 295

PREFACE

> Sine ira et studio.
> — Tacitus, *Annals*, 1.1

At the end of World War II the United States emerged as the hegemonic power in Western Europe and the Mediterranean basin. This ironic, although not entirely unpredicted, outcome to the European civil war of 1914–45 was an impressive display of the extent and diversity of the sources of American power. Never before had one society enjoyed such an overwhelming dominance in so many key areas of human endeavor. The United States, by virtue of its technology, its industrial base, its cultural creativity, its free institutions, and its capacity to absorb ideas, manpower, and output from other societies, spent the next half century expanding its role as the central player in international affairs. Because of the seamless integration of its various types of power—from the "hard" power of military force symbolized by nuclear bombs to the "soft" power of its culture—into a mutually supporting structure, the United States built upon success while shaking off the effects of bad policy decisions and negative internal and external events.

In securing a predominant role in international affairs, the United States has followed a political strategy laid out in Lampedusa's novel *Il Gattopardo* (*The Leopard*, 1958): "In order for things to remain the same they have to change." American hegemony, the critical objective, has been promoted by a conscious effort to foster change in other societies. In the immediate aftermath of World War II, the United States utilized such programs as the Truman Doctrine and the Marshall Plan, such organizations as the North Atlantic Treaty Organization (NATO), the General Agreement on Tariffs and Trade (GATT), and the World Bank and International Monetary Fund (IMF) to foster economic, military, and political integration and to raise standards of living among its allies. Modernization was a key element in the U.S. strategy to defend itself against the threat posed by its great power rival, the Soviet Union, and allied national communist parties.[1] To a large extent this strategy worked. The recovery of Europe's economy strengthened America's by creating a pole of trade, investment, and technological exchange. The integration process, a creative and remarkable European response to both addressing critical internal problems and redressing the imbalance of power between Europe and the United States, paid major benefits on both sides of the Atlantic. By securing peace at home and expanding its markets, "Europe" has reduced the defense burden on the United States while offering new opportunities to U.S. corporations. The complex and frequently unsuccessful way in which Europe makes political and security decisions reinforces Washington's dominant role in the realm of hard power and also offers Washington a quarrelsome but nevertheless useful junior partner.

The European response to American hegemony on the political level, a mix of cooperation and confrontation, has been relatively painless for both sides because so many of the concepts exported from the United States were simply American versions of ideas conceived in Europe. The process of "Americanization," the adaptation of political, social, and economic models that appeared in modern form in the United States, is really part of the larger process of modernization, or globalization, in which the United States plays a very significant role, albeit frequently that of the guinea pig of change. On the governmental, business, and individual level, Europeans have shown themselves quite capable of drawing specific lessons from the U.S. experience and applying them to their own societies in ways that permit them to preserve what is specifically Italian or Spanish or French or Portuguese about their cultures. American software coexists quite happily with European or Asian hardware; even such an execrated symbol of the United States as McDonalds has easily integrated into the framework of other societies due to a willingness on the part of both American exporters and European importers to modify the product to fit the circumstances.

European-American accommodation is not simply a state-to-state or industry-to-industry process. Were the United States only a major military power like ancient Rome or solely an economic giant, it might in fact have been absorbed by Europe's attractive culture and drawn to its clever postwar social compromise. Much nineteenth- and early-twentieth-century American literature testifies to the drawing power of that culture. However, the United States by the twentieth century was already on its way to establishing a major position in almost every area of Western cultural production: from literature, music, and theater on the high cultural plane to popular music, such as ragtime, swing, and later rock and roll and its multiple offspring, on the mass cultural plane. The American motion picture industry managed to command a dominant place in both high and mass culture. Throughout the twentieth century, the United States outpaced European cultural production by combining creativity in the arts with business acumen.[2]

The meeting between hegemonic America and unifying Europe is also an encounter with individual citizens. The basic American assumption has been that its production will be tested and modified in a marketplace dominated by individual consumers. American businesses, of course, like to place a thumb on the scale to encourage adoption of their products. Nevertheless, the consumer, in this case the individual European citizen, plays a critical role in determining what should be adopted from the American model. Individual citizen's economic and political choices have frequently exasperated European governments and elites, particularly French defenders of "cultural exceptionalism." While preserving the essence of their national identity, individual Europeans have largely embraced the major products of American innovation even as they have modified them to meet their special needs.[3] In the process, Europeans have effected subtle but important changes on American business and culture, in part by exporting modified American models back to the United States.

A central belief of U.S. elites is that their nation constitutes something of a universal social model, producing ideas, goods, and services that can be absorbed easily and profitably by other cultures. On the whole, U.S elites have found confirmation of this view in American experiences of the past 250 years. Still, the universality of the American experience is frequently called into question by both American and foreign critics. Europe, which constituted the most impressive success for the exportability of American models, was the United States' mother society. The validity of the latest edition of the American model of democracy, capitalism, multiethnicity, and cultural pluralism is continually tested. A particularly crucial challenge is now under way in the Middle East. In declaring a "war on terrorism" and invading first Afghanistan and then Iraq, U.S. president George W. Bush abandoned traditional and largely pacific methods of exporting American ideas, placing an unusually heavy reliance on military force. Whether force can promote democratic development is clearly an open question. Even the pugnacious Bush administration began backing away from its strategy.[4]

Among the many examples of U.S. utilization of its power to secure critical interests was post–civil war Greece, 1950–74. In choosing to intervene in a bloody civil conflict in order to defeat the insurrection, American officials sought, in the first place, to check the spread of Soviet influence and break the power of a national communist movement. They were simultaneously undertaking to modernize a nation that, although geographically a part of Europe, and led by a small, westernized elite, was, in the unflattering analysis of a French diplomat, a "Balkan society" that frequently acted more like an

Ottoman than a European polity. American support for Greece's government involved large-scale military aid, major investments of capital, and intermittent efforts to reform the political system. Modernizing the Greek army was the essential first step in defeating the insurgency but from the beginning was closely linked with economic assistance programs aimed at fostering levels of prosperity and consumption that would build social stability and weaken the grassroots appeal of communism. A modern, productive agricultural sector and improved communications systems, in turn, would allow Greece to slowly integrate into an expanding international economic system. Political reforms, which U.S. officials deferred until the insurrection was crushed in 1949–50 and then viewed largely as an exercise in electoral system management, before shelving them in 1953, should have guaranteed Greeks a controlling voice in decision making, completing the stabilization process and ensuring that change would continue along lines favorable to U.S. interests.

This book looks at the Greek response to American power. Poor, backward, but proud of their cultural traditions and possessing very sturdy institutions, including the family, a national identity built in resistance to foreign intervention, the Orthodox Church, and a firmly rooted, pervasive patronage political system, Greeks engaged in the same analysis of the benefits and costs of the American model as other peoples, adopting some things and rejecting others. Ultimately in the postdictatorship era, Greece arrived at a politically satisfactory solution: importing modernization through European institutions. Aspects of this process have been studied by others, most notably in William McNeill's work on the social impact of Greek modernization and in the contributions of a number of economists on America's role in restructuring Greece's economy.[5] This book looks at another critical element: Greece's incomplete political reconstruction. Between 1950 and 1974, Greece failed to create a stable democracy. This failure was largely the work of Greece's politicians, military, and monarchy, but the United States cannot escape some burden of responsibility for what went wrong in Greece, particularly because of its post–April 1967 acceptance of and eventual support for the military junta.

The United States and the Making of Modern Greece focuses on the methods by which American and Greek officials cooperated and struggled over the political future of Greece. It attempts, in the first place, to get the facts right: what happened, when it happened, and why it happened through a careful reading of available primary source material. Simultaneously it reconstructs how Greeks, in particular the political center-left and their eventual leader,

Andreas Papandreou, wrote Greece's contemporary history not only to ensure their rise to power, but also in defense of Greek culture against the threats posed by American power.

Greek resistance to American dominance, of course, was not simply cultural or intellectual. Greek foreign policy from 1954 onward frequently undermined U.S. aims, above all in its approach to the issue of *enosis* (union) with Cyprus. On other issues, too, Greek officials had a tendency to upset the presumed model in which the patron commands and the client obeys. This was particularly the case during the junta years, 1967–74, when Greece's military rulers ignored or outright rejected Washington's advice. The pattern emerged even as the civil war drew to an end and, ironically, the United States engineered electoral reforms that guaranteed a stable governing majority and helped propel Greece's leaders to a more independent stand.

The United States and the Making of Modern Greece is based largely on printed or manuscript archival sources: Greek, American, British, and French. The greater openness of Western European and U.S. archives and the limited availability of Greek sources give the book something of a bias toward the "American" viewpoint. To reduce this imbalance, U.S. sources have been used very carefully in the reconstruction and interpretation of frequently disputed events. Available Greek documents, memoirs, and public statements as well as Greek historical studies have been woven into the book's analysis. To provide further corrective balance, the book utilizes the documentation of two "neutral" observers: the British, whose close relationship with both states across decades created an unusual understanding of Greece and the United States, and the French, who can scarcely be accused of a pro-American bias or, for that matter, of much sympathy for postwar Greece.

Since this book is also about the writing and political exploitation of history, particularly the interpretation of Greece's recent past created by Andreas Papandreou and his allies, I have examined his memoirs and those of his associates with care. My intention has been to compare this recounting of events with the public record, first to determine the reliability of these works as history and second to demonstrate how these books were fitted into the political project by which Andreas came to dominate Greek politics.

The United States and the Making of Modern Greece is a response to curiosity. In the winter of 1965, I visited Greece for the first time. While public outrage at the political defenestration of George Papandreou had cooled, I had the opportunity to hear about those events from my hosts. On the morning of April 22, 1967, I turned to my Greek roommate, Christos Georgiou, for an initial explanation of the coup in Athens. Thereafter I read memoirs of participants, especially the Papandreous, for further enlightenment. In 1981, I had the serendipitous opportunity to be the first American historian to review U.S. State Department files and to write a paper discussing the events of 1964–67. Ten years later, as an editor of the series *Foreign Relations of the United States*, I returned to the subject, compiling documentation from a wide variety of U.S. sources into a long and, I believe, largely comprehensive look at the events of 1964–68. I spent too much of the next decade trying to extract the resulting volume from the clutches of the Central Intelligence Agency, the masters of a sophisticated and ongoing program of historical disinformation. With the release of this volume and the availability of Nixon-era records, I decided it was time to exploit my own experiences, including more than a decade of teaching modern Greece and Cyprus, and to see what conclusions I could draw.

In writing this book, I have relied on the advice of many scholars, including a number of Greeks and Greek Americans. None of them obviously bears any responsibility for my conclusions, but I would like to thank all of them for their comments. Special thanks are due also to the University of North Carolina Press, which took the time to procure two of the best possible readers for the manuscript, John Iatrides and S. Victor Papacosma. I benefited greatly from the care they lavished on the text.

Reference to Tacitus's claim to write history without prejudices or hidden agendas is intended to be ironic, but his statement should represent the ultimate if unreachable objective of historians. Herodotus's approach to the writing of history, combining criticism with recognition of the unique qualities of all the involved parties, has guided my approach to this and my other works.[6] I hope the book's readers will find it critical of but fair to all those involved: Greek, Cypriot, Turkish, British, and American.

Finally, I would like to briefly address the issues of bibliography and transliteration. All bibliographies are selective. In addition to listing all the manuscript collections, printed sources, and books cited in *The United States and the Making of Modern Greece*, I have added a small number of other titles that have influenced my thinking while strictly limiting books dealing with the broader contours of U.S. foreign policy, modernization theory, modern Turkish history, and many aspects of Greek and Cypriot political history. Transliteration is the hair shirt of anyone attempting to pass from one alphabet to another. No agreed upon single system of transliterating from Greek to English exists. Transliterations in this book generally follow the Library of Congress system, although I have tried to use the most common spelling of well-known Greek names. Elina Karmokolias of the Greek language staff,

Foreign Service Institute, reviewed and corrected my efforts. I am grateful for her kindness and suggestions. Also riding to my rescue in the last stages of the editorial preparation process were two talented and supportive friends, Professor Eric Terzuolo and Fynnette Eaton, who offered to read the final manuscript for both content and grammar.

I would like to dedicate this book to my friends and colleagues Elina, Elene, Achilleas, Maria, and Sofia, who opened up the Greek world to me in a very personal way, and to Alexis Papahelas, whose interest in the subject has never waned over the nearly two decades of our friendship.

ABBREVIATIONS IN THE TEXT

AKEL
: Progressive Party of the Working People (Cyprus)

ASPIDA
: (Shield) Officers, Defend the Fatherland, Ideals, Democracy, [and] Meritocracy

CIA
: Central Intelligence Agency (United States)

EAM
: National Liberation Front (Greece)

ECA
: Economic Cooperation Administration (Marshall Plan)

EDA
: United Democratic Left (Greece)

EEC/EC
: European Economic Community/European Community

EK
: Center Union Party (Greece)

ELAS
: National Popular Liberation Army (Greece)

EOKA
: National Organization of Cypriot Fighters

ERE
: National Radical Union (Greece)

ERP
: European Recovery Program (Marshall Plan)

EU
: European Union

GAF
: Greek Armed Forces

GATT
: General Agreement on Tariffs and Trade

GSEE
: General Confederation of Greek Workers

IDEA
: Sacred Band of Greek Officers

IMF
: International Monetary Fund

INR
: Bureau of Intelligence and Research, Department of State

JCS
: Joint Chiefs of Staff (United States)

KKE
: Communist Party of Greece

KKK
: Communist Party of Cyprus

KYP
: Central Intelligence Agency (Greece)

NATO
: North Atlantic Treaty Organization

ND
: New Democracy Party (Greece)

NIE
: National Intelligence Estimate

NSAM
: National Security Action Memorandum

NSC
: National Security Council (United States)

NSDM
: National Security Decision Memorandum

PAK
: Pan Hellenic Liberation Movement

PASOK
: Pan Hellenic Socialist Party

SOFA
: States of Forces Agreement

UNFICYP
: United Nations Force in Cyprus

THE UNITED STATES AND

THE MAKING OF MODERN

GREECE

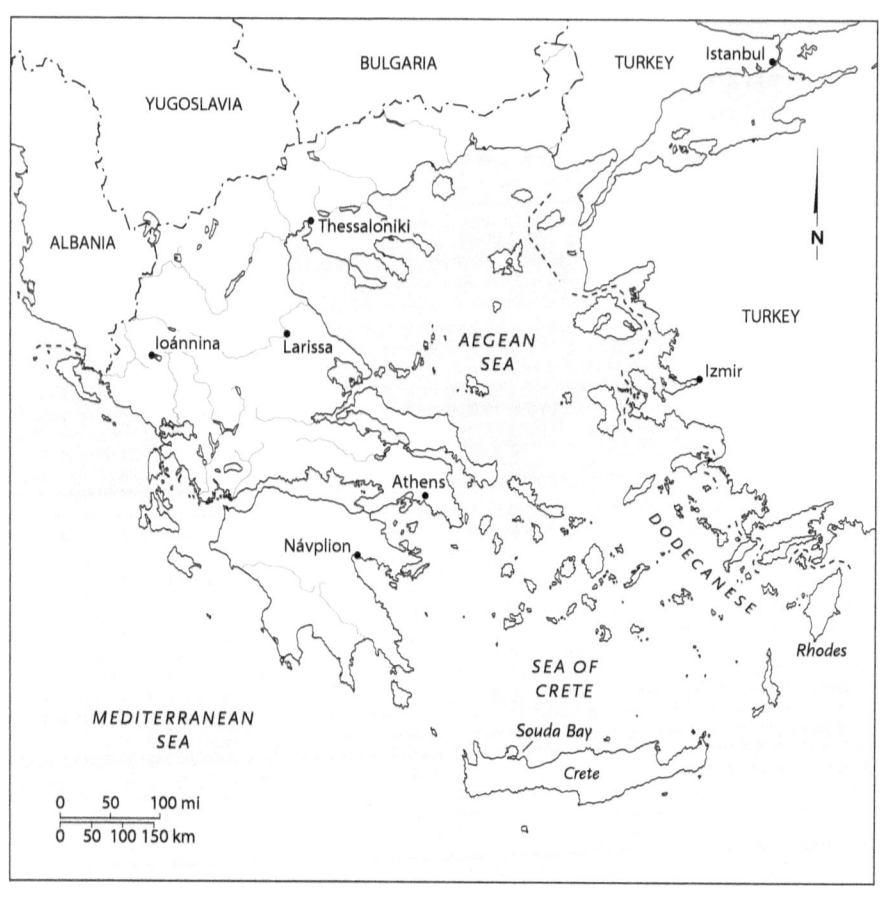

GREECE, 1950–74

INTRODUCTION

MANIFEST DESTINY MEETS THE MEGALI IDEA

> The very existence of the Greek state is today threatened by the terrorist activities of several thousand armed men, led by communists. . . . [T]he Greek government is unable to cope with the situation. The Greek army is small and poorly equipped. It needs supplies and equipment if it is to restore the authority of the government. . . . Greece must have assistance if it is to become a self-supporting and self respecting democracy.
> — Harry Truman, 1947

During the nineteenth century the United States and the kingdom of Greece were two models of expansionist nationalism. Both possessed supercharged ideologies that fueled and justified this expansion. Each enjoyed a good deal of nostalgic support from European public opinion even though their objectives frequently clashed with the interests of Europe's great powers. Each, moreover, achieved much of its expansionist agenda. The United States moved west to become a continental state. In what was in many ways a more surprising performance, Greece moved slowly but inexorably west to the Ionian Islands, north into Thessaly, Epirus, Macedonia, and Thrace, southward to Crete, east into the Aegean, and briefly back onto Anatolian soil.

TWO MANIFEST DESTINIES

American expansion enjoyed many advantages denied to Greece, but none was more important than distance. While, at various times, individual European powers looked with concern at the growth of the United States, their primary interests were closer at hand, and included a focus on the dramatic unraveling of the Ottoman Empire in the Balkans. American expansion was an intermittent worry. Moreover, U.S. growth was favored by intra-European power politics. Napoleon I sold the vast Louisiana territory to the emerging United States in 1803 when he concluded that maintaining a French position in the New World was not feasible. The British looked the other way as U.S. expansionists launched a war against a weak Mexican republic and seized another enormous chunk of the North American continent.

After 1850 the power of the United States was such that intervention to halt its growth only became possible during the first years of the American Civil War. The idea of permanently dismembering the United States appealed to many Frenchmen, particularly to Napoleon III, but Britain prudently checked the calculations and the resentments of a declining power toward a rising one.[1] Europe lost its last chance to significantly affect the course of American expansion. In 1867, the Russian Empire sold its Alaska territory to the United States, thus removing another great power from the North American continent. In the latter part of the nineteenth century the United States forced its way into Samoa, acquired Hawaii, and then rounded out its territorial expansion by roundly thrashing Spain and seizing its remaining empire.

"Manifest Destiny," the belief that the United States had the right, and indeed the duty, to take control of the North American continent, fueled American expansion. Manifest Destiny had its counterpart in the realm of foreign policy in the idea of the special "mission" of the United States, the model society, to spread democracy and free enterprise to a world that, by American lights, was singularly lacking in both and, in the process, to increase U.S. wealth and power. Throughout the nineteenth century, private citizens largely played the role of missionaries for the "gospel" of democracy and capitalism. Individual American officials encouraged these efforts, but the U.S. government prudently limited its involvement in nation building abroad. While perfectly willing to enter into short-term arrangements with foreign states, and to use force when necessary, the United States avoided long-term "entangling alliances" and quietly profited from informal arrangements with the United Kingdom that frequently put the muscle of the British fleet and British capital behind U.S. market-opening initiatives. In 1917, when tensions with Germany led to war, Woodrow Wilson melded traditional American concepts of foreign policy into a potent and intellectually coherent concoction and by adding the idea of the League of Nations, replaced traditional unilateralism with a new form of America-centric internationalism. The U.S. government, aided by American business and cultural elites, began to aggressively and, to some degree successfully, remodel the world to its liking, a process that continues.[2]

While they possessed an equally potent and expansive view of their national future, Greek leaders were hemmed in not just by their limited numbers, weak economy, and the difficult geography of the Balkans, but also by the realities of Europe's complex balance of power. In 1868 the U.S. representative in Greece commented admiringly: "This people can neither be crushed by their neighbor . . . nor set aside by the great powers of Europe by whom Greece is regarded as little more than a political nuisance."³ The Modern Greek state was born in a successful challenge (1821–33) to that balance of power. In one of the first modern examples of domestic public opinion influencing foreign policy formulation, public support for the Greek revolt in Britain, France, and to a lesser extent, the German states restrained the efforts of the more conservative powers to again impose Ottoman rule and then nudged the major powers into accord on an intervention to end the conflict and finally to create a Greek national state over the heated protests of the unwilling but impotent government of Sultan Mehmet II.⁴

Great-power support for Greece and its territorial ambitions had sharp limits. Stability in the Balkans was essential if the powers were to peacefully arrange the "Eastern Question," diplomatic shorthand for the careful management of the decline of the Ottoman Empire. The major powers were keenly aware that the ambitions of the tiny Greek state created a potential for disrupting that stability. The "Megali Idea" (Great Idea), a term coined in 1844 by Ioannis Kolettis but implicit in the dreams of Greek nationalists since the late eighteenth century, called for integrating all "Hellenes" (a suitably elastic term referring to those who were normally Greek speakers, Orthodox in faith, and inhabited territory once ruled by ancient Greeks or medieval Byzantines) into a single national state.⁵ In 1866, the U.S representative in Constantinople analyzed both their strategy and problems: "The Greeks cherish the hope of being able by force of arms, or political complications, to acquire the Turkish provinces of Albania and Thessaly, the majority of the populations of which profess the Greek religion and speak the Greek language. Whenever war occurs between the great states of Europe this ambition develops itself with an intensity that renders it almost impossible for the [Greek] government to preserve peace between the two countries. . . . [T]he condition of the empire is one calculated to awaken the keenest solicitude among all those . . . who apprehend that the fall of the Ottoman empire will be the prelude to one of the greatest and most dangerous wars in European history."⁶

Conflict in the Balkans could not be a local matter. The interests of three great powers were immediately in play. Both Austria and Russia had important territorial interests in the region. The United Kingdom, as the dominant naval power in the Mediterranean, would inevitably be involved in any Balkan conflict. France, too, had a major interest in the management of the Ottoman state. Greek efforts to create "disorder" in the Balkans provoked the French minister in Athens to complain that "the Great Idea is nothing more than the need for turbulence erected into a system." Sadly, the Count de Gobineau predicted, Ottoman corruption would hand its empire to the Greeks.[7]

Although the notion of inevitable Ottoman decline had been the guiding principle of European diplomacy since the eighteenth century, the "Turks" refused to accept their fate and repeatedly tried to revitalize their state through wide-ranging reform programs. As the nineteenth century progressed, the Ottomans played their diplomatic cards with considerable skill, getting a voice in decisions the Europeans might have preferred to make for them and resisting, frequently with force, and often with surprising effect, efforts by subject peoples or neighbors to dismember their state.[8]

As a result, Greek efforts to expand met with powerful resistance. Throughout the nineteenth century, Greece grew when and as the great powers saw fit. Greek efforts to move against the Ottoman state were smothered by diplomatic warnings, occasional territorial concessions, and even blockades and seizure of the port of Piraeus. Ottoman military power, reinforced by great-power pressures, forced the Greek state to back down on a number of occasions between 1854 and 1878. Greece's attempt to acquire Crete by force led to a humiliating military defeat in 1897. Nevertheless, the kingdom grew, if slowly. The British ceded the Ionian Islands (1864). The settlement of the Russo-Turkish war of 1877–78 worked out by the Congress of Berlin (1878) set the stage for an 1881 handover of Thessaly to Greece as part of the effort to limit Russian influence in the Balkans. Great-power intervention saved Greece from the worst consequences of its 1897 defeat and, by placing a semiautonomous Crete under the administration of a Greek prince, laid the groundwork for the Hellenic kingdom eventually to absorb the island.[9]

Early in the twentieth century, Greece finally achieved a key national objective without the humiliation of foreign intervention. The 1909 Goudi military revolt opened the way for Eleftherios Venizelos, a nationalist of enormous talent and energy, to reform the military and civil administration, enter into a series of deals with Balkan rivals, and in the chaotic situation created by the Italian war on the Ottoman Empire (1911–12), lead Greece into successful wars first against the Ottomans and then, in a new coalition including the Turks, against traditional rival Bulgaria (1912–13). The subsequent peace agreements left Greece in control of large parts of Epirus and Macedonia.

The outbreak of a war in Europe in August 1914 opened the door to further growth. However, Greek leaders were unable to agree on a strategy to achieve their objectives. These divisions provoked a political crisis, polarized the nation, and prompted great-power intervention. Venizelos, backed by the

Entente Powers, emerged victorious from the internal struggle and brought Greece quite close to the fulfillment of the maximum objectives of the Megali Idea: the incorporation of Thrace, Constantinople, and the Asia Minor coast, into a "Greece of two continents and five seas." Beginning in 1919, the Greek military began to occupy parts of western Anatolia. By 1920 Greek forces were marching into the interior of Asia Minor while Greek civil administration took hold of the costal areas. However, the rise of Turkish nationalism, waning Allied support, and the physical and economic exhaustion of the Greek nation after a decade of warfare led to a massive military defeat, the "Asia Minor catastrophe," in 1922. The Treaty of Lausanne (1923), with its forced exchanges of population and territorial surrenders, put an end to dreams of a great-power Greece, although not to all irredentism. Greeks continued to nurture hopes of incorporating the Italian-held Dodecanese Islands and the British colony of Cyprus into their state.[10]

A FRACTURED RULING CLASS

The defeat of 1922, while partially due to a weak economy and foreign "betrayal," was equally a product of divisions among Greece's ruling elite. By the early twentieth century, three basically antagonistic forces existed within the Greek political firmament: the political class, the monarch, and the military. The seeds of this split ran back to the Greek war of independence. The political class largely emerged from landowners (the primates), Greek-Ottoman refugee elites, and some local military chiefs and attempted to impose its control over another elite, the *kapetanios*, whose existing social and political role was reinforced by their leadership in the armed struggle against the Ottomans. The war for independence was frequently a civil war between rival social and military groups.[11] The European powers, anxious to restrain political turbulence, imposed the teenage Otto [Othon] of Bavaria as king of Greece to further both a centralization of power and social peace (1833). Over the next decades, the populations of the mountain regions decreased, and, thus, the pool of potential recruits for outlaw and guerrilla bands declined while the kapetanios successfully integrated into the political class. Nevertheless, banditry, particularly the odious practice of kidnapping for ransom, remained an accepted part of political maneuvering, and the bands operating along the frontier with the Ottoman Empire formed the spearhead of Greek expansionism. In a political system characterized by patronage and an emphasis on local issues, brigands played a powerful role. In 1870, the U.S. minister to Greece observed that the brigands "are known, not only to the government, in name and person, but mingle ... freely with the people of the villages. . . . The candidate for election to the chamber of deputies finds it in his interest to keep on good terms with one who can with such facility do him good or do him injury. He knows that if he denounced the outlaw without ability to crush him, he, his family, or his property will at some time or the other pay the penalty. . . . He finds that he has nothing to gain and everything to lose . . . and if he contents himself with simple neutrality, his political opponent . . . will secure the brigand's services and win the day."[12]

Greece's first "president," Ioannis Kapodistrias, and the kingdom's subsequent Bavarian rulers recognized that, as independent sources of military power, the kapetanios represented a threat to social stability. They began creating a national army, amalgamating former kapetanios and their soldiers into the new organization. However, the professional army suffered for decades from a lack of popular support and of professional training. In times of crisis, desertions by patriotic officers and men to irregular bands were frequent and widely approved. Resentment against the continuing presence of foreign officers and the desire to improve their own career possibilities combined with rejection at the autocratic rule of King Othon, prompted Greek officers to revolt and force the king to accept a constitution in 1843. Later, after Othon had proved incapable of abandoning his autocratic habits or of achieving Greek expansionist ambitions, the army played a central role in his ouster (1862). While these coups enjoyed support from civilian elites, and the Greek officer corps immediately turned power over to civilian political leaders, they created a dangerous precedent for further military intervention. Succeeding monarchs learned the important lesson that retaining a primary influence over military affairs was critical to their survival. Royal efforts to co-opt the military led to repeated conflicts with civilian authorities and with junior officers.[13]

Surveying the scene shortly after the installation of King George I (1864), the French representative in Athens commented that the division of powers between monarchy and parliament made their conflicts inevitable and frequently high-stakes games. The loser faced "the loss of all its prerogatives." Moreover, a weak party system invited royal intervention: "There are no political parties in Greece. Only personal groupings exist. In reality, few people are concerned whether King George or King Otho[n] reigns; still less if the government is constitutional or outside the rules; but everyone belongs to some group that rallies around a more or less influential figure, which is attached to the fortunes of the chief, and as issues of friendship, relationship, interests are the only ones that determine allegiance, they also decide desertions."[14]

Since parliamentary majorities were formed over matters of interest, not principles, the monarch found himself buying some deputies and distributing rewards to others. In 1909, the British representative in Athens reported on the cynical attitude of the king toward the "price" of his rule: "I was surprised to find that His Majesty made light both of the employment of jobbery in the administration and of influence in the courts of law." King George explained that "nothing could be obtained without influence" because corruption was "too deeply ingrained in the Greek character."[15]

Although nineteenth-century Greek politics were no more backward or corrupt than those of many other European societies, and Greece, as a result of the 1843 revolution, was the first European nation with universal male suffrage, parliament was plagued by the effects of patronage politics, weak party structures, and a badly managed education system. While spending little on primary education, successive governments encouraged middle-class Greeks to attend university, producing "doctors and lawyers in sufficient numbers for more than ten times the population of Greece. . . . Many [graduates] unable to obtain employment in their profession . . . take up politics and endeavor to obtain employment in the public sector . . . and constitute an element of mischief . . . by clamoring for frequent ministerial change, in the hope of securing subordinate official positions."[16] The parties were little more than floating coalitions of local interests captained by a few skilled deal makers. Initially referred to as the English, French, and Russian parties, by midcentury they were the "party" of Kolettis, Voulgaris, or Koumoundouros and later of Trikoupis and Deliyiannis, an indication of the dominating influence a few politicians and of the lack of a set of national policy objectives, save territorial expansion. The parliamentary parties proved quite capable of pushing forward laws that expanded patronage, including public works bills, and also increased the national debt, pushing Greece deeper into a humiliating dependency on foreign banks and governments. Further, parliament and the parties, along with the royal family, took the blame for the defeat of 1897.[17]

Parliament's relationship with the monarchy was murky. From 1843 until 1973, Greece labored under a variety of constitutions that left the monarchy largely outside of firm legal restraints. Efforts to restrain royal prerogatives invariably provoked the king to join political maneuvers, negating his essential constitutional role as *supra partes*, and placed him in the dangerous position of leader of a parliamentary faction. The deputies, who were legally responsible for their actions, were also expected to protect the monarchy from the costs of its errors. Tensions between king and politicians, particularly over foreign affairs, were frequent. At times, the king restrained political leaders from foreign adventures. Other times, the king, acting after minimal or no consultations with his ministers, pushed Greece toward dangerous foreign entanglements.[18]

The monarchy's privileged relationship with the military and with foreign powers, its deep involvement in the operation of the parliamentary system, and its frequent efforts to act with one foot outside the constitutional system exacerbated the tensions inherent in Greek politics. In 1909 a group of junior military officers revolted against both the king and the political elites, calling Eleftherios Venizelos from Crete to advise them on the reform of the state. The officers wanted to put an end to the corruption, mismanagement, and lack of national purpose that characterized the Greek constitutional system. They demanded a Greek military that was professionally capable of achieving major territorial expansion by force. Venizelos, whose objectives included advancing the Megali Idea and his own career, skillfully achieved a rapprochement with the monarchy and the restoration of parliament and its members to a central role in Greek public life. He built a national political movement, the Liberals, with a program of reform and territorial expansion. However, the Liberal Party was largely a coalition of local notables that relied on Venizelos's extraordinary charisma and political skill to achieve its objectives.[19]

Venizelos, the greatest Greek political leader of his era, left a very mixed legacy. Greece seemed incapable of political success without him but was equally burdened by the outsized programs he created, particularly in the realm of foreign affairs, and by the legacy of his management of public policy when in office. "Venizelos was Greece's greatest asset and, in the long run, its greatest liability. Without him Greece never would have won what it did ... without him it would never have tried to swallow so much."[20]

In 1915–16, Venizelos and King Constantine I provoked a crisis going to the heart of Greece's national interests and its constitutional system. In dismissing Venizelos twice, ignoring the prime minister's majority in parliament and country, the king placed his own judgment above the rules of parliamentary democracy. Venizelos responded by suborning the loyalty of the officer corps and encouraging the creation of a separate and rival provisional government in Thessaloniki. After France and Britain forced the king into exile, Venizelos split the officer corps with his patronage practices and committed Greece to the occupation of large portions of Anatolia, gambling on his ability to retain allied support. He was fortunate to lose the 1920 elections. His feckless successors, including a recalled King Constantine, were saddled with responsibility for a reckless policy of expansion that Venizelos had launched. Overall, Venizelos's wartime actions divided the officer corps and moved them to the center of politics, laid the groundwork for the 1922 Asia Minor military catastrophe and a massive surge of refugees from Anatolia, returned to the discredited practice of relying on foreign intervention, cast the electoral system into disrepute by gerrymandering, further undercut the shaky position of the monarchy, and weakened the position of parliament. On the other hand, Venizelos averted the worst through his handling of peace negotiations with a victorious Turkey, subsequently restored a measure of civility to relations between Greece and its powerful neighbor, and worked to repair the nation's economic and internal political position when returned to office in the late 1920s.[21]

After 1922 Greece engaged in the difficult business of redefining itself. The dream of great-power status gave way to the reality of a small state of limited power and influence, with a weak economy, a massive problem of refugee resettlement, and exposed borders. For the next half century, Greece struggled to establish a viable political and economic system and to defend itself against external threats. Internal political upheaval, military dictatorships, foreign conquest and occupation, mass starvation, a brutal civil war, and a repressive post–civil war administration followed in the four decades after the national catastrophe of 1922. Although post–World War II Greece enjoyed impressive economic growth, continuing divisions among its governing elites ushered in a seven-year military dictatorship. Finally, the extreme nationalists of the military junta intervened in Cyprus, seeking to annex this predominantly Greek island. Turkey responded with force, inflicting a stinging defeat on Greek and Greek Cypriot forces, carrying out an ethnic cleansing of the northern part of the island, and creating a partition.

The Cyprus humiliation led to the fall of the military regime, and Greece began a remarkable renaissance. Democracy was fully introduced and flourished. The economy continued to grow. Most importantly, Greece entered the European Economic Community in 1981, exploiting opportunities offered by economic integration and political security to firmly ground its democratic institutions. European integration has strengthened Greece's sense of identity with the West and fostered profound social changes.

The Cyprus debacle stoked intense anti-American feeling in Greece. The Nixon administration's open support for the military junta and subsequent inactivity in the face of the Turkish invasion produced a deep sense of betrayal among Greeks. After a lengthy estrangement, democratic Greece gradually became a very reliable U.S. ally and partner. Nevertheless, Greek-American relations remain very sensitive. Most Americans are unaware of and are puzzled by the sense of injury that many Greeks (and a portion of the Greek American elite) nurture. History, which is largely a nonfactor in U.S. public policy debate, plays an enormous role in Greek perceptions of current events. What British historian Romilly Jenkins has called the difference between "truth and ethnic truth" plays a central role in Greek perceptions of the outside world. Greek political discussion centers on "national" issues and national image. The Greek public and its leaders focus on Greek interests and are extremely sensitive to foreign criticism. A sense of inferiority to the West is often combined with a magnification of Greece's importance. Greeks tend to see their nation as locked into a subservient relationship with stronger states that consistently betray and humiliate them. Ceaselessly reiterated stories of past betrayals and a sense of the special nature of Greece (nurtured by the West's enthusiasm for ancient Greece) become part of the fundamental education of Greeks and factor into both its internal politics and its diplomatic dealings with other states.[22]

ANCIENT GREEKS OR BYZANTINES?

For the vast majority of West Europeans and Americans, Greece conjures up nostalgic images of the Parthenon and other remnants of fifth-century B.C.E. architecture, symbolizing an era when Athenian democracy created a model for modern politics. Simultaneously it can provoke thoughts of the warm, white sand beaches and clear blue sky and seas of this small but beautiful nation. For its inhabitants, Greece is a much more complex and continuous concept that embraces not only an ancient past and an increasingly prosperous present, but also two other civilizations, the Byzantine and the Ottoman empires, which provide the connective tissue of the Greek experience. While the Western view of Greece is largely discontinuous and focused on the territory that constitutes modern Greece (the southern part of the Balkan peninsula and adjacent islands), Greeks stress continuity, as exemplified by their language, and emphasize the role of the Eastern Roman (Byzantine) Empire (330–1453 C.E.), a state centered in the Balkans and Anatolia, in their national experience. Moreover, because of their confrontational relationship with modern Turkey, Greeks have daily reminders of four hundred years of domination ("the Turkish Yoke") by a Muslim state that, with considerable help from Western Crusaders, overthrew the Byzantine Empire.

Modern Greece owes its liberation in great part to the romantic visions of antiquity that inspired Western Europeans to aid the struggling revolutionary movements of the 1820s. Since the eighteenth century Greeks have cleverly played on the West's belief that its culture and political traditions are rooted in the ancient Greek experience and have secured special consideration for their nation. The European Community granted Greece membership in spite of its backward economy. Greece's reputation for political instability convinced Europeans to guarantee its apparently fragile democracy through membership in the community. This seemingly illogical act was a demonstration of how Western philhellenism has supported Greek national interests.[23]

In taking on the mantle of the successors of Pericles, modern Greeks have laid a heavy set of burdens on themselves. As one American writer observed, being Greek implies a daily effort to live up to the image of the Periclean super Greek. Moreover, in establishing the modern Greek state on the Periclean model, Greeks have emphasized discontinuity over continuity, leaving fault lines in their culture. For more than one hundred and fifty years the society struggled over the language question: whether to favor the use of street Greek (*demotiki*) or the "purified" version (*katharevousa*) that would restore a highly selective form of the ancient language to common use.[24]

Greek efforts to reconcile a glorious past with a less-inspiring present have not escaped the notice of some fairly influential critics. Western visitors, including members of the American intellectual elite, frequently left Greece with a less-than-favorable view of the modern nation. In 1867, Mark Twain spent a few days cruising through the Aegean and commented scathingly on the corruption, lack of attention to ancient monuments, and general desolation: "We saw little but forbidding sea walls and barren hills, sometimes surmounted by three or four graceful columns of some ancient temple, lonely and deserted.... Greece is a bleak, unsmiling desert, without agriculture, manufactures or commerce, apparently. What supports its poverty stricken people or its government is a mystery.... I suppose that ancient and modern Greece compared furnish the most extravagant contrast to be found in history. The classic Illisus is gone dry and so have all the sources of Grecian wealth and greatness."[25]

This sort of pointed criticism stung, and for many members of the Greek elite it was at best only partially mitigated by admiring celebration of Greece's folk culture by such writers as Henry Miller in his *Colossus of Maroussi*. A few years earlier, in an essay entitled "Free Spirit," George Theotokas, one of Greece's most important twentieth-century writers, complained that his nation, "backward, conservative and provincial," had failed to strike roots in the dynamic culture of the West, lamenting that "modern Greece has offered nothing to the intellectual culture of Europe" and has clung tenaciously to its Byzantine past.[26]

Debate over what Greece should adopt from Western models of thought, dress, and expression stirred controversy among the elites of the newly liberated nation and set elites against the mass of deeply conservative peasants. The Greek Orthodox Church, which had played an important role in creating and preserving the Hellenic character, fought, and on some issues continues to fight, the adoption of ideas from the West, insisting that to be Greek is, above all, to be Orthodox, that is, heir to Christian Byzantium. The church's hostility toward the West, rooted in theological differences with Roman Catholicism, is further inflamed by still-live memories of the "betrayal" that the West visited upon the Eastern Romans by sacking Constantinople in 1204 and by failing to come to the empire's aid in the years before the fall of Constantinople in 1453, even after extracting an agreement on church unity from the feeble successors of Constantine the Great. Catholic and Protestant proselytism among Christian Greeks (much of it by American missionaries) further enflamed the Orthodox leadership and faithful.[27]

The nineteenth-century church had other, more immediate, reasons for its opposition to Westernization. Greece's Catholic Bavarian rulers immediately cut the local church's organizational ties to the patriarchate in Constantinople and seized its wealth. An 1833 law set up the independent Greek Orthodox Church, directed by the archbishop of Athens but operating under the supervision of the state. The creation of a national church of Greece, which the patriarch reluctantly recognized in 1850, set a pattern for other emerging Balkan states to form national churches independent of Constantinople. The Ottoman Empire's Balkan territorial loses were simultaneously setbacks for the leadership claims of the Great Church of Constantinople.[28] Moreover, the Greek Orthodox Church became a critical tool in the government's efforts to establish the legitimacy of its claims to further expansion. In 1883 the U.S. minister in Greece observed that the "Hellenic point of view, although plainly contradicted by the facts, is that the population of Eastern Roumelia and Macedonia is entirely Greek, chiefly on the ground that hitherto they have been included in the Greek church [of Constantinople]."[29]

In creating a national church, the Greek government prevented Ottoman authorities from intervening in its internal affairs through their control of the patriarchate. They also created a powerful internal opponent of many aspects of their modernization policy. The church, with is ability to mobilize masses of Greeks, was and remains a formidable and frequently quite independent actor in Greek politics.[30]

Despite the church's objections, Greece after 1830 had to move in the direction of modernization, through the adoption of Western models of political, economic, and social organization, as a matter of national survival. No other realistic options existed for a newly created state that was small, weak, and badly in need of foreign assistance to maintain its independence. The Greek people's bloody war of national liberation had been a rejection of the cultural model under which they had lived for four centuries. The average Greek's desire to be rid of all vestiges of Ottoman rule led in the direction of adopting the political, bureaucratic, legal, and economic organization of the powerful states of the West. It also led to the adoption and hellenization of ideas of nationalism.

In addition to the creation of a national church, two other ideas that emerged from the Greek independence struggle had an impact on the history of the entire Balkan region up to our times: ethnic cleansing of Muslims and the parallel effort to implant a single national identity among diverse Christian ethnic groups. Greeks drove out or killed the Muslim population of their new state, seized their property, and proclaimed as a national goal the integration of all Greek-speaking Orthodox peoples into the new state by a process of territorial expansion. They simultaneously attempted to hellenize Christian populations inhabiting their newly acquired territories through combinations of suasion, education, and coercion. Other Balkan states followed similar practices and came into conflict with Greek nationalism. Greece paid a very high price for its actions when Turkish nationalism exploded in the early twentieth century and later when Bulgarian nationalists twice invaded and occupied parts of Macedonia.[31]

For more than a century, the glue holding together Greek society was the Megali Idea. Like many successful ideological constructs, the Great Idea was a marriage of basically conflicting objectives. While rooted in the Western notion of nationality, it also partook of the dream of the reconstitution of a Byzantine empire that would see Greeks ruling over not only ethnically diverse fellow Christians, but also Muslims. Its twin capitals were Athens, with its memories of antiquity and pull toward the West, and Constantinople, the seat of the medieval Byzantine state and of Orthodoxy.[32]

In attempting to shape policies that would achieve the Megali Idea, political elites in Athens fought over questions of strategy and tactics. Some politicians insisted that the expansion of the Greek state could be achieved on the cheap through opportunistic guerrilla warfare operations that took advantage of favorable international events. Others argued that achieving national expansion would require the patient creation of a strong Western state with an efficient bureaucracy, a powerful and modern military, and a supporting infrastructure of modernized agriculture, industry, and education. These reformers, incarnated in the figure of Kharilaos Trikoupis, found their efforts undercut by the intensity of the public demand for action to achieve national expansion. The leadership elites in Constantinople, above all the patriarchate, recognized that imposing such a Western national state over existing Ottoman society would dissolve the very glue that bound the Christian peoples of the empire. They dreamed of seizing control of the decaying Ottoman state from its ineffective Muslim rulers. However, they lacked the key to power: the Ottoman army's officer corps remained firmly in Muslim hands.[33]

The incompatibility of these visions, recognized by both Constantinople and Athenian Greeks, was temporarily submerged when the Macedonian conflict began in the early 1870s. The struggle for Macedonia continued until the final partition of that region in 1913, uniting all shades of Greek opinion against rival Balkan nationalisms and Ottoman control. In defending their claims to universality, the patriarch of Constantinople and Greek bishops in the Macedonian region found themselves working with Greek nationalists, many infiltrated from the kingdom, and bandit chiefs in a long battle against Bulgarian nationalism and Slavic dreams of self-determination. In this struggle, the Greeks were able to employ history (particularly the Alexander the Great legend), popular loyalty to the Constantinople patriarchate, and educational institutions, trade links, and guerrilla warfare with telling effect to build a Greek consciousness among large numbers of Macedonian Christians.[34]

HISTORY AND EXCEPTIONALISM

Neither the United States nor Greece would have enjoyed success in expanding their borders without a firmly rooted faith in their national "mission." A sense of exceptionalism is common to all nationalities, waxing and waning in relation to the difficulties particular people face. What sets Americans, Greeks, and certain other peoples like the French, off from the norm is the depth of their assertion of their special character and mission. The United States has never had its exceptionalism tested as deeply as has Greece. Greek leaders and, indeed, evidence suggests that the mass of Greeks retained an extreme degree of faith in their national mission in the face of centuries of foreign occupation and a long string of painful setbacks.[35]

History has long played an important role in sustaining Greek exceptionalism and the Greek national project. History serves as an equalizing mechanism that has allowed a weak Greece to extract concessions from stronger states and given Greeks psychological reinforcement in dealing with more powerful and successful societies. The intellectual background to the creation of a Greek nation owes a great deal to Greek diaspora merchant communities of Europe and to those Greeks engaged in the Mediterranean shipping trade. Diaspora Greeks, seeking Western comprehension of and aid for their coreligionists in the struggle against the Ottoman state, and wise to the views of their Western hosts, utilized images of the distant past and encouraged the Greeks of the Balkans to adapt to the West's mania for antiquity.[36]

In matters of history, Enlightenment Europe followed a long Western tradition that both glorified the ancient Greek past and denigrated the Byzantine state as a "decadent" descendant of the Roman Empire. Edward Gibbon perhaps best summarized Western thinking on Byzantium by dismissing it as embodying the "triumph of barbarism and religion."[37] Even the men of the Italian Renaissance, who began the West's romance with the ancient Greek world, had little good to say about the Byzantines, despite their dependence on scholars from Constantinople for training in the Greek language.

The Greek war of national independence provided a catalyst for the movement toward the West. The initial and unsuccessful revolt in the northern Balkans was a product of a "Byzantine" vision of a future Greek state and an indication of the profound influence of Western ideas. Alexander Ipsilanti, the revolt's major leader, wanted to create a Constantinople-based empire, modeled on Byzantine and Russian traditions, but was beholden to the conspiratorial organizational efforts of Greek merchants who were thoroughly imbued with the romantic nationalism of the West. The successful revolt in the Peloponnesus, while rooted in local grievances and enjoying strong church support, quickly developed sets of institutions, above all constitutions and parliamentary assemblies, appropriated from the Western dream factory.[38]

The stamp of Westernization was more firmly attached when the great powers created a Greek monarchy and placed a young Bavarian on its throne. King Othon's first decade of rule (1833–1843) centered around the emplacement of Western bureaucratic institutions, a state church, neoclassic architecture, a university, and urban planning in the new capital. When the 1843 military revolt sent Othon's Bavarian officers and advisors packing, the Greek political class adopted a constitution that in many aspects was the most advanced in Europe. On paper, at least, Greece was a modern European state. In 1875, the U.S. representative in Greece commented on the progress of its Europeanization: "In America we have been taught to regard Greece as part of Europe. The truth is that she is nominally in it without being a part of it. She has nothing in common with the European system, nor does she come into contact with the rest of mankind.... The busy currents of life and trade sweep past her interesting shores.... Athens [offers] abundant evidences of European taste and culture.... But Athens is an exceptional indication of the future possibilities of Greece... not a fair specimen of the present condition of the country at large. Whoever attempts to judge Greece by her capital will be guilty of egregious folly.... Within twenty miles of ... Acropolis and Parthenon, modern civilization vanishes like a dream."[39]

Throughout the nineteenth and early twentieth centuries European visitors echoed these views. Modern Greek prose, a product of Westernization, often reflected the contradictions between tradition and modernity. George Theotokas's *Argo* plays on the contrasts between a modern and western Athenian elite and the political and social practices of Constantinople at the time of the 1922 national disaster. Nikos Kazantzakis's reconstructions of rural and small town life, *Freedom or Death*, *Christ Recrucified*, and *Zorba*, focus on a society dominated by ideals derived from Ottoman times and from the church.

Historical writing about modern Greece has reflected the national divisions and ambivalence about the effects of Westernization. It has largely been produced not by professional historians (a small and quite competent band) but by social scientists of various types and by journalists. Theory (usually imported from the West) has played a major role in explaining Greece's past. Social science models, in particular, have enjoyed a long run in the Greek academe. Intense nationalism, of course, deeply affects Greek historical production.[40]

Certain hallmarks of Greek history writing are bound to strike even the most casual reader. One is hostility toward the national enemy, Turkey. A typical expression, a 1992 Ministry of Education primary school textbook, *Modern Greek History* [Στα Νεότερα Χρονιά], lays the blame for Greece's backwardness on the 400-year Turkish yoke, overlooking the complexities of collaboration of Greek elites with the Ottoman Empire as well as the contributions Greeks made to Ottoman culture. In portraying this part of their national past, Greek public education has stressed resistance to foreign occupation, not the mutually rewarding but morally ambiguous cooperation with conquerors. An effort to tone down negative stereotypes of Turks in one modern Greek history textbook collapsed in the face of church-backed nationalist protest.[41]

"Underdogism" is another consistent trait of Greek historical writing. Small or weak is equated with virtue while the large and powerful are naturally oppressors. The short story "History" by Vassilis Vassilikos (1996) provides an amusing but edgy reading of Greece's nineteenth century that reflects the underdog feelings of Greeks. In an academic version, *Foreign Intervention in Greek Politics*, the authors (two Greek Americans and a Greek political scientist) list foreign-imposed restraints on Greek freedom of action in domestic and international affairs. Intervention, however, was not a one-way street. Small and restrained as it was, the Greek kingdom actively meddled in the internal affairs of the Ottoman state until that empire's collapse, and subsequently, in pursuit of further national expansion, it supported an internal revolt against the British on Cyprus, while later, in trying to achieve Cypriot *enosis* (union) with Greece, the military junta repeatedly attempted to assassinate the (Greek) president of the island republic and finally overthrew him in July 1974. After the junta's collapse, Greek press and politicians laid responsibility on others. As one study of the teaching of history in Greece explains, telling the Greek story requires "removing responsibility for past negative events from Greek authorities and attributing it to other countries," thereby creating "xenophobic attitudes on the part of students."[42]

On a more ideologically sophisticated level, writing underdog history creates a powerful attraction toward Marxist or neo-Marxist models of historical explanation. Nikos Mouzelis, another Greek social scientist practicing the historian's craft, developed a class-based model to explain Greece's role as a "peripheral" or "semi-peripheral" part of the West. Influenced by Immanuel Wallerstein's work and by Andreas Papandreou's political assault on the West and his calls for a "third way" of development borrowed from non-Soviet socialist experiments (1975–85), Mouzelis stressed the exploitative nature of Western capitalism but laid equal blame on the small Greek economic elite who followed policies of self-enrichment at the expense of careful development of the Greek industrial economy, with a resulting increased dependence on the foreign factor.[43]

Conspiracy theory is an offshoot of feelings of powerlessness. In the Greek case, this tendency is increased by the reality that foreign governments have repeatedly intervened in Greek public affairs. What is usually missing in these analyses is recognition that Greek political elites have consistently sought to involve larger states in their internal affairs. John Petropulos's classic account of the origins of the modern Greek state, *Politics and Statecraft in the Kingdom of Greece*, underlines the degree to which Greek politicians solicited foreign involvement. In the 1840s and again in the 1860s, French diplomatic representatives in Athens criticized the Greek political leadership's tendencies to ignore the real issues of governance, especially internal reform, and rely on foreign intervention to achieve their expansionist political aims. Moreover, as the French minister cuttingly observed in 1866, "governmental and administrative anarchy" in Athens meant that Greeks inside the Ottoman Empire had little desire to be liberated by the Hellenic kingdom.[44]

Conspiratorial views of history find their rich soil in the relationships of Greek political movements and foreign governments. What is surprising about Greek conspiracy theory is its lack of sophistication, especially when compared with other Mediterranean states like Italy where the writing of conspiratorial history is an art form. Conspiracy history works best by stringing together a few documented facts, adding a rich layer of unsupported but believable supposition, and drawing conclusions. Greek conspiracy writers go the process one step further. They seem impelled to invent "facts" from whole cloth. Scholars provide support for conspiratorial history by failing to critically examine these claims or the sources for them. One example is a frequently quoted and quite entertaining story offered by memoir writer Philip Deane (Gigantès). During the early 1960s, Deane was assigned to the Greek embassy's press office in Washington with a portfolio that focused on public relations work. A major objective of his mission was to polish the image of the royal family, especially the domineering and ultra-conservative Queen Frederika. Deane, who subsequently became a supporter of Andreas Papandreou, claimed that during a 1964 meeting with Ambassador Alexander Matsas (at which Deane was not present) U.S. president Lyndon Johnson placed intense pressure on the Greek diplomat to accept the U.S. position on the need for direct talks between Greece and Turkey over Cyprus. When Matsas demurred, Deane continued, Johnson exploded: "Fuck your Parliament and your Constitution. America is an elephant. Cyprus is a flea. Greece is a flea. If those two fleas continue itching the elephant they just may get whacked by the elephant's trunk." Shortly thereafter, still according to Deane, Johnson called the Greek ambassador. The U.S. president informed Matsas that he was reading the secret cable the ambassador had dispatched to Athens on their just completed meeting and piled on further threats in an effort to break the will of the Greeks. While the Deane version makes good reading, and has been quoted frequently, U.S. documentation indicates that

Johnson was not abusive, although anxious to promote direct Greek-Turkish discussion. The president's daily diary shows only one presidential meeting with the Greek ambassador, June 11, canceling the possibility of a second confrontational meeting. There is, moreover, no record of a telephone call from Johnson to Matsas (or from Matsas to Johnson) at any time during the Johnson presidency. The idea of Johnson calling the Greek embassy and revealing that the United States was reading its most secret cryptographic information stretches credulity. (Although it plays well with a widespread and quite exaggerated Greek notion of the efficiency of U.S. intelligence services.) In the first place, cryptographic analysis of a foreign state's traffic is rarely instantaneous. In addition, material of this sort is distributed to the White House with great care for protection of sources. Even enraged U.S. presidents would be reluctant to reveal information of this type. Deane's memoir trades on Johnson's reputation for crude speech and unpopularity arising from his Vietnam policy. Deane's stories were part of a well-orchestrated campaign by Andreas Papandreou and friends to rally public support for the embattled exile leader. These inventions gained the status of fact largely because no one has taken the time to compare them with a long available public record. Conspiratorial stories, connected with traditions of nationalism and underdog history, make difficult U.S.-Greek relations more problematic.[45]

OIL AND WATER

When the United States decided on a major economic and military intervention in support of the monarchical and parliamentary government of Greece in the winter of 1946–47, it inherited an existing climate of opinion based on a highly nationalist reading of the past together with other, more immediate problems, such as economic chaos, military collapse, a repressive public administration, widespread corruption, and a disciplined and combat-tested communist-led insurrection.

American officials were quite aware of the severity of the Greek crisis. They had few illusions about the difficulty of the challenge. Lincoln MacVeagh, the U.S. ambassador in Greece, had been reporting on Greek affairs since 1933 and constituted an institutional memory of enormous depth. MacVeagh was unstinting in his analysis of the weakness of Greece's political and civil society.[46] The United States intervened in Greece as part of a larger strategy designed to thwart the geopolitical ambitions of the Soviet Union. State Department officer Joseph Jones recalled that the decision to take action to bolster Greece provided American diplomats with a psychological "release from the professional frustrations of years." Philhellenism, the common motivation in so many European approaches to Greece, weighed very little in the U.S. decision to aid the Hellenic kingdom. From Harry Truman downward, U.S. officials made no secret of the larger strategic objectives of their actions. The major goal of the costly Cold War battle that the United States would wage in Greece was containment of the Soviet Union. Because Greece was a weak and divided nation, American assistance would be plentiful, and corresponding American involvement in the administration of Greece would be intense. The Truman administration, having staked the nation's future on a "containment" strategy, permitted neither its political opponents nor its newly acquired allies in the Greek political class to obstruct U.S. goals. The Faustian bargain offered to the Greeks was long-term recovery in exchange for short-term U.S. domination.[47]

Greek political elites of the right and center eagerly seized upon the American offer. They had, after all, generations of experience managing foreign interlopers and trusted that they could deal successfully with their new overlords. Moreover, the Greek political and economic elites had no alternative. Defeat by the communist insurrection meant political and, probably, physical extinction. Schooled by decades of foreign intervention, Greek political leaders of all stripes continued to maneuver for immediate and personal advantage, creating the worst possible impression on their new foreign partners. From the beginning, the U.S. involvement in Greece was a search for reliable interlocutors among a Greek political class that frustrated and infuriated American officials with its apparent lack of a sense of national purpose or geostrategic interest. From the perspective of U.S. leaders, the Greek civil war had two fronts: one against the communist rebels, the other against their scheming Greek political allies.[48] The extremist right-wing elements of the government joined with the communists in polarizing Greek society through brutal repression of their political opponents. In February 1947, Paul Porter, the chief of the U.S. aid mission to Greece, warned Washington that the nation's governmental, administrative, and business elites were in a state of political paralysis, unwilling "to adopt any policies or to undertake any permanent reconstruction until international and domestic security is achieved" and waiting for U.S. action to remedy their problems. In an analysis reminiscent of those written a century earlier, Porter added: "There is really no state here in the Western concept. Rather we have a loose hierarchy of individualistic politicians, some worse than others, who are so preoccupied with their struggle for power that they have no time, even assuming capacity, to develop economic policy. . . . [J]ournalistic and commercial circles claim that there exists a high degree of corruption. The civil service is a depressing farce." Nevertheless, Porter concluded, with that optimistic American "naiveté" often derided by Greeks, "the situation in Greece . . . is very discouraging but not hopeless."[49]

Between 1947 and 1949, U.S. officials were able to make considerable progress on their two primary objectives: creating a Greek national army capable of countering a communist-dominated insurrection and beginning the reconstruction of the Greek economy. The U.S. shelved its efforts to "reform" Greek political practice, recognizing that the American presence already was so overwhelming that it threatened to repress essential Greek initiatives. U.S. officials urged the Greek political leadership to assume responsibility for salvaging their nation. Deeper U.S. involvement in Greek political affairs was counterproductive, U.S. ambassador Henry Grady argued, and the Greeks must "seek their own solution rather than be permitted to turn to the United States."[50] The Greek government's sudden and surprising victory in the civil war (spring 1949) opened a new phase in the relationship. With the communists vanquished and economic recovery under way, American officials confronted questions about what sort of political reforms could transform Greece from a dependent to a self-sufficient U.S. ally against the Soviet Union, which leaders could carry out those reforms, and at what price.

1

THE GREEK TAR BABY, 1950–1953

> It is of the utmost importance that we supervise the use of any funds made available to Greece; in such a manner that each dollar spent will count toward making Greece self supporting, and will help to build an economy in which a healthy democracy can flourish
> — Harry Truman, 1947

> Not only what Papagos said, but the tone in which he said it deeply disturbed me. In the vernacular he was telling us off. . . . My views were not requested.
> — Ambassador Henry Grady, 1949

Movies frequently provide Greeks and Americans with a basic understanding of recent history.[1] The postwar relationship between the United States and Greece was the subject of Takis Tzimis's "The Man with the Carnation" [Ο Άνθρωπος με το Γαρύφαλλο], a 1983 documentary-style melodrama with music by Mikis Theodorakis, released about midpoint in Andreas Papandreou's first term as prime minister of Greece. In a 1950 Greece staggering under the weight of repression, the courageous communist Nikos Beloyiannis returns from exile hoping to unite all "true Greeks" in a struggle against American imperialism. The repression, accompanied by uncontrolled violence, is imposed by the forces of the "Right," at the orders of the U.S. Central Intelligence Agency (CIA), whose Athens representative, the Greek-speaking "Tom," is a cinematic version of the legendary agency operative Thomas Karamessinis. Early on in the film, Tom asks one of his Greek interlocutors to fill him in on the activities of future dictator Col. George Papadopoulos, clearly already a key U.S. collaborator. Meanwhile, the unnamed U.S. ambassador, presumably John Peurifoy, carries on his efforts to bend the Greek people and their progressive prime minister, Gen. Nikolaos Plastiras, to the will of the United States. Plastiras's brave efforts to deal with the nation's pressing economic problems and to pacify a war-shattered people are undermined by the members of his government and the secret services, both lackeys of the United States. The idealistic Beloyiannis, betrayed by the Communist Party, is executed on American orders after a stirring courtroom speech in which he compares Greece's latest foreign masters with the Nazis. His martyrdom is an essential step in the recovery of national independence. Close-ups of tanks and a map of Cyprus at film's end reinforce the implied comparison with the subsequent struggles of Andreas and his father, George, against alleged U.S. intervention in Greece's affairs. The ultimate triumph of Andreas, his Panhellenic Socialist Movement (PASOK), and the Greek people over American imperialism is forecast.

Tzimis's film is a failure as both entertainment and agitprop. A more satisfying and entertaining portrait of the American experience in Greece in the early 1950s is Peter Sellers's "The Mouse That Roared" (1959), a tale of the ways in which small states successfully manipulate great powers. American efforts to create a stable, prosperous, and democratic Greece were a study in official frustration. While American officials, above all U.S. ambassadors Henry Grady and John Peurifoy, did possess the power to play a determining role in the direction of Greek postwar reconstruction, utilizing it successfully proved difficult. American power confronted Greek history. Intensely nationalist and wary after decades of foreign intervention, Greek politicians and public opinion resisted American efforts at persuasion. Heavy-handed U.S. interventions aroused public anger, defeating a primary American objective of reinforcing the legitimacy of the Greek government by reducing U.S. involvement in the nation's internal affairs. While eagerly accepting U.S. assistance, particularly the monetary variety, the Palace, the army high command, and Greece's political class were equally determined to utilize this aid for their own partisan ends. American efforts to scale back its economic and military assistance to the levels of 1947–49 were a paradigm of later U.S. foreign policy problems. Carefully hoarding its limited financial resources and applying them on the rational criterion of strategic importance was a good approach to foreign policy. Unfortunately, the United States, in Greece and elsewhere, wanted it both ways. While reducing aid and encouraging greater "independence" on the part of Greek elites, the United States simultaneously attempted to retain the level of influence its earlier investments had purchased. By 1952 as Marshall Plan assistance phased out and the size of the military assistance program declined, the United States began to lose its leverage over Greece's political leaders. It could not push them to reform, and it lacked viable alternatives to cooperating with these elites. Essentially, the Greek political class became a tar baby from which the United States could not disengage successfully, except on terms it was unwilling to accept.

The psychological impact of U.S. power remained strong even as its purse emptied,[2] but the United States was unable to achieve its objective of fashioning in a relatively brief time a long-term solution to the inherent problems of the Greek political system.

THE PROCONSULS

The image of U.S. ambassadors as proconsuls, an idea deeply ingrained in the Greek collective memory, recurrently revived by the Greek press, and thus probably not erasable, is in marked contrast with the realities of the early 1950s. Neither the liberal Henry Grady nor his conservative and controversial successor, John Peurifoy, fit the imperial mold. Grady, a veteran of the wartime Italian occupation, was particularly aware of the dangers of intense intervention in Greek politics and consistently pushed Greek authorities to assume more control over their affairs. Peurifoy, an experienced administrative officer with no background in Greek affairs, relied heavily on his staff for direction. His initial readings of Greek politics proved remarkably incorrect. One U.S. diplomat recalled: "He had no political sense at all." Both men were frequently in conflict with the semiautonomous parts of the American mission, above all, the Marshall Plan economic aid administrators and the U.S. military. Gen. James Van Fleet, who headed the military assistance mission during the civil war, remained in Greece through the middle of 1950. Van Fleet, whose very conservative views made him into a natural ally of the king and queen, was a source of continuous trouble for Grady. The CIA station under Karamessinis was more cooperative, but the chief of station's ethnic background inevitably attracted the notice of the country's elites, who hoped to find a more sympathetic interlocutor in a fellow "Greek." Greece's politicians, its military officers, and the Palace successfully played on divisions within the U.S. mission.[3]

A good part of the U.S. problem was its own anomalous role in Greece. Having effectively taken control of the Greek economy for the duration of the civil war, the Americans had accustomed their Greek clients both to feeding at the trough of U.S. aid and to receiving (and largely ignoring) U.S. directives and pep talks. U.S. officials, led by Ambassador Grady, were telling Greek political and military leaders, as well as King Paul, to take control of the internal affairs of their country and, as much as possible, to exclude the U.S. from their decision making. Greek leaders liked much of the message but had no intention of dealing the Americans out of their political maneuverings. The king had a taste for authoritarian politics. He frequently suggested installing Marshal Alexander Papagos, the popular commander in chief of the army, as prime minister of a government that would answer to the Palace and not parliament. In seeking U.S. support for this project, the king argued that it was the only way to defeat communism. Grady repeatedly intervened to dissuade the monarch from following through with plans for "extra-constitutional" governments. A few weeks before the end of the civil war, the king was again maneuvering to replace the politicians with a royal government. Grady headed to the Palace to put the brakes on this plot. Informing Washington of the results of this meeting, Grady stressed that he was trying to keep the United States out of Greece's internal affairs while steering Greek leaders toward democratic practices. He would be back at Tatoi Palace five months later to discourage another plan for establishing an authoritarian government.[4]

The Palace was not the only threat to democratic government. The Greek army was riddled with conspiratorial movements, one of which, the Sacred Band of Greek Officers (IDEA), epitomized the military's intense, long-term involvement in politics. Founded in 1944, IDEA was strongly nationalist and anticommunist, and its influence grew within the officer corps. It acted as the self-anointed guardian of the Greek state. At one time, IDEA opposed the extraconstitutional machinations of Plastiras. Initially wary of Marshal Papagos, IDEA was ultimately co-opted by the commander in chief.[5]

Another problem facing Greece's political system was the political weight of these two senior military leaders. Plastiras, a hero of the Greek left, and particular bête noire of the Palace, led the 1922 coup that ousted King Paul's father and sent his brother into exile. He had been involved in a failed 1933 coup. Although long out of uniform, Plastiras remained a symbol of Greece's praetorian political traditions, telling the U.S. ambassador in September 1951: "Of course, I'm terribly royalist nowadays. But I've kicked two kings out, and if at any time you want the present one to go, just let me know."[6] Marshal Papagos, the hero of the resistance to the Italian invasion of 1940 and victor in the civil war, was a man of the right who commanded the loyalty of the vast majority of the army officer corps and, until early 1951, enjoyed the support of the king and queen, who hoped to thrust him onto the political stage to counterbalance parliamentary parties and leaders, above all Plastiras.[7] Papagos's relationship with the royal family was complex, but he was ready to cooperate when it favored the objectives of the military. The king and queen apparently believed Papagos malleable enough to serve their interests.[8]

Greece's political parties were staunch defenders of neither democracy nor the national interest. Politicians of all factions attempted to utilize the U.S. embassy as a tool in their political maneuverings. They curried American support while their backers in the Greek press carried out an assault on U.S. management and objectives, complaining of "foreign intervention." Seeking U.S. backing for his candidacy, Plastiras assured embassy officials that as prime minister "he would take no move in foreign policy without the advice and consent of the United States."[9] Palace support for Papagos led politicians of both the right and center and their press allies to request embassy intervention against this threat to their positions.[10]

In the early spring of 1950, the Palace undermined the broadly based coalition government of Alexander Diomedes, which, in the judgment of U.S. officials, had made useful progress in reconstruction. Diomedes told sympathetic American diplomats that his fall was an effort by politicians allied with the Palace to create a new party of the right at the expense of both the conservative Populists and the centrist Liberals. He warned that this type of intervention would endanger the monarchy. King Paul installed a (nonpolitical) "service" government to carry the nation to new elections. The outcome of the March 1950 vote was not to royal taste. The center parties emerged victorious.[11]

Undaunted by the expression of the popular will, the royal couple began a full-court press to open the way for a Papagos government. Queen Frederika tried to win American support by writing to former U.S. secretary of state George Marshall. Meanwhile, a senior member of the royal household approached the embassy with a plan for a government that excluded Plastiras, the leader of the largest party of the center. Conservative allies of the Palace piled on other arguments, such as Plastiras's supposed softness toward the Soviet Union and dangers of his interference with the management of the army. The king summoned Grady to urge the creation of a coalition that would keep Plastiras on the sidelines. The ambassador responded that such an action would subvert the entire democratic process, rejecting the argument that Plastiras constituted the threat of excessive civilian control over the Greek military.[12]

Ignoring Papagos's willingness to serve under Plastiras, the Palace continued to resist nominating a prime minister. King Paul drew out discussions with party leaders as a way of undercutting the Plastiras candidacy while playing on the ambitions of the other principal leaders of the fragmented center, Sofokles Venizelos and George Papandreou. The king worked out an arrangement for Venizelos, the ambitious son of the great man, to form a minority administration. "This has come as considerable shock to us," Harold Minor, the U.S. chargé, reported. Venizelos formed his ministry "without the full support of his own party and with a clear understanding that his antics were viewed unfavorably by [the] Americans and British." Minor met with Petros Metaxas, the king's chief aide, to protest that the Palace's actions in handing power to a government representing only about 20 percent of Greek voters and led by an "intriguer" were violations of democratic procedure.[13]

The king and queen stood firm. Plastiras was a "republican, unreliable, stupid, and a fellow traveler." Venizelos ignored a private warning from Grady that the United States could not accept his minority government. The Greek embassy in Washington, acting on instructions from Athens, announced that the United States backed the new ministry.[14] Grady fumed: "It is easy to see what would happen if they could say the American ambassador has caused the fall of [the] government.... Our correctness here is being taken advantage of and we are drifting into political confusion. We can be neither dictatorial nor laissez faire but 'gentle persuasion' does not seem to be effective with irresponsible politicians and stubborn monarchs. We are all ... deeply concerned about effect on [the] ECA [Economic Cooperation Administration] program of political drift during [an] interval of six months or so it will take King to accomplish his very definite objective of getting Papagos in as prime minister."[15] The ambassador released a March 31 letter to Venizelos stating that with only twenty-seven months left in the Marshall Plan, the Greek government had to be able to act decisively on a broad range of politically unpopular domestic reforms. Without a stable government based on majority support, U.S. taxpayer aid would be frittered away, Grady continued, and thus, such assistance would have to be suspended. Venizelos, utilizing the Greek embassy, tried to rally U.S. backing for his continuance in office. When this ploy failed, he resigned, proclaiming himself the innocent victim of U.S. intervention.[16]

This incident underlined the practical difficulties of attempting to disengage from Greece's complex internal politics. The U.S. stake in Greece was too large in political and economic terms to simply ignore the machinations of the Palace and the political class. An American government that permitted foreign politicians to control U.S. funding and use its dollars for their partisan objectives would face serious domestic political criticism. Moreover, a Greece that failed to follow normal democratic political practice would largely undercut the rationale for the Truman Doctrine and other major U.S. foreign policy initiatives. Still, if the United States insisted on having the last word on Greek decisions, it would pay a heavy price, above all with Greek public opinion. In its April 4, 1950, analysis of the crisis, the embassy commented that Grady's intervention had "tremendous" impact. Greeks generally agreed with Grady's arguments but were angry that a U.S. action left their "dirty laundry . . . hung out in front of the world."[17]

American actions offended Greece's national pride and broke the unwritten rules of patronage that governed Greek society. The patron-client relationship as practiced in Mediterranean society was long-term and based on reciprocal if unwritten obligations. Greek politicians believed that by backing them in the struggle against the communists, the United States had entered into a permanent relationship. With that war over, they expected the Americans to continue economic aid at high levels. Greece's monarchs believed that they had a special relationship with the United States that constituted an extra layer of protection for their special constitutional status. Greeks generally believed that the United States had made an open-ended commitment of economic assistance. Accustomed by European philhellenism and their own unique historical experiences to see themselves at the center of world geopolitics, they were unwilling to accept the idea that, with the civil war over, Greece's objective strategic importance had declined. No Greek appears to have taken at face value repeated public and private American statements that both the aid and the level of involvement were short-term, designed only to get Greece back on its political and economic feet, to be followed by a rapid reduction of U.S. activity. In 1944, long before U.S. intervention was in anyone's plans, Ambassador MacVeagh explained Greek political reality to President Franklin Roosevelt: "No Greek will ever believe that a 'head man' can't do the things he wants to, whatever may be the rules, and no such 'head man' can survive in Greece."[18] U.S. efforts to reduce its commitment to Greece through selective interventions struck Greeks as absurd. Accustomed to foreign intervention as a logical means of increasing an outsider's control, they could not accept the idea that the United States intervened to extract itself from the complexities of Greek internal politics. Moreover, the targets of these interventions naturally took advantage of the opportunity provided to play the role of aggrieved defenders of national autonomy against the Americans. The idea that Peurifoy sought to impose a permanent U.S. control over Greece became ingrained in the national historical memory.[19]

The American evaluation of the strategic importance of Greece changed even before the Greek civil war ended. As a result, Washington aimed to speedily draw down the resources assigned to its small ally. By 1951, U.S. regional strategy focused on Turkey, "the strongest anti-communist country on the periphery of the USSR and the only one in the Eastern Mediterranean and Middle East area having the determination and capability of offering substantial resistance to Soviet aggression."[20] Strides made by Turkey toward a stable parliamentary democracy reinforced U.S. conclusions about that nation's potential and were in evident contrast with Greek political instability. By late 1951, U.S. officials, after considerable hesitation and in the face of opposition from several European member states, decided to support Turkey's request for full membership in the North Atlantic Treaty Organization. Greece's candidacy essentially depended on the decision on Turkey.[21]

The limited value of Greek military forces and the desire to reduce U.S. economic assistance as quickly as possible were key factors in the American effort to downsize the Greek military. By late 1948, the embassy was already pressing for a reduction in the size of U.S. military aid to the Greek army, arguing that such aid reinforced existing Greek dependency on the foreign factor and an accompanying reluctance to make decisions. Once the civil war was over, Grady informed the Greek government that since the royal army constituted a major drain on the nation's economy it had to significantly cut its forces. The following year, the United States took steps to remove one of the most active supporters of a large Greek military, recalling Van Fleet from Greece, and replacing him with an officer of lesser rank and prestige. Assistant Secretary of State George McGhee told the U.S. army's chief of staff that the move would "help us in our efforts to deflate Greek thinking in terms of their own importance."[22]

A small, well-equipped army capable of defending Greece's borders and of dealing with internal subversion fit well with the U.S. objective of restraining Greek tendencies toward irredentism. U.S. officials were divided about whether aggressive, public Greek border claims in the Balkans constituted a real threat to the uneasy peace of the region, but given the background of over a century of Balkan wars and unrest, as well as Greece's past record of treatment of its ethnic minorities, they wanted to curb any temptations for an "unreliable" and nationalist Greek political class.[23]

Efforts to reduce the size of the Greek military inevitably met stiff opposition. Greek political leaders resisted passively. The king and Papagos took a much more aggressive approach. Just as the civil war was ending, the monarch arranged a meeting between the field marshal and Grady in which the commander dressed down the U.S. diplomat and "demand[ed]" more U.S. aid.[24] The outbreak of the Korean War was a gift to the Greek military. By September 1950, with U.S. forces engaged in Asia and intelligence suggesting a Soviet thrust into Europe, the U.S. Joint Chiefs of Staff endorsed a higher manpower ceiling for the Greek army in spite of the drain this would entail for the Greek economy and for the impact of U.S. aid.[25]

As part of a program for turning its client into a respectable international presence, U.S. officials turned their attention to the Greek government's sullied reputation for failing to respect the rights of its political opponents. The Greek civil war was a bloody and ruthless conflict that began with the communist-dominated resistance movement, EAM-ELAS, exterminating its antifascist opponents. The Greek right repaid the left in kind with the murderous actions of "Security Battalions," while Nazi occupiers killed unarmed civilians and resistance fighters with equal fury. In the immediate postwar period, the right enjoyed an upper hand and unleashed a "White Terror" on the communist and noncommunist left. British officials in Greece were largely powerless to stop the bloodshed that, in turn, pushed the communists toward their 1946 insurrection. During the civil war, the Greek government's draconian treatment of prisoners became a major embarrassment for Washington. While recognizing the need for exceptional measures to deal with an armed insurrection, U.S. officials urged the Greek government to provide normal judicial processes for the accused. President Truman was among those worried about Greek judicial procedures and the executions. Greek leaders ignored American concerns, labeling them "intervention" in their internal affairs. Once the civil war was over, American diplomats nudged the Greek government to end martial law and executions. They tried to ensure that political prisoners on the island of Makronissos were afforded humane treatment. Gradually, these pressures succeeded in moderating Greek governmental behavior. "Grounds for legitimate criticism of Greek internal affairs have been lessened," a March 1950 NSC report declared, "although the functioning of the Greek governmental apparatus is likely to remain below Western standards and to pose continuing problems." Subsequently, the renascence of Greece's communist movement, operating within the United Democratic Left (EDA), and security concerns created by the outbreak of the Korean War led Washington to downplay human rights.[26]

The sense of urgency in U.S. dealings with Greek leaders was rooted in economic realities. The Marshall Plan constituted a one-time-only act of self-interested generosity on the part of U.S. taxpayers, and the claims of a worldwide struggle against the Soviet Union put severe limits on American financial resources. American officials repeatedly signaled the end of major aid to their Greek counterparts and to the Greek public. Greek insistence that its aid needs were too special to allow the United States to reduce assistance created a dialogue of the deaf. July 1950 comments by the U.S. chargé reflected the gap in understanding: "The Department may be as discouraged as I was to learn that the Greeks are again thinking of additional foreign assistance as the only way out of Greece's economic difficulties.... [T]he prime minister's remarks... indicate a lamentable lack of realism."[27]

Greek unwillingness to accept a change in either the size or methods of U.S. assistance was hardly surprising. Greece had long been a net importer of foreign capital. Since the nineteenth century, this money largely arrived in the form of loans negotiated with private investors by the Greek government and underwritten by state-issued bonds. Greeks had painful memories of the results of this form of foreign investment. Government default on bonds triggered foreign control over the economy. Even when the Greek government was in a position to exert a greater control over its finances, it faced the demands of foreign bondholders, including American investors, backed by their governments, for speedy repayment of overdue bond interest and principal. The overall effect was to stimulate Greek economic nationalism and to create a widespread and understandable public hostility toward foreign investment. At the same time, Greece could not achieve economic self-sufficiency and growth without some form of foreign assistance. Thus, the arrival of postwar U.S. aid was a godsend. In the first place, the Marshall Plan consisted largely of outright grants. While the United States insisted on retaining a strong degree of control over how the money was spent, it did not demand repayment. Second, the aid was a government-to-government arrangement that allowed Greek officials to play heavily on noneconomic factors in negotiating the level of assistance. Greece's very weakness and the threat posed by the communist insurgency, together with Washington's determination to ensure the Truman Doctrine's success, meant that Greece received an extraordinary high level of assistance during the period 1947–52. Ambassador MacVeagh had described prewar Greece as "a country operating almost completely under the principles of a planned economy."[28] Government-to-government aid like the Marshall Plan fit perfectly into a system that traditionally stressed government's role in planning and allocating resources and that reinforced the Greek political patronage system. Convinced of their exceptional strategic importance, Greek political leaders continued to believe that they could extract large amounts of U.S. aid.

In June 1950, a departing ambassador Grady tried yet again to employ the weapon of bluntness to convince the Greek foreign office and, through it, the country's politicians that the U.S. assistance program would soon end. The United States, he warned the Greek chargé in Washington, had nearly achieved its military and economic objectives in Greece. Greeks should not "kid themselves" that the U.S. government would continue: "to underwrite political confusion in Greece." President Truman was fed up with the politically self-serving actions of many Greek politicians that imperiled their nation's economic recovery. Grady's letter to Venizelos had been a warning to Greeks to act in their national interest before U.S. aid and patience evaporated.[29]

During the next few years, U.S. officials would repeat this message, U.S. economic aid would decline, and Greek leaders would continue to resist and protest aid cuts. Psychological and practical considerations led Greece's governing political and military elites to chart a different course from the one the United States wanted. The surprising and strong growth of the Greek economy in the 1950s shielded the country from the worse effects in the cuts in U.S. aid, and the United States abandoned its best leverage by cutting assistance. The Korean War forced a reconsideration of levels of U.S. military aid to Greece while ever-pragmatic U.S. officials sought a rapprochement with Greek elites that weakened the "reform-or-else" message. Then, to the intense relief of American officials, the unstable balance of power within the Greek elite was temporarily upset and a more effective government, enjoying a parliamentary majority, and capable of restraining the Palace, emerged.[30]

FROM PLASTIRAS TO PAPAGOS

Between 1950 and 1952, as U.S. officials played the frustrating, damaging, and usually unsuccessful role of referee in Greece's internal political struggles, they began to seek a way out through electoral engineering. The collapse of the traditional party of the right, the Populists; the self-destructive actions of the leaders of the center; the continuing maladroit activities of the Palace; and the emergence of Papagos as the key player in Greece's internal politics drove a change in U.S. strategy. External factors, above all the war in Korea and the decline in U.S. public support for foreign assistance, motivated the mission to seek a quick resolution of Greece's chronic political instability.

The decline of the traditional monarchist party was one of the factors that triggered increased Palace efforts to manipulate the political system. King Paul's attempts to create a Papagos ministry reflected his concern that the right needed a figure to rally around and his belief that Papagos was a reliable monarchist. After Plastiras formed a government in May 1950, the royal couple assured U.S. officials that they backed the new cabinet while at the same time they began undermining their new prime minister. They were ably assisted by Venizelos, who initially declined to enter the cabinet, and then headed off for a long "vacation" on the French Riviera, signaling his intention to topple Plastiras. In early July 1950, the Palace turned on the government.

Plastiras's decision to release 130 communist inmates from the Makronissos prison camp, a gesture of reconciliation, led to a clash with his minister of public order and coalition partner, George Papandreou. Press criticism of the government mounted. Plastiras's pacification plans and his desire to avoid a Greek commitment to the Korean conflict were clearly at odds with U.S. priorities. Sensing an opportunity to utilize the American factor, and taking advantage of Grady's reassignment to Iran, the Palace dispatched royal aide Metaxas to sound out the embassy about a new government. Arguing that Plastiras was an incompetent, Metaxas warned that the "Center government 'of which the Americans are so fond' has done absolutely nothing except undo the victory against the communists." Greece, Metaxas continued, needed "a strong man." Since none appeared available immediately, the Palace would give the politicians one last chance to form an efficient government before King Paul took control. U.S. chargé Minor, who was concerned about Plastiras's capacity to govern, nevertheless defended the government's record and reiterated the U.S. position that the government's fate had to be decided by parliament and the parties.[31]

Rebuffed at the embassy, the Palace turned to Van Fleet. The retiring chief of the military mission cooperated in a *New York Times* interview blasting Plastiras as a "communist." Venizelos and Papandreou, sensing a chance to topple their rival, then cooperated to force a government crisis. Minor hastened to see Plastiras, to assure him of U.S. noninvolvement in the crisis, and released a similar statement to the Greek press. While true, the claim of noninvolvement challenged Greek credulity in view of evident U.S. concerns about Plastiras's policies and, more glaringly, of Van Fleet's outburst.[32]

Venizelos replaced Plastiras, and the Palace maneuvered to turn power over to Papagos. The embassy began to rethink its approach to Greek political affairs. The Korean War had dramatically reversed U.S. priorities: "The international situation apparently dictates . . . abandoning hope Greece would finally be able to take road of peace, subordinating military and security considerations to sorely needed physical and moral recovery."[33] As usual, the Americans favored the creation of a broad coalition government to carry out a rearmament policy. Since the Palace's preferred solution, imposing Papagos, would violate the rules of parliamentary democracy, elections offered the best chance of building a stable government. "In this connection . . . it would seem desirable . . . to use the strongest possible emb[assy] influence to secure adoption [of a] majority system. We feel any new election under proportional representation system might tend to produce some polarization to left and right, but that no one party or effective coalition would emerge to form a stable government."³⁴

Since none of the major Greek political actors wanted to return to the polls so quickly after the spring 1950 elections, American officials found themselves back in the swamp of cabinet formation: urging various centrist leaders to cooperate, restraining the royal family, fending off Greek efforts to increase the size of their aid package as a *pourboire* for their cooperation, and swallowing a Venizelos government that lacked a broad parliamentary majority. The new ambassador, John Peurifoy, arrived in the middle of the negotiations and got a quick education in the complexities of Greek politics. The end result of this intense activity was a "government . . . by no means generally popular with press or public [that] affords little hope [of] efficiency or stability."³⁵

A November 1950 embassy review of the previous year painted a discouraging picture of six governments, of which only three had enjoyed parliamentary majorities, and seven months of inaction due to the lack of a cabinet with a governing majority. It concluded that, without new elections and a clear majority, Greece would never be able to effectively utilize U.S. assistance.³⁶

Thus, the inexperienced Peurifoy jumped at the plan outlined by King Paul a few days later. Anticipating the fall of Venizelos, the monarch offered to set up a service government, call new elections, and invite Papagos to form a party and contest the vote. The monarch pledged to give Papagos a free hand to form and direct his new party. Peurifoy was ecstatic: "We will either have elections from which . . . a really strong, able, and honest Papagos government will emerge, or when word of the King's plan leaks . . . we will have parliamentarians cooperating to the hilt among themselves and with our mission" to avoid elections. The State Department expressed greater caution, worrying about the center's future and the king's authoritarian predilection, but fell into line with the idea of elections and of a Papagos-led party, even as it stressed the need for replacing proportional representation with a voting system that would produce a reliable majority.³⁷

Ironically, Papagos proved to be the stumbling block to this solution. The marshal, still on active duty, appeared genuinely torn between his desire to develop an effective army and his political ambitions. His chief adviser, Spyridon Markezinis, an astute, abrasive and ambitious intellectual, favored a party open to the center and left. King Paul balked and in April 1951 reversed course, telling Papagos to stay out of politics and setting off a public feud with the chief of the armed forces. With its hopes again checked, the

United States decided to take another tack, pushing for a merger of Venizelos's Liberals and Plastiras's party as a step toward a stable majority.[38]

Tensions between the king and his chief of general staff became too intense for the two men to work together, and Papagos resigned in late May. Units of the Greek army revolted. Papagos intervened directly to restore order. Subsequent inquiries demonstrated that officers belonging to IDEA were responsible for the uprising. The government, however, took only limited disciplinary measures. Papagos opposed any action, and the U.S. military mission and embassy lined up squarely behind the marshal. The U.S. objective was restoring Papagos to command of Greek forces. Although this effort failed, the United States continued to insist that the government avoid action against the rebellious officers to protect the "GAF [Greek Armed Forces] from traditional Gr[ee]k political manipulation." Liberal leader George Papandreou took the same stand. Embassy concern about shielding the army from a power struggle that risked undermining the military chain of command, while understandable, ignored the question of how an army riddled with secret political societies could maintain its discipline.[39]

While no evidence of U.S. involvement in the revolt has ever surfaced and the episode worked against American interests, quick U.S. intervention in support of Papagos underlined its long-standing positive view of the marshal. The sharp political antennae of both the Palace and the political elite quickly and inaccurately translated this into support for the marshal's political ambitions. Encouraged by sensationalistic press reporting of the confused events of May 31, Greek popular suspicions of embassy machinations were aroused. For many Greeks the episode confirmed their belief in dark connections between U.S. "services" (the CIA) and IDEA.[40]

The upshot of the revolt was to place Papagos at the center of politics. Having resigned, the marshal could only settle scores with the Palace and his political opponents by forming a party and contesting elections. This placed the embassy in front of yet another dilemma. Papagos demanded elections based on a majority system, a key U.S. objective. Only George Papandreou agreed with the marshal. A consensus quickly emerged among other Greek politicians in favor of a reinforced proportional system that awarded a "prize" of seats to the party with the largest vote totals and that, while providing the stability the U.S. was seeking, would also ensure their political survival. The embassy had doubts about Papagos's impact on the political system: "[The] real disadvantage [of] Papagos entry . . . is [the] long term one which has hitherto persuaded [the] Dep[artmen]t and Emb[assy] to consider him a last card for use only in [an] emergency. [The] artificial and temporary crystallization of polit[ical] forces around [the] marshal will interrupt gradual normalization of Greek polit[ical] life."⁴¹ Instead of backing one faction, the embassy assumed its standard operational mode: suppressing concerns, circulating among Greek political factions, encouraging "moderation," avoiding opportunities for press speculation, and hoping that reinforced proportional representation would provide a basis for a two party system.⁴²

The elections of September 1951 failed to produce any of these happy outcomes. The campaign played out in the rough-and-tumble tradition of Greek politics. The Palace organized a press campaign against Papagos centering on his presumed IDEA connections. Venizelos, with the king's support, maneuvered to restrict the military vote. Papagos's Greek Rally won a plurality (34.6 percent and 116 of 258 seats). The marshal immediately demanded new elections under a majority system. He refused to enter any coalition, calculating that the alternative, a Plastiras-Venizelos government, would quickly collapse, forcing new elections. The marshal told a French diplomat that once the Americans realized that he could bring together a government with a stable majority, their efforts to avoid comment on Greek internal matters would evaporate in order to get a compact administration capable of carrying out reconstruction. As long as the Rally observed basic democratic procedures, the United States would have to throw its support behind him: the situation was too precarious for them to remain on the sidelines.⁴³

The Rally refused to vote in favor of Greece's new draft constitution, challenging provisions that expanded the Palace's role in the event of a "national emergency." After the usual deal brokering, the aging Plastiras replaced Venizelos as prime minister of a shaky center coalition. The government authorized Beloyiannis's execution, while carrying out a campaign of arrests of EDA members in order to appease public concern about a rekindling of the civil war.⁴⁴ To the intense frustration of the Americans, the prime minister was soon hospitalized with heart problems that kept him out of action for months. Heated exchanges over IDEA continued as the Palace and government threatened judicial probes and their press supporters sought to discredit Papagos. Once this issue had been milked, the king signed a decree giving amnesty to both IDEA and to those officers involved in the May 1951 revolt. Having created public paranoia, the political class tried to place IDEA back into cold storage. However, the group's origins, actions, and objectives remained a staple of Greek political debate for decades.⁴⁵

The political infighting in Athens caught the attention of Harry Truman, who expressed his concern to Secretary of State Dean Acheson after a February 8, 1952, cabinet meeting. Later that month Acheson, meeting with

Venizelos at the NATO foreign ministers summit in Lisbon, broached the subject of a broad coalition with Papagos. The State Department subsequently instructed the embassy in Greece to see what could be done to expand the base of the Plastiras government.[46]

The embassy was caught off balance when the king and Venizelos, in a bid to undercut Papagos, took advantage of Plastiras's illness to propose a revised electoral law that would reinstate straight proportional representation. Amused French diplomats commented that Greek political maneuvers again befuddled their American colleagues. The "Yanquis" could not create strong government without "troubling their scruples" by open intervention. More amazingly, "the republicans support the monarchy against the royalists who [back] Plastiras" in the effort to defeat Papagos.[47] Peurifoy, who had hoped to avoid new elections, hastily released a press statement opposing the move. He reiterated the standing U.S. position: a proportional system "with its inevitable consequences of continuing governmental instability, would have a disastrous effect upon the efficient use of American aid." Plastiras crawled out of his sickbed to block the plan at a cabinet meeting. Although Peurifoy had avoided endorsing a majority electoral system, the anti-Papagos element of the Greek press and political establishment ignored Plastiras's actions and focused on this latest example of U.S. "intervention," claiming it represented foreign endorsement of Papagos. Peurifoy, who wanted to avoid such an endorsement, made the best case he could to Washington: "We have warned our Greek friends many times in [the] past that [the] issue of [the] electoral system [is] so critical to [the] effectiveness of [the] U.S. aid program [that] we would be obliged to state our position publicly if the need arose." The ambassador admitted that his actions would only increase public resentment of U.S. "controls." He promised that the mission would attempt to limit its future interventions but justified his actions: "There are times when our intervention in the interest of US policy and the US taxpayer must be prompt, firm and decisive."[48]

Peurifoy recognized that he had crossed a critical line. Adding to his discomfort, the Greek cabinet voted to reject U.S. "intervention." A furious King Paul invited the British government to intervene to offset U.S. influence. Anxious to preserve his standing with the State Department, and perhaps his job, Peurifoy assured Assistant Secretary of State William M. Roundtree: "I trust that as long as I remain in Greece I am through issuing statements although one can never be sure."[49] The State Department endorsed Peurifoy's action. The embassy tried to repair a public relations debacle by insisting that its statement was advice. A final decision on the Greek electoral system belonged to the political parties.⁵⁰

By the summer of 1952, another ministerial crisis was imminent. George Papandreou was secretly working with Papagos to topple the government and in late July engineered the defection of two deputies, thereby depriving Plastiras of his majority. Independently, the U.S. government became convinced that a currency reform was essential for Greece's economic well-being and, of course, that such a major initiative required a stable majority. This, in turn, would mean new elections. Having undercut the Plastiras ministry, Papandreou then provided it with a lease on life when the king informed him that the proposed plan for currency reform was linked to a massive cut in U.S. aid. Peurifoy tried to minimize the public relations damage by unveiling the U.S. plan. The king and queen suddenly appeared at the U.S. embassy, a quite extraordinary break with protocol, to lobby Peurifoy against supporting Papagos. However, both the State Department and the embassy had decided that Greece had to have new elections, and the ambassador pushed hard for them in his off-the-record meetings with Greek politicians. The Greek parties and Palace began maneuvering over the text of a new electoral law that would limit their potential losses.⁵¹ The result was a majority-voting law supported by Plastiras and Venizelos and, ironically, opposed by Papagos, who objected to provisions that would deprive many soldiers (and women) of the right to vote. The marshal expected to do well with both groups, and his opponents agreed. Greece went to the polls for the third time in three years in November 1952.

The November 1952 elections marked a turning point in U.S.-Greek relations. The Greek Rally won 49 percent of the popular vote and 247 of the 300 seats in the Boule (legislature). The center was eviscerated. Plastiras lost his seat. Although the EDA received 10 percent of the vote, it failed to elect a single deputy. For the first time since World War II, Greece would be governed by a single party. While the Greek Rally, like its centrist opponents, was less an organized party than a group of ambitious politicians united by the desire to be in on a division of spoils, Prime Minister Papagos combined considerable practical experience in military and foreign affairs with strong leadership qualities. Papagos's victory effectively reduced the Palace's influence and created the basis for a decade of stable rule by conservative Greek politicians who shared most U.S. objectives on both the international and the domestic plane. Even before the election American officials were confident that they could finally break the embrace of the Greek tar baby and enter into a more normal relationship with Greece. Whatever the outcome of the vote, the United States would "internationalize" responsibility for Greek recovery. In September 1952, the embassy forecast the postelection establishment of relations "on approximately the same basis as our relations with other NATO countries.... We should and presumably will continue to exercise guidance and leadership of a very important character but it should tend to become increasingly fraternal rather than paternal."[52] Aid and the Cyprus issue replaced the frustrating struggle over internal political reform at the center of the Greek-U.S. relationship.

FROM A (AID) TO C (CYPRUS)

The relationship between the United States and the Papagos government was certainly more businesslike and "normal." It got off to a bad start in the spring of 1953 as the recently elected Greek government sent its first high-level mission, led by Markezinis, to Washington for consultations with the recently installed administration of Dwight D. Eisenhower. Peurifoy sent the obligatory telegram to Washington stressing the need for special sensitivity to Greece's desire for economic aid. A "financial commitment" would encourage close US-Greek cooperation and prevent an erosion of parliamentary support for Papagos. The Greek deputy prime minister got plenty of official time, meeting with both Secretary of State John Foster Dulles and Eisenhower, but no financial commitment. Dulles took an immediate dislike to Markezinis and nearly destroyed the air of amity the State Department hoped to create by redrafting the official communiqué after Markezinis had released it to the Greek press. At the end, following an emotional outburst by the Greek leader and a partial retreat by the dour Dulles, "another Greek tragic-comedy" ended.[53]

A Dulles meeting with Papagos in Athens increased the level of personal cooperation. However, the new American administration saw no reason to respond favorably to Greek requests to increase economic assistance. Eisenhower had come to office pledged to reduce federal spending and shared the Truman administration's general strategic outlook, including its view that Greece constituted a limited strategic asset. When, in June 1953, Papagos coupled an offer to send Greek troops to Korea with a proposal to grant the United States basing rights on Greek soil, Eisenhower commented that he saw no reason to connect these advantageous offers to an increase in economic support. In a personal message, the U.S. president accepted the Papagos offers without offering a quid pro quo.[54]

On the domestic affairs side, Papagos ran the country with a minimum of consultation with the United States. When Peurifoy, reflecting the accentuated anticommunism of the Republican administration, raised the issue of Greek internal policy, Markezinis, whose government had displayed its bona fides by depriving thirty-nine KKE (communist party of Greece) members of their citizenship, told him that the EDA represented no immediate threat and that his government would not dissolve it. Papagos politely but firmly told the U.S. chargé that he would control military affairs. The Greek government decided on and announced the creation of a new national intelligence service, the Κεντρική Υπηρεσία Πληροφοριών or KYP, without informing the American embassy. The government's decision to enact a major reform of the civil service, long a target of U.S. criticism, raised American suspicions about Papagos's motivations and goals. The Rally government met one key U.S. objective when it enacted a currency reform.[55] While pleased with both the drive and effectiveness of the new government, embassy officers were concerned about the lack of a capable opposition as well as the government's apparent determination to eliminate the center as an electoral alternative. Without a democratic-center opposition, seepage of votes to the EDA seemed inevitable. Moreover, the government appeared content to encourage a swing to the left as a way of creating a permanent parliamentary opposition and thereby ensuring the Rally's long-term hold on power. A similar process was already under way in Italy. On the other hand, resurrecting the center appeared nearly impossible. Plastiras died in 1953. Papandreou defected from the Rally coalition and, after the obligatory secret negotiations, announced that he and Venizelos would join forces. Peurifoy had no desire to deal with Venizelos, concluding that the United States should not encourage centrist unification but simply wait on events and "hope that somehow the country is rugged enough to carry on."[56]

The other loser was the Palace. The royal family refused to accept any eclipse of its powers. Hoping to reclaim a central role, the king insisted on the prerogatives of his position: an expensive new yacht and an official visit to Washington. Both moves clearly spelled trouble for Papagos, especially an American visit in which the king and queen could be counted on to try to undercut the prime minister. In the meanwhile, the queen reignited her simmering personal vendetta against Peurifoy by publicly snubbing his wife. Peurifoy's subsequent recall, though apparently unrelated to the incident, led to an outburst by the prime minister in which he "launched into a diatribe against the Palace. . . . Papagos declared that the time had come to determine whether [the] constitutional government of Greece has decisive influence over Greek relations with the US and that 'this means open warfare between [the] Palace and [the] government.'"[57]

Peurifoy's last official act was, ironically, an attempt to mediate between the government and Palace. Nevertheless, he could depart for his next and most controversial posting in Guatemala with a sense that the relationship between Washington and Athens largely had become normal in terms of diplomatic practice. The U.S. footprint in Greece internal politics was drastically reduced. On the other hand, the issue of U.S. aid was firmly entangled with questions of military cooperation. In offering "sweeping" basing rights, Papagos shrewdly tried to draw the United States into a larger expenditure on Greece. Creation of the bases would force the United States to pay for major infrastructural development. Simultaneously, the Greek government declared that it was incapable of supporting a military force of the size that both the United States and NATO wanted. Greek defense minister Panagiotes Kanellopoulos informed Harold Stassen, head of the U.S. foreign assistance program, that only increased U.S. aid for Greek development could keep Greece's defense expenditures at required levels. When the United States instead cut its aid, Papagos reduced the size of the Greek armed forces.[58]

Personal temperament aside, Papagos's determination to extract a price for continued Greek cooperation reflected his growing political difficulties, above all the question of British control over the island of Cyprus. By mid-1953 the future of the island was becoming an issue no Greek government could ignore. Papagos took it up with visiting British foreign secretary Anthony Eden in June 1953. The dyspeptic Eden refused to discuss the issue. He then added insult to injury by telling Papagos that Greece had no claim to the island, as the only ties between Greeks and Greek Cypriots were those of religion and language. "Papagos seemed disappointed," the understated British minute of the meeting commented. More likely he was stunned that the British would acknowledge the basic element of the Greek claim to Cyprus, a common national identity, only to dismiss it. Papagos decided to pursue Greece's objectives by confronting the British at the United Nations. This strategy was a confession of weakness. Lacking leverage over the more powerful British, Papagos attempted to create it by rallying anticolonial feelings. Queen Frederika tried her hand at diplomacy by writing Prime Minister Winston Churchill that Britain ought to grant Greece enosis (unification) with Cyprus in order to avoid injuring the feelings of her subjects. Churchill replied that British possession of Cyprus was not negotiable and that Greece should recognize that the situation favored its interests.[59]

The contending parties, especially Greece, looked to Washington for assistance. U.S. officials wanted no part of the issue. A January 1955 National Intelligence Estimate for Greece reinforced their calculations by declaring: "Although the *enosis* issue is likely to be a continuing irritant in Greek relations with the UK, Turkey and the US, it is unlikely that Greece's alliance with these powers will be strained by this or any other issue."[60] In the long history of CIA misjudgments, few analyses have been more mistaken or more pregnant with difficulties for the United States.

2

NO REPORT FROM CYPRUS IS EVER CHEERFUL, 1950–1959

> Both strategically and commercially Cyprus appears to me the least important of the Turkish islands, full of interest as it certainly is to the historian and the antiquarian. Without harbors, unhealthy, occupied by a population whose habits, fixed for generations past, will alter little for generations to come, it offers no attractions for colonization . . . professional, commercial or financial pursuits.
> — U.S. minister at Constantinople, 1878

> Difficult and disloyal
> — Cyprus governor general Sir Richmond Palmer, 1939

On July 22, 1878, the first British governor of Cyprus took control of the island from its former Ottoman rulers at Larnaca. "Having caused my commission to be read," the high commissioner, General Lord Wolseley, "took the oaths of allegiance and office and assumed the government of Cyprus" to the "cheers" of representatives from its Christian and Muslim communities.[1] British rule, which was legally a loan of the island from the Ottoman state, was thus installed on a people with two millennia of experience with outside governance. The island's new rulers had acquired what they conceived as a strategic outpost in the eastern Mediterranean capable of restraining Russian and Ottoman power and, with it, responsibility for the welfare of people whose economic backwardness and mutual mistrust were deeply rooted.

"A DIFFICULT AND DISLOYAL PLACE"

Cyprus was, and is, an island with a majority Greek population. After nearly four centuries of rule by Western states, the island fell to Ottoman conquerors in 1571. The victors introduced the Muslim faith, along with a new set of overlords, by settling members of the victorious army and converting a portion of the indigenous Orthodox population to Islam. The island

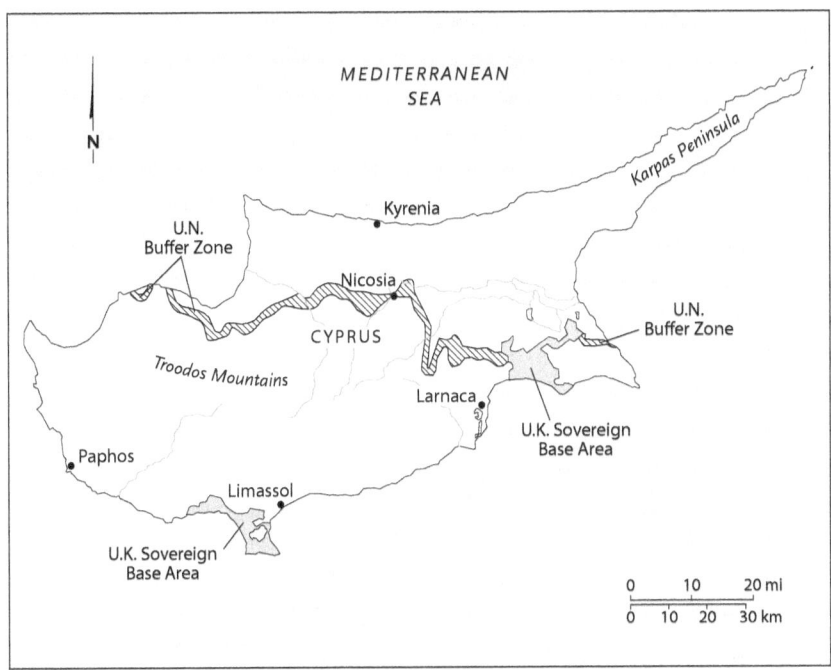

CYPRUS

was a provincial backwater, largely ignored by its Ottoman overlords, save for collecting taxes and suppressing the occasional popular revolt.

The Orthodox Church of Cyprus, an autocephalous part of the Eastern Church, administered the affairs of the Christian population (*millet*) for the Ottoman rulers and preserved and developed a strong sense of faith and Greek identity among the island's ethnic majority. Overall, that population was poor, uneducated, and rural. The limited reserve of education and administrative experience on the island was portioned out among churchmen, their lay assistants, some merchants, and a small Muslim administrative, commercial, and upper class. A majority of the Muslim population lived in the same poverty as their Christian neighbors but enjoyed the psychological reinforcement that came from believing they belonged to a conquering people. They also enjoyed the advantages conferred by sharia (Koranic-based) law in their relationships with the Christian community.[2]

British administrators immediately set to work to bring the island's legal code into conformity with Western standards, establishing an effective police force and court system and expanding public education. In 1882, they oversaw the first free elections in Cyprus's history. However, as the island's high commissioner admitted in an 1897 address to the Cyprus Legislative Council, "No vast strides have as yet been made in material progress." Having acted to provide a level of self-government to people who were "European," the British had neither the resources nor the interest to deal with the island's poverty. During the next half century, the colonial government made important infrastructural improvements while leaving the job of economic development largely to a limited number of Cypriot entrepreneurs.[3]

The British also inherited a deeply rooted ethnic conflict, fueled by the disagreements and resentments of the island's small Christian and Muslim elites. British decisions on the educational system and on the administration of justice ended the privileged administrative and political position the Orthodox Church had held under Ottoman rule, setting up an immediate conflict with the island's most powerful institution. Introducing Western law and a democratic assembly also upset many Muslim Cypriots because it underlined their minority status and loss of cultural hegemony. The colonial government balanced the number of judges on a given case equally between the two communities and colonial representatives, ensuring that any controversial decision lay in presumably impartial British hands. It assigned seats in the assembly to the Turkish Cypriots and apportioned employment in the local civil service between the two communities. These reforms failed to calm Turkish Cypriot concerns and exacerbated tensions between the Christian and Muslim populations of the island. By the early part of the twentieth century, Christian-Muslim conflicts were close to the surface. The 1912–13 war between Greece and the Ottoman Empire provoked violent clashes between the two communities. The legislative assembly became a scene of pointed exchanges between Christian and Muslim. "The debate, which began with genuine desire on the part of all parties . . . to work harmoniously together . . . ended . . . acrimoniously;" the high commissioner reported in 1913, "but, considering the hopes and fears which dominate the Moslem and Christian sections of the population . . . it is hardly surprising."[4]

The British declaration of war on the Ottoman Empire and subsequent formal annexation of Cyprus offered the Greek community the opportunity to press its agenda while placing the Turkish population in a difficult position. During the 1915 assembly session, the Greeks crafted a resolution to force the Turks to endorse both Britain's war and their demand for the "union" (enosis) of Cyprus with Greece. The Greek Cypriot resolution praised the British war effort and its past services to Greece and urged Britain to complete this work by ceding their island to the kingdom of the Hellenes. Greek representatives demanded that the Turks support the resolution as proof of their loyalty to the colonial power and their respect for the will of the Greek

Cypriot majority. Turkish leader Irfan Bey responded that while loyal, "he wasn't a certifying officer." Greek members were outraged. "The sentiments expressed by both sides are quite satisfactory from our point of view," one Colonial Office bureaucrat commented, "Irfan Bey is a witty member who always maddens the Greeks whose eloquence lacks humor."[5]

The British initially sent a regiment of Maltese troops to the island to deal with the possible ethnic clashes but withdrew these forces in late 1915, and Cyprus remained quiet during the war. The British focused on securing cooperation from the two antagonistic ethnic communities, not on inflaming their rivalry. Their objective was to create an imperial elite whose loyalty was to the British crown rather than an ethnic community. As part of this approach they encouraged talented young men, Christian and Muslim, to study in London and then return home to take up influential civil service posts. A divide-and-rule strategy carried obvious risks of provoking intercommunal violence that would undermine colonial rule. Moreover, the British felt they were dealing, at least in the case of the Greek Cypriots, with a people whose "European" character necessitated different treatment and more "democratic" administration. Cyprus's advisory legislative body and locally staffed administration permitted Greeks and Turks to participate in their own government. Ultimately, the aim of this exercise in self-rule was to maintain British control by creating a Cypriot elite that supported the empire. If either community refused to accept London's control, a local legislature would become divisive, and the legitimacy of British rule would be challenged.[6]

The British inadvertently created a cause for division when, in October 1915, they offered Cyprus to Greece in exchange for its participation in the war against Germany. The Greek government turned down the offer, and the British subsequently withdrew it. However, the offer made both Greeks and Greek Cypriots believe that a deal could be made, fueling nationalism and unrest among the island's majority community. The United Kingdom had no intention of permitting discontented Greek Cypriots to undermine its rule. While the island hosted few British troops and lacked a suitable harbor, its proximity to Turkey and to the Middle East led the War Office to insist on its regional strategic importance. Moreover, in the wake of its victory in World War I, the British government faced a series of challenges to its rule in colonies, such as India. Withdrawing from one of its colonies would fuel nationalist agitation throughout the empire. Early in 1919 the U.K. embassy in Greece warned that Britain, having signed on to the ideas of self-determination and nationality championed by U.S. president Woodrow Wilson during the war, now faced a contradiction between its proclaimed values and the reality of its widespread empire. Foreign secretary Lord Curzon dismissed granting enosis as "soft hearted." However, the British colonial dilemma grew more evident as Greek Cypriots continued to press for union with Greece.[7]

During the 1920s, the Orthodox Church adopted a more confrontational strategy in its struggle for enosis. British officials continued to insist that the movement was largely confined to the urban elites and that the "troublemakers" were a minority. It could point to a number of Greek Cypriots who collaborated with Turkish Cypriots in the colonial administration and who supported British rule as well as to the generally peaceful relations between the two ethnic groups in the countryside. The movement supporting enosis was a minority but a particularly effective one. The church commanded the ultimate loyalty of the vast majority of Cypriots. The lay element of the movement, closely tied to the hierarchy, included a number of forceful and capable organizers. The increasingly powerful Cypriot Communist Party (KKK, later AKEL—Progressive Party of the Working People), although suspicious of both nationalism and the "capitalist" Greek state, had little choice but to back enosis.[8]

Fortunately for British rule, the prewar push toward enosis peaked at the moment when Greece was incapable of providing any international assistance. Venizelos returned to power in 1928 and had to cope with the world depression and Fascist Italy's imperial ambitions. He had no interest in provoking a conflict with Greece's major protector. The living symbol of Greek territorial ambitions prudently refused to respond to press demands for action on enosis. Prodded by London, the Greek government scaled back its overt and covert support for Cypriot demands when the situation on the island exploded into a violent confrontation.[9]

Ironically, the October 1931 outbreak of violence in Nicosia extracted the British from one sticky situation only to entrap them in another. The increasingly effective actions of the church in promoting enosis had put the colonial government on the defensive. As Colonial Office officials glumly recognized, Greek Cypriot demands for enosis were a legal exercise of their right of free speech. The British had no effective means of stamping out Greek "subversion." As long as proponents of enosis acted peacefully, they could neither be tried nor jailed. Even the most limited efforts to monitor church-sponsored political activity ran afoul of British privacy laws and aroused British press criticism of government infringement of the basic rights of its subjects. Governor Sir Ronald Storrs complained that, while the Greek Cypriots were openly organizing to undermine British rule, he lacked any effective legal means to prevent their actions.[10]

The Greek Cypriots played into the government's hands with a spontaneous uprising in October 1931. Once pro-enosis Cypriots had acted in an illegal manner, London could respond forcefully. British forces were called in from Egypt as a mob burned down the governor's mansion and the rioting spread to other towns. The government arrested a number of Greek Cypriot leaders and sent ten, including two of the island's three bishops, into exile. Even so, Storrs warned, the effort to decapitate the Greek Cypriot leadership was only partially successful and brought with it a new problem: "There can be no question now of bringing these deported persons back for trial in Cyprus. It is extremely doubtful whether any convictions could be obtained." Greek Cypriot agitation for the return of the exiled "martyrs" became a major headache for the colonial government. They became symbols of resistance to British rule.[11]

The Greek Cypriots, however, also lost. London suppressed the elected legislative council and imposed direct rule on the island. Moreover, the riots intensified Turkish Cypriot apprehensions about the Greek Cypriots' long-term objectives. Turkish elites, aware of the Greek state's role in the long and brutal ethnic cleansing of the Balkan Muslims the previous century, could only wonder what fate awaited them if the island passed under Greek rule. They repeatedly appealed to Britain to maintain the status quo. Simultaneously, the effects of a successful nationalist revolution in Turkey encouraged them to develop a deeper ethnic identification. The Cypriot Muslim community rapidly became a Turkish one, and encouraged by the local Turkish consul, they began looking to an as-yet-unresponsive Ankara for support and meanwhile loyally cooperated with the British administration.[12]

After the riots, Colonial Office policy actively sought to cut the roots away from pro-enosis activity. It replaced the "weak" Storrs with a series of more "forceful" governors. The British placed a special tax on the Greek Cypriots to cover the costs of post-riot reconstruction. They rejected calls for a return to free elections, interned a number of Greek Cypriots, and intermittently imposed press censorship. The colonial administration carefully monitored the church for signs of nationalist activity and tried to reduce its influence among the Greek Cypriot community.[13] Believing that the church was best undermined by the growth of prosperity and accompanying secularization, Storrs's successor, Gov. Richmond Palmer, urged the Colonial Office to undertake major economic projects, including school construction, designed to boost prosperity and increase urbanization. Meanwhile, the colonial government sought to further undermine the church by impeding the election of a successor archbishop to Kyril III (ob. 1934) and by shutting down its political-funding operations.[14]

In spite of momentary flights of optimism, Palmer acknowledged that the battle against enosis forces was not successful. The church refused to crumble and, in fact, solidified its hold on many Christian Cypriots through its determined battle against colonial administration. The Greek-language press was an effective critic of the colonial government and spread pro-enosis propaganda. The British media joined in the assault, to the intense discomfort of the Colonial Office. The British administration found itself increasingly isolated. Palmer warned: "The future of Cyprus as a British colony will become more and more difficult if this continues."[15]

World War II gave the hard-pressed British a bit of respite. They denied the Greek government-in-exile's request for refuge on the island, transporting it to Egypt and then South Africa. With Greece totally dependent on Britain for its liberation, the Church of Cyprus became more malleable, reducing its agitation and providing a carefully modulated support to the British war effort. War-generated prosperity helped to calm political passions without affecting the basic situation. One colonial official acknowledged the "absence of any general and fundamental sentiment of British loyalty" on the island, while another lamented that: "No report from Cyprus is ever cheerful."[16]

Once the war was over, enosis agitation began to slowly pick up steam. However, a critical element was missing. Greece plunged into a civil war. Without Greek support, enosis remained a local issue, attracting little international attention. In spite of their success at harassing the British, Greek Cypriot leaders had no strategy for forcing their exit. Cyprus simmered, but British authorities believed they could retain control of an island that seemed increasingly valuable as their Middle East interests faced unprecedented challenges. In 1948 they attempted to introduce a new constitution and restore self-rule. Pro-enosis forces, led by the church, rejected the offer, demanding "self-determination." Early in 1950, the church organized a cleverly rigged "plebiscite" in which 96 percent of Orthodox Christians voting opted for enosis.[17]

The British position began to deteriorate seriously in 1950. The "plebiscite" crystallized the debate around the issue of "self-determination." With the civil war over, Greek public attention gradually began to refocus on Cyprus. Greek concern grew in response to events in Cyprus, beginning with the plebiscite and nurtured by a highly nationalist press. Initially, the crown and Greece's political elites tried to avoid the issue until British missteps aroused their "philotimo" (pride), most notably in 1953, when Anthony Eden refused to discuss Cyprus with Prime Minister Alexander Papagos. In the summer of 1950, the Cypriots elected the plebiscite's manager, Michael Moskos, a thirty-nine-year-old monk, as Archbishop Makarios III. The charismatic new church leader, who also assumed the role of political representative of the Greek Cypriot community (ethnarch), understood that Cyprus would attain some form of self-rule only by mobilizing international pressure on Britain. A student of both Machiavelli and Archimedes, Makarios planned to use the United Nations to achieve leverage over the Greek and British governments: driving the first into full support and then utilizing Greece's membership in the UN to place the Greek Cypriot demand for self-determination on the international body's agenda. Makarios's success in internationalizing the Cyprus issue nearly tore apart the United States' primary alliance system, the North Atlantic Treaty Organization (NATO), put diplomatic relations between Britain and Greece into a prolonged deep freeze, and created powerful antagonisms between Greece and Turkey. Inevitably it drew the United States into a prolonged engagement with the Cyprus issue and created enduring tensions with Greece over what the Greek ambassador in Washington characterized as a U.S. "betrayal" of its obligations to a small ally and client.[18]

BETWEEN A ROCK AND A HARD PLACE

Greek Cypriot claims were difficult to resist precisely because they held the moral high ground. Self-determination was a basic human right, recognized by the U.N. Charter and by repeated U.S. public statements. Majority rule was an equally unchallengeable principle of democracy. In theory, the United States, which supported decolonization as a part of its foreign policy, might have backed the Greek Cypriot position. Instead, the U.S. government avoided endorsing either side's claims, urged the Greek and Turkish governments to avoid inflaming the Cyprus question, and encouraged the British to deal with the Cyprus problem.[19]

U.S. reluctance to become involved with Cyprus had many motivations. In the first place, the Greek Cypriot position was not as unchallengeable as its proponents argued. The Turkish Cypriots were more than a "minority." Both Ottoman and British imperial policy had recognized their status as a separate "community" living on the island with a Greek community. Turkish Cypriot and, subsequently, Turkish leaders insisted on recognition and maintenance of this legally and customarily recognized status with the special rights of self-administration it conveyed. Moreover, given both the background of ethnic violence on the island and Greece's disturbing historical record in treating Muslims in the Balkans and post–World War I Asia Minor, an arrangement for enosis would require some form of special protection for the Turkish minority on Cyprus. The Greek Cypriots resolutely refused to offer the sorts of guarantees that Turkish Cypriots or the Turkish government would accept. Outside mediation appeared to be the best way to arrive at a compromise between the two communities, but neither Greece nor Turkey nor Britain was inclined to act as a deal maker.[20]

British control of the island was sanctioned by treaty arrangements. However, in an age of nationalism and decolonization, their claim to rule Cyprus rested on exceedingly shaky moral and legal foundations. The Foreign Office doubted that the colony was worth retaining. Nevertheless, the British government decided to hold on to Cyprus. It made two arguments in support of continued rule. First, London claimed that the island was of great strategic value not only to Britain, but also to the West. Second, the British insisted that their withdrawal would bring with it intercommunal violence that would tear apart the social fabric of the island and invite intervention by the Soviet Union. To bolster this claim, the British could point to the size and influence of AKEL.[21]

The argument for the strategic value of Cyprus appeared to find support largely among the U.K. chiefs of staff. Lacking good ports, Cyprus had not played a major role in British imperial defense policy from 1878 onward. British took control of Egypt and its great port of Alexandria in 1884, largely negating the usefulness of Cyprus as an advanced base in the eastern Mediterranean for the next sixty years. The island played no significant role in either world war. However, the Egyptian revolution of 1952 and subsequent expulsion of British bases, combined with the greater importance of air power, gave Cyprus renewed strategic possibilities. With its control of the Suez Canal in jeopardy and nationalism threatening its position throughout the Middle East, the credibility of British claims regarding the value of Cyprus bases improved. Additionally, the United Kingdom had a major signals-intelligence operation on Cyprus and provided a listening post to its American ally.[22]

In 1956, the Suez crisis finally put the British thesis of the strategic importance of Cyprus to a test, with mixed results. The island served as a mobilization point for expeditionary forces. Aircraft operating out of Cyprus supported the Anglo-French invasion of Egypt, in spite of some successful Greek Cypriot sabotage actions on military bases. In the aftermath of its Suez setback, with Anglo-American relations under the worst strain of the postwar era, Prime Minister Harold Macmillan met with President Dwight D. Eisenhower in Bermuda. In discussions about Cyprus, the British leader abandoned the claim that Cyprus's strategic role required continued colonial status, proposing instead that a few permanent bases would be adequate to Western needs.²³

If history and current events argued that Cyprus was of limited strategic value, then the last line of defense for a British colonial presence was ethnic conflict. Here, the British were on increasingly firm ground. The intransigence of the Cypriot ethnic communities was growing. Greek Cypriot terrorism directed against the British colonial administration, against Greek Cypriots who supported British rule, and, ultimately against Turkish Cypriots poisoned intercommunal relations. Extremist Turkish Cypriots gained the upper hand in their community. The support the two "motherlands" gave "their" Cypriots fueled ethnic tensions. The British were losing control of Cyprus but could continue to argue that their presence alone prevented a bloodbath. Moreover, a civil war on the island would likely provoke war between two NATO allies.²⁴

Neither Greece nor Turkey had a legal claim to Cyprus. Turkey had abandoned its legal rights in 1923 by signing the Treaty of Lausanne. Greece never had any legal claim. Both states, nevertheless, advanced strong arguments about their rights to a say in the island's future. In January 1958 letters to Eisenhower, the Greek and Turkish prime ministers invoked ethnic nationalism in remarkably similar terms in advancing their claims. Greece's Constantine Karamanlis underlined his nation's "duty towards her oppressed children," while Turkey's Adnan Menderes stressed the "future and fate of our brothers on Cyprus."²⁵ For Greeks, the integration of Cyprus was a final step in a nearly 150-year national unification process. The Turkish case, given its apparent abandonment of Cyprus in 1878 and 1923, was a bit more difficult to make. Greek Cypriot and Greek leaders underlined the apparent contradiction in Turkey's position. The Turks responded that their renunciation of Cyprus had been based on the assumption that Britain would maintain control of the island. As early as 1951, the Turks laid a diplomatic marker with Washington. Any change in the status quo, Ambassador Feridun Erkin informed the State Department, would require Turkish assent. Moreover, the Greek Cypriot struggle to obtain union with Greece roused strong nationalist feelings among Turks. In late August 1955, the U.S. mission in Turkey forwarded an analysis of public opinion warning that government efforts to stir up public interest in Cyprus had struck a responsive chord. A "very genuine" apprehension about the island gripped all segments of Turkish society, and the public mood was ugly. Within two weeks, the Turkish government lost control of anti-Greek demonstrations it had organized. Given an opportunity by Turkish police, inflamed nationalists conducted a brutal pogrom against Greek minorities in Istanbul and Izmir.[26]

Each state buttressed its position with other arguments. Greece claimed that failure to achieve enosis would undermine its pro-Western government and give the Soviet bloc a strategic advantage in the Eastern Mediterranean. Turkey also stressed geopolitical arguments, based on a paranoid view of Greek intentions and Cyprus's position less than forty miles from the Turkish coast. Insisting that Athens was reviving the Megali Idea, Turkish spokesmen "firmly oppose[d] further Greek territorial expansion at what they fancy to be Turkey's expense." Menderes warned Eisenhower that "since 80% of the Greek population [of Cyprus] is known to be communistic," enosis would deliver the island to anti-Western forces and create a major threat to Turkey. A Turkish presence on the island could best and perhaps only be achieved through its partition.[27]

In July 1956 Vice President Richard Nixon returned from a visit to Turkey to report to the U.S. National Security Council that the Turks "had a positively pathological attitude on the Cyprus problem. The prime minister had even gone so far as to suggest that if Cyprus was joined to Greece, the Turks would go to war to prevent it."[28]

Tensions between Greece and Turkey grew as result of their diplomatic tactics, their readiness to support violence, and the actions of Great Britain. The Greek government backed the terrorist campaign for enosis, and the Turks responded by organizing and supplying Turkish Cypriot paramilitary bands. The Greeks initially sought to freeze the Turks out of talks over Cyprus, arguing that they had abandoned any right to a say in the island's future by signing the Lausanne treaty. They wanted direct talks with Britain and a parallel set of negotiations between the British colonial administrators and Greek Cypriots. Britain, on the other hand, insisted that Turkey had to have a role equal to that of Greece, citing the presence of a Turkish community on the island and counting on Turkish support for its efforts to hold on to the island. Later, as the British sought a formula to reduce their responsibility for the island, they would look to the Turks as potential partners.[29]

The British lost their best chance to arrange a peaceful settlement of the island's problems by deporting the one man capable of speaking with authority for the Greek Cypriots. British mistrust of Makarios was natural. They knew that the archbishop had contacts with and provided financial support to Colonel George Grivas and his terrorist movement, EOKA (National Organization of Cypriot Fighters), in their attacks on British citizens and administration. Grivas, a sociopath, was an effective guerrilla leader. EOKA's activities altered the balance of power on the island, strengthening Makarios's hand, but simultaneously lessened the archbishop's room for maneuver. Early in 1956, the British governor, Field Marshal Sir John Harding, decided that talks with Makarios had reached a dead end. The archbishop would not accept a formula to deal with Turkish Cypriot concerns, was trying to drive a wedge between the United Kingdom and Turkey, and would not condemn terrorism.[30] In March 1956 the British arrested Makarios and exiled him to the Seychelles.

Makarios was an extremely difficult personality. Driven by conflicting objectives and operating under extreme pressure from the fanatically nationalist and violent Grivas as well as his backers within the Orthodox Church, the archbishop adopted a torturous negotiation style that further complicated the chances for settlement by undercutting Harding's trust. Nevertheless, he was the Greek Cypriot leader. With Makarios in exile, the British had no authoritative interlocutor. Moreover, on the critical issues of the future of Cyprus, Makarios showed flexibility. An informant close to Makarios told U.S. officials: "[The] archbishop's ultimate objective is to achieve complete independence for Cyprus with freedom to make its (his) own choice—not necessarily simple enosis on Greek terms."[31] Makarios's personal ambitions frequently diverged from the pursuit of enosis. As the leader (ethnarch) of the Greek Cypriots, he would not simply hand over the island to the political class in Athens and permit Cyprus to become a backwater in the Greek state. Makarios's relationships with Greek leaders were always complex and tense. As head of an autocephalous church, his relationship with the postunification Greek church created potential difficulties, given both state control over the national church and the leadership claims of the "Archbishop of Athens and All Greece." An independent church in an independent state might provide a better stage for Makarios's abilities and ambitions.[32]

The British decided to treat Makarios as "the origin and foundation of all terrorism in Cyprus." London argued that his removal would permit it to crush EOKA and with it Greek Cypriot dreams of enosis. In March 1957, Macmillan privately assured Eisenhower that the "archbishop . . . is the Bourbon of Cyprus. . . . [E]vents in the island and in the world are surging past him. Harding has beaten terrorism militarily, and the world now recognizes that Cyprus is an international problem" that could be settled by an arrangement between the United Kingdom, Greece, and Turkey without reference to the island's ethnic majority.[33] In reality, Makarios's arrest, detention, and subsequent exile in Greece created a major impasse to negotiations. Karamanlis faced plotting to depose him and hand the prime minister's job to the Cypriot ethnarch. As a result, he refused to make any arrangement without Makarios's blessing. The exiled archbishop's presence in Athens after March 1957 meant that Karamanlis viewed the ethnarch's immediate and unconditional return to Cyprus as the first step in a settlement. The Turks took Makarios's exile to Athens as a sign of weakening British resolve and responded by ratcheting up their already hard-line stance.[34]

Throughout the 1954–58 Cyprus impasse, all the major players appealed to Washington for support. In spite of an obvious U.S. interest in successful resolution of this extremely complex issue, Washington maintained its distance, settling for one unsuccessful probing mission. Resolving Cyprus called for an extremely skillful, persistent American diplomatic initiative. None was forthcoming.[35]

American Cyprus policy operated on a series of calculations based on a hierarchy of values and interests. U.S. reluctance to become involved in the Cyprus issue was partially rooted in its leader's distaste for the nationalistic politics of Greece and Turkey as well as for the imperial calculations of Great Britain. In the course of creating a successful Western national state, Americans substituted "civic" for ethnic or "tribal" nationalism. The monocultural nationalism of Greece and Turkey emphasized exclusion and had a long history of violence. American nationalism, despite its racism and nativist streak, was inclusive, based on the conviction that individuals, whatever their ethnic background or religious faith, could become loyal and contributing citizens. At the same time that Greeks and Turks were disputing dominance over a small island, the United States was peacefully absorbing two large territories with multiethnic populations, Alaska and Hawaii. The American "empire," unlike the British version, grew on the basis of the free choice of territories to seek association and with the understanding that new member states of the union would be largely self-governing. In contrast with the British model, the states of the American union sent a political and administrative class to Washington to govern the United States.[36]

A second source of U.S. uneasiness over Cyprus was the damage the Cyprus quarrel was doing to the NATO. In a 1951 discussion with Makarios, the U.S. ambassador to Greece, John Peurifoy, underlined the danger that the Cyprus dispute would weaken the Western alliance and urged the archbishop to recall that the "common struggle" against communism required a "common front." In February 1957, Secretary of State John Foster Dulles complained of weariness with the Cyprus issue to a high-level delegation from Turkey: "The three interested parties were putting something of lesser importance ahead of the greater issue," containment of the threat posed by

Soviet authoritarianism through mutual cooperation, and until they were "prepared to make some compromises," Dulles did not feel that the United States "had any responsibility to continue its efforts to find a solution" to the problem.[37] By embroiling themselves in a quarrel created by aggressive racial nationalism and old-style imperialism, three U.S. allies were ignoring the entire purpose of the Western alliance, undercutting support for it among their populations, and making multilateralism more difficult to justify to an American public steeped in traditions of unilateralism.

A hierarchy of concrete interests also influenced U.S. calculations. The United States placed an exceptionally high premium on British cooperation, particularly in the eastern Mediterranean and Middle East. Despite its postwar economic and military decline, Britain retained significant military force and intelligence-collection capabilities, enjoyed excellent contacts with regional elites, possessed local experience, and shared a set of common values and interests. American policy makers sought to nudge the British toward decolonization in Cyprus while in the process avoiding damage to British prestige or vital interests.[38]

Turkey was another important strategic partner that, in the eyes of the Eisenhower administration, required careful stroking. Turkey's democratic development had stalled. The authoritarian tendencies of the Menderes government and economic corruption reinforced by government regulation were growing. In the mid-1950s, most U.S. officials regarded enosis as the inevitable, and probably the best, outcome of the Cyprus crisis. A Cyprus under Greek control would offer basing rights to NATO and keep the Soviets out. As a result, the United States tried to move Turkey away from insisting on the status quo. In August 1955, the Americans warned the Turks that world public opinion was coalescing behind Greek Cypriot demands. The "right to self-determination is hard to oppose." Cyprus could stand on its own feet economically, and no matter how strong or weak an individual Greek government might be, time was on the side of the Greeks. The subsequent Turkish demand for partition found little support in Washington. Turkish proposals called for handing over approximately 40 percent of the land to 18 percent of the population. U.S. studies estimated that an ethnic division of the island would require shifting nearly two hundred thousand people and would open up the issue of the fate of Muslim and Christian "holy places," further exacerbating tensions between the two communities. Clearly, "the majority of the population" would reject partition.[39]

In 1955 the U.S. ambassador in Athens, Cavendish Cannon, warned that Cyprus, as "the central national issue," threatened Greece's newly constructed political stability. The State Department understood that a peaceful settlement in Cyprus was the best tool for mooring Greece securely in the Western alliance and reinforcing its internal stability.[40] The Greeks made such a deal difficult. By 1955 Greece was backing a low-intensity war with Britain, the most important U.S. European ally. Papagos's decision to bring the Cyprus issue before the United Nations further roused Greek public opinion. As frequently happened in the nineteenth century, Greek politicians found it impossible to resist the combination of demanding territorial expansion and utilizing a "national" issue for domestic political advantage. Greek efforts to justify their Cyprus position would have been much more credible in American eyes if the state radio had not conducted an aggressive campaign encouraging anti-British and later anti-American public demonstrations and demanding enosis. Moreover, Greece provided a logistical base and financial support for Grivas's terrorist campaigns against British citizens. The Greek Orthodox Church, part of the state structure, backed the use of violence against the British administration on Cyprus while also fomenting anti-Americanism. Contacts between Grivas and the top Greek political leadership were constant, going through the Greek consulate in Nicosia. It should have come as no surprise to Greeks that the British were extremely angry or that the Turkish government and public opinion, recalling past humiliations at the hands of Greece, soon adopted a hostile position.[41]

Fortunately, Greek inflexibility on the Cyprus issue peaked under Papagos. The Greek prime minister took a very aggressive line after his September 1953 rebuff by Eden. By 1955, Papagos, terminally ill but holding firmly to power, had dug Greece into a deep hole. Public Works Minister Karamanlis, whom the king had privately approached about succeeding the ailing and absent prime minister, told his cabinet colleagues that Greece must adopt a new approach or face diplomatic isolation and political defeat. For Karamanlis this meant coming up with a Cyprus policy that would win U.S. support by acting as a partner rather than an antagonist to its NATO allies Britain and Turkey. Cyprus was important to Greece, but maintaining its position in the alliance was paramount. Moreover, Karamanlis recognized that, as the weakest and least strategically important of the involved states, Greece had fewer cards to play. He hoped to gain an American declaration of support for enosis by developing a sense of shared strategic interests, above all the need to preserve Greece's political stability, while he employed patient diplomacy to win Turkish and British acquiescence to unification.[42]

This approach made life difficult for Greece's leader. The United States, although privately urging the British to talk with the Greeks about Cyprus, took two actions guaranteed to worsen the situation for Papagos's successor. It blocked U.N. consideration of the Cyprus question and then responded in an "evenhanded" manner to the September 1955 riots in Istanbul and Izmir, chiding the Greeks, who justifiably felt themselves the victims of Turkish misdeeds, and failing to publicly censor those responsible. These actions, which enraged Greek public opinion, made forging a compromise all the more difficult.[43]

Karamanlis tried to articulate a less confrontational policy, while avoiding the public concessions that would bring him into conflict with Makarios and Greek public opinion. He insisted that Greece support the just desires of the Greek Cypriot majority but suggested that improved relations with Turkey could open the way to a deal that protected Turkish interests. British colonialism, he asserted, was a thing of the past, and Greece stood ready to assist the United Kingdom in escaping from it. Cyprus, the prime minister stated in March 1956, would utilize its right to self-determination to enter the democratic family of nations with a constitution that guaranteed the rights of the Turkish Cypriots. In April, he suggested that NATO should be the mechanism through which decolonization and self-determination could operate. Privately, he assured U.S. representatives that Greece would support continued British basing rights and, in a refrain that would characterize Greek diplomacy for two decades, pledged to reign in Makarios and pro-enosis forces. He also promised that, assuming a plebiscite on the island endorsed enosis, Greece would protect the Turkish minority, meet Turkey's security interests, and offer "generous economic privileges to Turkey and Great Britain."[44]

The United States was unwilling to lend the type of support that Karamanlis needed to settle Cyprus on terms that best met Greek needs. Karamanlis wanted the Eisenhower administration to twist arms, specifically those of the Eden government and Makarios. The Greek prime minister was frustrated by the refusal of British authorities to talk directly with Greece but was unwilling and realistically unable to abandon Greece's role in backing Grivas. He wanted the United States to take on the critical role of confronting Makarios, something he could not do because of Greek public support for the archbishop. In exchange, Karamanlis was ready to accept a solution creating an independent Cypriot state, leaving the door open for later union with Greece. He warned that failure to provide him greater U.S. aid would probably mean his political defeat. Dulles agreed. Karamanlis bitterly complained about the lack of U.S. support for his peacemaking efforts and for his political career. Eisenhower and Dulles were unmoved. In a rare discussion about Cyprus, the two men sketched out the parameters of their policy: "The

Sec[retary] said the Greek-Turkey thing was a mess. The Pres[ident] said the Greeks were demanding [that] unless we take their side, they will be tough. The Sec[retary] said . . . the British . . . dragged the Turks in and got them excited so the issue is considered Greek-Turkish and not Greek-British. The Pres[ident] said Cyprus never belonged to Greece."[45]

The policy that emerged from these considerations bore the mark of John Foster Dulles. Eisenhower had little interest in Cyprus, regarding it as an annoyance. Dulles favored a cautious, low-risk approach that stressed secret negotiations between the three nations involved, aimed at compromise, kept the United States in the background, and until early 1957, expected, but did not encourage, Greek Cypriot achievement of enosis. Karamanlis repeatedly tried to pin down Under Secretary of State Robert Murphy on the specifics of a U.S. plan for a Cyprus settlement. He failed because the Eisenhower administration had no plan, nor was it willing to take the lead in promoting a solution. When Taylor Belcher, U.S. consul at Nicosia, urged a more active U.S. role, the Greek desk replied that such a radical shift was unlikely, as the policy "reflects the secretary's thinking pretty accurately."[46]

Dulles aimed at a solution that would meet Greece's minimum objectives but simultaneously compensate Turkey. In February 1958 he told the new U.S. ambassador to Greece, James Riddleberger, "It was pretty clear that the island was Greek." Partition was a "basically bad" solution, but "the Turks had a good case regarding Cyprus when they put it on a basis of security" and "had to be satisfied on this aspect of their claims . . . by something more than a paper guarantee . . . conceivably . . . by a Turkish base on the island."[47] Dulles felt that the British, too, needed only basing rights on Cyprus. In the event of a settlement, the United States would require some form of authorization from Greek or Cypriot authorities to maintain its own signals-intelligence operation on the island, but there was little apparent concern about this issue. Karamanlis was on record as supporting NATO basing. Makarios, who repeatedly signaled his desire for close cooperation with the United States, was ready to meet this basic U.S. objective.[48]

While containing Greek diplomatic initiatives and moderating Turkish intransigence were important problems for Dulles, the main thrust of his activity was convincing the British to make concessions. Eden proved to be especially difficult. He frequently dug in his heels, insisting that the problem lay in Athens and urging the United States to put pressure on its Greek ally to make concessions. Dulles and Eisenhower declined and warned the British that they were losing leverage by relying on Turkish support. Britain, the president wrote to Eden in June 1956, had to retain a free hand to make the compromises needed to settle the Cyprus question. Moreover, the British would have to deal with Makarios. When Macmillan replaced Eden as prime minister (December 1956) in the wake of the Suez disaster, the U.S.-U.K. dialogue became more intense, and British tactics changed. Where Eden resisted, the supple Macmillan offered his diplomatic interlocutors a show of British flexibility, as he unveiled a series of proposals, each designed to retain maximum U.K. control over the island.[49]

Since Dulles was convinced that a public airing of disagreements was counterproductive, he tried to scuttle Greek efforts to bring Cyprus before the United Nations. By 1956, the United States recognized that this effort was damaging its interests and decided to stop blocking discussion, opting instead, for neutrality in U.N. votes on Cyprus. The Greeks were only mildly encouraged by this change of position. Greek foreign minister Evangelos Averoff-Tossizza recalled that he was unsure if the latest American position was "genuine" or "hostile" neutrality. The preferred U.S. international setting for discussions was NATO. By early 1957, the Untied States envisioned a double-track strategy with the three involved states talking inside NATO, while the British and Greek Cypriots resumed their long-suspended dialogue. The Greeks, while open to some role for NATO, were still resisting the sort of talks that would reinforce the Turkish claim to parity in the solution of Cyprus. They preferred the United Nations as a venue for talks and as a bully pulpit from which to organize international pressure on the British to force a compromise.[50]

Makarios was the key to any successful dialogue. At Bermuda in March 1957, both Eisenhower and Dulles put intense pressure on the British to release the archbishop from his internment as the first step toward resuming negotiations. Macmillan agreed but parried the U.S. effort by refusing to let Makarios return to Cyprus. At the same meeting, Eisenhower, whose understanding of military strategy was difficult to challenge, subtly undercut British claims over the strategic necessity of Cyprus. He told Macmillan that, even without Cyprus, the West had enough Mediterranean bases to ensure its security. The island was strategically useful, not essential.[51]

Even after illness and death removed Dulles from the management of U.S. foreign policy, the Eisenhower administration refrained from major involvement in settling the Cyprus issue. In spite of unrest among State Department diplomats who believed that the United States had a major stake in a Cyprus deal, the policy remained to "avoid involving the United States in a settlement that will require significant . . . economic or military support."[52] Britain's willingness to support the long-term costs of holding on to Cyprus wilted.

In June 1958, following the failure of two other British initiatives, Macmillan came up with a new proposal for a Greek-Turkish-British "tridominium" to control the island until a final solution was arranged. The Greeks rejected the idea, and to their surprise, so did the Turks. Macmillan then announced that the program would be implemented without Greek participation on October 1, invited the Turks to join in the administration of Cyprus, and essentially abdicated responsibility for a final settlement to the Greeks and Turks. At the same time, Turkish Cypriots, realizing their Greek Cypriot enemy was on the defensive, unleashed a set of riots in Nicosia and other towns reminiscent of the 1955 Istanbul-Izmir attacks.[53]

The Macmillan proposals acted like a cold shower on Greece's political leadership. Karamanlis tried and failed to secure U.S intervention to block the idea. Facing isolation, and a solution worked out by Britain and Turkey that surely would involve partition of the island, the Greeks shifted policy to accommodate reality and keep Greece in the Cyprus game. As early as the summer of 1957, one senior Greek diplomat argued that Athens had to rethink its strategy, accept the increasing irrelevancy of Britain to a final Cyprus deal, and approach the Turks. Karamanlis already had begun to question the value of the U.N. in achieving a solution. Macmillan's action forced a bilateral approach on Greece. On September 19, 1958, the Greek prime minister explained the new realities to Makarios. The archbishop responded that Karamanlis had to utilize Greece's most effective weapon, threatening withdrawal from NATO, to force an American intervention and a solution favorable to enosis. The Greek leader rejected this suggestion, telling Makarios that Greek security interests were and would remain his primary concern. The Cypriot ethnarch departed, warning the Greeks that he would publicly attack this policy. The following day, however, the surprising Makarios told British parliamentarian Barbara Castle that he would favor "guaranteed" independence for Cyprus, in effect accepting Turkish equality in deciding on the island's future and abandoning enosis. The Greek leadership was stunned. Makarios's concessions had undermined their bargaining position before they began talks with the Turks.[54]

Backs to the wall, the Greek government, aided by some unexpected diplomatic finesse on the part of the Turks, managed to forge a compromise—independence without self-determination—that they and the British agreed offered the only way out of the Cyprus impasse. The London-Zurich Pact of

February 1959, the fruit of Greek-Turkish bargaining, would heavily influence subsequent U.S. efforts to settle the island's problems. The three powers imposed the settlement on the two ethnic communities. The agreements covering Cyprus recognized Turkey's claims to parity on Cyprus, created an independent ("partnership") state based on the existence of two essentially equal ethnic communities, forbade either enosis or partition, and under certain circumstances permitted British, Greek, or Turkish military intervention to preserve this status quo. Both self-determination and majority rule were swept aside. Makarios, who had helped engineer this settlement, craftily held the loyalty of his base by a public show of his reluctance to sign the agreement. The October 1959 National Intelligence Estimate for the new republic of Cyprus gloomily forecast: "Independence will not eradicate serious tensions between the Greek and Turkish communities. The settlement is replete with provisions which will tend to perpetuate divisions.... Though the new constitution will prohibit enosis, sentiment for union with Greece will persist not only in Cyprus but in Greece.... The island's stability will depend in great part on whether the Greek and Turkish governments continue to exert moderating influences on the two Cypriot communities."[55]

WINNERS AND LOSERS

The London-Zurich agreements rewarded Britain, Turkey, and the Turkish Cypriots at the expense of the Greek Cypriots and Greece. In spite of committing a seemingly endless series of missteps, the British succeeded in getting free of the island while retaining extensive basing rights. They had blocked self-determination, and thus enosis, through negotiations with Greece and Turkey. Relations with Turkey were strong. Its costs were the loss of a colony and a period of difficult relations with Greece in exchange for bases and a more smoothly functioning Near Eastern partnership with the United States. The value of Cyprus to the British plunged during the decade. Suez had demonstrated the island's strictly limited basing value. In the early 1950s, British leaders had insisted they could never surrender it, but by 1960, they gladly left. The empire was finished, and British public opinion was largely happy to see its end. Macmillan helped to prolong Conservative rule by withdrawing.[56]

The Turkish government secured its claim to a central role in determining the future of Cyprus and protected its ethnic minority on the island. It even improved its relationship with Greece. The Turkish Cypriot community was the biggest potential winner. The London-Zurich accords gave it effective legal parity with the majority Greek community. However, securing its interests, especially its economic well-being, required it to cooperate with the Greek Cypriots across a range of issues. Unfortunately, Turkish Cypriot leaders retained their deep mistrust of the Greek Cypriots, utilized their veto powers to force further concessions, and thereby reinforced support for their most dangerous enemies among the Greek Cypriots, Grivas's EOKA veterans.

The Greek Cypriots, particularly EOKA and the Orthodox Church, were the most obvious losers. Although British colonial administration was gone, their drive for enosis had been blocked. An independent Cyprus could enjoy neither self-determination nor majority rule. Instead, the Greek Cypriot majority, having bested the British Empire, settled into protracted negotiations with the Turkish Cypriot minority, whose now internationally recognized legal status as equal partners in the administration of the island was backed by the armed might of Turkey. Ironically, but perhaps inevitably, Makarios emerged from the enosis struggle reinforced. He was not only the symbol of resistance to the British, but also the man most Cypriots believed could achieve union with Greece. Whatever the depth of Makarios's own ambivalence about that union, he publicly played the champion of enosis with gusto, worsening relations with the suspicious and nervous Turkish Cypriots.[57]

Constantine Karamanlis had inherited a weak hand from Papagos, played it with considerable skill, and in the end opted for a settlement on Cyprus that protected Greek political interests as well as his own. Lacking military power, located hundreds of miles from Cyprus, and having no allies, the Greek government elected to use the United Nations as its primary tool to provide support for the Greek Cypriots. The policy succeeded in embarrassing the British, but Greece was unable to convince Washington to back its case, and faced with an aroused Turkey, it settled for the possible: independence. Greece's position in the Western alliance was more critical to Greek conservatives than was the unlikely possibility of enosis. Karamanlis presented the deal to the Greek public as "interim" but certainly realized that the London-Zurich agreements made enosis improbable even in the long term.[58]

The United States had a foot in both the winning and losing camps. It won because the NATO alliance held together and because its key ally, the United Kingdom, escaped from its misadventure with its considerable military power and its prestige largely intact. U.S. relations with Turkey remained strong. However, Greek-American relations would never be the same. While the United States and Karamanlis governments quickly patched up their differences, the average Greek's feeling of betrayal was intense. An American living in Athens during the 1950s recalled: "Every Greek political party wanted Cyprus. . . . The best chance, the Greek electorate decided, lay with the party known to favor a strong alliance with the United States. . . . [T]hat party won; the Greeks did not get Cyprus. . . . In their anger they have stoned American buildings, burned American flags, attacked American citizens."⁵⁹ U.S. Information Agency polling (October 1957) showed that while favorable opinions of the United States remained high among educated elites, the "average" Greek was angry over the situation in Cyprus and, as a result, doubtful of the benefits of the Western alliance. A preference for neutrality in the East-West struggle held a 10 percent advantage over membership in the NATO alliance. Anti-Americanism, while still held in check by "the Greek picture of Uncle Sam as well-meaning, rich, kindly, but a bit stupid," was fed by anger over U.S. Cyprus policy. With the British withdrawal, the United States would increasingly become the focus of public frustration over the Cyprus situation.⁶⁰ Cyprus joined the theme of "intervention" in a bill of indictment that many Greek intellectuals, the Greek left, and ultimately Greek public opinion were preparing against the United States, the patron that had betrayed them. A third element in this emerging indictment was the relationship of the "Americans" with the "Right:" a decade of close collaboration between the United States and the Papagos and Karamanlis governments.

3

THE RIGHT, 1953–1963

> We are passing through a period when our influence and prestige among the Greek people and with the Greek government are undergoing a reassessment and readjustment in a changed world situation. We can no longer be as certain . . . that we shall have Greece's support in foreign policy matters that are critical to us.
> — U.S. embassy in Greece, November 1957

The decade 1953–63 was the golden age of U.S. relations with Greece. Despite the strain created by the Cyprus question and strong disagreements on the size of U.S. aid, the Greek and American governments shared basic objectives, above all confronting and containing the power of the Soviet Union while promoting Greek economic growth and integration into the Western economy. John Owens, a junior diplomat assigned to Greece in 1960–66, recalled: "Of course it was a wonderful time to be an American diplomat in Greece. The degree of our influence was great. The prestige . . . was great. . . . Greece itself was prospering." W. Tapley Bennett, the deputy chief of the U.S. mission in the late 1950s and early 1960s, agreed: "It was so exuberant, the whole atmosphere. . . . The pace was just electric."[1] Even as U.S. diplomats enjoyed their Greek adventures, however, the two states were moving apart. As the Greek political class pushed for enosis, fueling an already angry public opinion, it became a prisoner of this issue, less inclined to listen to Washington's concerns. For the United States, Greece's fate was no longer a critical issue. It focused on other problem areas: Berlin, the Middle East, East Asia, and, increasingly, South East Asia.

At the center of U.S. contentment with its relationship with Greece was the stability of the Greek government led by two strong prime ministers, Alexander Papagos and his successor, Constantine Karamalis. From John Peurifoy (1953) through Henry Labouisse (1963), six successive U.S. ambassadors enthusiastically endorsed the two men's leadership as the best option for advancing U.S. interests and, above all, for the successful integration of

Greece within the Western community. This judgment was largely shared in Washington. Nevertheless, an important distinction existed. As Dulles's conduct of Cyprus policy demonstrated, Washington's support for the two leaders was tempered by larger interests as well as by the limits of U.S. ability to meet Greek demands, above all their aid requests. In the end, successive U.S. administrations were unwilling to accept arguments made by the two Greek prime ministers, and their enthusiastic supporters at the U.S. embassy in Athens, that Papagos and Karamanlis were absolutely essential to the achievement of U.S. objectives or internal political stability. Dulles was ready to accept Karamanlis's fall as part of the price of pursuing U.S. policy interests in Cyprus. President John F. Kennedy, although favorably impressed by the Greek prime minister, turned down repeated Greek requests for higher levels of aid. When Greek foreign minister Evangelos Averoff insisted that Karamanlis was the glue holding Greece together, and that U.S. failure to provide assistance at higher levels would mean a return to the chronic instability of the early 1950s, Secretary of State Dean Rusk responded that "while he was fully aware of Mr. Karamanlis's great value to Greece and to the Alliance . . . one would not want to think of the future of a NATO country in terms of one life."[2] Washington stood aside as Karamanlis's hold on power crumbled.

FROM PAPAGOS TO KARAMANLIS

Papagos's three-year administration of Greece placed the country in a political straitjacket. The 1953 elections neutered the traditional parties of the right and left, weakened the major factional chiefs, assured Papagos a high degree of personal control over politically ambitious military officers, and left the monarchy largely frozen out of the normal political process. The situation could not endure for long. George Papandreou's defection from the Papagos camp and the subsequent break between Papagos and Markezinis, his chief adviser, were the first signs of the return to politics as usual. The prime minister's handling of Cyprus offered the opposition an opportunity to sap his public support. King Paul maneuvered to create a government crisis. In July 1954 he told newly arrived U.S. ambassador Cavendish Cannon that he favored immediate elections. When Cannon replied that no evident reason existed for a return to the polls just eighteen months after Papagos's triumph, the king suggested broadening the cabinet with men loyal to the Palace. The process of "normalization" sped up as Papagos's health declined. Concerns about military intervention grew as officers in the Sacred Band of Greek Officers, or IDEA, the military nationalist group, openly managed parts of the government. Shortly after Papagos's death in October 1955, the Central Intelligence Agency's representative told a meeting of the National Security Council that the prime minister's passing meant "the probable end of . . . relative political stability" in Greece.[3]

Papagos was not essential to continued political stability. Karamanlis, a forceful but relatively junior minister, took control, formed his own party, isolated potential rivals, won three elections, and governed Greece effectively for eight years. His selection by King Paul, the subject of considerable speculation by contemporaries and historians, was part of a successful effort by the monarchy to return to its central role in the political process. The king could scarcely hide his impatience to replace the autocratic and hostile Papagos with a more malleable successor. The choice of Karamanlis, a man with a reputation for competence, and plenty of political rivals, was designed to make the Palace once more the fulcrum of Greek politics. Paul "twice indicated his determination to call on Mr. Karamanlis" to CIA representatives, a clumsy way of sounding out the United States on its views of his nominee.[4] No one in Washington appears to have objected.

As Karamanlis built his personal power base at a steady pace, he faced a series of challenges from political rivals as well as both domestic and international crises. A domineering but aloof and austere personality, he was skilled at self-promotion and distributing patronage and ruthless in isolating potential internal rivals. As minister of public works and then as prime minister, he utilized the opening of new roads, bridges, and plants to identify himself with the public's desire for a speedy modernization of Greece. Nevertheless, Karamanlis's hold on power was never totally secure. Initially, he could rely on strong support from the Palace. His relations with the military high command seemed to improve with time. IDEA's influence waned during the Karamanlis years, a testimony to the prime minister's ability to meet the demands of the Greek army. (He served as minister of defense until 1961.) Moreover, the prime minister's hold on power was solidified by the nature of the political opposition. The center, whose leaders, ironically, included many of Papagos's former lieutenants, remained weak and divided. A majority of Greeks consistently rejected the communist-dominated United Democratic Front (EDA) as an unacceptable alternative for governing the country.[5]

Economic growth, the most important aspect of the postwar era, was a double-edged sword for Karamanlis. During the 1950s, Greece was in the midst of a massive population movement from the countryside, with its very limited prospects, to the promise (and ultimately the reality) of a better life in urban areas, above all Athens. Karamanlis could take some credit for the growth of the economy but also faced criticism for the limited assistance government provided families and individuals facing the painful personal dislocations of internal migration. The prime minister, who admired the dynamism of U.S. society, the productivity of its economic system, and the pragmatism that characterized its political action, hoped to adapt them to Greece and was an enthusiastic promoter of growth. He told former assistant secretary of state George McGhee that his objective was a "rapid expansion" of Greek industry (specifically steel and mining) and the tourist sector. Karamanlis admitted to his guest that pursuing such development policies with limited funds meant that Greece's rural population, "the backbone of political stability," would continue to be left out of the prosperity. Since small landholders were both the core of anticommunist sentiment in Greece and the bedrock of Karamanlis's political strength, the prime minister argued that the Greek and U.S. governments shared a common interest in assisting them. Foreign investment, preferably in the form of direct U.S. aid, was the best way to stabilize the Greek situation while firming up Karamanlis's personal position.[6]

The U.S. embassy shared Karamanlis's analysis of Greece's needs. With the prime minister hard-pressed over Cyprus, the embassy argued throughout the 1950s that Washington should make some concrete gestures that would provide Karamanlis support.[7] The Eisenhower and subsequent Kennedy administrations were willing to provided limited support, but Washington saw a different Greek reality. A 1957 National Security Council review of policy toward Greece concluded that growing "economic strength and political stability" had fostered "a sharp reduction in American aid and . . . an increased sense of Greek independence. These developments have been healthy for Greek-American relations. Greece has been especially anxious to reduce the appearance of dependence on the United States." While Greek self-assertion was creating serious problems for the NATO coalition as a result of its Cyprus "irredentism," the United States retained its ability to influence Greek behavior because it provided the shield against the threat posed by the Soviet Union and its Balkan satellites and because, given the limited size of the Greek economy, its military would require continued U.S. defense assistance. The United States should seek the "continuation of rule by conservative and moderate groups," Greek participation in NATO, and the "lessening of Greek irredentism."[8]

This optimistic reading of Greece's stability and economic growth potential led U.S. officials to insist on more cuts in the aid package. A week after the National Security Council's assessment, Eisenhower, acting on the recommendation of the State Department, informed Karamanlis that U.S. aid would be further reduced. The State Department's analysis argued that: "The prime minister overstates the consequences of reduced aid." Even the embassy allowed that Karamanlis exaggerated his political weakness as a ploy to win U.S. support for his policies. Moreover, as a mid-1956 National Intelligence Estimate concluded, in the unlikely event of Karamanlis's fall, the U.S. relationship with Greece would remain firmly grounded. Overall, Washington preferred a policy that would avoid being too closely tied to the political future of one man, even the capable Karamanlis.[9]

The other factor influencing U.S. optimism about Greece was the weakness of the internal communist threat. Until the 1958 elections, U.S. officials regarded the KKE-dominated EDA as a nuisance, even while worrying that it might be able to exploit the Cyprus issue to increase its support. In the event that EDA became a substantial threat to Greece's Western orientation, the U.S. could count on the Palace, police, and military to limit its influence. A November 1955 analysis of Greek internal security commented that, as a last resort, the "military clique, IDEA . . . would undoubtedly use its influence against the formation of a government in which communists had a dangerous degree of power."[10]

Thus, the U.S relationship with Karamanlis was considerably more nuanced than his political opponents and subsequent Greek writers have suggested. In addition to providing very limited backing to Greece's Cyprus initiatives, the United States reduced its aid, and even in the case of the U.S.-Greece Status of Forces Agreement (SOFA), Washington was slow to heed embassy advice to speed up negotiations on a less intrusive accord. Following the revision of the SOFA, Ambassador Ellis Briggs, who wanted to lower the U.S. profile, butted heads with the Defense Department over both the size of its mission to Greece and the extensive privileges that mission enjoyed.[11] Demands from American holders of prewar Greek bonds for a definitive settlement of their long-standing claims for repayment also bedeviled U.S.-Greek relations. Responding to the bondholders' political pressure, Washington pushed Greece to honor its debts. Karamanlis, for domestic political reasons, demanded a settlement on Greek terms. In August 1960, Briggs acknowledged that, given the political imperatives motivating both sides, "extracting [a] debt settlement seems about as difficult as pulling out a walrus tusk with tweezers."[12] The two governments disagreed about U.S. access to the Greek tobacco market. Karamanlis stood firm against U.S. entreaties, insisting that Greece's application for association with the European Economic Community required it to limit U.S. privileges.[13] A further irritant was the level of U.S. defense support for Turkey. While U.S. officials were preoccupied with bolstering Turkey, a "frontline state" that faced the threat of direct Soviet attack, Greek leaders foresaw the likelihood that Turkey's U.S.-supplied firepower could be turned on them or on Cyprus.[14]

Both the embassy and Greek political leaders argued that the damaging psychological impact of American actions required Washington to provide greater levels of U.S. aid and to make other concessions. The 1956 embassy report "The Influence of Emotion on Greek Policy" warned that irrational behavior was a "deep-seated and serious disease of the Greek body politic." Embassy Sigmund Freuds expressed concern about a society "caught up in an emotional vortex" caused by the "sense of abandonment" and "even betrayal" Greeks felt over the Cyprus issue. The following year, the embassy argued that anticipated deep cuts in U.S. aid would have a serious effect on the collective Greek psyche. A March 1957 report to the Senate by former U.S. diplomat Norman Armour, which criticized Greek investment strategy, provoked a firestorm in the Athens press and embarrassed Karamanlis. In early 1958, the embassy reported the "indignant and piqued" response of Greek officials and press to the announcement of U.S. aid reductions. Karamanlis himself complained of being "taken for granted" by Greece's allies. Averoff and Karamanlis were convinced that both the embassy and the CIA worked against his National Radical Union (ERE) party during the 1958 elections. Briggs complained about the prime minister's "pathological suspicions" and his "tirades" directed at both the United States and Greece's European allies. His successor, Henry Labouisse, reported that Karamanlis's "bad moods" and feelings of being "misunderstood" hampered efforts at cooperation with the Greek government.[15]

U.S. officials in Washington were largely shielded from the immediate impact of Greek outbursts and chose to interpret them as signs of "strengthened self-confidence," although Under Secretary of State Christian Herter allowed, with evident surprise, that he had never seen an absorption with an issue similar to the one Greeks displayed over Cyprus. The Americans seem never to have fully understood the impact of the "even-handed" response to the 1955 anti-Greek riots in Constantinople and Izmir. U.S. officials were also in a position to avoid the daily criticisms of a Greek press, with its "layers of willful fabrication and misinterpretation" that were the bane of U.S. diplomats. Finally, personal meetings between senior officials were usually free of displays of Greek, or American, intemperance. Eisenhower, Kennedy, Karamanlis, Dulles, Herter, Rusk, and Averoff respected each other and recognized that they shared major common interests.[16]

Thus, in the face of some major differences of opinion, the overall relationship between the U.S. and Karamanlis governments worked for both sides. Karamanlis was aware of the limits that Congress placed on foreign aid spending and assisted the Americans in reducing the impact of assistance cuts on Greek public opinion as well as in highlighting occasional positive readjustments in U.S. funding. The United States recognized the tremendous difficulties Karamanlis operated under, and, within the limits imposed by complex alliance arrangements and economic commitments, attempted to meet some of Greece's more basic demands. It also recognized that, given the weakness of the center opposition and the peculiar problems posed by the Greek monarchy, Karamanlis represented the best guarantee of domestic political stability and continued Greek participation in Western defense. While the United States failed to meet Greek demands for support on Cyprus, it was not opposed to enosis. U.S. officials did not press Greece to take Jupiter missile bases in the late 1950s in deference to Karamanlis's political situation. Karamanlis, for his part, continued to urge higher levels of assistance but gratefully accepted what was offered, tried to prevent further cuts, and lined up with the United States during its 1959–63 clashes with the Soviet Union. In return, the United States demonstrated its backing for Greece in a 1961 confrontation with Bulgaria. The Kennedy administration worked to create a "crazy quilt" of international economic and military aid for Greece and, despite some initial Greek hesitation over the plan, succeeded in winning donor support from both NATO and the Organization for Economic Cooperation and Development (OECD).[17]

THE OLD MAN AND THE CENTER

More than any other factor, the U.S. tie to Karamanlis was secured by the lack of a viable democratic alternative. Between the center's 1953 debacle and the 1958 elections, the United States avoided any involvement in the reconstruction of an opposition. Concern about the effects on its relations with Karamanlis of open intervention in Greek internal affairs, combined with a lingering distaste for opposition leaders, above all Venizelos, led to a policy of noninvolvement. The results of the May 1958 elections, however, changed American views and those of Karamanlis as well.

Greece had returned to proportional representation for the 1956 elections, on the basis of an agreement brokered by the Palace that changed the electoral system in exchange for the center parties' pledge not to cooperate with EDA (which they broke). The U.S. embassy, which had no desire to repeat the Peurifoy experience, made no comment. American officials were surprised by the outcome of the 1958 parliamentary elections. While the total votes for EDA and the center parties were nearly equal, EDA, with 24 percent of the vote, won 78 seats, largely at the expense of the center, which got 36 seats with 21 percent of the vote. The finger-pointing over this outcome was vigorous. Karamanlis blamed the rise of EDA on U.S. Cyprus policy. CIA chief Allen Dulles put the blame squarely on the voting system. The U.S. embassy was more cautious in its judgment, blaming the center's defeat on a variety of internal political problems, Karamanlis's management of election issues, and his failure to directly attack EDA. However, it warned that "Greece is confronted with an unprecedented polarization . . . [the] fight for the center is just beginning. On the outcome may depend Greece's hopes for political stability."[18]

In this atmosphere of crisis the CIA stepped forward and with support from the embassy undertook a major covert-funding operation in Greece. Political counselor Daniel Brewster recalled that the "CIA tried to scare the bejesus out of us . . . and warned us things were going downhill."[19] The agency was well positioned to undertake this operation. It had developed major contacts among Greek elites during the civil war. After the conflict, the CIA retained its interest in intelligence gathering and in reforming the Greek secret services. A large station in Athens and its active subsidiary operation in Thessaloniki engaged in intelligence gathering throughout the Balkans. Since communist dictatorships effectively limited U.S. intelligence activities inside their borders, Greece became an important platform for signals and technical intelligence and the collection of information from defectors as well as for mounting espionage operations inside the Iron Curtain. The value of the intelligence the agency accumulated in Greece was fairly limited. Greece was an open society with a free press, and contacts with most members of the nation's elites frequently were easier for diplomats than for CIA officials, who operated under a variety of self-imposed restraints. Where the agency enjoyed a special advantage was in its privileged contacts with the royal family and with the leadership of the army. These sources, which the CIA guarded jealousy, were obviously important to the United States. Because of the size of the Athens station, both the diplomatic and military missions in Greece provided "cover" for CIA agents, increasing its influence and contacts with the Greek officer corps. The well-funded agency naturally enjoyed a privileged relationship with Greek intelligence, providing training and exchanging information.[20]

In addition to gathering Greek and Balkan political and military intelligence, the CIA's Athens station had a number of priority missions. With the cooperation of the Greek army and Greek intelligence it set up a NATO "stay behind" operation. NATO strategy was to absorb an initial massive Soviet attack that would drive allied armies back from their national borders. Small groups of highly trained local forces would remain behind enemy lines to collect intelligence, engage in sabotage, and prepare for an eventual counterattack. During the first decades of the Cold War, coordinating the preparations and training for stay behind operations was a major CIA responsibility.[21]

Another CIA European operation that had a Greek component was its attempt to undermine communist control of trade unions. In Greece, the agency, in cooperation with the American Federation of Labor, created a program of support for democratic trade unionists after the civil war. Given the rather rudimentary state of Greek labor organization, this program tried to create an alternative between communist trade unionists and government-backed union leaders within the structure of the GSEE (General Confederation of Greek Workers), the officially recognized national labor federation.[22]

The decision to make Greek elections a priority intelligence operation appears to have been taken only after the 1958 vote. By this time the agency had considerable experience with programs of covert funding for democratic parties in France, Italy, Germany, and other parts of Europe. The value of such funding was always hard to determine, but the agency retained great confidence in its ability to "surgically" intervene in support of selected candidates. The program was not designed to support Karamanlis or the ERE per se. Instead, its objective was to undercut support for EDA candidates by funding the activities of candidates from either the ERE or the center who appeared capable of defeating communist-backed politicians. Funding was limited, and the program itself, although in place on a permanent basis, was activated on the eve of elections. The Greek operation, like other CIA covert actions, was subject to regular review as Washington monitored its effectiveness.[23] Karamanlis probably had only limited knowledge of the specifics of the plan, but as the head of one of the parties receiving support he was undoubtedly aware of its outlines.

U.S. documentation points to December 1958 as the date of authorization for an expanded and aggressive CIA election program. Karamanlis had decided to contest EDA forcefully in spring 1959 local elections. The embassy began planning for a series of "psychological" operations based on public opinion surveys designed to pinpoint vulnerable EDA candidates and defeat them by employing the press and other forms of information dissemination to discredit the far left. Aided by initial favorable public response to the conclusion of a deal on Cyprus, the ERE won. However, its victory took place largely at the expense of centrist candidates. By adopting a reinforced proportional representation system, the government encouraged the formation of heterogeneous coalitions. The EDA, which exchanged its support for some centrists for Venizelos's backing of certain of its candidates, avoided the sort of pummeling that both the United States and Karamanlis intended. Most embarrassingly, EDA candidates, with support from the center, won the mayoralty in Athens and Piraeus.[24]

Both Karamanlis and the Americans drew the same conclusion: defeating the EDA required resuscitating the center by reunifying it.[25] While no evidence exists that they coordinated their efforts, some form of informal agreement to pursue assistance to the center evidently existed. Given Karamanlis's deeply suspicious nature, U.S. officials would have avoided acting at cross-purposes to the prime minister on an issue of such importance to his future. Moreover, the embassy and ERE's leader shared a common objective: a center that would suck electoral support from EDA without ever taking power. Karamanlis told U.S. officials that he was willing to lose "some seats" to the center in the effort to build the sort of "opposition" Greece needed.[26]

From the U.S. perspective, the first problem in resuscitating the center was one of leadership. Embassy officials retained a lively mistrust of Venizelos, whose flirtations with the EDA and press attacks on embassy collaboration with Karamanlis were a continuous source of irritation. The alternative, George Papandreou, roused little enthusiasm, particularly among senior U.S. diplomats. Papandreou himself was a bit dubious about the possibilities of a reunified center: "Whenever I start out as a collaborator with Venizelos I end up as his victim."[27] The year and a half following the center's 1959 election defeat were marked by a slow reconstruction of unity. Reconciliation between Venizelos and Papandreou was difficult. These efforts, while closely monitored and encouraged by embassy officials, were the work of Greek political leaders. Papandreou was miffed by a lack of U.S. support. His primary contact, junior diplomat Monteagle Stearns, reported that: "He misses no opportunity to urge his indispensability on the embassy, which he sees as a deus ex-machina which can, if it only will, resolve the contradictions of the star-crossed opposition."[28]

Venizelos remained a difficult collaborator for both Papandreou and the embassy, complaining that Papandreou failed to make the concessions to clinch a deal. Like Papandreou he wanted the United States to intervene in support of his ambitions. In January 1961 Venizelos addressed an open letter to President-elect Kennedy demanding he intervene in support of the center and against Karamanlis. Venizelos followed up this initiative by attacking the new president for receiving Karamanlis at the White House in April. The embassy reminded him that Karamanlis was visiting Washington as prime minister of Greece and that Venizelos was acting a bit illogically by complaining about alleged U.S. intervention at one moment and then demanding it the next.[29]

Eventually, Papandreou gained the upper hand and Venizelos entered a new coalition party, the Center Union (EK) as the number two man. This reunified party then carried out a spirited campaign for the October 1961 elections, emerging with 31 percent of the vote. EDA support dropped to 15 percent. U.S. ambassador Ellis Briggs enthused that Greek voters had "slapped down the communists so hard their teeth rattled."[30] Karamanlis, too, was highly satisfied with an election that left him firmly in control and with an opposition dominated by the mutually suspicious Papandreou and Venizelos. The situation seemed perfect for the perpetuation of ERE government.

The leaders of the EK were perfectly aware of Karamanlis's plans, particularly his designs to consign them to the role of a permanent opposition party. Papandreou had reasons to try to foil them as quickly as possible. Neither the ERE nor the EK possessed the discipline and structure of a strong party. ERE remained an extension of Karamanlis. Its power and discipline rested largely on his demonstrated ability to win elections and his repeated purges of potential challengers. EK had inherited many of the prime minister's ambitious would-be successors, who now hoped to replace Papandreou as leader of the opposition. To retain control of his party, the seventy-three-year-old EK chief needed to oust Karamanlis as quickly as possible. To secure power, Papandreou, calculated, he needed to provoke an intervention by either the Palace or the "American factor" to force elections.[31]

Papandreou's tactic for holding his own allies in line and building pressure on the Palace and the Americans was to continue the electoral campaign after the vote. Charging that the ERE had rigged the vote, Papandreou announced he would conduct a "ceaseless struggle" for new elections, organizing mass demonstrations and boycotting parliamentary activity. While foreign observers generally dismissed Papandreou's charges as overblown, enough evidence of small irregularities emerged to give them credibility. Papandreou milked these reports with considerable skill and utilized his formidable oratorical and tactical political skills, including a flair for dramatic gestures, to keep the issue alive, if not always on the front burner, for the next two years.[32]

Ellis Briggs, one of the oldest and most experienced American ambassadors, was the perfect foil for Papandreou's moves. "Ellis Briggs had been in

Latin America too long; he was someone who took things over. . . . Briggs wanted Karamanlis and the right wing ERE to win and he was open about that."[33] The U.S. ambassador was infuriated by the Center Union's boycott of the opening of parliament. His new year's 1962 message to the U.S. community in Greece included a passage that the opposition argued was an endorsement of Karamanlis's election fraud: "We are among a people who believe as we do in personal freedom and in the dignity of the individual; elections here . . . testified to these beliefs." The French embassy judged Briggs's comment "somewhat imprudent," less for its content than for offering the opposition a tempting opening: "The veritable rage which the [opposition] manifested over an affair that was quite minor . . . tends to prove that the day has not yet arrived when a coherent and responsible opposition could take control, without risking the future of Greece."[34]

Briggs's reaction to Papandreou's conduct reflected the generally low opinion senior American officials had of the Center Union's chief. These opinions did not immediately change when Briggs departed in early 1962. American diplomats gave little credence to Papandreou's changes. "[T]he official . . . impression was that there was no more fraud and violence than there had been in most Greek elections, in fact probably less."[35] However, Papandreou was on firmer ground when he charged that the Greek military, acting on orders from its chief of staff, General Vassilios Kardamakis, "bent every effort to deliver a heavy vote for [K]aramanlis." A pattern of police and military involvement in elections stretched back to Karamanlis's first run in 1956. In 1961, however, the military and police actively encouraged the vote for the ERE instead of simply "discouraging" rural electors from supporting the EDA.[36]

The involvement of Greek army officers in support of ERE's electoral campaign inevitably aroused Greek suspicions about the U.S. role. The close ties between the CIA and the Greek military were hardly secret. Briggs's comments helped to fan these suspicions. "Papandreou went over Center Union charges of illegal intervention by military and security forces in the last elections" reported one U.S. official. "He said that he was convinced that the U.S., willingly or not, had played an important role in this. . . . [W]e wanted him only as the leader of the opposition . . ." The Center Union's leader believed that the "efficiency" of the operation proved that Americans, not Greeks, conducted it: "Perhaps not the embassy, but certainly your secret services."[37]

The CIA's secret election-funding programs undoubtedly played a role in grounding Papandreou's suspicions. "Covert operations" of this type were impossible to hide by their very nature. Too much money passed through too many hands to avoid information leaks. The Greek press had little difficulty in uncovering the outlines of the operation and drawing its own conclusions. Briggs's mistrust of Papandreou and support for Karamanlis were well known.

Although the CIA distributed its money to both EK and ERE, Center Union politicians exploited the covert-funding reports to portray themselves as victims of foreign manipulation. Privately, EK leaders demanded that the United States now level the playing field by abandoning Karamanlis and throwing its support to the Center Union.[38] Papandreou publicly raised the ante by talking of a "revolution" against the "quasi-dictatorial" rule of Karamanlis. He dragged the royal family into the campaign by attacking their lavish spending and by tying Palace adviser and Karamanlis ally General Constantine Dovas to the 1961 election fraud. By mid-1962, Papandreou was confidently predicting victory in elections he believed he could force within a year.[39]

Like Papandreou's bouts of confidence, the "ceaseless struggle" waxed and waned as a political issue. British diplomats, who outdid the Americans in skepticism about the opposition, repeatedly judged the campaign a "dead horse," only to see Papandreou successfully resurrect it. In 1962 George Papandreou's claims about U.S. involvement in the "electoral coup" finally provoked the embassy reaction he wanted. Henry Labouisse, the new U.S. ambassador, decided to personally replace the departing Stearns as the EK chief's interlocutor, the surest sign of Papandreou's rising significance. In November 1962, the U.S. ambassador addressed the question of American support for Karamanlis during a meeting with the EK leadership. Labouisse "entertained no doubts about the loyalty of Center Union leaders to Greece's Free World alliance." It had been fully displayed during the October 1962 Cuban Missile Crisis. "He wanted the Center Union leaders to realize that the United States had no intention of intervening in the internal affairs of Greece." The ambassador concluded that U.S. policies aimed at strengthening Greece's economy and military posture. "[W]e believed that political stability was essential if these objectives were to be realized."

His listeners were skeptical. Stefanos Stephanopoulos, a pro-Western former foreign minister, responded that a difference existed between political stability and governmental stability and that Karamanlis's continuance in office would likely damage both. George Papandreou claimed he wanted "no favors" from the United States. He repeated his charge that Americans were involved in the 1961 election "fraud." When Venizelos objected that no evidence existed to support this theory, Papandreou responded that Greeks generally believed that the embassy and the Palace were cooperating to keep Karamanlis in power and to freeze the EK into permanent opposition.

Venizelos, assuming a new, and undoubtedly congenial, role as mediator between the Americans and the opposition, concluded the EK presentation by taking a moderate position: "[He] would like to make a personal remark about the role of the embassy . . . in Greek internal affairs. . . . The Center Union did not seek American intervention in Greece's internal affairs. However, this did not mean that the embassy could not give 'advice' to the political leaders when the situation called for it. The United States was the acknowledged leader of the Free World, and its leadership could—and should—be exercised in this way." Venizelos ended his presentation, one that drew no objections from his fellow EK chiefs, by stressing that the Center Union was interested in U.S. views. Seizing this opening, Labouisse replied that the United States wanted the EK's push for elections to stay within legal bounds and pledged that he would continue to consult with the opposition.[40]

The session with Labouisse illustrated both the growing unity of Center Union leaders, convinced that they were positioned to topple Karamanlis, as well as their enduring divisions. A few months earlier Papandreou had complained to Stearns that he remained "alone in his own party" and mistrusted his fellow EK leaders, above all the supple Venizelos. Venizelos's emergence as mediator reflected his desire to marry his access to the Palace with improved relations with the Americans and to strengthen his internal party position. For his part, Labouisse, who, like his president, favored Karamanlis's continued leadership of Greece, recognized that the EK had a chance to attain power and sought to reposition the United States in a neutral stance.[41]

While trying to neutralize embassy support for Karamanlis, Papandreou's allies were busily reconstructing their personal relations with the Palace. Simultaneously, EK spokesmen applied direct pressure on the king either to back off from his longtime support of Karamanlis or repeat the historic error of placing the monarchy's role and fate at the center of an election campaign. The EK's carrot-and-stick strategy, a product of division among its leaders, achieved a first success in January 1963, when the Palace pushed the pro-Karamanlis army chief of staff Kardamakis into early retirement.[42]

A ROYAL ANACHRONISM

In September 1962, U.S. vice president Lyndon B. Johnson visited Athens for meetings with Greece's political leadership. The opposition boycotted LBJ's visit to emphasize its claim that Karamanlis's government was illegitimate. LBJ's talks with the prime minister went well, and on his return to Washington, the American vice president joined the ranks of cheerleaders for the ERE leader. Johnson advised Kennedy: "[We] can not allow . . . Karamanlis to fall before an irresponsible opposition because of our termination of defense support."[43] It soon became evident that opposition to Karamanlis was coming as much from the Palace as from the center.

U.S. relations with the Greek royal family were complex. Since 1947, successive U.S. ambassadors had come away with initially positive readings of the royal couple. The king and queen were quite adept at presenting themselves as "adults" surrounded by a brood of squabbling and immature politicians. They offered close and informal collaboration with the embassy. Moreover, their devotion to the Western alliance, while a matter of political self-preservation, was sincere. Still, successive U.S. ambassadors inevitably realized that the royal family was largely out of touch with the needs of their subjects and as absorbed in their own self-serving maneuverings as the much-criticized politicians. The conservative and snobbish social views and ostentatious lifestyle of the royal couple were out of step with the views of an egalitarian and relatively poor Greek society. The monarchs generally acted more as leaders of the "political royalists" than as a unifying force above politics. In fact, the king and queen thrived on the political instability that allowed them to manipulate public policy. On the whole, the Palace did not serve key U.S. objectives for promoting stability in Greece. The monarchy's position was slowly eroding, and it was declining into irrelevance due to its "inability or unwillingness to surround itself with able and politically competent advisors, and . . . to identify itself with [the] basic social and economic aspirations of the Greek people."[44]

Aware of the negative judgments coming out of the embassy, the royal couple tended to keep their contacts limited to the ambassador and to cultivate other elements of the U.S. mission, above all the CIA. The chief of station normally enjoyed easy entrée to the Palace. The king and queen appear to have concluded that the agency had a direct line to the Eisenhower White House. The queen assiduously cultivated CIA director Allen Dulles, the brother of John Foster Dulles, and NSC files indicate she had some success in passing along her views through this channel. The queen developed a passion for nuclear technology that led Briggs to a derisive comment that Frederika, whose education had never reached high school level, suffered from "atomic delusions."[45]

By late 1961, the king and queen, egged on by a coterie of "old-guard politicians" managed to personally antagonize both Karamanlis and Papandreou. The queen carried on a long-standing personal vendetta against Karamanlis and his young wife. The royal couple encouraged twenty-one-year-old Crown Prince Constantine to call Papandreou seeking support for the government's electoral law. Papandreou resented "what he regarded as the irresponsible manner in which the king and queen (who he assumed had put 'the boy' up to the call) were attempting to deal with serious matters of state."[46] Ellis Briggs, who actively cultivated the royal couple throughout his mission, regarded them as an "anachronism" and repeatedly warned that they were out of touch with reality. He prophetically forecast that the monarchy, "a tree with such shallow and insubstantial roots is likely . . . to be overturned."[47]

The ouster of Karamanlis was typical of the royal couple's inability to look to its best interests. The prime minister could be difficult. He was a prickly personality. Over the years, he had succeeded in limiting the royal role and increasing his personal control over both public administration and party politics. But he was a monarchist. Nevertheless, the king and queen decided that Karamanlis would have to go. On January 31, 1963, the queen told the CIA's chief of station that despite his "great ability," Karamanlis "is becoming increasingly hard to get along with and occasionally shows bad judgment," including an "ineffectiveness in protecting the Crown from public criticism. . . . Thus, the time may be approaching when elections and a new government are in order." The queen, of course, expected to replace Karamanlis with another conservative leader. She characterized Papandreou as an extremist and Venizelos as a "slippery opportunist" who sought Palace backing against Papandreou.[48]

Despite her fears that political instability could provoke a communist upheaval in Greece, the queen plunged into further political adventure, confident that the crown enjoyed the backing of both the Greek army and the United States. She might have been less sanguine had she known of plans for a military coup organized around the recently retired Kardamakis. In a discussion with a U.S. military attaché, the former chief of the Greek general staff expressed concern that Karamanlis would be ousted and sought U.S. support for a coup. Surprised U.S. officials, who had believed that Karamanlis had moved the military out of politics, tried to discourage the plotters. Karamanlis, too, got wind of the plot and moved to quash it. Nevertheless, the plan, involving three future leaders of the 1967 military junta, was a warning of the fragility of the Greek political system and the threat that the monarchy's actions posed to Greek democracy.[49]

Papandreou simultaneously turned up the pressure on Greece's monarchs. In March he boycotted ceremonies celebrating the one hundredth anniversary of the royal family's installation. (Venizelos prudently left Athens for his home in Crete to disassociate himself from this maneuver.) In a letter to the king, Papandreou repeated his charges of electoral fraud and warned that by supporting an "illegal" government, the royal family was endangering its future. The time had come for the king to dismiss his prime minister. When the king declined to act, Papandreou's press allies claimed that the United States had intervened to prevent royal action. The French ambassador commented that the tone of the unsubstantiated center-left press reporting and editorials would have done credit to a "communist newspaper."[50]

The monarchs provoked a crisis with Karamanlis in the summer of 1963. The prime minister's personal position weakened after police informers murdered EDA deputy Gregory Lambrakis during a May rally in Thessaloniki. The murder and its initial investigation called into question the government's competence and honesty as well as its control over Greece's security forces. The killing's political motivation seemed to substantiate George Papandreou's charges. Karamanlis's government was badly shaken. The royal couple leaped at this opportunity to oust the prime minister. Some months previously, protestors had advanced on the queen during a visit to London. Now the king and queen announced that they would make a "private" trip to the British capital to see Queen Elizabeth. Karamanlis opposed the visit. He noted that further protests against the royal couple would harm Greece's international image. In addition, Karamanlis reminded the royal couple that the prime minister had responsibility for managing Greece's foreign policy. The king and prime minister met, disagreed, and then released separate statements outlining their positions. Ominously, the crown prince was a frequent spectator at these displays of royal power and indifference to constitutional precedent. The king and queen stood firm. On June 11, after consulting the cabinet, Karamanlis resigned.[51]

Karamanlis's resignation set off furious maneuvering. The former prime minister announced that he was going into voluntary exile in Switzerland in order to permit the formation of a new government majority. Karamanlis wanted elections that he hoped would take advantage of improved public opinion polls which followed his clash with the king. The royal couple supported the speedy formation of an ERE government under Panagiotis Pipinelis to pass a new election law and began a flirtation with the Center Union. George Papandreou insisted that the nation could only go to the polls with a nonpartisan ("service") government in power. He threatened to boycott elections run by a Pipinelis ministry. The EK's leader got his way, aided by royal pressure. Pipinelis guided a revised election law that met EK demands through parliament and resigned. A neutral ministry under economist John Paraskevopoulos took Greece to the polls. Karamanlis returned to lead his party after stating that he was determined to define and limit the royal family's role in politics. U.S. officials hoped that Karamanlis would be returned to office but maintained strict neutrality during the election campaign. On November 3, Papandreou's Center Union won a plurality of 42 percent and 138 seats, thirteen deputies short of a majority. Karamanlis went into exile in Paris. The EK's leader, now prime minister, provoked a parliamentary crisis after securing agreement from the king to call new elections.[52] Shortly thereafter, the queen and Foreign Minister Venizelos visited Washington for the funeral of President Kennedy. Frederika confidently assured President Johnson that Greece was under royal control: "The 'present crowd' (the new government) were a little nervous because they had attacked 'us' (presumably the Royal Family) while they were out of office. But they were learning that they could work with 'us' and she did not foresee any great trouble."[53] Venizelos assured U.S. officials of Greek loyalty to the Atlantic alliance and of the new government's desire to "eliminate" friction on Cyprus by reform of its constitution. "His government would be content to see not Cyprus as a part of Greece but a second Greece in Cyprus."[54]

The era of the "Right" was over. With Karamanlis's firm hand removed, Cyprus reemerged as a major international problem while the monarchy and the political elite drew each other into a confrontation that paved the way for military intervention. Greece was about to enter into the political turbulence perpetually feared by American officials.

4

BLACK MAK: CYPRUS, 1960–1964

> We must convince Black Mak to reverse course.
> — Robert Komer, February 1964

> Makarios [is] a stinker of the first water. He wants a central government in Cyprus that would rob the Turkish minority of its rights. Makarios seemed to rely on a Soviet promise that it will keep the Turks from invading the island.
> — Prime Minister Sir Alec Douglas Home, February 1964

On April 25, 2004, the day after Greek Cypriots had overwhelmingly voted down a plan for a settlement of the division of Cyprus proposed by U.N. secretary-general Kofi Annan, a cartoon appeared in *O Fileleftheros*, one of many Cypriot newspapers calling for rejection. U.S. president George W. Bush asks British prime minister Tony Blair: "What shall I do, Tony, if one side votes yes and the other no?" Blair, displaying a map of Cyprus, replies: "Divide and rule." The belief that the United States and Britain malevolently work against the interests of the Greeks of Cyprus, together with an exaggerated sense of the importance of the island to the Anglo-American allies, are items of faith among the island's Greek citizens. Greek Cypriots might be excused for this belief. Their own press and Greek-language histories of the island's postindependence era have dwelt on the supposed centrality of Cyprus in the Cold War and on the assumed preoccupation of the United States with events on the island. Moreover, this Cypriot-centered view of the world has been reinforced by the contributions of a few English-speaking authors, most notably the essayist Christopher Hitchens[1] and, more recently, two British journalists, Brendan O'Malley and Ian Craig, in *The Cyprus Conspiracy*, the subtitle of which, "America, Espionage, and the Turkish Invasion," summarizes their view of events that led to the 1974 division of the island.

In all of these versions, U.S. policy toward Cyprus is assumed to be consistent and based on high-level interest in maintaining strategic control of the island. O'Malley and Craig describe their "search for the real story . . .

a conspiracy by America . . . to divide the island" rooted in "an astonishing international plot, developed from a blueprint first evolved under British rule . . . the goals of which were finally realized in 1974." This plot, rather than ethnic hatred, led to the partition of Cyprus.[2]

Conspiracy theories win popular acceptance on the island because they absolve Greek and Turkish Cypriots, as well as their Greek and Turkish backers, of the burden of responsibility for events leading up to the Turkish invasion of 1974. They also do real damage to the historical record. U.S. policy toward Cyprus in the decade following independence was anything but consistent. It ranged from near indifference under Dwight Eisenhower to efforts at nation building under John F. Kennedy, from reactive crisis management during the first year of the administration of Lyndon B. Johnson to a grudging acceptance of Archbishop Makarios in the later part of LBJ's presidency to, ironically, Richard Nixon's embrace of Makarios as a critical factor in eastern Mediterranean stability. While Cold War considerations were basic to the shape of U.S. policy, other factors, including a desire to ameliorate ethnic tensions, also played an important role. U.S. attitudes toward enosis were as contorted as those of Makarios. The Johnson administration initially believed that enosis combined with compensation to Turkey was the best solution to the island's problems. Later it would promote national independence through ethnic reconciliation. Partition was never a U.S. objective.[3]

Cyprus in the 1960s was largely the story of the complex maneuvers of the Cypriot president. Caught between a powerful communist party, the Reform Party of the Working People (AKEL), and the ultras of the former EOKA (National Organization of Cypriot Fighters), and determined to perpetuate his dominance of the Cypriot state, Makarios left the door open to enosis but simultaneously created an independent Greek Cypriot–dominated state. He planned to weaken the left by promoting economic development, paid for with foreign assistance. In the meantime, he held AKEL in line by exploiting tensions among the Turkish Cypriots over the issue of majority rule. The archbishop-president kept the pro-enosis EOKA right in line by placing its youthful leaders in his government and, in violation of the London-Zurich agreements, trying to impose a centralized government over the Turkish Cypriots. While joining the "nonaligned" camp of states in the Cold War, he attempted to build a "special relationship" with the United States by granting Washington's major desire, basing rights, and sought economic assistance in exchange. In a calculated gamble, Makarios unleashed military operations against the Turkish community to break its resistance to Greek Cypriot dominance, counting on the United States to prevent a Turkish military response. He used the issue of majority rule and memories of the Cypriot struggle against the British to build support among the former colonial states who dominate the U.N. General Assembly.[4]

Makarios's strength lay in the support he enjoyed among both the Greek Cypriots and a majority of Greeks. Makarios's popularity made life difficult for the Karamanlis government, which had a major interest in making the London-Zurich agreements work to improve its relations with Ankara and to protect the remnants of the Greek community of Constantinople. The opposition capitalized on Karamanlis's moderation to undercut government support. As a result, when George Papandreou, one of Karamanlis's most outspoken critics, came to power in late 1963, he had little margin for maneuver on Cyprus. From late 1963 through mid-1965, as the Cyprus situation boiled over, Makarios won frequently grudging support from Athens. He took advantage of the weakness of a minority government in Ankara as he aggressively pushed forward with his plans. While tactically brilliant, Makarios's activities divided the island, set Greeks and Turks on a confrontation course, provoked the great powers, above all the United States, into a deepening involvement in Cyprus, undercut the Greek Cypriots' dominant position, and ultimately frustrated Greek desires.[5]

NATION BUILDING

The Eisenhower administration had little time for and less interest in the affairs of an independent Cyprus. In the months following the London-Zurich accords, as Makarios wrangled with British representatives over the final treaty arrangements governing the transfer of power to a Cypriot government, U.S. policy was to avoid any major economic commitments and to rely on the British to secure it continued basing rights inside U.K. sovereign territorial areas. The drawn out nature of the talks put off the establishment of an independent Cypriot state until mid-August 1960, by which time Eisenhower and most of his major subordinates were awaiting November U.S. election returns and retirement from public life.[6]

While the United States continued to insist that Cyprus was primarily a British problem, Makarios, with greater realism, was seeking an expanded relationship with the reluctant Americans. U.S. officials ignored repeated signs of London's desire to severely limit its involvement in an independent Cyprus, such as a British suggestion that the United States arm the Cypriot army envisioned in the London-Zurich agreements. The Macmillan government's decision to legalize AKEL (over U.S. protests) was another indication of its desire to be rid of the Cyprus question. The U.S. continued to press the British to take "the lead role" in an independent Cyprus.⁷ Makarios's handling of the negotiations leading to independence showed that he agreed with London's assessment: Britain was a part of Cyprus's past.⁸

While Washington tried to avoid involvement in Cyprus, Makarios utilized every opportunity to win concessions from the Americans. The archbishop won the presidential election in December 1959, but his leadership of the Cypriot nation was taken for granted, and from his first days back in Cyprus following his long exile, he was at the center of diplomatic activity. In his initial meeting with U.S. consul general Taylor Belcher in March 1959, Makarios requested $20 million in U.S. economic assistance. In October 1959, the Greek Cypriot ethnarch quite reasonably laid down his markers by insisting that, while he had no difficulties with informally approving the presence of U.S. intelligence facilities, he could not commit future governments to a continuation of existing arrangements. Only direct talks leading to a treaty between the United States and Cyprus could preserve access to these rights. Makarios also insisted on payment for U.S. rights to build a communications relay station on the island. Shortly thereafter, Makarios asked that the United States provide arms and equipment for a Cypriot army and then sought U.S. mediation in stalled base talks with the British. The Eisenhower administration dodged these requests, providing the new Cypriot state with a small technical assistance program and some food assistance. Makarios, in turn, ignored U.S. suggestions about taking action to control AKEL.⁹

The U.S. attitude change markedly when John Kennedy assumed the presidency in January 1961. The new administration was actively seeking to expand the number of America's allies in the Cold War. As part of this program, it embraced decolonization and tried to convince the U.S. congress to increase foreign assistance for economic development. Cyprus caught the young president's eye as a state that could be anchored in the Western camp through support of economic development and settlement of its ethnic divisions. This program of nation building began in August 1961 when Kennedy, in National Security Action Memorandum 71, instructed the Department of State to provide a full report on the Cyprus situation. The focus of the president's concern was the growing power of AKEL. While Greek Cypriot politics were already factionalized and a number of political leaders had emerged, Makarios's dual role as ethnarch and head of state retarded the development of parties. A majority supported the archbishop who, as a symbol of Greek Cypriot unity, avoided creating his own political movement. As a result, the communists commanded the only disciplined political movement on the island. Makarios, in his role as Greek Cypriot spokesman, avoided divisive political actions and focused instead on creating a coordinated program of economic assistance that would involve the three guarantor powers, the United States, and other Western allies. In September 1961, Kennedy approved a plan for an expanded CIA role in combating AKEL and instructed the State Department to step up efforts to bring the guarantor powers into agreement on an economic assistance package.[10]

Missing from this U.S. initiative was recognition of Makarios's central objective. In a March 1961 meeting with U.S. secretary of state Dean Rusk, Cypriot U.N. ambassador Zenon Rossides delivered the message that the London-Zurich agreements were "in many ways divisive." Increased economic aid might help to ameliorate the problems the accords created, but ultimately the Greek element of the Cypriot government wanted liberation from the straitjacket created by the constitution and the Treaty of Guarantee.[11]

Throughout the first year of its existence, the island republic gave clear signs of being incapable of functioning effectively. Greek Cypriot leaders' treatment of Turkish Cypriot representatives was often tactless. The Turkish Cypriots utilized their constitutional powers to restrict the ability of the majority Greeks to operate in the interest of their constituents. The Turks were unable to fill all the civil service posts allotted to them but refused to permit Greek Cypriots to occupy them. Efforts to create an army broke down after the Turks insisted on separate ethnic units. In December 1961 the Turks refused to approve a national budget. The two sides fought over the terms of a bill designed to integrate separate Greek and Turkish municipal administrations into unified city councils. Early in 1962, Makarios announced his determination to "revise" the Cypriot constitution. British officials warned Washington of the dangers and approached the Greek and Turkish governments to head off potential trouble.[12]

Kennedy invited Makarios to Washington for talks. The invitation was a major boost for the prestige of both Cyprus and its president. Symptomatic of the Greek Cypriot approach, Makarios arrived in Washington without any Turkish Cypriot spokesmen in his official party. The Greek Cypriots told concerned U.S. officials that the Turkish Cypriot diplomat stationed in the United States would represent his community. During the talks, the archbishop outlined Greek Cypriot complaints about Turkish Cypriot behavior, sought greater aid, and left open the possibility of a deal on a communications relay station. JFK affirmed his support for the London-Zurich accords. The U.S. public image got a temporary boost among Greek Cypriots and a corresponding loss of prestige among the Turkish minority.[13]

Vice President Lyndon Johnson got an eye-opening introduction to Cyprus realities during an August 1962 visit to the island. The U.S. vice president pushed Makarios for action against AKEL. The Cypriot president explained the difficulties entailed by such an approach and then "closed his eyes . . . and said another party might be formed some day, but there was plenty of time before the next elections." Seeking a higher payment, Makarios deftly blocked a deal on a communications station by invoking Cypriot neutrality. Johnson next met with Turkish community leaders. They complained about Greek behavior and Rauf Denktash, president of the Turkish Communal Chamber, explained their strategy. Turkish Cypriots would be ready to create a common set of national institutions but only after they had built their own institutions and could approach the Greek side on the basis of parity. Denktash urged the United States to channel its aid through "communal chambers rather than the central government" to ensure that the Turks received their fair share and to reinforce Turkish political autonomy.[14]

NATION DESTROYING

Charles McCaskill, a veteran Cyprus watcher, recalled that in the first years of independence the Cypriot national flag was regarded as a "nuisance" in a land where Greek and Turkish national colors were the preferred means of expressing identity. A few weeks after independence, the British high commissioner warned London that the prospects for melding Greek and Turkish Cypriots into a single nationality were discouraging. The Cypriot's independence celebration had a "flat" quality. No one seemed very enthusiastic about the republic. Former EOKA fighters were engaging in a limited but worrying number of payback killings of their Greek opponents. The economic situation of the new nation was not promising. Pressure from Greek Cypriot extremists limited Makarios's options, while the position of Turkish Cypriot leader Fazil Kutchuk was weak. Three months later, the high commissioner commented that both communities rejected the concept of a single Cypriot people. The Greek Cypriots did not disguise their sense of superiority, while the Turkish Cypriots were ever more determined to assert their sense of separateness.[15]

Glaufkos Klerides, Makarios's sometime ally and later president of the republic, recalled that the frustrations caused by the imposition of the London-Zurich accords on Greek Cypriots and the resulting assertiveness of the Turkish Cypriots "coupled with the everyday irritations of a cumbersome, *sui generis* constitution . . . led the Greek Cypriot leadership to impatient, unwise, and premature acts" that inflicted new wounds on both Cypriot communities. Makarios, the essential leader for Greek Cypriots, was the worst possible choice to guide a multiethnic state. As ethnarch he personified the idea of enosis and thus could not command trust among Turkish Cypriots. During the first three years of independence, his actions and statements held the loyalty of Greek Cypriots at the cost of compounding Turkish Cypriot mistrust. By filling his cabinet with former EOKA fighters, Makarios reinforced the message that he was president of one community, not the entire population, and undercut the idea of an independent republic. Turkish Cypriot leaders drew the logical conclusion that they should prepare for partition.[16]

The London-Zurich Accords, however, were designed to place the island in a straitjacket of constitutional and international law. The "Basic Structure" (constitution) recognized the equality of the two communities (article 1), effectively negating the large majority Greek population. It provided each community with an absolute veto over actions of the other. Constitutional revision required a two-thirds majority of both communities' parliamentary representation. Moreover, the document's "basic articles" could not be modified. The constitution preserved the millet system of division and administration on confessional lines by granting each community a "communal chamber" that had the right to impose taxes as well as "exercise authority in all religious, educational, cultural, and teaching questions" and on all matters of "personal status." The chambers oversaw the activities of communal sports, charities, coops, credit organizations, and professional associations. Civil judicial issues involving members of one community were tried in courts representing that community. Most importantly, the Basic Structure banned both enosis and *taksim* (partition). The Treaty of Guarantee, signed by Cyprus, Greece, Turkey, and the United Kingdom reinforced the ban: the maintenance of the island's "independence, territorial integrity and security" was the common objective of all the contracting parties. The three "Guarantor Powers" had the right of intervention to prevent either partition or unification with Greece. Both Makarios and Turkish Cypriot leader Fazil Kutchuk accepted these restrictions for their respective communities. Less than five years later, the archbishop was looking for a way out of the deal.[17]

Makarios's December 1962 decision to confront the Turkish Cypriots over the municipal government issue was brinksmanship. His growing list of demands enjoyed wide support among frustrated Greek Cypriots, determined to enforce their "majority rights," but brought him into confrontation with all of the Guarantor Powers. All three were disturbed by the Cypriot president's failure to curb the power of AKEL. While they accepted the archbishop's decision to place Cyprus in the nonaligned camp, they could not ignore the anti-Turkish nature of the move. Karamanlis's Greece, in particular, opposed any radical moves by the Greek Cypriot leader. Its relationship with Turkey had speedily improved after the London-Zurich accords. In addition to increasing Greek security, cooperation over Cyprus led to a marked improvement in the position of the Orthodox patriarchate in Istanbul. Turkish leaders told their Greek colleagues that they were ready to cooperate in pressuring the Turkish Cypriots to adopt a more cooperative attitude in their talks with the Greek Cypriots. The close cooperation between Athens and Ankara provoked a Makarios visit to Greece in the fall of 1962. The archbishop wanted to remind Karamanlis of the depth of his Greek public support. The event went as Makarios planned, with mass demonstrations for enosis, but failed to affect Karamanlis's policies. Ignoring the political risks, the Greek prime minister continued to support the London-Zurich accords and to pursue cooperation with Turkey. As long as Karamanlis governed in Greece, Makarios would have to go it alone in his confrontation with the Turkish Cypriot community.[18]

The attack on the London-Zurich accords and Makarios's challenge to Turkish Cypriot rights to self-government provoked a confrontation between the Greek Cypriots and the Turkish government. The lack of a firm U.S. response may have encouraged Makarios to think he could drive a wedge between the Americans and Turks. U.S. ambassador Fraser Wilkins believed that Makarios was using the municipalities issue to force a general compromise and suggested granting the archbishop some leeway to pursue a deal. Officials in Washington, as usual, wanted to avoid a direct intervention in Cypriot affairs. Such interventions always had the potential to upset one side or the other, and Washington was at that moment engaged in sensitive negotiations with Turkey to remove nuclear-armed Jupiter missiles from Anatolia, replacing them with submarine-launched Polaris missiles. Such a replacement would reduce Turkey's already limited control over the decision to use nuclear weapons and remove a deterrent weapon from Turkish soil. Washington's leverage over Turkey was weakened at the moment when Ankara began to react angrily to Makarios's provocations.[19]

U.S. officials placed their hopes for peacefully resolving the situation on Greek and British diplomacy. Averoff immediately proposed a one-year extension of the existing municipalities' arrangement. The Americans appealed to their British allies to take the lead in promoting a cooling off. The British, who blamed Makarios for stirring up trouble, countered with a suggestion of a joint U.S.-U.K. initiative. Washington had concluded that Makarios's immediate objective was not enosis, but exercising full sovereignty on the island and that he was counting on the United States to restrain Turkey and prevent a split in NATO. The Kennedy administration decided on a coordinated approach toward the archbishop, reiterating American support for the London-Zurich accords and for direct intercommunal negotiations to settle differences between the two parties. Greece then stepped forward to restrain Makarios, to the intense relief of Washington. Averoff told the archbishop that the Karamanlis government would honor the London-Zurich agreements and that it was ready to accept the domestic consequences of aligning itself with Turkey against Makarios's actions.[20]

The archbishop, however, had no intention of changing course. Karamanlis's June 1963 resignation strengthened Makarios's determination to force the issue. Moreover, George Grivas and his followers inflamed Greek Cypriot public opinion, and their president responded to the pressure. Brushing off Klerides's arguments that, with proper incentives, the Turkish Cypriots would cut a deal, Makarios decided to seek a confrontation, confident that "nothing terrible will happen." On June 21 he handed Ambassador Wilkins a memorandum stating that the London-Zurich agreements were not working and that, as a result, his government would seek to implement major changes in the constitution together with suppression of the Treaty of Guarantee. The Cypriot government would initially approach the Guarantor Powers with its demands, but if they were not met, Greek Cyprus intended to void the treaties through sovereign action.[21]

Washington, once again, was slow to react to Makarios's moves. Wilkins insisted that the archbishop was floating a "trial balloon" designed to leverage the United States into supporting revisions in the London-Zurich accords. The State Department initially accepted Wilkins's judgment. The tendency to do nothing was reinforced by the firm reaction of the Greek government of Panagiotis Pipinelis to Makarios's proposals. Robert Komer of the National Security Council staff was less sanguine. An activist by nature and, like many Kennedy appointees, highly skeptical of the State Department's willingness to carry out presidential policy, Komer began to agitate for intervention in the Cyprus dispute, warning that Makarios had embarked on a dangerous course and that the State Department's "complacency" and "optimism" meant that the United States was in danger of seeing the situation in Cyprus spin out of control. He spent the next four months prodding his superiors and the State Department to take a stiff line with Makarios. In October he convinced national security adviser McGeorge Bundy and the president that the situation needed forceful action. On October 17, President Kennedy signed National Security Action Memorandum 266 warning that Cyprus was on the verge of an internal blowup and asking for policy recommendations to prevent a clash between Greek and Turkish Cypriots that would jeopardize NATO cohesion.[22]

Under White House prodding, the State Department quickly came up with a set of proposals that were designed to meet some of Makarios's demands by persuading Turkey to make concessions. However, the horse had already fled the barn. Neither Makarios nor the Turkish government was prepared to accept Washington's proposals. Turkish prime minister Ismet Inonu's government, a politically shaky coalition, had little room to maneuver and argued that Makarios should not be compensated for creating a crisis in which he was acting as representative of one community and not as president of all Cypriots. Makarios, in spite of the outbreak of sporadic intercommunal violence, raised the ante by informing the American embassy that he had a list of ten specific constitutional modifications to table before Turkish Cypriot leaders. Armed with a statement from the British high commissioner endorsing reforms, and reinforced by Greek elections that produced a more pro-enosis government under George Papandreou, Makarios informed the Greeks that he had British support and then presented his proposals (now thirteen in number) to Turkish Cypriot vice president Kutchuk on November 30.[23]

Kutchuk promptly rejected Makarios's proposals. More ominously, the Turkish government publicly condemned the "Thirteen Points" a week later. The NATO coalition supporting London-Zurich began to crumble. Although the newly installed Papandreou government initially warned Makarios about the dangers of trying to overturn an international agreement such as London-Zurich, it subsequently began to reverse course. Papandreou wanted the king to call new elections for early 1964. Initially, he had hoped to shelve Cyprus by warning Makarios not to act. However, the temptation to use the Cyprus issue against opposition from the National Radical Union (ERE) proved irresistible, particularly since Papandreou had taken a pro-enosis line during his "Ceaseless Struggle" campaign of 1961–63. During late November talks in Washington, Venizelos lined up behind Makarios's demands for revisions in the Cyprus constitution. The Turkish government dug in on its position: no concessions to Makarios until he respected the basic rights of the Turkish Cypriots outlined in the London-Zurich agreements.[24]

Continuing the approach he had adopted with Karamanlis, Makarios, in offering his Thirteen Points, presented the Greek government with a fait accompli. Less than a month later, he again acted without warning Athens. On December 22, another outbreak of violence in Nicosia triggered a Greek

Cypriot military action outlined in the Akritas Plan, a document drawn up by Makarios's interior minister, Polykarpos Georkadjis. Heavily armed Greek Cypriot militia began an offensive designed to crush Turkish Cypriot independence. Turkish Cypriot militia units successfully defended enclaves in Nicosia and key villages. Both sides suffered heavy casualties, and Turkish Cypriot resistance appeared likely to collapse without reinforcement. Turkey reacted energetically, seeking diplomatic support and preparing for military action. Britain and the United States tried to create a unified position that would end the fighting and lay the basis for a negotiated settlement. The Greek interim government under John Paraskevopoulos urged Makarios to restrain his men and assisted in brokering a cease-fire shortly after Christmas. The British invoked the provisions of the London-Zurich agreements and summoned a conference to meet in London to find a way out of the Cyprus impasse. Makarios made his position clear to Greek officials when they tried to arrange a peace mission by George Melas, a respected senior diplomat. The archbishop handed the Greek representative in Nicosia a paper with a list of weapons. If Melas came to Cyprus he should bring along the listed weapons.[25]

"A STORY . . . TOO SAD FOR TEARS"

Looking back on the Cyprus crisis of 1963–64, former Greek foreign minister Evangelos Averoff compared it to the 410 B.C.E. Athenian disaster in Sicily, appropriating Thucydides's conclusion that it was a story "too sad for tears." The behavior of the tragedy's protagonist, Makarios, recalls the ancient dramatic theme of hubris. Gifted with an exceptional intellect, wonderfully skilled at political maneuver, and with a remarkable capacity to calculate and successfully take risks, Makarios, with the support of the overwhelming majority of Greek Cypriots, guided his nation into a bloody and avoidable tragedy. Along the way, he repeatedly outmaneuvered the British, Americans, Greeks, and Turks as well as AKEL, Grivas, and his EOKA followers, the Turkish Cypriot leadership, and the hierarchy of the Cypriot church. From George Papandreou to George Papadopoulos, successive Greek prime ministers tried and failed to "control" Makarios and achieve enosis. At last, the exasperated ultras of the Greek military junta resorted to force, deposing Makarios, and opening the way for Turkey to partition the island. At every turn in his remarkable career, Makarios rejected compromise in favor of playing a zero-sum game that kept him at the center of Cypriot political life. He persisted in efforts to impose Greek Cypriot dominance over their unwilling Turkish Cypriot neighbors until it was too late. In the end, both he and the

Greek Cypriot people paid a spectacularly high price for his refusal to permit any reduction of his personal power and independence.[26]

Makarios's tactical brilliance was on display in the weeks following the December 1963 outbreak of civil war on Cyprus. He defeated an Anglo-American effort to pacify the island and retain alliance unity by placing a NATO force there. The Cypriot president realized that permitting such a peacekeeping force (even with some form of U.N. sanction) would exclude the possibility of support from the Soviet bloc and nonaligned states. Moreover, Turkey was a NATO member state, and the Anglo-American proposal opened the way to Ankara's increased military presence on the island, an idea that all strands of Greek Cypriot opinion rejected. At the January 1964 London conference, Makarios, assisted by a weak interim Greek government, blocked the NATO option and threw the issue into the hands of the U.N. Security Council, where Cyprus's leverage was the Soviet veto. He planned to win U.N. General Assembly backing to nullify the London-Zurich agreements.[27]

On January 25, 1964, as the London conference staggered to its unsuccessful end, the Johnson administration decided to commit the United States to an active role in forging a Cyprus settlement. British inability to manage their contentious treaty partners had Johnson complaining that "the British are getting to where they might as well not be British anymore if they can't handle Cyprus."[28] At a meeting of senior advisers, Under Secretary of State George Ball pressed for a U.S. military commitment to head off war and pacify the island. This option was totally unattractive to the new president. Johnson, scarcely two months in office, weighed down with an escalating conflict in Vietnam and the need to present himself for reelection in November 1964, was not going to send in the marines. He instructed his aides to mount a diplomatic offensive and to continue to press the British to take the leading role in working out a solution. The following day, the U.S. president instructed Ball to arrange a "special mission" to Britain, Greece, Turkey, and Cyprus headed by a senior U.S. official.[29]

Johnson ultimately tapped Ball for the Cyprus mission, pairing the activist under secretary of state with another dynamic personality, NSC Cyprus expert Komer. Former assistant secretary of state Raymond Hare described Komer as a "spark generator": "He . . . had some really good ideas. But he had a lot which were speculative; so obviously you had to winnow [them] out."[30] Komer was convinced that Makarios was a threat to U.S. interests in the region and had to be stopped. Ball, who developed an abiding dislike of the archbishop while visiting Cyprus, adopted this view. Some months later, these two men partnered with Dean Acheson, the forceful and arrogant former secretary of state, to forge a Cyprus solution. By keeping Makarios out of the negotiation process, these experienced foreign policy makers handed the archbishop the leverage he needed to kill their project with skillful diplomacy.[31]

Ball set out on his peacemaking mission in mid-February. The London conference had collapsed, and Makarios turned to the United Nations and the Soviet Union for assistance. The relationship between Greece and Turkey lay in ruins with Athens convinced that its erstwhile partner was planning an invasion of Cyprus and demanding that Washington prevent such a move at all costs, even by positioning its navy in the way of an invasion fleet. Ankara, meanwhile, was talking partition. The Cypriot government, its Turkish members having walked out, acted solely in Greek interests, insisting that all issues were negotiable as long as Turkey abandoned its treaty rights to intervene in Cyprus. Both the Greek and Turkish governments were convinced that the United States favored the interests of the other state and, as a result, were deeply suspicious and resentful.[32]

Ball headed for Nicosia by way of the three allied capitals, attempting to provide reassurance and deter both Greece and Turkey from the use of military force. He flew to Cyprus on February 13 for stormy interviews with Makarios. The ceasefire had broken down, and while battles raged all over the island, Ball and Makarios dueled over the nature of a peacekeeping mission. "I told off Makarios and his extremist ministers in a manner unfamiliar to diplomatic discourse," and, not surprisingly, "we reached complete deadlock."[33] Ball returned to Washington convinced that the best solution to the Cyprus issue was an accord over the island's future negotiated by Greece and Turkey.

Johnson had reached a similar conclusion after talks with Queen Frederika and British prime minister Alec Douglas Home. Ball warned that Turkey was readying an invasion; the queen had told LBJ that Greece was prepared for war. While the British offered to supply troops for a peacekeeping force, they remained adamant about avoiding the lead role in seeking a Cyprus settlement, preferring a U.N. lead. At Ball's suggestion, on February 20 the president sent letters to both Inonu and George Papandreou. Papandreou's electoral victory, Johnson suggested, gave him "the necessary freedom of action" to deal with Cyprus. The American president urged Greek-Turkish cooperation to save the NATO alliance and pacify Cyprus and to establish a "new partnership" with Inonu based on direct talks between the two states. Ambassador Henry Labouisse, who delivered the Johnson missive, brought along both assurances of U.S. "neutrality" between its two allies and pledges that Johnson would restrain Turkey. Papandreou promised to restrain Makarios and "enforce discipline on Greek Cypriots." However, the Greek prime minister "smilingly added" that "if the US fully supported . . . 'right' [justice] we [the Americans] would have to take sides—Greece's—for the London Zurich Accords had created an impossible situation." He wanted to remove both Greek and Turkish military contingents from Cyprus to undermine the provisions of the London-Zurich agreements. Papandreou suggested sending Grivas back to Cyprus to weaken Makarios's position and win control over irregular forces from the Cypriot president.[34]

The Johnson-Papandreou exchange was the beginning of a long effort to find common ground on Cyprus. The United States recognized that Greece's cooperation was its best and indeed only means of exercising leverage over Makarios. American officials, concerned about upcoming U.S. elections and the threat of the expansion of Soviet influence in the eastern Mediterranean, found the London-Zurich formula ideal for managing the crisis. Greece and Turkey would take advantage of their privileged legal positions and influence on the island to decide the future of Cyprus, peacefully marginalizing Makarios and reinforcing NATO unity. The United States would limit its involvement. At this early stage, American policy makers did not have a plan for a Cyprus settlement but trusted the Greeks and Turks to find a solution.[35]

Unfortunately, the London-Zurich model was unacceptable to the Greeks. Papandreou had spent the previous two years criticizing it. Bilateral discussions with Turkey risked again placing Greece in the position of making public concessions. Moreover, Papandreou had nothing to offer the Turks. He was seeking immediate enosis, an idea that had absolutely no appeal for Ankara. Plus, for all his talk about "control," Papandreou had little leverage over Makarios. Greek public opinion remained passionately pro-Makarios, and the military engagements of that winter only strengthened support for the archbishop. However, the prime minister may have felt that he possessed some leverage over the United States. Greek analyses suggested that Greece could insist on greater concessions for its security contributions to NATO. While these papers argued that the United States might be willing to provide more military aid, the prime minister may have decided that he could play on Greece's supposed strategic value to extract U.S. assistance on Cyprus. Papandreou wanted the United States to deliver Cyprus to Greece by convincing the Turks that a Cyprus under Greek rule was the best way to undercut Makarios. A deal with Turkey would mean that Papandreou had achieved a major goal of Greek nationalism, unifying the "big island" with the "national center." Such a political coup would almost certainly solidify his hold over both his party and the Greek nation. It would also limit Makarios's role in a unified state by upstaging him as the champion of Hellenism.[36]

Papandreou and Makarios were playing for high stakes. If the Greek leader achieved enosis, he would strip Makarios of influence and power. The moment seemed right. Papandreou was operating with fewer restraints on his conduct of foreign policy. His smashing electoral victory could be presented as a mandate for Cyprus action and had momentarily silenced potential internal party critics. King Paul was dying of cancer. His son, Crown Prince Constantine, who succeeded to the throne in early March 1964, was inexperienced. In a February 26, 1964, letter to the Cypriot president, Papandreou insisted that he would take the lead in Cypriot affairs, negotiating an agreement permitting enosis and instructing Makarios to follow his lead. The Greek Cypriot leader could not condone a situation in which the fate of his people was decided in Athens. A Greek-Turkish deal on enosis was totally unacceptable to Makarios. He was unwilling to permit any Turkish role in the final settlement. Moreover, he bridled at the arrogance of George Papandreou and other Greek leaders who treated him as a subordinate who must follow the direction of the "national center." As a result, Makarios formally agreed to the general principle of Greek leadership but did not permit coordination between the two governments. He kept the Greek government in the dark about his moves until the last minute and never requested agreement from Athens. Over the following sixteen months, Makarios outmaneuvered both Papandreou and the Johnson administration. The Greek prime minister concluded, correctly, that Makarios aimed to undermine him.[37]

Ironically, the key weapon in Makarios's armory was the threat of Turkish military intervention. American policy makers feared both its immediate and long-term effects. A Turkish attack would be bloody and almost certainly partition the island with all the ensuing human tragedy of ethnic cleansing. It would probably ignite a Greek-Turkish war that, at a minimum, would weaken both states and seriously damage, if not destroy, NATO's so-called Southern Flank. By keeping pressure on the Turkish Cypriot community, Makarios forced the United States to restrain the Turks and to defend the continued existence of a Cypriot state. The cost to the Americans was a worsening relationship with Turkey. The archbishop emerged as a hero to both the Greek Cypriot and Greek public as he twisted the Turkish tail while Washington held Ankara on a leash. One of the constants of Makarios's strategic outlook was his certainty that, in the end, the United States would protect him from the worst effects of his provocations. This calculation held true for over a decade.[38]

Assessing the situation from Nicosia in April 1964, the newly arrived U.S. ambassador, Taylor Belcher, suggested that the United States accept the Greek Cypriot position on self-determination and use its support for some form of enosis to ensure the security of the Turkish minority. Belcher's suggestion found support from the U.S. ambassadors in both Athens and Ankara, who, however, stressed the need for a realistic quid pro quo for Turkey.[39] The problem was George Papandreou. The Greek prime minister was convinced that success was about to fall into his lap without him having to make any concessions. Even as renewed fighting elevated tensions on Cyprus, an ebullient Papandreou told Labouisse (April 10) that the outlook for speedy realization of enosis was so good that he was concentrating on moves to avoid humiliating Turkey. Papandreou's plan called for the United States to force the Turks to accept the dissolution of the London-Zurich agreements and recognize the complete independence of Cyprus. Then a plebiscite could follow that would endorse enosis. Makarios would be sacrificed to the "cause of Hellenism." Papandreou reversed himself on sending Grivas back to Cyprus, saying he feared it would cause divisions among the Greek Cypriot majority. In late April he and Makarios met in Athens to plan a common strategy, in which Papandreou traded a pledge of Greek military support for the Greek Cypriots in exchange for promises that the archbishop would support enosis and that Greek Cypriot irregulars would avoid further provoking the Turks.[40]

Papandreou kept his part of the bargain, secretly flooding the island with Greek troops. By midsummer, between eight and twenty thousand Greek soldiers were positioned on the island in violation of the London-Zurich accords. In addition to giving Greece a bargaining chip in talks with the Turks and with its other NATO allies, the presence of this force provided Papandreou with a potential tool finally to exercise some control over Makarios and, if necessary, to deal with AKEL. It gave credibility to Greek talk of defending the island. Of course, such a move also begged for a counter by the geographically contiguous and more powerful Turks and increased Ankara's determination to retain its treaty-authorized garrison on the island. Since one of the archbishop's major objectives was evicting that force, Papandreou and Makarios were both engaged in brinksmanship but with conflicting aims and approaches that were bound to sow confusion and increase the possibilities of miscalculation.[41]

The situation in Cyprus already was confused. The U.N. peacekeeping force there (UNFICYP) had only limited forces and authority. It was designed to keep the two warring camps apart but only through mediation. If one side refused to cooperate, UNFICYP had no authority to intervene. The peacekeepers operated in an extremely dangerous environment, in which they tried to protect civilian populations without becoming caught in the crossfire between warring militias. Their local peacemaking efforts frequently failed. Fighting broke out and subsided only to start again at other locations. Hundreds died or were wounded that winter. The tenuous ties between the two major ethnic communities snapped under the pressure of warfare. Turkish Cypriot leaders, having withdrawn from the national government, began creating independent local administrative bodies. Meanwhile, U.N. diplomats and peacekeepers struggled to deal with outbreaks of violence, Turkey and Greece edged closer to armed conflict, Makarios defied both Turks and Turkish Cypriots, and the major powers maneuvered offstage as part of their ceaseless Cold War conflict. All the involved players laid blame on the others. Positions hardened, reducing the hope for a negotiated settlement. Andreas Papandreou recalled that relations between Greece and Turkey hit a low point while George Ball warned Secretary of State Rusk that "all this confusion is made to order for Makarios, who has already shown a notable capacity to do mischief. . . . Time is not on our side as both [Turkey] and [Greece] seem in [a] mood to force [the] issue . . . blowing up the island." Fortunately, Ball added, George Papandreou was as fed up with Makarios's antics as the United States was, and cooperation with him might offer a means of dealing with the threat to peace from Nicosia.[42]

U.S. efforts to maintain neutrality between two important allies clearly were not working. In early May Senator J. William Fulbright visited the region as a presidential emissary. The visit got an equally cold reception in Athens and Ankara, particularly from the overheated press of the two nations.[43] Even before Fulbright returned to the United States, Ball had already concluded that the United States needed a plan to support its diplomatic initiatives. He too began to think about enosis as the most effective way to checkmate Makarios. Agreement to such a plan, he argued, would have to be purchased from Turkey through some form of Greek concessions that offered Ankara security by placing the island under NATO supervision and prevented "a Cuba off their shore."[44]

The difficulty was finding a concession large enough to satisfy Turkey without making Papandreou appear to have traded away something of value. Greek public opinion viewed the Cyprus issue in the same zero-sum optic as Greek Cypriots. Convinced of the "justice" of their claim to Cyprus, few Greeks would tolerate paying for something they were convinced was theirs by right. Not surprisingly, "all Greek politicians, government and opposition, stand as one on this issue." Papandreou had virtually nothing to offer in exchange for enosis. Greek Cypriot hostage taking added to the fury of public opinion and to sense of impotence among Turkish leaders. Makarios, while trying to use the United Nations to destroy the London-Zurich accords, simultaneously was seeking arms from the Soviet bloc to enforce his control over the rebellious Turkish Cypriots.[45]

At the beginning of June, the Turks decided to invade. President Johnson stopped them, employing the "diplomatic equivalent of an atomic bomb" (Ball). The American president warned Prime Minister Inonu that if Turkey used force it would be acting without NATO support and would face the possibility of Soviet reprisal. Further, Ankara would be responsible for the Greek Cypriots' likely bloody retaliation against largely unarmed Turkish Cypriots. Johnson reminded the Turks that U.S.-supplied weapons could not be used in such an invasion. This "brutal" display of American power humiliated a major U.S. ally and, to intense U.S. irritation, once again saved Makarios from his own excesses. It also opened the way for a major U.S. initiative to find a Cyprus solution.[46]

Tucked at the end of LBJ's letter to Inonu was an invitation to visit Washington for talks. U.S. diplomacy tried to entice both the Turkish and Greek leaders to meet under U.S. auspices. Inonu quickly agreed. Papandreou proved difficult. Ball headed off for Europe to consult the British, deliver the formal invitation to Greeks and Turks, and lay the groundwork for a joint meeting. Convinced they held the winning hand, Papandreou and his ministers displayed a confidence bordering on the delusional. Papandreou insisted that the United States, Turkey, and NATO had no options left, that only enosis would prevent the creation of a "Mediterranean Cuba." Foreign Minister Stavros Costopoulos agreed and added that Greece would make no territorial concessions to Turkey in exchange for enosis and also would insist that the patriarchate remain in Istanbul, although it might be open to some population exchanges. Direct talks could follow discussions at the United Nations and would simply formalize the deal. The Turks behaved like spoiled children, the foreign minister concluded. Washington had to bring them to their senses.[47]

Johnson's take on Cyprus was quite different. While Greek leaders believed that American intervention had decisively tilted the Cyprus problem in their direction, their American counterparts all agreed that the Greeks had simply won a reprieve and that only quick action could stave off a Turkish military operation. Moreover, Johnson felt that, since he had held up the Turks, it was up to Greece to do something to facilitate a settlement: "I think that the last thing we want . . . is to let me be the peacemaker. . . . I think we ought to carry it right to Athens and Ankara. . . . Now that's my country boy approach."⁴⁸

Johnson tried his country boy diplomacy on Greek ambassador Alexander Matsas (June 11) without notable success. The meeting was vintage Johnson. He conducted a full court press that displayed both his knowledge of the situation and determination to pressure the Greeks into accepting his basic point, that Greece and Turkey needed to start talking about a Cyprus solution: "If I can't get you to talk, I can't keep the Turks from moving," he interjected as Matsas tried to move the discussion away from tactics to Turkish behavior. Relentlessly, Johnson brought the Greek ambassador back to the question of talks. When Matsas surfaced the idea of an independent Cyprus, the president responded that that would be a matter for Greece and Turkey to settle. "The President observed that negotiating with Makarios was impossible. Makarios wasn't interested in the security of the West. But Greece, the US, and Turkey were. Matsas interjected that Greece could not negotiate without Makarios. The President indicated that the Cypriots would have to be consulted at some point."⁴⁹

While U.S. officials worked themselves into a frenzy over Greek intransigence and the damage it would do to the NATO alliance, Turkey continued to show an accommodating face and a readiness to discuss Cyprus with the Greeks. By the time George Papandreou, accompanied by his son and adviser, Andreas, arrived in Washington on June 24, 1964, the two sides had diametrically opposed views of the next step on Cyprus. Three days of meetings in Washington and at the United Nations in New York constituted a dialogue of the deaf. The American side pressed for immediate direct talks with Acheson as mediator. Papandreou countered that talks would fail and war become inevitable. The Greek leader, schooled in the use of the past as a tool of achieving Greek objectives, exploited the occasion to improve his public image in Greece: wrapping himself in the national cause, claiming a readiness to fight, and giving his rendition of Metaxas's 1940 "Oxi" [No surrender] declaration before his stupefied hosts. The Americans pleaded, badgered, and prodded without success. As diplomacy, the meetings were an unmitigated disaster. The only concession Papandreou made was that U.N.-mediated talks between representatives of Greece and Turkey were possible. An Acheson role, the key to a successful outcome in the U.S. view, was left in the air.⁵⁰

Ironically, Ball was the one U.S. official who expressed optimism after the meetings, predicting that Papandreou would come around to a compromise after milking all the domestic political benefits from his "firm" stand against the United States. There was, however, little sign of Greek give in the days immediately after the Washington "discussions." Papandreou, in search of allies, stopped off in Paris on his way home and got a chilling reality check. French president Charles de Gaulle brushed aside Greek complaints about American pressure and told Papandreou not to stir up trouble and to get control of Makarios. Once home, Papandreou coldly responded to a follow-up message from Johnson, labeling it "more of the same" and telling U.S. chargé Norbert L. Anschuetz that Cyprus was not a Greek-Turkish problem. He upped the ante by dispatching Grivas, whom Ball described as "a fanatic fortunately anti-communist," to Cyprus to wrest control of the Greek Cypriot forces from Makarios. Grivas's return could only increase Turkish anxiety about a Greek plot to achieve enosis.[51]

The sole Greek concession was permitting the Acheson mediation to begin under a U.N. cover in Geneva (July 11–September 1). From the start, Acheson sought a deal based on enosis with some form of compensation for Turkey. He dismissed both partition and federalism as unrealistic. He tried to convince the suspicious Greek side that a relatively small Turkish base did not constitute partition. Acheson was very firm on the need for local government autonomy for the Turkish Cypriots, stressing that guarantees for minority rights were essential to a deal. Acheson's plan was to induce some movement on the Greek side, and Papandreou gradually rose to the bait. Foreign Minister Costopoulos and then the prime minister suggested trading off the Dodecanese island of Kastellorizon for Cyprus. George and Andreas Papandreou traveled to London to see whether they could round up British support for their position. A more subdued Greek prime minister tried to draw out his bottom line. He wanted to maintain the unity and effectiveness of NATO and thus would do everything possible to avoid a war with Turkey, even postpone a Cyprus solution. He could accept Turkish bases on Kastellorizon and the participation of a Turkish contingent on Cyprus under cover of a NATO base. ("NATO with a fez.") Greece was ready to provide whatever minority guarantees were necessary to achieve enosis. Pledging to "deliver" Makarios's backing for a solution, and to respect British control of the sovereign base areas after unification, Papandreou argued that U.N. support for an independent Cyprus could be ignored in order to reach the greater goal of "Natofication" of the island. Pressed by his skeptical British hosts to explain how he would control Makarios during the process of unification, the Greek prime minister replied that "a Greek flag would defeat Makarios." All that was needed to bring off enosis was American readiness to defend the island against Turkish military threats.[52]

Throughout July and August Acheson sought a deal by making concessions to Greek demands and trying to whittle away the Turkish position. In late July, the U.S. mediator circulated a first memorandum summarizing the positions of the two sides and suggesting areas where compromise would work. The so-called first Acheson Plan immediately made its way into the hands of Makarios, who was visiting Athens. The archbishop held a press conference to denounce the proposal and released the document as proof of an American attempt to sell out Greek interests. The Papandreou government compounded its gaffe in leaking the document to Makarios by confirming the accuracy of the text. Labouisse warned that the incident showed that Papandreou was not a free agent and that Makarios, who had a spy in the prime minister's office, had effective control over Greek policy. Moreover, the episode demonstrated that "Basically Makarios is opposed to enosis, but will not publicly admit it." An embarrassed and enlightened Papandreou, who shared Labouisse's estimate, offered to stage a coup against Makarios. "Instant enosis," as the prime minister outlined it, would "eliminate" Makarios and establish a NATO base under Turkish command. Greece would offer full guarantees of security for the Turkish Cypriot population. When Labouisse reminded Papandreou of the inherent difficulties of such an approach, the Greek prime minister responded that he would ignore the United Nations and move against Makarios. Papandreou tried to line up Grivas's backing for instant enosis based on Acheson's memorandum.[53]

The tempest surrounding the Acheson Plan offered opportunities that both Turkey and Makarios seized. The Turks stiffened their demands. Makarios lined up backing for a U.N. resolution affirming the independence of Cyprus and Soviet pledges of support in the event of a Turkish invasion. Predictably, Grivas, with Greek Cypriot troops now under his command, unleashed a new offensive against the Turkish Cypriot enclaves in the northwest part of the island. As predictably, Makarios utilized the attacks to drive a wedge between Greece and Turkey simply by declining to call off his commander. The Turks struck back with air assaults on Greek Cypriot positions. U.S. ambassador Belcher, who had approached Makarios before the strike, alerting the Cypriot leader of Turkish intentions, got his hands slapped by Washington for breaking a diplomatic confidence. Washington urged the Turks to calm down, which they did after delivering this forceful message to Makarios and the Americans. The Greek Cypriots pulled back. Fearful that the Turkish attack would kill any chances of a deal, Acheson appealed to Papandreou (through Labouisse) to offer some sort of base leasing arrangement. Ball, who felt the Greeks had done useful work in finally getting Makarios to stand his forces down, hinted at the need for U.S. military intervention. With U.S. elections less than three months away, Johnson rejected the idea. Diplomacy remained the only tool the United States would employ to deal with Cyprus.[54]

Papandreou and his ministers recognized that sending back Grivas had been a serious error. They now had two out-of-control leaders on Cyprus. Makarios was appealing to the Soviet Union for help while Grivas threatened to resume military operations. Grivas argued that Makarios was the primary stumbling block to enosis and wanted Athens to break with the ethnarch. Both Washington and Athens were in a panic. Still, the Greek leader insisted that the Acheson proposals could not be sold to his electors because they would create de facto partition. Labouisse approached the king, who agreed to convince the opposition leadership to support a deal based on Acheson's proposals. Acheson redrafted his paper to meet Greek demands and worked over the Turks to secure more concessions to the Greek position. By August 15, after further talks with both sides, the U.S. mediator concluded it was time to pull the plug on his effort. The two states were too far apart.[55]

Ball, who wanted to oust Makarios as soon as possible, refused to give up, and for another fortnight he and Acheson conceived of one scheme after another designed to meet Greek demands and somehow bring Turkey along. Papandreou, who also felt that the situation was out of control, arranged for a "crown council" meeting of the senior party leaders to secure their support for a coup against Makarios while simultaneously sending a trusted aide, Defense Minister Petros Garoufalias, to Nicosia to win Makarios's agreement to instant enosis based on the second revision of Acheson's proposals. The Cypriot president refused to go along. After weeks of angry rhetoric, Makarios, like most Greek Cypriots, was convinced that Acheson was aiming at partition. He pointedly reminded Garoufalias that the Turkish army was too close to permit him to approve a plan for instant enosis that could trigger an immediate invasion. He did not intend to act on the basis of security assurances from the United States. Nor would he play the hero and expose his people to advance Greek interests. Fearing that Papandreou might unleash a coup against him, Makarios became even more active in seeking arms for his police forces. What limited trust that had existed between Athens and Nicosia evaporated. From his post in Nicosia, Belcher had consistently warned Washington of the impossibility of a deal without Makarios's inclusion and blessing. His reward was to be cut out of much of the critical diplomatic exchange.

Now, he forwarded Makarios's self-congratulatory and accurate estimate of U.S. diplomatic performance. The archbishop was brutally realistic: "Papandreou will accept anything I agree to but I don't necessarily agree with any decision he may make." The State Department had gotten the cart before the horse by failing to consult him first and then excluding Cyprus from the Geneva talks. Makarios concluded with expressions of resentment at U.S. moves and mistrust of U.S. objectives.[56]

Ball dished out one more-extreme scenario after another while lashing out at the Greeks. Acheson counseled realism. Komer accepted defeat. He ruefully admitted to the president that the archbishop had outmaneuvered Greece and the United States and that the available policy options looked to be largely ineffective. George Papandreou, too, realized that he had lost the battle with Makarios. Achieving enosis against the will of the Greek Cypriot leader was beyond his political strength. The impossibility of a bloodless coup, the limited capabilities of Greek troops, and the effect on his political position if Greek soldiers killed Greek Cypriots while imposing enosis had finally dawned on the Greek leader. If the United States could not deliver Cyprus on Greek terms, then it was time to make a retreat and lay the blame on Washington and Ankara. In an August 25 discussion with Labouisse, the two Papandreous poured out their resentments. Andreas blasted the "despicable" Greek and Greek Cypriot press, while his father laid blame on the Turks and added that "he would be more than delighted if [a] coup d'etat for unconditional enosis would be achieved in which case Makarios would be his captive. . . . He was willing to eliminate Makarios." For now, however, he would have to live with the archbishop. A well-organized campaign of government leaks to the pro-Papandreou press assured that the Americans would become the fall guys for the latest failure to achieve enosis.[57]

THE SNAKE REFUSED TO DIE

Even after officially throwing in the towel, Greek and American officials continued to exchange suggestions on how to achieve enosis. On September 8, Ball tried to revive the effort with a plan to have Turkish troops seize the Karpas Peninsula while the Greeks took control of the rest of the island. President Johnson rejected the idea. Cyprus would return to the diplomatic back burner. The violence cooled off as Makarios readjusted his strategy to new realities. After his close call with enosis by coup, the archbishop avoided tempting fate again, particularly with the dangerous Grivas back on the island. Makarios's Soviet backing evaporated after Nikita Khrushchev's October 1964 ouster as prime minister and party leader. A final solution of the Turkish Cypriot problem would have to wait. Wearing away a surrounded minority's will to resist seemed a surer tactic.[58]

Badly burned, the Americans took their distance, while the Greek and Turkish governments slowly began to address the issue bilaterally. In February and again in March 1965, George Papandreou suggested reviving the Acheson Plan. U.S. officials had no desire to have Papandreou as a partner in a further mediation. In any case, Greece soon plunged into a major domestic crisis, ending with Papandreou's ouster (July 1965), and his successors eventually decided to pursue direct talks with Turkey. By December 1966, Greece and Turkey appeared to be close to an agreement based on "compensated" enosis, involving Greek concessions in exchange for unification with Cyprus. But then a more severe political crisis shook the Greek state, ultimately triggering a military coup. Once the military junta ("the Colonels") felt firmly in control of Greece, it returned to the bargaining table, only to discover that the Turkish government had raised the ante. A summit meeting in September 1967 produced a major humiliation for the Colonels. The Greeks, without consulting Makarios, offered a deal based on the Acheson proposals. The Turks demanded more territory than Athens was ready to offer. Two months later, Grivas ignited a confrontation by attacking a Turkish enclave. Makarios, as usual, emerged from the crisis in an improved position. He correctly calculated that the United States would intervene to remove Grivas and to ensure that Turkey did not attack Cyprus. The Greek junta paid the cost of Grivas's misjudgments. It was forced to withdraw the troops Papandreou had placed on the island and to recognize the validity of the London-Zurich agreements, including the independence of Cyprus.[59]

The events of 1964–67 highlighted a critical weakness in both the Greek and the American approach to Cyprus. Both states underestimated the degree to which Greek Cypriots had developed their own specific identity. Barrington King, a U.S. diplomat stationed on Cyprus between 1964 and 1967, recalled: "Greek Cypriots were funny about enosis. If you asked them, they would say yes, and if you said 'You don't really want it,' they would become extremely angry. But, in fact, I am sure they did not want it because they knew the Greeks looked down on them."[60] During the Greek Cypriot struggle to end colonial rule, union with Greece, an idea blessed by the church and full of historical symbolism, seemed the best solution. Enosis became synonymous with self-determination. Once the Cypriots had independence and self-rule thrust upon them by a foreign diktat, however, the attraction waned. Makarios was clearly out in front of his countrymen in seeing the benefits of independence, but a growing portion of the Greek Cypriot population gradually embraced such a solution. By mid-1967, the British estimated that only 20 percent of Greek Cypriots were actually committed to enosis. The vast majority appeared unsure of whether enosis or independence offered the best situation. Makarios, who certainly sensed the same divisions of public opinion, avoided committing to either view in order to preserve the unity of Greek Cypriots in the face of the real threat of a joint Greek-Turkish intervention. A strategy of public statements favoring unity with Greece but practical independence in foreign and domestic policy offered the best plan to ward off external intervention.[61]

The 1963–64 crises over Cyprus bolstered Makarios's leadership of the Greek Cypriot community. In besting the United States, Greece, and Turkey by alternating delay and sudden action while making a set of impossible but seemingly reasonable demands, Makarios demonstrated how a small state could take advantage of the openings provided by the conflicting interests of larger powers. With his prestige at its height, he was able to calm the island, deflate the immediate threat from Grivas (further embarrassing the general's patron, George Papandreou), and maneuver Cyprus away from enosis. Makarios, the British high commissioner opined, was employing "skillful propaganda" to "reduce the Greek Cypriots to such a state of confusion that they will reject enosis in the name of enosis." Greek ambassador Menelaos Alexandrakis recalled, however, that Makarios consistently underestimated both Turkey's ability to control the Turkish Cypriots and its readiness to use force while simultaneously overestimating the value of the United Nations in achieving his goals. These misjudgments would cost Cyprus dearly.[62]

The Cyprus crises of 1964 were a major setback for the United States. The U.S. tilt toward Greece's position failed to satisfy either the political needs of George Papandreou or the demands of Greek public opinion. The ERE, not wishing to be outmaneuvered by Papandreou, took a more radical position on Cyprus, largely abandoning Karamanlis's stance and reinforcing the Greek sense of betrayal by the Americans. Andreas Papandreou began to emerge as a major player in domestic politics through his use of the Cyprus issue. Equally important, the tilt was not unnoticed in Turkey, and U.S.-Turkish relations entered a long period of tension. Anti-American feeling was stoked by the subsequent release of Johnson's June letter to Inonu. Three years later Cyrus Vance's effort to prevent a Turkish invasion of the island rekindled resentments. The United States, in Turkish eyes, was not acting as an ally or even a neutral player, but as the protector of Greece and Makarios. Its treatment of Turkey was reminiscent of European behavior during the late Ottoman Empire.[63]

U.S. officials learned a difficult lesson about the need to deal with Makarios. The archbishop, the ultimate political realist, was only too happy to improve his ties with Washington, and during the late 1960s Makarios's cooperation on intelligence issues was noted with appreciation by U.S. officials. Vance's treatment of Makarios during the 1967 crisis was markedly different from that accorded him by Ball, Acheson, and Komer in 1964.[64] Discussions with the Cypriot president did not aim at marginalizing him, but at winning his approval or at least his neutral cooperation with a plan to defuse the crisis. Gradually and grudgingly, the Johnson administration began to recognize Makarios's role as an independent player and sought to manage its relationship with him carefully.

The biggest losers in the 1964 confrontation were the Turkish Cypriot community and the Greek government. The Turkish Cypriots found themselves literally surrounded by Greek Cypriot military forces and unsure of the level of support Ankara could provide. The presence of a U.N. peacekeeping force provided them only limited security. With Makarios and Grivas struggling for the support of pro-enosis opinion, Greek Cypriot willingness to keep the peace was not a sure thing. The subtle hard-liner Rauf Denktash elbowed aside Fazil Kutchuk as leader of his community, and the Turkish Cypriots dug in to resist Greek Cypriot demands.[65]

The Papandreou government dealt a body blow to the sense of common interests that tied together Greeks and Cypriot Greeks. The Greek leadership's constant public demands that Cypriots follow the direction of the national center, combined with its enosis-at-all-costs approach and frequently deceptive efforts at a diplomatic settlement, created the impression that Athens was all too willing to sacrifice Cypriot interests to its own goals. Typical of the Greek attitude was Foreign Minister Costopoulos's comment: "It doesn't matter what President Makarios thinks." George Papandreou instructed his ambassador to "cooperate" with Grivas but to "handle" (control) Makarios. While the archbishop was never likely to agree to enosis, the Papandreou government sped up the process by which Greek Cypriots began to see their destiny as different from that of Greece.[66]

The Papandreou government's handling of the 1964 crisis was opportunism gone awry. At the end of its erratic maneuvering, the Greek government had managed to damage its relations with all of its key NATO partners. Karamanlis's patient efforts to create the basis for a Greek-Turkish agreement on Cyprus lay in ruins. Athens enjoyed no credit with Turkish leaders, who now were committed to the use of force on Cyprus if the situation warranted. The British, too, drew the conclusion that Papandreou could not be trusted.

American comments on the Greek government were equally scathing, but U.S. officials realized they would have to live with George Papandreou. Still, by the autumn of 1964, the United States had little reason to trust Papandreou and even less to take actions that would support his continuance in office. Papandreou's subsequent Cyprus maneuvers only strengthened these convictions.[67]

The last point was particularly important because of the changed U.S. perception of Greece's new monarch, Constantine II. With great reluctance the young king had rounded up opposition support for Papandreou during the last phases of the Acheson mediation. The prime minister's management of the crisis convinced Constantine that he had to replace Papandreou as soon as possible.[68] While U.S. officials steered clear of involvement in this internal political matter, they appear to have emerged from the political drubbing they took with an enhanced respect for the careful way in which the king played his role and for his moderation. In contrast with George Papandreou, who seemed ready to destroy the Western alliance to gain Cyprus, the king clearly viewed NATO as key to Greek security and thus critical to its foreign policy calculations. The twenty-five-year-old monarch, for all his inexperience, appeared much more mature in judgment and steadier than the seventy-six-year-old prime minister or his forty-five-year-old son and heir apparent.

5

COUP D'ÉTAT, 1964-1967

> The Ceaseless Struggle is not only history. It is both present and future.
> — Andreas Papandreou, April 1965

> The hour of the unknown colonel is arriving.
> — Spyridon Markezinis, February 1967

In June 1963, Guy de Girard de Charbonniere, the French ambassador in Athens, analyzed the "American presence in Greece" for his superiors in Paris. By announcing that it would terminate all its grant-aid programs the United States was moving further away from its role as protector power. "Since 1952 we can document no U.S. [internal] interventions, and our files are quite complete." The United States, of course, remained by far the most significant foreign presence in Greece. Its military assistance programs enabled the Greeks to field and pay for a respectable modern army. Its economic assistance programs helped Greece avoid balance-of-payment problems while they fueled economic growth. Overall, U.S. private capital had played a relatively limited role in the Greek economy, with the exception of the movie industry. Films, however, played a significant role in a strong American cultural presence. While the era of an American "protectorate" was over and Greece enjoyed "full sovereignty and independence," state and society were extremely sensitive to U.S. views.[1]

This positive assessment of the U.S. role in Greece, reflecting success in reducing American commitments while maintaining U.S. influence at a premium, as well as the stability of Greece's democratic experiment, was being overtaken by events even as the French ambassador wrote. Karamanlis's resignation, the election of George Papandreou, the Cyprus crisis, and a harsher internal political climate plunged Greece into a crisis that divided its ruling elites and ultimately sparked a military coup. As the major Greek political factions turned to it for assistance, the United States reluctantly and slowly assumed a mediation role. The inability of U.S. officials to promote a resolution of Greece's internal political problems (or to resolve the Cyprus question) left many Greeks disillusioned. The patron seemed to act against their national interests.

TWO OLD MEN AND "THE BOY"

After Karamanlis's June 1963 ouster, King Paul and George Papandreou were the key players in Greek politics. Both wanted to end the former prime minister's long domination of public life, and while neither had a particularly high opinion of the other, they cooperated over the ensuing seven months to open the way for fair elections and two Papandreou victories. In the first of these contests, Papandreou and the Center Union (EK), capitalizing on political fatigue with Karamanlis, won a plurality of votes (42 percent to 39.3 percent for the National Radical Union [ERE]) but not a majority of seats in parliament. In a gesture to both the Palace and the military, Papandreou announced that he would reject the support of the United Democratic Left (EDA) and form a minority government. Karamanlis planned to force him to govern from that position. However, the ERE's chief, who was uncomfortable as leader of the opposition, then elected to go into exile a second time (December 9), anointing as his successor a trusted lieutenant and relative by marriage, Panagiotes Kanellopoulos. Karamanlis and, at least initially, Kanellopoulos saw the arrangement as temporary. The ERE's founder would return to lead the party at the appropriate time. In the meanwhile, ERE would pay back its antagonists, employing extreme nationalism and obstructionist tactics like those the EK had used against it after the 1961 vote.[2]

Karamanlis's plans for weakening his opponent collapsed because the king was unwilling to go along with them. The Greek monarch privately complained that he was being "blackmailed" by Papandreou's hints of renewed assaults on the monarchy but seems also to have recognized that public sentiment demanded a change in government and to have accepted pledges of good behavior from the EK leadership. Meanwhile, the newly installed prime minister continued to operate as though he were running for political office. He accused Karamanlis's government of using the intelligence services against him and announced that he wanted new elections in January. Papandreou offered an ambitious electoral program of "people power" (*laokratía*), including higher wages and tax cuts. Simultaneously, he attempted to pack the civil service and military with EK supporters, turned on the spigots of government spending, and mounted a relentless public attack on ERE leaders. French diplomats were appalled: "The Western varnish applied to this country by more than a decade of civil stability has cracked, the political customs and manners are tending to become again Balkans-like or even oriental." Even Papandreou's allies expressed concern. However, the opposition was knocked off balance and quickly resigned itself to defeat. After rejecting a suggestion by King Paul for a national unity government to deal with Cyprus, Papandreou handed in his resignation on December 20. The king dissolved parliament and called for new elections.[3]

George Papandreou's second electoral victory, February 16, 1964, reflected his shrewd use of issues, especially Cyprus, and of patronage as well as widespread public enthusiasm for his gestures of reform and liberalization. The EK emerged with a majority of 171 seats and 52.7 percent of the popular vote. The ERE and Markezinis's Progressives combined for 35.3 percent of the vote and 107 seats (99 ERE deputies).

U.S. officials watched the political maneuverings with detachment. Although Henry Labouisse strongly favored Karamanlis's reelection, officials at the "State Department were determined to keep strictly out of the present Greek political troubles and to adopt a rigid policy of non-interference." Washington believed Papandreou had good prospects of winning and expected a "more independent" Greek foreign policy under the EK that nonetheless would keep Greece securely tied to NATO. Indeed, the new prime minister pledged that "his government 'will be more pro-American than the previous one.'" Moreover, the embassy thought it had a trusted ally within the prime minister's inner circle. American deputy chief of mission Tapley Bennett and Andreas Papandreou assiduously courted each other throughout the long electoral season.[4] Analyzing the effects of the Center Union's February 1964 triumph, the State Department's Greek desk commented: "With Andreas Papandreou . . . at his side, we can expect [George Papandreou] to take constructive attitudes toward Greece's problems. We expect Andreas to have increased responsibilities and greater influence. . . . On balance we can expect those who participate in the Papandreou government to be friendly to the U.S., and perhaps more so, compared to those in [K]aramanlis's government."[5]

Since George Papandreou had pledged to pursue an activist Cyprus policy and promote internal reforms, he chose ministers capable of providing reassurance to business, the Palace, the military, and NATO allies. One of these intermediaries, Sofokles Venizelos, died during the campaign. Shortly after Papandreou's second victory, King Paul succumbed to cancer. The ailing Venizelos's political stock had been declining. Nevertheless he had constituted a powerful restraint on Papandreou. King Paul, frequently a source of Greek political instability, had a sense of limits and the ability to get along with Greece's political leaders. His son, Constantine II, was well meaning but burdened with a public reputation as a playboy and limited experience in the complexities of Greek politics. Moreover, he was under the influence of Queen Frederika, whose imperious temperament and reactionary political views had been a source of trouble in the past.[6]

The "boy" king would have to contend with two old men in a hurry. The new monarch's relations with both major parties were problematic. He was suspected of playing a role in Karamanlis's ouster, and both he and his mother were known to be hostile toward the return of the domineering former prime minister. The Palace's relationship with Papandreou remained to be worked out, but both major party leaders were in a combative mood. Papandreou was anxious to solidify his control over both the EK and Greece, while Kanellopoulos was trying to hold on to party leadership in the face of a parliamentary group whose loyalty was first to Karamanlis and next to their own ambitions. Karamanlis's long-distance management of ERE affairs inevitably left Kanellopoulos in a precarious position. To assert his leadership, Kanellopoulos was attracted to potentially risky maneuvers. The temptation grew as the party recovered from the initial disorientation caused by the loss of its leader and two election defeats. From his exile in Paris, Karamanlis urged his lieutenants to confront Papandreou.[7]

The EK, meanwhile, acted "more like a party running for office than a governing party. Papandreou's own admission that he is more comfortable in opposition than in power seems to be borne out." The cabinet, composed of "elderly liberal politicians . . . almost entirely from the more conservative elements of the Center Union," included party barons and one interesting appointment, Andreas Papandreou, as minister to the prime minister. Foreign diplomats praised the "brilliant economist" who would inject some new thinking into an uninspired cabinet. Unfortunately, the prime minister's unconcealed ambition to promote his son to party leadership fueled discontent within his party, canceling Andreas's potential for modernizing Greek politics and the economy.[8]

George Papandreou encouraged the pro-EK press to unleash campaigns against the United States over the Cyprus issue, against the judiciary for its putative ties to the ERE, and against the opposition for "corruption." Labouisse remonstrated with Papandreou over EK press treatment of an ally. Opposition leaders were enraged by the tone of attacks on them. Inside parliament, the government frequently coordinated its assaults on the ERE with the EDA, raising questions about its anticommunist bona fides. A series of measures designed to open up Greek society, including repatriation of communist civil war veterans, and the reduction of police presence at public demonstrations, achieved their immediate goal of expanding civil liberties after more than a decade of strict police control. They also sowed a great deal of ill will among the opposition and heightened fears of communist penetration in Greek politics and society.[9]

Papandreou's press strategy was effective. Evangelos Averoff admitted that the government's popularity grew as it successfully exploited "scandal" charges against the ERE and pledged a "real" national solution to Cyprus. Papandreou appeared to be siphoning off part of the EDA's voting base. As he simultaneously closed off avenues to the right, however, concern grew within his own party, while the extremist wing of the ERE expanded its influence. Moreover, by reducing pressure on the communists, Papandreou stoked discontent among a military leadership that was already worried about his efforts to shake up the high command and intelligence services as well as by his Cyprus policy. Concerns about the communist threat in Greece were almost certainly overstated. Nevertheless, Papandreou needed to address them if he was to retain the loyalty of senior officers.[10]

Moreover, the pro-EK press was not under his full control. Press barons like Panos Kokkas and Christos Lambrakis were independent operators who promoted the careers of ambitious Center Union leaders like Constantine Mitsotakis and were ready to turn on more conservative ministers like Petros Garoufalias or on the prime minister himself. They encouraged headline-creating party infighting. Disagreements over press coverage and the division of patronage sparked a series of short-lived internal party revolts. The ambitious Mitsotakis carried out a determined war against his likely rival for party leadership, Andreas Papandreou. Meanwhile, party barons allied to resist George Papandreou's efforts to impose discipline on the EK.[11]

By the autumn of 1964, foreign observers and the opposition were expecting the Papandreou government to collapse under the weight of its mistakes. The effort to achieve enosis with Cyprus had failed. The government lacked a coherent legislative program. George Papandreou was having a difficult time holding together the factions within the EK. The king's mounting impatience with his prime minister was no secret. Nevertheless, Papandreou basked in popular support. He stamped out internal party revolts, placated his ministers, revived his son's floundering career, managed to smoothly maneuver his old enemy, General Constantine Dovas, out of the role of political secretary to the king, and launched a renewed offensive against the ERE's leadership with more corruption charges. In February 1965 the prime minister announced that an internal investigation of the security forces had uncovered a "Pericles" plan, the blueprint for Karamanlis's electoral "fraud" of 1961. These charges caught the opposition off guard. Panagiotis Papaligouras, the former ERE minister of economic coordination, fretted that Papandreou was on the verge of destroying Greece's internal security forces and putting the country into a deep recession but admitted that the prime minister was positioned to call new elections and win them handily.[12] Then, in May, Grivas handed hard-pressed conservatives a political time bomb that permitted them to oust Papandreou's government, at the cost of plunging Greece into a constitutional crisis.

THE PRODIGAL SON

In a meeting with defense minister Garoufalias, a confidant of Papandreou but also the Palace's man inside the cabinet, Grivas charged that Greek intelligence officers stationed in Cyprus had created a conspiratorial group, ASPIDA (Officers, Save the Fatherland, Ideals, Democracy and Meritocracy), with the objective of moving the army to the left. According to Grivas, the conspirators' leader was Andreas Papandreou. Armed with documentation provided by the Greek commander on Cyprus, Garoufalias informed the cabinet and, on his own responsibility, privately discussed the information with the king.[13]

ASPIDA had the look of a political setup. A pro-Papandreou faction undoubtedly existed within the Greek intelligence service (KYP). The prime minister and his son, who were very suspicious of the KYP's ties to the ERE, were packing it with their supporters. One of its founders, Aris Bouloukos, stated that ASPIDA aimed to break the control of anti-Papandreou officers over the army. However, the means by which the scandal came to light left plenty of room for doubt about the threat it posed. Grivas was a political opponent of the Papandreous. Garoufalias, despite a long association with the prime minister, was one of the most conservative members of the cabinet. His decision to take the matter directly to the king undoubtedly reflected the officer corps' mistrust of political meddling by the Papandreous. The opposition's exploitation of ASPIDA was as aggressive and well orchestrated as Papandreou's use of other issues against them.[14]

George Papandreou needed to handle the situation carefully. The Greek army had long been infested with conspiratorial groups, but ASPIDA was different. For conservatives, its left-wing character summoned up memories of the interwar factionalism in the army and the Greek civil war as well as fears of communist infiltration. The group had no direct relationship to George Papandreou, who was apparently unaware of its existence.[15] Nevertheless, his son was implicated publicly. Any attempt to protect Andreas would deepen tensions inside the prime minister's already frayed party and government.

Moreover, issues of political control over military intelligence were bound to rouse concern in the Palace, which ultimately relied on the army's loyalty for its institutional survival. In late January 1965, the king told Labouisse that Papandreou had created a "mess" but that he would stick with his popular prime minister as long as he did not "tamper with the army as he has with the gendarmerie."[16]

George Papandreou decided to stare down both his internal critics and the opposition, relying on his personal popularity to force his colleagues into line and to discourage his opponents. Papandreou calculated that the threat of his resignation would place the king in a situation eerily similar to 1915–17, when his grandfather, Constantine I, had provoked a "national schism," his own exile, and almost brought down the monarchy. In the polarized situation created by the resignation of a prime minister with a large popular and parliamentary majority, new elections inevitably would turn into a referendum on the monarchy. The deeper the crisis became, the more the Papandreous built their strategy on a return to the ballot box. Their calculations minimized the possibility that the king and their opponents inside the EK and in the ERE would coalesce around a strategy of postponing elections.[17]

The great irony of the 1965 crisis was that it resuscitated Andreas Papandreou's badly damaged political career while finishing both George Papandreou and the EK as political forces. In the five years since his 1959 return to Greece, Andreas Papandreou had done little to suggest that he would become the central issue in either internal politics or U.S.-Greek relations. His father had lobbied hard and successfully for Greek government financial support for the economic institute that Andreas had launched with U.S. foundation and government money. As head of the Center for Economic Research, the younger Papandreou served informally as an influential adviser to his father and kept a low profile that befitted his U.S. citizenship and his role as a "scientific" adviser to the Greek state. The center's Keynesian approach to Greece's economic development dovetailed with the mixed-economy model favored by Washington. Andreas Papandreou, the American embassy noted approvingly, had formed a squad of young, U.S. trained technicians eager to modernize Greece.[18]

Elected to his father's traditional seat in February 1964, the younger Papandreou joined the government as minister to the prime minister and then moved into the position of alternate (deputy) minister of economic coordination. He ran into internal political problems in the summer of 1964.

The ERE began attacking his youthful involvement with Trotskyism, claiming he was still a communist. His chief party antagonist, Constantine Mitsotakis, mobilized press attacks on Andreas's management of public spending. Andreas hastily resigned on November 11 when press investigations of a sex and bribery scandal began to focus on him.[19]

As many of his most impassioned defenders admitted, Andreas Papandreou was maladroit. Even a more experienced politician would have had trouble. Andreas was parachuting into a complex domestic political situation. The Center Union political barons held together because of a common lust for power. His father's open desire to groom Andreas as his successor roused the animosity of the older men as well as Mitsotakis. In nearly two decades as a privileged member of the U.S. academic elite, Andreas had shown little interest in Greece's fate and missed the formative experiences of his rivals: the war, occupation, civil war, and political struggles of the 1950s. EK leaders regarded him as little more than an intrusive import from the United States in an era when Greeks generally were weary of overarching U.S. influence.[20]

Compounding personal rivalries, policy issues created friction within the EK and between the Papandreous and the U.S. government. Andreas Papandreou, with sporadic support from George Papandreou, tried to nudge the party and nation toward the "center-left." He frequently went far beyond the modest objectives of his father. Cultivating the party's youth organizations, intellectuals, and labor, the younger Papandreou organized a center-left within the EK, intensifying party divisions and fanning fears that he aimed at a popular front coalition with the EDA. Inevitably, this strategy brought Papandreous into conflict with both the Palace and anticommunists inside and outside the EK while it also aroused concerns at the U.S. embassy.[21]

Andreas consistently argued that a reforming center-left would reduce the appeal and size of communism in Greece. Twenty years later, François Mitterrand utilized the same tactic to hollow out the French communist party. However, the approach was untested, and given both Andreas's political missteps and the recent history of civil war in Greece, an opening to the left was a hard sell. British and French diplomats argued that while the EDA followed the Papandreou line on domestic issues, the cost was identifying the Center Union with the far-left and accelerating the dissolution of the EK to the advantage of the EDA. Western and Greek observers feared that the EDA would co-opt the EK's voting base.[22]

Moreover, in the effort to assert his Greek identity, Andreas found anti-

Americanism, with its inevitable association with the far-left, an irresistible part of his political toolkit. Initially, Andreas appears to have felt that his American ties could be used to forward the aims of his father. In 1961 he visited the Kennedy White House in a bid for support against Karamanlis. In 1962 he courted the president's brother, Edward Kennedy. Both efforts failed. To retain his job, Andreas had to issue a flat denial that he had engaged in any political activities in Washington.[23]

Andreas's relations with U.S. officials began to sour after his father's official visit to Washington in June 1964. Andreas was angry at the treatment the Papandreous received. He began sniping at the embassy and, in the fall of 1964, played a leading role in forcing the recall of the U.S. Information Agency's Athens branch chief, Vincent Joyce. Next Andreas gave an interview to *Le Monde* (October 5) in which he charged the United States with promoting plans to partition Cyprus and tried with success to lay the blame for his subsequent resignation from the government on the "Americans."[24]

The *Le Monde* interview provoked a U.S. embassy reevaluation of its relationship with Andreas. Labouisse commented that the statements did not reflect the views of the cabinet majority, but "I do believe, despite Andreas's rather weak protestations . . . that reportage probably reflects rather accurately his own orientation and unfortunately his influence with his father is a factor determining high-level . . . Cyprus policy."[25]

Andreas's subsequent claims that his exit was the result of U.S. pressure widened his confrontation with the embassy. The story was taken up in the press and parliament. American officials were taken aback: "The prime minister's failure . . . to denounce charges of U.S. intervention in his son's resignation—charges which he knew were patently false—is inexplicable." Labouisse issued a flat public denial. The following day, George Papandreou reluctantly confirmed the ambassador's statement. The damage to already limited U.S. trust in both Papandreous was serious.[26]

The incident marked a turning point both in Greek internal politics and in U.S.-Greek relations. Andreas Papandreou had reinvented himself. The "American" who had parachuted into Greek public life utilized the Cyprus issue and anti-Americanism to mold a new image as a steadfast defender of the national interest against the "foreign factor." He carefully cultivated his "anti-American" image for the next three decades while staying in fairly constant contact with U.S. officials. The younger Papandreou's exploitation of Cyprus in this political metamorphosis profoundly disturbed internal political enemies and was a focus of American concerns. U.S. officials regarded the elder EK leader as weak but reliably pro-Western. Over the next two years they developed a healthy respect for Andreas's maturing political skills, together with the belief that his move to the left portended EK collaboration with and eventual capture by the EDA.²⁷

THE "COUP" OF JULY 1965

In the months preceding the ASPIDA crisis, it was easy to underestimate Andreas Papandreou's strengths. His efforts at a comeback were largely limited to a visit to Cyprus and initial steps in defining himself as Greece's anti-American politician par excellence. His father maneuvered his return to the cabinet in March 1965 as deputy economics minister, stoking Andreas Papandreou's rivalry with Mitsotakis for control over economic policy and the succession to George Papandreou.²⁸

ASPIDA exploded two months later. Andreas's many party enemies saw an opportunity to finish off his still embryonic political career and not incidentally checkmate George Papandreou's efforts to impose his personal control over the governing coalition. The battle lines were drawn both within the EK and between the Papandreous and what Andreas, the privileged son of a political grandee, regularly denounced as the "Establishment." ASPIDA also touched a particularly sensitive nerve with the king, who suspected that it represented an effort by the Papandreous to undermine his relationship with the army. Overcoming his hesitations, Constantine decided to confront the prime minister.²⁹ Questions of personal power and constitutional precedent mixed together to produce a lethal cocktail.

The king's decision was made simpler by encouragement from the ERE and from within the EK. By mid-June discontent with George Papandreou's political style was rampant. The prime minister again baited opposition leaders with threats of indictments in a scandal involving the public power agency. Military discontent fomented by ASPIDA focused on Andreas Papandreou. Coup rumors abounded.³⁰

U.S. officials expected George Papandreou to survive the crisis. The prime minister enjoyed wide popular support. The king had no intention of going beyond constitutional limits.³¹ However, the situation deteriorated in late June and early July. George Papandreou decided on a confrontation with the king to break out of the ASPIDA crisis. He aimed to force Constantine to call new elections. With a renewed popular mandate, the prime minister could reduce the king's role in public life, achieve control over the military, extract his son from a politically embarrassing situation, and strengthen his hold over the EK. His political opponents and EK rivals aligned with Constantine to oust George Papandreou and avoid elections. In accepting the challenge, King Constantine placed the monarchy in a perilous position. Once again a Greek king became the leader of a political faction. If he lost the confrontation, the monarchy would become largely symbolic or be abolished.[32]

Throughout the crisis, American officials sought to keep their options open by avoiding any public involvement. Greek politicians of all stripes just as eagerly dragged the "American factor" into the conflict to create support for their objectives. In late June 1965, Greek Desk Officer Richard Barham arrived in Athens for a regularly scheduled orientation tour. The embassy arranged talks with political leaders from all parts of the political spectrum. He met with Andreas Papandreou on June 27. The following day, Barham had a discussion with *Eleftheria* editor Panos Kokkas, Mitsotakis, and two other EK deputies. On June 30, he met Kanellopoulos.[33] In all three meetings, the Greeks laid out their plans for the upcoming confrontation. Andreas Papandreou warned that a stunning defeat awaited the king. George Papandreou expected to resign and also counted on the king to try to create a new government to avoid elections. The Papandreous were confident the royal maneuver would fail. Taking no chances, the Papandreou government prepared the battlefield, using the press and state radio to rally support. Kokkas and Mitsotakis, fishing for American backing, centered their fire on Andreas but admitted that for the moment they had no alternative but to back his father in the confrontation. Kanellopoulos outlined a strategy to avoid elections following Papandreou's resignation: a government of EK defectors supported by ERE.[34]

American officials quietly sought to head off a confrontation, fearing that street violence might provoke a military coup.[35] On June 30, Papandreou told chargé Norbert Anschuetz that he would remove defense minister Garoufalias and the army chief of staff, General George Gennimatas. Anschuetz responded:

> I am concerned at implications of [a] confrontation between the Palace and gov[ernmen]t over question of military leadership. US interests in the stability of Greece as well as our continuing contributions to [the] Greek armed forces are [the] basis of legitimate interest in this question. I entirely agree with [the] PM that politics should be kept away from the armed forces. While I agreed that [the] gov[ernmen]t[,] not [the] king[,] is responsible for policy determination, I am also aware that modern Greek history shows clearly that [the] king has over a period of time acquired a generally recognized interest in [the] armed forces. Any severe shock to

this delicate balance of powers could be dangerous and might even risk raising [the] basic issue of regime. This would be tragic for Greece. For this reason I earnestly hope that a solution satisfactory to both parties could be found.... I expressed concern that [the] departure of both Garoufalias and Gennimatas might create [a] profound reaction in [the] Palace and perhaps certain opposition circles.[36]

George Papandreou ignored Anschuetz's appeal for caution and directly challenged the king by demanding the portfolio of minister of defense, in effect, taking charge of the investigation of ASPIDA and his son. The CIA's station chief, Jack Maury, telephoned Washington to report that a "worked up" king would reject both the removal of Gennimatas and George Papandreou's assumption of the defense portfolio. If the prime minister held firm, Constantine planned to "fire" him.[37]

On July 8 the king brought the crisis to a head with an intemperate letter to his prime minister. A biting exchange of correspondence followed. Anschuetz met with Andreas Papandreou to encourage a compromise aimed at ending all political activity in the army. On July 12, the pro-Papandreou press charged that Barham and Mitsotakis were conspiring against the "Old Man of Democracy." "The whole effort fitted in neatly with . . . efforts to drag the United States factor into this domestic political problem," embassy officer Daniel Brewster lamented. "We have little doubt that this is one of the principal aims of Andreas Papandreou. . . . it will not be long before the U.S. is tarred with responsibility for much of what has been going on over the past month."[38]

On July 15 the prime minister flew to the royal summer palace on Corfu where the young king and his wife awaited the birth of their first child. At the end of a brief meeting, George Papandreou announced he would resign. Without awaiting formal communication of this decision from the prime minister, King Constantine appointed EK deputy and speaker of parliament George Athanassiades-Novas as Papandreou's successor, securing control of state radio and public security forces. The king expected his new prime minister to form a majority with the support of the ERE and a large number of EK defectors. Novas could barely find enough EK "apostates" to form a ministry. Most EK deputies played for time, calculating that quick elections would return the "Old Man" and leaving it up to the king to create a majority they could join after a vote of confidence. George Papandreou, meanwhile, easily won the battle of public opinion, rallying the press, labeling the king's action a "royal coup," and putting thousands of demonstrators into the streets. The

Papandreous turned to their Washington contacts, appealing to liberal members of the Johnson administration to support the ousted prime minister. The king stood his ground and refused to call new elections after Papandreou defeated the Novas government in a vote of confidence and then strangled a challenge from Stefanos Stephanopoulos. The king raised the ante by turning to one of the leaders of the EK's left, resistance veteran Elias Tsirimokos. Further EK defections followed, but Papandreou held enough deputies to defeat the second attempt at a coalition government (August 28). In spite of this victory, Papandreou was no closer to his goal of new elections. The king and his allies applied every possible combination of pressure and inducement to pry more deputies away from the EK. Mitsotakis vowed that Papandreou would never return to power under any circumstances.[39]

From the beginning of the crisis, both British and French officials strongly opposed George Papandreou's return to power. American diplomats moved more slowly from neutrality. Publicly, the United States labeled the crisis an "internal affair." However, the embassy was not enamored of a new Papandreou government, and as the crisis continued, concerns about street violence and military intervention led U.S. officials in Athens to provide discreet private support to efforts to create a coalition of ERE deputies and EK defectors. Andreas tried to check embassy involvement by attacking foreign intervention. U.S diplomats were caught in a bind. Public confrontation polished Andreas's image as a nationalist. Nonconfrontation confirmed his claims. American frustration grew as Andreas built his popular following. Anschuetz began laying the groundwork for a covert intervention, warning Washington that the crisis had spun out of control, that the EK was drifting leftward, and that communist elements in Greece stood poised to take advantage of the mutual weakness of George Papandreou and the king. Kanellopoulos, alert to both the danger of a coup and the possibilities the split in the EK provided the ERE, proposed a compromise at a September 1 meeting of the crown council. He would form a government with EK support and then carry the country to early elections. Papandreou initially rejected then accepted the offer. By this time, however, ERE's deputies had refused to go along with their leader.[40]

Following the failure of Kanellopoulos's compromise, and facing the uncertain prospect of a Stephanopoulos attempt to form a coalition government, the embassy proposed covert U.S. intervention. This CIA plan involved providing cash payments to EK deputies who broke with Papandreou and supported Stephanopoulos. The proposal was sent to Washington, where senior officials rejected it. McGeorge Bundy, the president's national security adviser, opposed meddling in Greek internal affairs, especially when the bulk of reporting did not support embassy contentions. The proposal was tabled, and the Greeks were left to work out their own solution. The frustrated Papandreous and their allies claimed that the United States was responsible for Stephanopoulos's narrow, scandal-tainted, victory in the vote of confidence.[41]

THE HOUR OF THE UNKNOWN COLONEL

Stephanopoulos proved to be the Lazarus of Greek politics. Despite his government's narrow majority, constant infighting within his coalition, and his own ill health, Greece's septuagenarian prime minister held on to power for sixteen months, until George Papandreou, Kanellopoulos, and the king secretly agreed to unseat him. The tenacity of Stephanopoulos's grasp on power forced the king and Papandreou to compromise. George Papandreou's objective remained new elections. He could only gain them through a deal with the Palace and Kanellopoulos. The king needed to extract himself from the center of a political controversy through a deal with Papandreou. Kanellopoulos hoped to finally secure a hold on the ERE with an election triumph. Alone among conservative leaders, and outside observers, he insisted that his party could defeat the EK.

Initially, Greece's political leaders failed to find common ground. The king hoped to ride out popular discontent and wait for the calming effects of patronage to weaken political support for the Papandreous. George Papandreou launched a second "ceaseless struggle" that held his party firmly in line but made compromise more difficult. With his rivals out of the EK, Andreas Papandreou's political fortunes waxed. He was now the clear successor to his father and had little incentive to compromise.[42] Moreover, as Margaret Papandreou recalled: "a conflict between father and son began to smolder. ... the old man had all his life been center stage; he was unable to play a supporting role.... Andreas assumed a leadership role, often making decisions without consulting his father. Andreas's father considered him ungrateful, impulsive and disrespectful."[43]

The crisis of 1965 made the career of Andreas Papandreou. Fighting for his political life, he mustered formidable skills to survive. A talented orator, a gifted improviser, a man with a clear and simple message, Andreas rallied a sizable element of Greek public opinion behind the EK and his political ambitions. He supported his father's bid for power and simultaneously emerged as his most obvious rival for leadership. While George Papandreou's declining health played some role in this process, Andreas was overtaking his father largely because of his readiness to take risks. He challenged the Palace, the military, the economic elite, the great power protector with no apparent concern about the consequences of his heated rhetoric, winning over growing segments of Greek public opinion.[44]

In November 1966, one senior American diplomat complained: "It is difficult to keep up with the almost endless stream of words ... from Andreas." There was little new or original in the package of ideas Andreas offered Greeks. He borrowed indefinable concepts, such as "people power," a favorite expression of his father, and played upon nationalist obsessions with "foreign intervention" as well as traditional Greek resentment of the privileges of the Palace and other elites. He gave voice to the deeply rooted desire of many Greeks for closure to the civil war experience, a fairer division of the benefits of economic development, and some form of protection against the impact of urbanization. His economic formulas were decidedly moderate. Andreas mixed his ideas into simple but effective slogans that capitalized on widespread resentments. Basically, Andreas called for democratic change and economic modernization carried out by a mass-based political party. He painted a vision of a new Greece, industrialized, with fairer income distribution, open to both Europe and the positive effects of foreign investment, carrying out a foreign policy that would achieve a "Greek solution" to Cyprus and resist the power of both Turkey and the United States, defended by a national army that no longer answered to the Palace but to the elected government. He advocated eliminating the special privileges of the crown, the high command, and the economic elites. Those who resisted democratic change would lose their positions. This message, forcefully delivered, helped mobilize broad support for the EK. Not surprisingly, the monarchy, the military, and the business elite chose to interpret his challenge to their entrenched positions as a call for communism. Andreas's aggressive rhetoric, his abrasive personality, and his position as an outsider combined to make dialogue with the right difficult. George Papandreou should have been able to fill that role. But he had tarnished his "old boy" credentials during his four-year quest for power and assault on the ERE.[45]

Greece's political system was at a crossroads. Karamanlis had modernized the economy and infrastructure. Resistance to his efforts to bring key institutions, especially the monarchy and military, under the full control of an elected government caused Karamanlis's fall. George Papandreou's management of the government, with its emphasis on symbolic concessions to the left, sharpened the inherent crisis. Andreas's rhetoric and actions made the situation dangerous. Conservatives began to question whether reform was too dangerous to Greece's stability. By questioning the value of Greece's alliance with NATO, Andreas Papandreou reinforced a sense among moderate and conservative Greeks, and among Greece's major allies, that he was moving toward communist positions. Private efforts to convince political opponents and foreign allies of his moderation were undercut by the rhetoric that enhanced his domestic support. U.S. nonintervention policies further unhinged the country. Conservative Greeks recognized that the foreign protector power was very reluctant to provide them with the level of support they wanted, while Andreas's backers, seduced by the rhetoric of Kennedy's New Frontier, were angry over American failure to support the EK leader's formulas for reform and modernization.

American officials recognized the difficulties of a nonintervention policy. They hoped to see the Greeks reach a compromise solution that would resolve their political crisis. In a November 1965 analysis, the embassy observed that, in the event of George Papandreou's return to power, the apostates and the king's immediate advisers would be the primary targets of a new EK government while the army would face a purge of many senior officers. The king, too, would lose power, while the United States would have to deal with the younger Papandreou's continued anti-American outbursts. Still, his father regarded the United States as Greece's key ally and was no radical. The real danger lay in the reaction of the military to the return of the Papandreous. The king had toyed with an "extra-constitutional" solution but was wary of military intervention. The generals, however, might act independently to save their careers and the army's special role in Greek public life.[46]

In the face of an internal deadlock, Greek leaders looked to the "American factor" to broker a deal that would achieve their objectives. The king, without informing his government, wrote directly to President Johnson seeking economic and, by extension, political support. The Papandreous continued to cultivate the embassy. Anschuetz remained the primary contact with Andreas Papandreou; the new U.S. ambassador, Phillips Talbot, met frequently with his father.[47]

Anschuetz and Andreas Papandreou talked twice in a three-week period in late 1965. In both meetings Andreas, exuding confidence and personal charm, stressed that cautious changes would follow an EK election victory. He downplayed his anti-American outbursts, admitting that he "may have been imprudent." Anschuetz was not convinced. Meetings with Andreas Papandreou underlined the American dilemma. A U.S.-arranged compromise leading to new elections might achieve the desirable goal of avoiding a military intervention but end up harming the interests of those elements of Greek society that had traditionally cooperated with the United States, all to the benefit of a politician capable of aligning his party with a communist-dominated EDA.[48]

To counter American reluctance, George Papandreou worked on U.S. officials with two messages. The first was that he, not his son, was in control of the EK and could be counted on to follow a moderate course that would protect the Palace and other conservative interests. The second was his readiness to prove his bona fides by making a deal with the king in exchange for early elections. Confirming that his wrath would fall on the apostates, George Papandreou discounted rumors of coup preparations, stating that the king would keep his officers in line. As 1966 progressed, he indicated a willingness to bury the contentious issue of control of the military, suggesting that on his return to power he would appoint a defense minister who enjoyed Constantine's confidence.[49]

The embassy declined to act as a conduit between Papandreou and the king. Andreas was the reason. Talbot outlined his concerns: Andreas's ties with EDA, the growth of his left-wing faction within the EK, and his continuing public attacks on the United States. The power struggle between the two Papandreous continued, and Andreas had the ultimately winning advantage: his youth. Approaching eighty, George Papandreou would not be leading his party or nation too much longer. The embassy would maintain ties to both Papandreous to have a "constructive influence," not to facilitate their joint or individual political objectives.[50]

The longer the Greek political crisis continued the more difficult nonintervention became for the United States. American officials were uneasily aware that a prolonged crisis meant that the "EDA and the communist movement in general may ... profit."[51] The EK defectors were as eager to drag the "American factor" into their political wars as the Papandreous were. Finally, George Papandreou would not last forever, and U.S. officials had to weigh the options of quickly finding a modus vivendi with the elder Papandreou or later facing a government led by his son.[52]

The United States could temporize because, during the summer of 1966, Greece's politicians were working toward their own solution. The king reached out to Karamanlis, seeking advice and suggesting that the ex-prime minister return to Greece to take charge. Karamanlis rebuffed the offer, telling the Palace to make a compromise with the EK's leader. George Papandreou, showing greater concern about a military intervention, continued looking for a path to early elections. George Mavros returned to politics, mounting a leadership challenge to Andreas Papandreou within the EK. ERE rank and file grumbled about the price they were paying to support an "apostates" government incapable of decisive action on the major issues facing Greece, including Cyprus.[53]

In late September, the king told Talbot that George Papandreou, using a go-between, had floated the idea of a nonpolitical "semi-service" government lasting six months and enjoying the support of the EK, to take Greece to new elections. The king wanted an "objective" observer to see if a deal was possible. Talbot was cautious, fearing a royal effort to utilize the "American factor" in Greece's complex political game. Nevertheless, the ambassador saw signs of a political thaw. In spite of Andreas's attacks, or perhaps because of them, the king realized that his position and the future of the monarchy depended on striking a deal with the Papandreous.[54] Making a deal required bridging the immense mistrust created by a year of angry political rhetoric. The United States, which enjoyed the relative trust of the king, and as such was attractive to the Papandreous, was gradually drawn into the role of intermediary.[55]

At a September 29 meeting, the Papandreous asked the U.S. to serve as mediator. They promised that the EK would not form a popular front with EDA, that Greece would retain its membership in NATO and special ties to the United States, and outlined their proposal for a nonpolitical government as the bridge to new elections.[56]

Such a deal was within reach. The military's much-awaited report on ASPIDA appeared at the beginning of October. Its efforts to link the plot to Andreas Papandreou were "weak and inconclusive."[57] One of the "apostates," defense minister Costopoulos, told Talbot that the time was ripe for a U.S.-sponsored reconciliation between the king and Papandreou followed by elections. Costopoulos believed that a new Papandreou government would operate within constraints that would make its rule tolerable for all. The major objective must be to avoid a dictatorship, a sentiment Talbot seconded.[58]

Two days later, Kanellopoulos told Talbot that the ASPIDA case had backfired on conservatives by turning Andreas Papandreou into a hero while polarizing Greek politics. Kanellopoulos revived his plan to form an ERE-led government to liquidate the ASPIDA affairs and revise the electoral system prior to a new vote. The ERE's leader was concerned about a coup. He was preoccupied with his political future and increasingly ready to gamble with Greece's. ERE barons were restless as Karamanlis continued to criticize his successor's leadership and strategy.[59]

CIA reporting confirmed that the threats of a military intervention were not simply press speculation. Senior and midlevel Greek officers were actively plotting a coup with some support from the chief of the army general staff. The extreme right wing of ERE encouraged the military to act while seeking a green light from the embassy. Former prime minister Panagiotis Pipinelis and Progressive Party leader Spyridon Markezinis were ready to lead an "extra-parliamentary" government.[60]

In early December, Greek political leaders acted. Kanellopoulos, George Papandreou, and the king's adjutant, Major Michael Arnaoutis, met secretly. They agreed to the creation of another interim government under economist John Paraskevopoulos, supported by both the ERE and the EK. The interim government would push a new election law through parliament. Then the king would call elections. The deal was signed on December 18. Two days later, Kanellopoulos withdrew the ERE's support from the Stephanopoulos government. On December 22, the king swore in Paraskevopoulos.[61]

Pleasantly surprised, Talbot commented: "our best posture is to enjoy the holidays while the various Grecian political pots are boiling. They need no stirring by us." Many ERE leaders were upset by Kanellopoulos's move. Karamanlis was contemptuous of the king's political amateurism. The Americans watched with amusement as the target of George Papandreou's insistence on secrecy writhed in discontent. Andreas Papandreou had been excluded from the negotiations. His efforts to torpedo the deal collapsed in the face of his father's determination. The younger Papandreou, however, preserved his political base with an open, if short-lived, defiance.[62]

On the surface, Greek political life calmed down. Andreas accepted his father's decision. George Papandreou and Kanellopoulos cooperated to support Paraskevopoulos and prepare for new elections. The elder Papandreou expressed satisfaction with the arrangement in mid-March. The Palace, however, was uneasy. The deal rested on Kanellopoulos's assurances that he could limit the size of the EK victory and force Papandreou into coalition with ERE. A Papandreou majority appeared more likely. Andreas's continued attacks on the "Establishment" unnerved the king's advisors. On January 28, 1967, the CIA's Maury talked with an edgy chief of the king's political office, Dimitrios Bitsios. Focusing on Andreas's latest public attacks, Bitsios argued that the younger Papandreou "was serving the purposes of the communists and the Soviets" and urged the United States to abandon its neutrality and support those seeking to stop the EK. Maury replied that no evidence existed of Andreas's collaboration with the communists. Bitsios asked point-blank whether the United States would support "extreme measures." Maury responded that the "U.S. reaction would be extremely unfavorable."[63]

Concerned about a crown-sponsored coup, knowing the mood of the military, and believing EK victory likely, Talbot endorsed a CIA plan for a "limited covert political operation." The February 11 plan aimed at reducing the size of the Center Union's anticipated victory by "encouraging support for certain competitive elements," apparently candidates within the EK as well as in the ERE. The idea was to limit the number of seats allocated to Andreas Papandreou's followers, thus damaging Andreas's standing within the party, and simultaneously to force the EK into a coalition that would restrain any radical tendencies. The plan offered protection to Greek political institutions, including the monarchy, and gave assurances that Greece would remain within NATO. Ambitious and probably unrealizable, it required a sophisticated level of manipulation that the CIA rarely achieved. To justify this proposal, the embassy and CIA station stressed the depth of Greek political polarization.[64]

The NSC's 303 Committee on covert operations, chaired by presidential advisor Walt Rostow, met twice to discuss the proposal. A majority of committee members were unconvinced by Maury's presentation of the plan. At the March 8 meeting, Rostow wondered if the threat justified risky intervention in Greek affairs. Ambassador Foy Kohler, the State Department representative, pointedly inquired if the embassy and station "were attributing more potential to Andreas than he deserved." At a second meeting Maury again failed to convince a skeptical Rostow, Cyrus Vance, or Kohler that Andreas Papandreou posed an overwhelming menace. Rostow observed that there were "other examples of leftists settling down after an election." The committee passed the plan to Secretary of State Rusk, who rejected it on March 14. "He believes that the possible political gain is outweighed by security risks. He commented that if the dual-national Greek-Americans are concerned about the prospects and if $200–300,000 will make the difference, they should have no trouble raising that sum themselves without involving the United States."[65]

Meanwhile, the preelection battle heated up. In speeches on February 9 and March 1, 1967, Andreas Papandreou expanded his attacks on both the Palace and the United States, triggering the first public display of American animosity toward the EK's second in command. Meeting with Talbot on March 17, George Papandreou disassociated himself from his son's more recent public outburst, pledged to publicly repudiate Andreas's charges of U.S. interference in Greek affairs (and delivered on this promise), and reiterated that the EK would not form a coalition with EDA. The elder Papandreou added that he was supporting a revised election law that would actually favor the ERE. He warned that a group of reactionaries, a "junta," that included Garoufalias, Pipinelis, retired General Constantine Dovas, and the queen mother, were pressing the young monarch to suspend the constitution. The trip wire would be an EK-sponsored amendment to the electoral law extending Andreas's parliamentary immunity from arrest through the upcoming election.[66]

Talbot confirmed the existence of the "junta" and its plans to avoid elections. He reported disquieting news that the military was ready to implement an intervention plan (Ierax 2) in support of a royal dictatorship but that "there is no evidence that [the] army leadership is actually plotting to create conditions leading to a deviation from [the] constitution." Moreover, the "key and still uncertain element . . . is [the] attitude of [the] king," who wanted to "avoid extremism." The Palace continued to be badly rattled by Andreas's rhetoric. Greek intelligence was circulating a report that a deal already existed between the younger Papandreou and the EDA for a postelection coalition. The king, who wanted an ERE victory, suspected that Kanellopoulos lacked the ability to manage the elections or a postelection government. At the same time, he was unwilling to grant amnesty to Andreas Papandreou.[67]

The modus vivendi between George Papandreou and the king collapsed the following week, when the ERE and Paraskevopoulos rejected Papandreou's demands for amnesty. The EK withdrew its support from the government, and the prime minister resigned. The parliamentary confrontation exposed Kanellopoulos's limited tactical skills. Besieged by challenges within his party, he lacked Karamanlis's firmness or charisma. The political crisis fueled party and Palace appeals for ERE's self-exiled founder to return from Paris. To counter these internal challenges, Kanellopoulos insisted on ERE-administered elections to improve his party's chances and save his leadership.[68]

Kanellopoulos won the king's approval for a plan to form a coalition government with the "apostates," and on April 3 the monarch asked him to serve as prime minister, simultaneously pledging to dissolve parliament if he failed to create a majority. This effort to blackmail the "apostates" into a coalition was designed to give Kanellopoulos leverage to make a deal with Papandreou: a coalition government of national unity based on an accord for early elections under ERE management. Talbot commented: "In our view, [the] decision . . . is the most important move the young king has made. . . . It may prove to be his worst." In granting Kanellopoulos his mandate, the king had aligned himself with a minority party and again betrayed the apostates while also rousing an intensely angry response from the EK. Although both George Papandreou and Constantine wanted to resolve the crisis, mutual mistrust made compromise difficult.[69]

Kanellopoulos's alliance with the king triggered action by a group of middle-level military conspirators. The conspiracy was long-standing. The CIA began collecting precise information on it in 1964. (The apparent source, journalist Nikos Farmakis, most likely was passing it along on the instructions of the coup plotters as part of an unsuccessful bid for U.S. approval.) The conspiratorial group's chief planner, Col. George Papadopoulos, and other radicals had been shifted out of Athens at various times by previous governments to avoid trouble. However, whether by plan or inattention, they were called back to postings in the capital. The conspirators pressed their general officers for intervention. No senior Greek officers appear to have paid sufficient attention to their activities or to have reported them up their chain of command to civilian authorities or the head of state. U.S. officials ignored the sudden evaporation of information on the Colonels' conspiracy because they were focused on the plans of the king and his senior officers. Their assumption, and that of the Greek army's high command, was that the Colonels would follow their chain of command and act only on orders from the Palace.[70]

Unfortunately, the Colonels could act independently of their superiors. Brigadier Stylianos Pattakos, the most senior plotter, had command of tank units at the Goudi military reservation in Athens. In late March the conspirators convinced themselves that elections would produce either an Andreas Papandreou–EDA triumph or street violence that would spark civil war. They agreed that only military intervention could solve Greece's problems. According to Pattakos, the decision to launch the coup occurred in early April. The rhetoric of Andreas and George Papandreou and "hysteric" press coverage convinced the officers that the communists would take power after an EK victory. Pattakos labeled Kanellopoulos's April 3 assumption of power a "coup." The conspirators began final planning. They chose the night of April 20–21 because most key political leaders would be in Athens where they could be rounded up easily.[71]

Armed with instructions from Washington to prevent military intervention, Talbot met with Constantine on April 9. While assuring the monarch that the United States viewed the possibility of an Andreas Papandreou–led government with deep concern, Talbot "stated the inability of [the] USG[overnment] to give assurances of support to [the king] and noted our traditional opposition to dictatorial solutions." Constantine probed for a clearer sign of U.S. intent, raising the danger Andreas Papandreou posed to Greece's NATO membership. Talbot avoided a reply but drew out a statement of royal intent to avoid precipitate action until May. Talbot concluded: "It was clear that [the] young king believes his throne and Greece's attachment to the West to be at stake. He has concluded that only [a] near miracle can save him from [a] final choice of yielding his country to Papandreou, or establishing a dictatorship." The king was looking for American support. "We share [the] king's fear that events in Greece [are] approaching [a] climax. . . . we have found little taste for compromise in any quarter."[72]

EK leaders, however, treated the crisis as if military intervention were unlikely. Andreas ridiculed the idea of a military coup. Margaret Papandreou recalled that, despite ample warnings from U.S. officials, her husband and his lieutenants were convinced that the king controlled the army and that, in any case, the United States would prevent a coup.[73]

On April 13, the EK and the "apostates," joined by Markezinis's Progressives, defeated the Kanellopoulos government in a vote of confidence. The prime minister dissolved parliament and called new elections for May 28. The parties dug in. George Papandreou was in a belligerent mood. Meeting Talbot prior to the dissolution, he labeled Constantine the "king of ERE" and threatened that after an EK victory he would treat the king as the defeated head of a political movement. If the Palace tried to install a dictatorship, Papandreou threatened, it would face a civil war. He insisted that only the appointment of a neutral government would calm the political tempest. The Palace was in an equally truculent mood. Analyzing the scene on April 14, Talbot warned: "I regret to report [that the] time has come to hoist urgent storm signals." The aging George Papandreou lacked the vigor to control his party. In the likely event of an EK victory, an Andreas Papandreou–led or –managed government would threaten Greece's internal political stability and U.S. interests. In order to avoid a military coup, the United States would have to put heavy pressure on the Palace, the military, and Greece's right-wing politicians. However, the probable beneficiary of U.S. actions, Andreas, was likely to dismantle "traditional Greek institutions and policies" while leading the country "even deeper into [a] Nasserite posture."[74]

Washington took a less dramatic view. On April 20, Deputy Assistant Secretary of State Lucius Battle instructed Talbot to approach George Papandreou with a U.S. proposal to reach an accord with the Palace. If Papandreou was unwilling to approach the king, Talbot should offer to serve as intermediary.⁷⁵ Washington had concluded that it could live with a Papandreou government. Unfortunately, tanks were already moving out of the Goudi military reservation.⁷⁶

PICKING UP THE PIECES

In an April 21 telegram to Washington, Ambassador Talbot bemoaned the "rape of Greek democracy." Successive generations of Greeks have blamed the United States for that rape, and in 1981 elections Andreas Papandreou capitalized on this belief. The Americans, particularly the embassy, shared responsibility for the events of 1967. However, placing the Americans at the head of the list of culprits for the collective suicide of the Greek political establishment is to reverse the order of responsibility. The Colonels, the generals, a young and inexperienced king, his advisers, ambitious politicians led by the aging George Papandreou and the insecure Panagiotis Kanellopoulos, and, above all, Andreas Papandreou vie for the distinction of most culpable. Andreas Papandreou's mixture of unbridled ambition, irresponsible action, and explosive rhetoric created a situation that the Colonels exploited to overthrow a parliamentary system they despised. The king and his advisers brought Greece to the edge of calamity by mobilizing the military for unconstitutional action. Stephanopoulos, Kanellopoulos, and George Papandreou provided textbook examples of a long tradition of politicians placing personal ambition and pride (*philotimó*) over the national interest. Neither did Karamanlis do his country any good by his resolute sniping at both the inexperienced Constantine and the insecure Kanellopoulos from a comfortable Paris exile. He helped polarize the political situation at a moment when Greece needed leaders to find some form of workable compromise.⁷⁷

All elements of the Greek political establishment skated determinedly along the edge for such an extended period that they should not have been surprised that the military intervened. The head of state was engaged in open conflict with the leader of the political majority. Rumors of coups were a regular feature of the press. From 1965 onward, all of the political players, as well as the diplomatic colony, were constantly and carefully calculating the possibility of a coup, yet no one focused on the existence of a military conspiracy that involved well-known radicals.

Two months prior to the coup, the French ambassador analyzed the American dilemma. Despite claims from the left, the United States had been following a generally restrained line in dealing with a deteriorating internal political situation. However, given the special role that the United States had played in Greece since 1947, it could not simply look the other way as the country slipped into political chaos. In their efforts to prevent the Greek system from melting down, U.S. officials had worked to restrain the right's tendency to turn to the military for political solutions and simultaneously stayed in close contact with the Papandreous to restrain provocative actions. Efforts, particularly by Anschuetz, to moderate the behavior of the "untrustworthy, ambitious, imaginative" and "brilliant" Andreas, had failed. Facing the possibility of an EDA-dominated government, democracy would play a secondary role in U.S. calculations. Ultimately the United States would come down on the side of stability.[78]

Stability, however, might only be possible at a price too high for the Greek people to bear. Confronting the likely collapse of a friendly constitutional regime, U.S. officials failed to make their opposition to a coup firm enough to discourage the Palace and the military. American concerns about an "extra-constitutional deviation," though repeatedly stated in private, were largely canceled out by an all-too-public obsession with Andreas Papandreou. What Greek leaders heard was a confusing "no, but" that encouraged them to interpret U.S. intentions to serve their particular interests. The weight of responsibility falls on the embassy. The Johnson administration, obsessed with Vietnam, normally ignored Greece. The State Department's Bureau of Near Eastern and South Asian Affairs, although holding responsibility for Greece, was, as its name indicates, more interested in Arab-Israeli and Indian-Pakistani issues. In the absence of firm leadership, the embassy was unusually free to form policy in collaboration with the small group of "Greek hands" in the Office of Greek, Turkish, and Iranian Affairs. The constant shuffling of these officers between Athens and Washington assured that those in the capital were as thoroughly infected by anti-Andreas feelings as their collaborators in Greece. As a result, U.S. policy was rarely subjected to the sort of critical analysis that twice led the State Department and the White House to reject embassy-CIA plans for covert interventions. The "country team" in Athens never seems to have taken to heart Washington's caution.[79]

In the end, the United States got exactly the solution it had wanted to avoid. U.S. officials neither encouraged nor supported the coup of April 1967. Once it happened, they found themselves dealing with a brutal, repressive, and incompetent regime whose leaders wrapped themselves in the mantle of NATO and pointedly told their American interlocutors: "we are your allies whether you like us or not."[80]

6

THE ANDREAS VERSION, 1967–1973

> My concern, as you can readily appreciate, is that the Papandreou version of events becomes a part of our modern mythology.
> — Vincent Joyce, 1966
>
> The colonels supported both by the Pentagon and the CIA beat the generals and the king to the punch on April 21, 1967, through the forceful seizure of power and the establishment of a military dictatorship.
> — Andreas Papandreou, 1970

About 556 B.C.E., the Athenian tyrant Peisistratus made a remarkable political comeback through what Herodotus judged "the silliest trick recorded in history." Driven from power by two rival political clans, he hired a beautiful and extremely tall village girl named Phye, fitted her with a suit of armor, placed her in a chariot, and, after posing her in a suitably striking manner, had one of his supporters drive her into the city proceeded by heralds announcing that the goddess Athena was bringing Peisistratus back to govern. The Athenians, taken in by the ruse, restored their former ruler. Herodotus, seemingly both embarrassed and amused at the gullibility of fellow Hellenes, commented that the "Greeks have never been bumpkins; for centuries they have been known for superior wit; and Athenians are known to be the most intelligent Greeks, nevertheless this ridiculous trick was played [successfully] on Athenians."[1]

Andreas Papandreou achieved his political resurrection with similarly inventive and impressive piece of legerdemain. By 1968, Andreas's brief political season appeared over. Arrested and charged with treason, then exiled, the younger Papandreou was reviled not only by the junta, but also by his political opponents and many former allies as the man chiefly responsible for the collapse of Greek democracy. Even his father disavowed him. He had scant contacts with internal operations of the Center Union (EK) and lost his bid to lead its exile activities. His newly created Pan Hellenic Liberation Movement (PAK) had a small following, and its calls for armed resistance found little resonance inside Greece while convincing many exiles and most foreign governments that Andreas was as irresponsible as ever. Throughout the seven years of junta rule, Andreas played a marginal role in exile politics and virtually none in internal Greek affairs.[2] Yet he returned to found a political party that quickly became the major opposition force and, after 1981, governed Greece for most of the next fifteen years. Andreas Papandreou rode to power by appealing to Greek voters' traditionally strong nationalism and responding to a postjunta sense of deep humiliation and betrayal by mixing slogans such as "people power" and "Greece of the Greeks" with demands for independence in foreign affairs, together with economic ideas and historiography borrowed from European and third-world socialism as well as U.S. academe. He successfully directed these concepts against internal opponents ("the Right") and their presumed foreign backers ("the Americans"). Papandreou and several of his closest collaborators wrapped this potent mix into a retelling of the events leading to April 21, 1967. The Andreas version continues to enjoy enormous success. During the 1990s, Papandreou's leadership became the subject of widespread criticism not only by his political opponents, but also from former allies and scholars. His management of Greece's economy, his frequent compromises on foreign policy and domestic reform, his failure to carry out a socialist reorganization of the Greek state, the cult of personality that surrounded him, and even his personal lifestyle were the targets of penetrating criticism.[3] However, his shaping of the history of the events that led to the 1967 coup has taken root in the collective consciousness of the Greek people in spite of some well-argued criticism from both the right and the left. This account, in which Andreas and his father George Papandreou were the victims of a conspiracy carried out by the right-wing Greek "Establishment," with support and at times direction from the United States, has solidified its status as revealed truth.[4]

Greek belief in the Papandreou version, as well as public indifference to the objections posed by its few challengers, has multiple sources. Democratic societies frequently prefer to avoid dealing with the wide implications of thoroughly purging previous dictatorial regimes. As a result of the many catastrophic events their nation endured during the twentieth century, Greece's leaders gradually developed a carefully honed sense of the damage purges could do to the social fabric. Charges that deflected responsibility away from the Greek officer corps, as well as those elements of the state bureaucracy and middle classes that supported or benefited from the regime, were gratefully accepted at face value. National pride, too, plays a role in seeking to bury past disgraces as quickly as possible. Moreover, Andreas Papandreou's claims about the nature both of the monarchical regime that governed Greece and of U.S. support for many of its leading officials had a solid base in fact. Andreas's version benefited from American revisionist historiography that underlined the degree to which the U.S. government's pursuit of its international objectives diverged from its stated ideals as well as from a widespread human tendency to see small states as virtuous victims of the evil machinations of larger powers. Moreover, Andreas Papandreou, a man of considerable intellect, wrote and spoke persuasively. However, the U.S. government made the most significant contribution to the success of the Andreas version: validating Papandreou's charges by its behavior during the junta's seven-year rule. While the Johnson administration tried to keep some distance from the coup, it accepted George Papadopoulos and his fellow conspirators as allies against the Soviet menace.[5]

ANDREAS WRITES THE HISTORY OF HIS TIMES

Early on the morning of April 21, 1967, Greek military units arrested Andreas Papandreou as part of a general roundup of political leaders. He was confined first at the Goudi military reservation and ultimately at Averoff Prison in Athens until the end of December 1967. Initially, many feared that the military conspirators would execute the younger Papandreou without trial. Even after Greece's new rulers announced they would try Andreas for treason, concern for his personal safety remained high, prompting both the Johnson administration and many American liberals to pressure the junta to secure good treatment.

In this crisis, Margaret Papandreou emerged as Andreas's dedicated and skilled political partner. Fearing for her husband's safety, she laid siege to U.S. embassy officials from the early morning of April 21. Mistrusting the very people she relied on to save Andreas, she successfully mobilized his many friends in the United States to apply pressure on both their government and the Greek junta to preserve Andreas's life and secure his release. At the same time, she attempted to rally Andreas's supporters to create a resistance movement inside Greece.[6]

The U.S. embassy and Johnson administration were Margaret Papandreou's willing allies in the effort to save Andreas's life. In spite of widespread animosity toward Andreas's policies, most senior U.S. diplomats knew him personally and had no desire to see him physically harmed. Moreover, he was a former American citizen and the father of a family of American citizens. In the first hours after the coup, Ambassador Philips Talbot warned Greece's new military rulers that harming Andreas could seriously damage their efforts to build a relationship with the United States. Thereafter, U.S. diplomats worked to secure Andreas's release, along with that of other political figures, as part of their effort to nudge Greece back to constitutional democracy.[7]

Andreas's release occurred once the junta had solidified its hold on power. By June, the Colonels had concluded that a public treason trial would serve to inflate Andreas's political standing. Thereafter he lived in a political limbo, widely blamed by Greeks for the coup, while the junta prepared to exploit his release to improve its image. Margaret Papandreou was trying to reclaim Andreas's citizenship, citing a pending U.S. court case involving another naturalized U.S. citizen who renounced and then reclaimed citizenship. Sending Andreas to the United States would respond to American pressure for his release and simultaneously dump a controversial former politician in the Johnson administration's lap. The junta calculated that such a move would further deflate Andreas's damaged public image.[8]

Andreas, who was desperately seeking release from prison, was simultaneously using his limited opportunities to mend fences. In September, two of his emissaries arrived in Paris to seek a working rapport with Constantine Karamanlis, while both he and Margaret were in contact with King Constantine and with Danish prime minister Jans Otto Krag. The younger Papandreou turned his formidable charm on an old adversary, C. L. Sulzberger of the *New York Times*. Margaret maintained an edgy relationship with the U.S. embassy. Andreas assured all his interlocutors that he was now a supporter of constitutional monarchy and would back a Karamanlis-led government of national unity as part of program to restore democracy. Neither Karamanlis nor the king wanted an alliance with Andreas, but Constantine tried to secure his release.[9]

The king's amateurish and unsuccessful countercoup of December 1967 revealed the extent of Andreas Papandreou's isolation. George Papandreou (and most other political leaders) worked in collaboration with the monarch, attempting to swing NATO governments behind the effort. Although the elder Papandreou actively sought support for the king throughout Europe, he never trusted his son or daughter-in-law with information on the plot or his involvement. Margaret, meanwhile, could not organize armed resistance. Both failures pointed to a widespread public indifference to both military rule and the return of the old political class. In the first months after the coup, Greek and foreign observers noted general public relief that the nation's squabbling political leadership had been swept away. Few Greeks were ready to risk their lives battling a well-trained army to restore either the Papandreous or the king. A majority looked to Karamanlis, the one politician free from the taint of provoking the coup and the only one possessing a track record of successful governance, to restore stability and democracy.[10]

After foiling Constantine's coup effort, the Colonels decided on a wide amnesty to demonstrate their power, quiet foreign critics, and empty the jails of harmless political opponents. Andreas Papandreou was among the prisoners they released. Determined to organize political action against the junta, and fearful of a second arrest, he decided to leave Greece. A first step was a fawning interview with Stylianos Pattakos, the interior minister, to request a passport. Always posed to attribute the worst possible motivations to their opponents and clinging to an exaggerated idea of American influence over the Colonels, the Papandreous tried to dupe the U.S. ambassador and expedite the release of Andreas's passport by pledging to avoid future political activities. During a January 9, 1968, meeting with Talbot, Andreas repeatedly thanked the ambassador for U.S. efforts to save his life, stressed his determination to stay out of politics, and tried to justify his anti-American sallies by claiming that "he had not attacked U.S. policies as an enemy, but rather as a member of family." Acknowledging that the embassy had made extensive efforts to maintain close contacts with the EK prior to the coup, Andreas encouraged Talbot to actively engage the junta. Papandreou pledged to avoid comments that would exacerbate internal U.S. debates over Greece and to avoid stirring up extremists inside Greece. Talbot offered to expedite a U.S. visa for Papandreou and assured him that taking a Greek passport would not prejudice Andreas's claims to U.S. citizenship.[11]

EXILE

Andreas Papandreou's consistent duplicity repeatedly undercut support for his political activities in exile. U.S. officials, who never requested that Andreas stay out of politics, were neither surprised nor concerned when the younger Papandreou launched a new public career at a press conference only minutes after his flight from Athens touched down in Paris. The performance simply confirmed U.S. officials' views that Andreas Papandreou was fundamentally dishonest. Nor were they alone. American friends like Carl Kaysen, while willing to aid efforts to secure his personal safety, had written off Andreas as a demagogue. Karamanlis kept his newly released political rival at arm's length, declining Papandreou's requests for a meeting. The British Labour Party and Foreign Office also shunned the Greek exile on grounds of his unreliability and anti-Western views. From Greece, his father privately urged him to avoid ties with EDA, to find ways to cooperate with Karamanlis, and to refrain from attacks on his fellow exile, the king. Reacting to the creation of PAK, George Papandreou added: "Political leaders do not head up conspiratorial organizations" and urged his son to work within the EK.[12]

Andreas followed a different strategy. Publicly he attacked the United States for its dealings with the junta and Karamanlis and the king for their supposed role in setting up the dictatorship. Simultaneously, he continued making private approaches to both the Americans and the ERE's former leader, offering collaboration. Initially, Papandreou hoped to rally European public opinion to the antijunta cause and to utilize this support to leverage a change in U.S. policy. Andreas was convinced that if the United States publicly broke with the Colonels their regime would fall. He privately suggested that Karamanlis then return to lead a short-lived interim government of national unity while publicly denouncing the same idea. In talks with Karamanlis's representative, he denied that he had ever criticized the former prime minister. Karamanlis dryly commented that Andreas posed a "real problem" for exile political efforts: he could not be ignored, nor could anyone trust or work with him.[13]

After 1970, Andreas Papandreou settled into a more consistently radical stance. Unable to take control of the EK in-exile, and lacking strong support for PAK, he returned to the New World, seeking to rally Greek American and U.S. liberal backing from Canada. As professor of economics at York University in Toronto, he was able to provide for his family and remain close to the United States, where a small but highly supportive network backed him. Simultaneously, he reached back to his Greek roots, taking a much more active role in the diaspora community than he had during his previous twenty-year residence in North America. Abandoning any hope of influencing U.S. policy, Andreas proclaimed that only armed resistance and revolution could restore national dignity and root out the evils of Greek society. The United States was the enemy of Greece's national independence. A revolutionary Greek government had to expel both America and NATO from its soil to end U.S. "occupation." Karamanlis had always been America's man and thus could not be entrusted with leadership of the postjunta Greek government. In fact, the former prime minister would only worsen Greece's situation. Calls for his return to power were part of an American plan to maintain its dominance in Greece. Beginning in 1969, Papandreou demanded the abolition of the monarchy as part of a revolutionary solution to Greece's democratic reconstruction. In early 1974, as the junta's position deteriorated, Andreas's rhetoric became as apocalyptic as it had been in the months prior to the 1967 coup.[14]

DEMOCRACY AT GUNPOINT

Andreas and his supporters immediately recognized that ousting the junta required mobilizing the support of international public opinion. The United States played a special role in their strategy. Greece's most powerful ally had the necessary economic and political force to make it difficult for the junta to continue in power but was embroiled in a divisive internal quarrel over the direction of its foreign policy. President Lyndon B. Johnson's Vietnam policy had become the central issue of American politics. By 1967, LBJ had lost the support of part of his liberal political constituency. As American war losses mounted, so did the level and viciousness of anti-Johnson rhetoric. The U.S. university system was a hotbed of antiwar sentiment and the launching pad for much of the criticism of his policies. Moreover, groups of American historians, among them William Appleman Williams and his students at the University of Wisconsin, Ivy League–educated semi-Marxists like Gabriel Kolko at the University of Toronto, and sophisticated radicals like Walter LeFeber of Cornell, were formulating different versions of a general critique of American foreign policy that placed a special emphasis on its economic exploitation of smaller nations. "Revisionist" assaults on U.S. foreign policy met with a furious response from liberal Cold Warriors like Arthur Schlesinger Jr. and from former government officials like Dean Acheson. The debate spread from academic publications to the editorial pages of major U.S. newspapers and newsweeklies and into the discussions of the foreign policy elite. While the subject of this exchange was the origin of the Cold War, the Vietnam War, and by extension situations such as that in Greece, were basic subtexts. Something was fundamentally wrong with American foreign policy, the revisionists argued, and political opposition to the war and to the foreign policy of the Johnson administration was an essential step in correcting the problem.

Andreas Papandreou, with his widespread contacts in the U.S. academe, seemed ideally positioned to seize on American discontent to move forward his plans for toppling the junta. Beginning in 1967, Andreas's academic and political allies pointed to Greece as an example of wrongheaded American intervention in support of reactionary political elites. Stephen Rousseas, a Greek American economist, was the pioneer in this effort. In articles in the *Nation* and *Ramparts*, subsequently incorporated into *Death of a Democ-*

racy: Greece and the American Conscience (1967), Rousseas portrayed Andreas Papandreou as a liberal reformer whose patriotic efforts to better conditions in the land of his birth were frustrated by conspiracies hatched by reactionary Greeks, the king, the U.S. embassy, and the CIA. Laying down a boilerplate for subsequent books, Rousseas opened with a dramatic recounting of the coup, then provided an analysis of recent Greek history before tracing the conspiratorial machinations against the two Papandreous that led to the coup. After charging that the United States was behind the April 21 coup, Rousseas somewhat illogically admitted that the Colonels' action was unexpected and denounced the American government for not leaning hard enough on the king to prevent it. He concluded his appeal to the "American conscience" by predicting the outbreak of civil war.[15]

Rousseas's book had its impact on an already sympathetic U.S. left. It encouraged Papandreou and his supporters to turn out more books, each hewing fairly closely to the Rousseas model but directed at different U.S. and West European audiences. John Katris's *Eyewitness in Greece* (1971), framed as an honest journalist's perspective, claimed to offer the late George Papandreou's viewpoint. In fact, it provided a fairly steady criticism of the "Old Man's" moderate political outlook. The book's real hero was Andreas Papandreou, an idealist and doughty fighter against foreign intervention. Claiming the United States followed a calculated policy that led to the coup, Katris called for cutting off American aid as the only means of ousting the junta.[16]

A notable feature of Katris's memoir was the introduction of new pieces of "evidence" that had accumulated since the coup and subsequently became part of its folklore. One was a statement by Tom Pappas, a right-wing Greek-American businessman and major Republican Party fund-raiser, that he was a CIA "agent." A second issue, more germane to the story of pre-April 21 U.S. policy, was a column by liberal journalist Marquis Childs reporting that, at a secret "mid-February" 1967 meeting, U.S. officials decided to do nothing to impede a coup. The story, which melded together information on the March 8 and 13, 1967, meetings of the NSC's 303 Committee on covert operations, was inaccurate in its key points (see chapter 5). However, in keeping with its policy of not discussing intelligence matters, the Johnson administration never denied it, and Margaret Papandreou would make frequent references to it. Katris repeated Andreas Papandreou's July 1968 claim to the *New York Times* that in 1961 the CIA had actively offered support to Constantine Karamanlis's ERE.[17] These charges became part of the evolving mosaic that the Papandreou camp used to place responsibility for the junta on foreign shoulders.

Andreas and Margaret Papandreou published their memoirs of the April 21 coup in 1970. Margaret's is more revealing about the motivations behind her husband's actions and internal family dynamics. It is impassioned, contains small but significant deviations from the story Andreas tells, and simultaneously offers both an insider's and an outsider's version of events. Margaret's portrayal of herself as a politically innocent Midwestern American woman is somewhat at odds with her past in Democratic Party politics and public relations work. She admits Andreas's role in inciting the 1967 coup. Her comments about the failure of the Greek people to rise up in support of Andreas and George Papandreou subtly undercuts her claims of overwhelming public support for the EK leaders. Some rather gratuitous shots at the Greek national character are included. Overall, however, the book is perhaps the most effective presentation of the Papandreou case.[18]

Andreas Papandreou's *Democracy at Gunpoint* offers readers the story of an idealistic university professor emerging as a fiery political leader of his people and a "thoughtful statesman" seeking liberty for Greece. Memoirs by their nature place the writer at the center of events, even when the writer's role is peripheral, and Andreas takes full advantage: inflating his early activities and, naturally, glossing over mistakes. In this self-portrait he paints himself as an articulate critic of U.S. policy long before he adopted these positions. In those places where *Democracy at Gunpoint* can be compared with the archival record, it is inaccurate, frequently to the point of invention. His Greek critics had an easy time picking apart the book's many inconsistencies. Nevertheless, *Democracy at Gunpoint* succeeded in creating support for antijunta actions in both the United States and Europe, and, most importantly, when subsequently translated into Greek, it built Andreas's image as a resistance leader. It remains a critical point of reference for understanding Papandreou.[19]

Democracy at Gunpoint marks a public turning point in Andreas's attitudes toward the United States. By 1970 he had abandoned all hope of influencing the Nixon administration's Greek policy. This attitude was becoming widespread among Greek elites as they watched the American government craft a policy of support for the junta. Andreas's views and those of an increasing number of Greeks began to converge. If Andreas Papandreou had been out of sync with Greek public opinion in 1967, by 1971 they were moving in lockstep as both focused on the U.S. responsibility for the coup and everything that followed. As one Greek intellectual observed at the time, "Andreasism" was alive in Greece even before most Greeks had connected Andreas with such views.[20]

In *Democracy at Gunpoint,* Andreas integrates most of the themes he would use to ride to power a decade later. While many were already part of his rhetorical armory, the way in which he marshaled them marks a significant break in his political thinking. He married Marxist economic and historical analysis to a stridently nationalistic and anti-Western perspective. Greece, he argued, had been systematically subjected to foreign rule through the cooperation of a privileged Greek elite ("the Establishment") with the United States. Greek efforts to free itself from this oppressive control, led by George Papandreou (and his son), had polarized the situation and forced the United States into alliance with military extremists. The April 21 coup was a CIA orchestrated plot to suppress democracy. Having cynically turned his army against the king, the United States abandoned Constantine when he foolishly tried to restore his personal power. Seeking to impose political control and to gain economic mastery over Greece, the United States suppressed Greece's old ruling class, replacing it with a new military-dominated elite determined to solidify the status quo. Andreas, through PAK, was coordinating a national resistance while rallying European and American opponents of U.S. imperialism for the restoration (or introduction) of true democracy in Greece.[21]

In this analysis of the origins of U.S. involvement in Greece, Andreas exploited a number of academic works that painted the Truman Doctrine as imperial intervention rather than the far-sighted and generous action traditionally portrayed in American and Greek rhetoric and memoirs. Seeking to make inroads among the left wing, Andreas adopted a neutral position on the civil war, ignoring the ideological issues of the confrontation and stressing the horrors of Greek fighting Greek. In his comments on the 1950s, Andreas charged Karamanlis with direct involvement in an American project to turn Greece into a "colony" and a Cold War "garrison state." Recognizing John F. Kennedy's enduring popularity, he claimed that the assassinated president had changed America's Greece policy in a positive manner, aiding George Papandreou's reforming efforts. The Johnson administration, however, had subjected Greek interests to the requirements of its confrontation with the Soviet Union, in particular through its treatment of the Cyprus issue. Only the determined resistance by the Papandreous had prevented a national disaster. As a result, the United States had decided to oust the elder Papandreou and destroy Andreas's political career by concocting the ASPIDA scandal in collaboration with the Palace and the EK's right wing. American efforts had succeeded in toppling George Papandreou and even in creating fissures between a father and his devoted son, but in the end, the elder Papandreou had shifted to the progressive course advocated by his son and finally anointed Andreas heir to his political movement and objectives.[22]

Even as he assumed his father's reformist mantle, Andreas proclaimed his own "socialism." While blessedly free from Marxist jargon, and contemptuous of the Soviet Union as the U.S. peer in oppressing small states, the memoir presents Andreas Papandreou as seeking a "third way" between American-style capitalism and Soviet command economics and politics. Andreas's search for political backing honed in on European social democrats. The governing Swedish socialists originally had helped to create PAK, and a number of EK and PAK supporters operated from West Germany where the Social Democrats of Willy Brandt held power. Andreas rejected the European integration efforts that social democrats throughout Western Europe were embracing. Papandreou initially had argued that membership in the European Economic Community was essential for Greek political stability and economic growth, but by the mid-1960s he had begun to question the free-market economic model and publicly expressed doubts about the West's pluralistic democracy. His somewhat contradictory solution to the problem of interest-group conflicts in democracy was a mix of decentralization and state planning directed by a tightly disciplined political movement and a national leader. Andreas Papandreou's third way to resolving Greece's problems fed largely off nationalism, underdog traditions, and a reading of history that melded Marxist analysis with Greek exceptionalism. Postjunta Greek socialism would be considerably more Greek nationalist than European social democratic and more Andreas Papandreou than Karl Marx.[23]

THE UNITED STATES VALIDATES THE ANDREAS VERSION

On the morning after the Greek coup, Daniel Brewster, the director of Greek affairs at the Department of State, entered the office of Secretary of State Dean Rusk to update his boss on unfolding events in Athens. Reacting to Brewster's agitation, Rusk admonished his deputy to control his emotions: "Don't get so excited; this is my ninety-first coup." Brewster, a veteran "Greek hand" responded: "This is different, [Its] the cradle of democracy." He ruefully recalled: "That didn't impress particularly." Already presidential adviser Walt Rostow had forwarded a memo to LBJ, with the suggestion that "At some point . . . we should express regret—even if softly—that the [Greek] democratic process has been suspended." Preoccupied with the war in Vietnam and its domestic consequences, the president and his senior officials (as well as most west European foreign offices) showed little interest in Greece's fate. In a May 20, 1967, dispatch to the Foreign Office, Britain's embassy summarized the view current among most NATO government representatives: the Papandreous had led Greece into the existing "mess." Their "foolishness" paralleled that of the king, whose political future was very grim. No viable alternative to military rule appeared to exist for the foreseeable future. Both Greeks and the West were going to have to learn to live with the junta. *New York Times* foreign correspondent C. L. Sulzberger captured the motivations behind the disinterest in Greek affairs: "All the U.S.A. stands for has been hurt by this; but not our national interests. The U.S.A., like the king, has passively accepted the coup."[24]

OPERATING IN A FOG

U.S. policy began to unfold in the chaotic hours following the putsch. As he and his startled staff stumbled into their offices in the early morning of April 21, 1967, Phillips Talbot tried to find out what had happened, and who was in control of the coup and Greece. By early afternoon, Talbot knew that traditional U.S. interlocutors had been swept from power. At 5 A.M. that morning, King Constantine confessed to a military attaché sent to Tatoi Palace that he had "no clear idea of what was happening." The shaken young monarch wanted support: "They are headed this way for me. Get word to the Sixth Fleet. Get word to Washington and have them send your army in." A few hours later, after an initial meeting with the coup makers, the king, "blazingly angry," told Talbot that "neither he nor [the] general officers control [the] Greek army tonight. 'Incredibly stupid ultra right wing bastards, having gained control of the tanks, have brought disaster to Greece.'" With Greece's military and political leadership in custody, Talbot needed to create some line of communication with the country's new rulers. He set up a meeting with the newly installed civilian prime minister, Constantine Kollias, to "strongly" insist on the restoration of "normal life," as quickly as possible, and the protection of detainees, to underline U.S. support for the king, and to stress U.S. interest, as Greece's chief source of economic and military support, in what followed.[25]

Talbot immediately determined that in talking to Kollias he was dealing with a figurehead. The prime minister and the chief of the army staff, General Gregory Spandidakis, were able to guarantee the safety of Andreas Papandreou and other prisoners but insisted that the army had acted to prevent a communist takeover and that, for the moment, no plans existed for a return to constitutional government. Talbot suggested that Washington take a "fairly starchy posture" but remain in contact with the junta, publicly "regret" the coup, and marshal its support behind the king as the "focus for restoring normalcy." The U.S. ambassador let his own feelings show: the "rape of Greek democracy" was an event its people would "long rue."[26]

In Washington, caution was the immediate response to the Greek tragedy. Rusk decided to avoid any statement, an idea Rostow endorsed. The State Department instructed Talbot to encourage the king to stay in Greece, arguing that he was in a position to extract significant concessions from the coup makers that could place Greece on the road to the restoration of a constitutional state. Finally, on April 28, Rusk publicly seconded the king's call for a return to democracy and urged the junta to release its political prisoners.[27]

No U.S. official in either Washington or Athens ever seriously considered using military force to oust the Greek junta, a decision that many Greeks resented and others took as proof of U.S. involvement in the coup. On its face, the idea of attacking a NATO ally, with the probability of serious loss of life among civilians as well as U.S. and Greek armed forces, was a nonstarter. The Johnson administration, with well over a quarter million soldiers bogged down in an unpopular war in Vietnam, was not about to seek congressional and public support for military action against an allied nation. Even if the president had concluded that force was needed, it would take months to build a popular consensus for such action. Moreover, threatening to use the military could have serious consequences, particularly if the United States was unwilling to back up its threats and the junta called its bluff. Such a threat could unleash a wave of Greek nationalism that would reinforce the junta. In lieu of a military confrontation with a regime composed of "limited, politically inexperienced, tough-minded no-nonsense types" who had full control of the Greek army, the Johnson administration decided to display its opposition by using stronger private rhetoric and by cutting off shipments of heavy weapons. Defense Secretary Robert McNamara made a very firm statement of U.S. desires for the quick restoration of democracy to General Spandidakis at the May NATO ministerial meeting in Paris. The United States, which did not seek NATO support to put pressure on the junta, instead limited its contacts with the Colonels and the Greek military to "working levels" and tried to reinforce the king's leverage by making him the principal contact between American and Greek governments.[28]

Then and now the most hotly debated question was whether Washington had exhausted its ability to manipulate the Greek crisis and restore democratic government short of the use of force. CIA chief Jack Maury believed that the United States could have exerted more effective pressures in the early days through a direct confrontation with coup leader George Papadopoulos. Based on Kollias's nervousness during his meeting with Talbot, Robert Keeley of the embassy political section (and future ambassador to Greece) believed that a show of force by the Sixth Fleet would have been sufficient to cause the junta to crumble. On the other hand, C. L. Sulzberger, one of the first Americans to have serious discussions with the coup leaders (April 28 and 29), left convinced that the Colonels were tough enough to hold on to power in the face of any U.S. moves. The junta's leaders displayed little interest in U.S. concerns or actions either in April 1967 or thereafter. Pattakos, the first of the coup makers to meet with Talbot, did not even bother to ask about U.S. intentions. He told the ambassador that the junta would carry out its program before handing over power. "Just remember," he told a U.S. military officer, "we are with you whether you want us or not."[29]

The junta's Greek opponents and their liberal allies in the United States consistently argued that a firm policy, centered on the total denial of military aid, would cause the collapse of the junta. A majority of American diplomats as consistently argued that the United States could not oust the junta with pressure and that such actions would do serious harm to Western defense capabilities. Both may have been right. A total or near total break with the junta would have seriously embarrassed the Colonels but might not have toppled them. Other willing arms suppliers were readily available, specifically France. On the other hand, a public break with the junta would have served U.S. interests much better over both the long and short term. It would have placed heavy pressure on the Colonels to depart the stage quickly and would have given the Greek people both hope and a point of reference in their resistance to the dictatorship. When Greece was liberated, the United States would have garnered Greek public respect. The patron would have delivered for its client. Instead, the Americans opted for the worse of all possible solutions, doing the minimum necessary under LBJ in order to maintain their immediate influence over Greece. Feeble American diplomacy scarcely reflected U.S. power or its proclaimed ideals.[30]

Added to American caution was its lack of information about Greece's self-imposed leaders. Keeley recalled that during the first days after the coup: "We were working overtime trying to figure who the Colonels were; no one knew them. We had no bio-data on them; they didn't speak English; they were not a part of our military circles." (Some twenty-five years later, when I had the opportunity to review still-secret CIA files, I discovered that the agency had scant information on the coup's leader, George Papadopoulos, prior to April 21, 1967, and worked furiously to assemble reliable biographical data in the days thereafter.) The Colonels preferred to operate behind the screen provided by Kollias and the king, to disguise how they shared power as well as the identities of the "revolutionary" leadership.³¹

Pattakos's role as the junta's contact with the embassy was natural. Alone among the Colonels he had undergone a military training program in the United States during the 1950s. Moreover, he had a brother living in Detroit and a nephew serving in the U.S. Army. Deeply religious, intensely nationalist, and frequently unintelligible to his U.S. interlocutors, Pattakos, whom the classicists at the French embassy dubbed "miles gloriosus," was tough, small-minded, bombastic, and given to mystic pronouncements.³²

Col. Nikolaos Makarezos, number three in the collective leadership, was largely a puzzle for U.S. officials for months after the coup. He avoided contacts with foreign officials, and his role as minister of economic coordination kept him largely out of the spotlight as he dispensed government patronage, thereby building ties to the business community. The United States had an equally difficult time deciphering the political ideas of such "hard-liners" as Ioannis Ladas and Dimitrios Ioannides. Ominously, these men and many of the captains who worked with them were more radical than the junta leadership.

George Papadopoulos emerged as the dominant figure in the junta. Prior to the coup, CIA informants had fingered him as one of the inner circle guiding the dissident officers' movement. As minister to the prime minister, Papadopoulos effectively controlled the day-to-day functioning of Greece's government. His accessibility grew in the days following the coup, but his dominant role in the leadership was cemented only after he took over as prime minister in mid-December 1967. Humorless, fiercely nationalistic, self-confident, and cunning, Papadopoulos had rarely traveled outside Greece and preferred behind-the-scenes manipulation, at which he was a master, to the give-and-take of democratic politics.³³

Papadopoulos's precoup ties with the CIA have been a source of intense speculation. During the early 1960s he had served for two years as a liaison officer between the CIA and its Greek counterpart, the KYP. Alexis Papahelas has documented an effort by the Athens station to build a good working relationship with Papadopoulos during this period. Available U.S. documentation indicates that he was not particularly close to the station either before or after his tour of duty with the KYP. Given his fierce nationalism and prickly personality, Papadopoulos was an unlikely tool of the CIA. His subsequent disdain for American interests (see chapter 7) is the best measure of Papadopoulos's views on dealing with the U.S. government: he wanted cooperation on his terms. Far from being used by the Americans, Papadopoulos sought, with success, to manipulate his U.S. interlocutors. The dearth of reliable intelligence information on Papadopoulos and coup preparations in the months leading up to April 21, 1967, is the most telling demonstration that this experienced conspirator carefully controlled his dealings with American espionage.[34]

BETTING THE HOUSE

By the beginning of May, U.S. officials were placing their hopes for a speedy return to democracy on the shoulders of King Constantine. Karamanlis, with some cautionary remarks, including a stress on expanding the arms embargo, endorsed this general approach during a visit to Washington and later in a November discussion with a senior U.S. diplomat. In view of the king's record, this was a risky bet, but given the limited political capital the Johnson administration could invest in Greece, it was probably the only alternative to accepting the junta. U.S. officials had been impressed by the coolness Constantine had shown in the first weeks after the coup, taking it as a sign of greater maturity. Throughout the remaining months of 1967, U.S. officials, with Talbot taking the lead, attempted to coach the king in his duel with the junta, trying to calibrate how far he could push for concessions while at the same time urging caution in his moves. The king, meanwhile, sought advice not only from his American allies, but also from other Western nations and from Greek politicians, including Karamanlis. While free with his advice, Karamanlis avoided the sort of public endorsement the young monarch craved.[35]

Throughout his short career, Constantine had displayed a marked tendency to act abruptly and to prefer confrontation to patiently undermining his political foes. He had moved precipitously against George Papandreou in July 1965 and March–April 1967. In dealing with the junta, Constantine displayed the same tendency. U.S. officials wanted the king to concentrate on securing a junta commitment to a timetable for writing a constitution and then for holding elections. In spite of their growing concern that the arms embargo was having a negative impact on Greek defense capabilities, they continued to wield it in order to pressure the junta toward the return of constitutional government. The king, however, was concerned that he had only a limited amount of time to regain control of the army before the junta purged his supporters in the officer corps and solidified their dictatorship. In late July, the embassy reported that the king was convinced that a confrontation was imminent and that he was being encouraged in this view by a group of active-duty and retired senior officers who were simultaneously seeking U.S. backing for a countercoup. Hoping to gauge the level of American support for a move against the junta, the king arranged an informal visit to the United States.[36]

Carefully briefed on the damage that a precipitate move could cause to U.S. efforts to nudge Greece toward a constitutional solution, Johnson tried to restrain the king. Constantine told the president that a military confrontation was likely during the winter of 1967–68 and asked whether he could count of military support or, at the least, public backing. LBJ responded that military support was out of the question and that any public statement of support would have to be decided on the basis of the "facts on the ground." The king also requested the renewal of U.S. military assistance to strengthen his position, suggesting an announcement be tied to continued progress in the restoration of democracy. Johnson struck Constantine as "sympathetic and concerned," but he avoided any commitment on aid until he could consult the U.S. Congress. The U.S. president expressed his concern about the fates of Andreas Papandreou and other political detainees, and the king promised to do what he could to secure their release.[37]

The king left Washington in a positive frame of mind, apparently convinced of an ultimately favorable American response to action against the junta. In fact, U.S, officials were of two minds about Greece's future. On the one hand, they wanted a restoration of democracy, if it could be achieved without violence. On the other hand, they were accommodating themselves to the likelihood that the military regime would hold on to power for some time. The arms embargo, which the administration imposed in haste in the days after the coup, was poorly designed. Arms needed for Allied defense against the Warsaw Pact were cut off, while the small arms needed to repress the Greek population continued to flow to the junta. The hoped-for psychological impact of the arms embargo was limited because press censorship left the Greek people unaware of U.S. action. Moreover, however unsavory, the Greek government was eager to cooperate within NATO and was resolutely anticommunist. The June 1967 Six-Day War, in which the junta aided supply efforts for Israel, won favor at the Pentagon. U.S. officials worried that France would try to leverage U.S.-Greek difficulties to create further problems inside NATO and take over the U.S. role as primary arms supplier. President Johnson declined to go along with initial recommendations to lift the embargo. Talbot, who had been the first to throw in the towel and suggest improving ties with the junta, fretted that the military government was now strong enough to take a confrontational line with the embassy. While official policy remained to support gradual regime change, French and British diplomats reported that the Americans were perplexed about how to deal with the Colonels and increasingly unsure whether either the arms embargo or an arm's-length policy were working.[38]

COLLAPSE

With the future of the dynasty at risk, the king made another daring move on December 13, 1967, by launching a coup against the junta. As early as September, the British ambassador had noted a fairly widespread belief that the king could rely on the Third Army Corps in Macedonia in any confrontation, adding that some politicians were convinced that just the threat of facing this unit, Greece's best equipped, would bring down the junta. The Colonels appeared weakened as a result of their bungled November 1967 confrontation with Turkey over Cyprus (see chapter 8). Cautiously urged on by Karamanlis, who viewed the situation as bleak, and time for action as limited, and probably misjudging the support he could expect from Washington, Constantine launched his coup without proper concern for security. While the Colonels had kept information on their plans tightly under wraps, the king, in seeking broad support from Greek political forces, had virtually announced his plans to the world. Certainly the junta was not caught unawares. Its telephone taps and surveillance were unremitting. Public speculation on a royal coup was widespread. The Colonels reacted swiftly to an ill-planned effort to restore constitutional rule.[39]

Early on the morning of December 13, by prearrangement, the king met with Talbot. Handing over a tape recording for broadcast on U.S. Armed Forces Radio, he informed the ambassador that the countercoup was under way. Constantine then bundled his family, prime minister, and assorted aides into two aircraft and headed north to military bases in Larissa and Kavala. For the next twenty-four hours, the United States lost contact with the monarch. Talbot, whose instincts were to support the king, had no information to feed his more cautious superiors in Washington as he sought to justify such a course of action. CIA efforts to make contact with the king failed. Meanwhile, the Colonels, who had both ambassador and king under surveillance, called Talbot to their command post to demand an accounting of his involvement in the coup effort. The U.S. envoy truthfully told them that he had not been involved in the planning, but his position was badly compromised with the regime. During the early morning hours of December 14, Talbot, now armed with a very limited authorization to nudge the junta into surrender, discovered that the Colonels were confident that they controlled the situation and were in no mood to deal with the king.[40]

Also during the morning of December 14, the king fled to Rome. The United States had to reassess its approach to the military regime in Athens. Talbot advised capitulating to the reality on the ground: with its "ace in the hole" in Italian exile, the military evidently loyal to the junta, and the Greek people likely to accept a regime that had displayed its strength, "no possible alternative to the coup group now existed"; the United States would have to regularize its relationship. Somewhat illogically, Talbot argued that a regime that showed little interest in democracy could produce a return to constitutional rule.[41]

Convinced that they had the upper hand not only in Greece, but also in their relationship with the United States, the Colonels sought a direct dialogue with Washington. The December political amnesty was a sign of their desire for an opening. In early January, Greek American businessman Tom Pappas delivered a personal letter from Papadopoulos, now prime minister, to President Johnson, laying out the junta's case. The Greek government was committed to the goals of the "Free World" led by the United States. The "revolution" of April 21 had averted a communist-led civil war. The junta had imposed a "temporary" suspension of the constitution, but "the regime of this country—democracy together with a hereditary sovereign—will remain unaltered" and a new constitution would soon begin the process of political normalization. Greece's government would determine the timing of a return to constitutional rule.[42]

Washington wasted little time in taking up the Colonels offer. On January 13, the State Department instructed Talbot that it wanted a "normalization" of relations with the junta. While the message insisted that the United States would continue to press for a speedy restoration of constitutional government, it also announced a decoupling of pressures to achieve that end. On February 2, Talbot conveyed the new policy to Papadopoulos together with an invitation to visit the aircraft carrier Franklin D. Roosevelt when it arrived in Piraeus in mid-February. The Greek ambassador in Washington commented that, weakened by its Vietnam problems, the United States had abandoned any effort to effect regime change and henceforth would deal with the "friendly" regime in Athens that had shown its ability to consolidate power. Talbot assured his bosses that "given US interests in Greece, [the] absence of acceptable alternative[s] to [the] present regime, and our incapacity to legislate Greece's future, I see no practical alternative." Using an argument that would win the day for the next six years, he added that only a program of renewed military assistance could prop up the more moderate elements within the junta and lead to an eventual restoration of democracy.[43]

The U.S. government had begun its slide down a slippery slope into the embrace of the junta. With Talbot in the lead, and despite a measured skepticism among officials in Washington, the Johnson administration began to substitute a policy of suasion for the use of carrot-and-stick tactics in seeking its objectives. While the restoration of democracy remained a primary objective of administration policy, it was now premised on a belief that such actions as the arms embargo were having no effect and should be abandoned. The United States, C. L. Sulzberger argued, had to find a way to work with Papadopoulos to achieve democracy. This view found increasing resonance among policy makers. As the process of constitution writing advanced, American officials comforted themselves that the policy was working. At the same time, they began to stress the need for reinforcing Greece's "strategic facilities" to face the Soviet Union. The Soviet invasion of Czechoslovakia gave the new policy a shove forward. In October 1968, President Johnson abandoned his earlier reluctance and agreed to release 40 percent of the military assistance program materials frozen in April 1967 in order to strengthen NATO capability to resist further Soviet moves. Ted Couloumbis of American University, an antijunta activist with good contacts throughout the U.S. government, found that while many American policy makers were highly sympathetic to the plight of Greeks, they had a hard time reconciling their concerns about international stability with support for the restoration of democracy in Greece. The longer the junta held on to power, the greater the American concern that its collapse would be followed by an anti-Western government that would lead Greece into the Soviet bloc.[44] According to this logic, successful resolution of the Greek situation depended on a highly improbable decision by the Colonels to begin democratization.

In one of his final messages from Athens, retiring ambassador Talbot signaled his recognition that suasion was not working on the junta. Having approved and simultaneously suspended Greece's new constitution, the regime was stiffening its resistance to the restoration of democracy. Papadopoulos's tone changed from one of requesting concessions to demanding them, noted an irritated deputy assistant secretary of state Stuart Rockwell. Greece's military rulers were convinced that they held Greece in solid control and that the incoming conservative administration of Richard Nixon would support their continued rule.[45] The Nixon administration's unwavering backing for the junta in turn would provide a convincing validation of Andreas Papandreou's version of history, reinforce his claim to power, and ultimately open the way for precisely the sort of political solution to Greece's problems that Americans of all political persuasions had feared: a Greek government pursuing an anti-NATO agenda while cozying up to the Soviet bloc and radical regimes in the Third World. As this scenario became reality, American officials had no one to blame but themselves.

7

DANCING WITH THE DICTATORS, 1969–1974

> Kanellopoulos, Mavros, and Averoff came to me in a group to express deep thanks, saying I had played a major role in the return of democracy to Greece.
> — Henry Tasca, July 1974

> When the junta took over . . . the United States allowed its interests in prosecuting the Cold War to prevail over its interests—I should say its obligation—to support democracy.
> — Bill Clinton, November 1999

In the spring of 1971, the State Department's Bureau of Intelligence and Research (INR) forwarded a study to Secretary of State William Rogers analyzing the longer term consequences of the Colonels' regime. Estimating that the military dictatorship could continue for another five years, INR commented that the costs to the United States of continuing junta control of Greece would largely arise from a widespread public perception that the American government was its primary source of foreign support. The damage would be serious, but Greece's need for U.S. cooperation in security, economics, and foreign affairs was great enough that the American government could accept the consequences of association with the Colonels.[1] Richard Nixon, who took control of America's foreign policy in January 1969, apparently shared the strategic outlook offered by the INR. The new president inherited a Greek policy that had failed to achieve its stated objective of moving that nation back toward constitutional government and had generated strong criticism from NATO allies, U.S. liberals, and Greece's democratic opposition. Nixon was unimpressed by the criticism. During the next five and a half years, the president and his national security advisor, Henry Kissinger, capably and, at times, enthusiastically assisted by America's ambassador in Greece, Henry Tasca, locked the United States into a close relationship with the military junta. By late 1974, Nixon's successor, Gerald Ford, and his chief policy advisor, Kissinger, were dealing with the consequences of a projunta policy: a hostile democracy in Athens, an angry Turkey, a divided Cyprus, and full scale-rebellion in the U.S. congress fueled by policies like those in Greece and Cyprus that threatened to strip the executive branch of considerable autonomy in the conduct of foreign policy. Although INR's broad analysis proved correct, the costs of embracing the Greek junta were higher than anyone in the administration appears to have calculated. The effects of Nixon's policy have plagued U.S. relations with Greece and Greek Cypriots for more than three decades.[2]

DIVIDED AND DISORIENTED

The king's failed coup was more than a disaster for the monarchy. It left the Greek opposition to the junta without a toehold in the national government. The king, the British embassy lamented, had "delivered Greece into the hands of the Colonels," who quickly stripped away all legal restraints and completed their takeover of Greece's bureaucratic and political institutions. While they had not turned Greece into a "concentration camp," the country's new rulers continued a process begun in April 1967, building an arbitrary regime that utilized indiscriminate arrest, imprisonment, and, at times, torture as means of control.[3] The opposition was divided. Foreign governmental criticism, at least the criticism that mattered to the Colonels, was largely stifled by Greece's continued active participation in NATO. By coopting Panagiotis Pipinelis as foreign minister, the Papadopoulos regime acquired a skilled and widely accepted public representative. Karamanlis worried that other conservatives would follow Pipinelis's example, providing the dictatorship with greater legitimacy. While he and his fellow exiles, including the king and Andreas Papandreou, maneuvered for influence, their divisions kept the opposition abroad as weak and disoriented as that in Greece.[4]

The sense of weakness only increased opposition leaders' psychological dependence on Washington. Karamanlis complained that Greeks were waiting for Washington to impose a solution instead of working on a common policy and seeking European backing. Simultaneously he sought a privileged relationship with the new administration.[5] Inevitably opposition concerns, as well as those of the military rulers of Greece, centered on the character and interests of the new U.S. president and his chief advisers. The death of Nixon's predecessor and former patron, Dwight D. Eisenhower (March 28, 1969), gave them the opportunity to probe the intentions of the new team in Washington. The junta dispatched Pipinelis and Pattakos at the head of an official delegation to the funeral. King Constantine hastened to Washington to present his case to the new U.S. president. Andreas Papandreou sought British Labour party assistance in gaining entrée to Nixon, while Karamanlis sent informal representatives to sound out the Americans.[6]

All sides agreed that the arms embargo was the critical issue for the future of U.S.-Greek relations. The junta wanted it lifted as much in recognition of its legitimacy as for military considerations.[7] The opposition wanted it extended in the hope of toppling the dictatorship.

In pressing its case with the Nixon administration, the junta enjoyed a number of advantages. The CIA station and military mission in Athens had speedily developed a favorable view of the Colonels because of their loyalty to NATO. The prominent Greek American businessman, presidential confidant, and fund-raiser Tom Pappas was an enthusiastic supporter of the dictatorship. The president, too, had a favorable opinion of the junta. In June 1967 Nixon had visited Athens as a private citizen. Pattakos headed up a Greek team that threw out the red carpet for the ex-vice president. Carefully briefed by the U.S. embassy, Nixon urged the junta to return to democratic government but significantly told the Colonels that he did not favor using American pressure to achieve this objective. He left Athens with a positive impression of the new regime, and the junta played up the visit as a sign of U.S. support.[8]

The Nixon administration gave the first indications of its policy during the Eisenhower state funeral. The United States recognized the king as Greece's head of state. (The junta had not deposed him after the countercoup. It appointed a regent to substitute for Greece's absent sovereign.) Legally, Constantine was the head of the Greek delegation to the Eisenhower funeral and could expect a meeting with Nixon. The State Department recommended that the president receive the monarch with full honors for "substantive discussions." The president's briefing paper for the proposed meeting cautioned that any conversation with the king likely would be "difficult." It suggested that Nixon avoid making "any commitment to help the king regain his throne," and if Constantine asked for help to return to Greece, Nixon should tell him to "make his own arrangements."[9]

The White House ignored State's recommendations. Neither the president nor his chief advisor trusted the nation's professional diplomats. Nixon exchanged a few words with the king during a formal reception and met privately with Pattakos. During their conversation, Pattakos assured the president that "they would continue to be friends even if the United States did nothing for them and they understood the stoppage of arms supply." Nixon responded that policy toward Greece was under review but that in the future the United States would be involved principally with external issues not internal ones, assurances that the Colonels craved. In a subsequent meeting with Foreign Minister Pipinelis, an ally of the king, Kissinger commented that he was sorry that the president had been unable to meet privately with Constantine but that Nixon could not permit himself to be placed in the middle of Greece's "internal quarrels." He did not explain how meeting with Pattakos conformed to this formula but praised the leaders of the junta as "men of vision."[10]

The king was shunted off to a private meeting with Vice President Spiro Agnew. The young monarch urged the United States to tie the extension of further military aid to Greece to firm guarantees by the junta to implement the 1968 constitution. Warning that the junta would be in power for a long time, he stressed that the United States needed to maintain close contacts with the opposition.[11] Subsequent approaches to the White House by former prime minister Constantine Karamanlis and leftist leader Andreas Papandreou met rebuffs.[12]

Reviewing U.S. options in the wake of the Eisenhower funeral, Harold Saunders, the National Security Council's specialist for Greece, outlined a series of policy scenarios and suggested that the Nixon administration follow a line similar to that of its predecessor, attempting to work with the junta but stressing the need for a return to democratic government. Nixon's friend Tom Pappas urged the United States to open diplomatic channels to the junta, arranging a meeting between the chief of the Greek army, General Odysseus Angelis, and Agnew, at which the general lobbied for the restoration of full military aid.[13]

The president's predilections became evident to his advisors in June. The NSC staff prepared a decision memorandum that would permit a limited extension of military assistance to Greece. As was customary, the paper offered the president three options: a full cut off of aid, the staff-endorsed idea of a limited aid package, or a full restoration of aid. Nixon read the paper attentively, annotating it. He then checked the option that would restore full aid to the junta. Kissinger and his chief aide, Alexander Haig, convinced the president to hold off: they wanted to carefully prepare U.S. and NATO public opinion, as well as members of congress, before resuming arms assistance.[14]

By the fall of 1969, the Nixon administration had formulated its policy toward Greece. Ignoring the repeated pleas of opposition leaders and its own NATO allies to keep the arms embargo active, as well as evidence of the junta's preoccupation with the issue, Nixon's team decided that the embargo was an ineffective tool for motivating change in Greece's internal politics and decoupled military aid from the question of the return of constitutional government. This decision was formalized in November 1969 but was carefully concealed from the public. A final announcement would await the dispatch of a new ambassador to Greece and a report in which he stated that the restoration of aid was critical to U.S. interests.[15]

OUR MAN IN ATHENS

The new U.S. ambassador, Henry Tasca, was the ideal man to carry out this policy. A career foreign service officer of very conservative views, Tasca had a knack for finding powerful patrons to advance his career. During World War II he had served as hatchet man for Secretary of Treasury Henry Morgenthau in a particularly bitter confrontation with the British over policy toward Italy. After a series of prestige postings in Europe, he served as ambassador to Morocco, where he befriended Richard Nixon as the latter struggled to resuscitate his political career. The decision to appoint Tasca reflected the Nixon administration's desire to have a tough, politically reliable, and experienced diplomat in a country where it could expect conflict over policy with U.S. liberals. While nominally part of the State Department's chain of command, Tasca enjoyed direct "back-channel" communications to the White House. Following its normal operational procedure, the Nixon White House cut off the State Department from decision making on issues of special concern.[16]

The Senate confirmed Tasca as ambassador on December 19, 1969. He departed for his posting with a set of instructions, National Security Decision Memorandum (NSDM) 34, approved by the president on November 14. Tasca was to tell Prime Minister George Papadopoulos that Nixon was prepared to resume normal arms shipments and that any sort of movement toward "a constitutional situation" would hasten the arms deliveries. The ambassador was further instructed that the arms resumption would take place after he had reported on the Greek response. In public comments, Tasca was to stress the "overriding U.S. security interest" in aiding the Greek military. He was also instructed to develop relationships that would enable him to push Greek leaders for democratic reform. Nixon told Greek ambassador Basil Vitsaxis that he wanted to avoid intervention in Greek internal affairs, expressed sympathy about the regime's negative press coverage, and suggested that steps toward the restoration of democracy would ease U.S. difficulties in assisting the junta.[17]

Tasca quickly discovered the limits of the Nixon administration's commitment to democratic reform. In one of his first acts as ambassador, he cabled Washington to object to a visit by U.S. Apollo 12 astronauts. Such a visit, Tasca commented "would be interpreted by the G[overnment] o[f] G[reece] as one more significant indication that U.S. reservations about [a] lack constitutional government in Greece are essentially pro forma." Kissinger overruled the ambassador: "But that's what the president wants."[18]

Washington displayed little interest in democratic reform in Greece; the junta had even less. Tasca held a first "cordial" meeting with Papadopoulos on January 26, 1970. He opened his presentation by stressing the importance that the United States placed on Greece's participation in NATO. He then switched to the issue of democratic reform, noting the widespread opposition to the junta existing in the United States. Papadopoulos interrupted to explain that it would not always be possible for Greece to listen to "our great friend" on internal issues. No linkage was possible, the prime minister continued, between Greece's NATO role and its internal affairs. The Greek government alone would determine the pace of implementing constitutional change.[19]

The junta was clearly in closer symphony with Washington's instructions than was the U.S. ambassador, who ignored the lack of enthusiasm for democratic reform in the White House. Pressed on the issue by the State Department's Bureau of Near Eastern and South Asian Affairs and by European colleagues in Athens, he attempted to secure concessions from the dictatorship. In a meeting with the Dutch ambassador to Greece, Carl Barkman, Tasca commented that the junta would be in power for a long time and that the United States needed to assure its continuing membership in NATO as a matter of priority, discounting the probable damage to Greek military effectiveness caused by large-scale purges of the senior officer corps. Barkman warned the U.S. envoy that the junta had capitalized on his arrival to build the impression it had Washington's backing. He also underlined European concerns about the use of torture to a "largely uninformed" Tasca. In order to counteract the impression of full U.S. backing for the regime, Barkman suggested that Tasca meet frequently with opposition leaders and join his European colleagues in pressing for the return of democracy. "I hated lecturing but Tasca asked for it," the Dutch ambassador confided to his diary.[20]

In March, Tasca sent back two reports on the Greek situation that constituted the bedrock of his approach for the next four years. In the first, the ambassador analyzed the dictatorship. He found it collegial in character and noted the important role of Brigadier Dimitrios Ioannides, the chief of the military police, in connecting Papadopoulos, "the undisputed leader," to the junior officers, "who pulled guns on their superiors on April 21 or December 13 [1967]" and whose careers and personal safety would be threatened by a return to democracy. Their line was: "No elections, no king, and forward with the aims of the revolution." Papadopoulos was the "best choice" to guide Greece back to constitutional government but, the ambassador argued, had little room to maneuver. Nevertheless, Tasca concluded that the United States would have to back Papadopoulos.[21] Left unanswered were two key questions: how would Papadopoulos carry the junior officers with him, and why would he want to try? The same possibility of punishment hung over his head with greater force. He had planned and instigated the coup and was ultimately responsible for the widespread human rights violations in Greece.

Tasca's second message, his long-awaited "Report on Greece" (March 31), was designed to provide the rationale for ending the arms embargo. Tasca concluded that the junta was "here to stay," that the arms cutoff was ineffective in influencing its internal behavior, and that the Greeks would get the arms elsewhere (France), thus reducing U.S. leverage. Therefore, the United States should lift the suspension and continue to press for constitutional reform. Tasca was "satisfied that the Greek government does indeed intend to move forward, albeit at its own often reluctant pace, with its programs to implement the constitution [of 1968]." Backing up Tasca's analysis was an April 7 letter from Papadopoulos to Nixon promising "normalization" in the form of a plan for a return to constitutional government. The Tasca report served as the justification for the president to approve the resumption of arms supplies as soon as the domestic and international political situation permitted. The NSC authorized Tasca to inform the Greek government of the policy shift prior to its announcement.[22]

The U.S. approval flew in the face of the junta's repeated public affirmations of its determination to stay in power. In late April, interior minister Pattakos ruled out even municipal elections. "Most unhelpful," the State Department commented to Tasca.[23] Nevertheless, on September 22, 1970, the department announced the resumption of military aid to Greece. "Although the United States had hoped for a more rapid return to representative government in Greece, the trend toward constitutional order is established . . . [and] recent events in the Eastern Mediterranean have underlined the strategic advantages which Greece affords NATO on its southern flank."[24]

Shortly before Tasca's arrival in Athens, Michael Llewellyn Smith, a British diplomat, wrote that the Greek internal opposition to the junta had reached the end of its options. The king's failed coup had destroyed its hopes of removing the Colonels through military action. Efforts by a few former party leaders to create a working relationship with the junta and gradually move it to democracy ended when Papadopoulos put off elections. The remaining hope, action by United States, was a long shot. The Greeks had overestimated both the power and will of the Americans. "The junta will not be overthrown by foreigners." Nevertheless, both Greek elites and a majority of the Greek people, recalling past American interventions, continued to hold out hope of U.S. action against their rulers. The long delay in appointing a new U.S. ambassador seemed to indicate that the Nixon administration had doubts about the regime. Announcement at year's end of Tasca's arrival inflated hopes of a forceful American intervention in favor of democracy. The Nixon administration wasted little time in disabusing Greek democrats. The pro-Western former minister George Ralles bitterly complained that Washington "laughs at us" and that Tasca was treating the opposition like "trash." King Constantine, who supported a resumption of arms assistance, was "browned off" by his treatment by Nixon and lamented that he had lost all access to official Washington. Senior diplomats inside the State Department as well as members of Tasca's embassy staff were strongly opposed to the policy and its consequences but had no influence on White House decision makers or on the ambassador. Moreover, despite a few prodemocracy gestures, European governments, including both Britain and France, believed that the junta would hold power for years and adopted policies similar to those of Washington. The Greek sense of isolation and betrayal grew and focused on the Americans.[25]

In a January 1970 meeting with Nixon, British Prime Minister Harold Wilson strongly backed a policy of working with the junta in NATO-related issues while ignoring its internal actions to avoid alienating the Athens regime. Passive Western acceptance of the Colonels discounted their narrowing base of domestic support. Greek public acceptance of the junta, especially in the cities, had long evaporated. While some businessmen were willing to go along and, of course, a thoroughly purged army remained loyal, the Colonels' support was largely limited to traditionally conservative peasants and was maintained primarily through heavy doses of patronage spending. The junta exploited the tolerance shown by Western governments, above all the United States, to tramp down resistance among its own people by claiming that it had the unwavering support of the NATO alliance. In October 1970, the State Department's Bureau of Intelligence and Research issued a classified internal "Intelligence Note" on Greece that was highly critical of the Nixon administration's policy of embracing the junta. The Note warned that the combination of a resumption of military aid and high-level U.S. official visits "will have the effect of convincing Greeks of whatever political persuasion that the U.S. has at last found in Greece the kind of regime it prefers to deal with." Deputy National Security Advisor Alexander Haig ordered the Note suppressed.[26]

SQUARING THE CIRCLE

For the next three years, Tasca struggled to carry out his interpretation of U.S. policy in the face of Greek noncooperation, congressional investigation, State Department pressure, and limited White House interest. He was handicapped by an autocratic personality that alienated many embassy staff members. He expressed his frustrations to Barkman and by late 1972 was angling for another appointment. Ironically, Tasca's skill at finding powerful patrons frustrated his efforts to escape from Greece. By 1970, he had an important ally in Tom Pappas. Pappas convinced Nixon that Tasca was essential to promoting U.S. interests in Greece. As a result Tasca was still in Athens in mid-1974 when Henry Kissinger desperately needed a scapegoat for his failed Cyprus policies.[27]

Tasca's views of a proper policy were frequently stated: give the junta all the means needed to meet its NATO security requirements and then rely on Papadopoulos to carry forward with a program of democratization. Despite his mounting doubts about the ability or willingness of Papadopoulos to carry out reform, Tasca became a cheerleader for the prime minister. He encouraged the junta to improve its public relations efforts, defended its failure to carry out promises of reform to Washington, attacked its critics, pressed for the earliest possible resumption of military aid, and doggedly attempted to move the junta toward implementing constitutional reform. Once arms aid resumed, Tasca concentrated most of his efforts on reform. Embassy reports on the regime's internal divisions, textbook examples of good analysis, pointed to precisely the conclusion Tasca avoided: the junta would never relinquish power willingly.[28]

Tasca's passion for promoting the regime also meant that he largely ignored the views of the internal opposition, failed to consult with either the king or Karamanlis, until forced to do so by the State Department, and played down regime human rights violations. The embassy never seriously analyzed the fighting capability of the U.S.-supplied Greek armed forces. Despite plentiful evidence that the combat capability of the army, in particular, suffered from continuing purges of the officer corps, the U.S. embassy took the line that "morale . . . is quite high."[29]

In early 1971, Nixon administration actions prodded a Democratic Party–

controlled congress into a high-profile investigation of the policy. At the same time, the U.S. Navy had begun to campaign for the "homeporting" of a carrier group in Athens, a move sure to increase the identification of the United States with the junta. Relations between the military government of Greece and the government of Cyprus and its leader, Archbishop Makarios, worsened. Athens pursued enosis. The Greek Cypriot president preferred to lead an independent state.

In February, a staff study team from the Senate Foreign Relations Committee visited Athens to prepare a report on U.S. policy. Tasca lobbied the Greek government, seeking its cooperation and stressing the potential for using the visit to improve the junta's public image by either ending martial law or by releasing political prisoners. The Greek response was negative, and after initially agreeing to meet with the Senate staffers, senior junta officials, including Papadopoulos, refused to receive them. The situation was not improved when the staffers sought information on Greek military preparedness and the embassy, acting under instructions from the Pentagon, refused to provide it. This confrontation only increased the determination of liberal Democrats to spotlight the administration's policy toward Greece. One of the junta's most determined foes, Congressman Benjamin Rosenthal (D-N.Y.), chairman of the Subcommittee on Europe of the House Foreign Affairs Committee, announced public hearings.[30]

The evident and politically embarrassing unwillingness of the junta to change course provoked a policy review in Washington. Tasca, while admitting that Papadopoulos had failed to live up to his pledges, urged continuing his approach. The internal review did not endorse any policy changes. The only alternative Nixon administration officials offered to dealing with the junta was resuscitating an alliance with the king. They concluded, however, that Constantine was "weak, superficial, vacillating, ill prepared" and, thus, unsuitable for a serious role. On March 16, the State Department instructed Tasca to nudge Papadopoulos into lifting martial law. The junta leader responded that public calls by the U.S. secretary of state and his deputy for the restoration of democracy were "most unfortunate."[31] Nixon reassured the junta that the secretary of state's criticisms did not represent his policy with a phone call to a Washington dinner honoring General Odysseus Angelis, the Greek Defense minister. "Other countries give us regiments of words. Greece gives us regiments of troops."[32]

Congressional discontent with the administration's Greek policy simmered. In Athens, a group of Greece's former political leaders accused the United States of abandoning its moral responsibilities and protested the lifting of the arms embargo. A month later, U.S. commerce secretary Maurice Stans arrived in Athens bearing a friendly letter from Nixon. In his public appearances, Stans praised the junta. The House leadership called public hearings that would provide the junta's U.S. and Greek critics a platform to attack Nixon policy. Tasca volunteered to return to aid the administration's rebuttal of its Democratic critics.[33]

Prior to his testimony in Washington, Tasca took action to blunt some of the most evident criticisms of his work. He expanded contacts with opposition leaders and finally flew to Rome for a meeting with King Constantine. The ambassador's sudden change of front failed to impress the former political leaders. Tasca had never disguised his disdain for the "old politicians," who largely reciprocated the feeling.[34]

The House hearings provided the platform junta opponents sought. Junta critic Ted Couloumbis offered a careful presentation that stressed both Greek opposition to the Colonels and the damage Nixon policy was doing to long-term U.S. interests. Margaret Papandreou, representing her husband, used the forum to rehash charges of U.S. backing for the coup. The most incisive testimony came from Tasca's personal bête noire, exiled journalist Elias Demetracopoulos, who underlined the unreliability of Greek armed forces. The drawn out hearings finally concluded in early August with Tasca's appearance. The ambassador stonewalled his critics, refusing to directly respond to questions regarding the chronology of the administration's decision to restore military aid. Richard Nixon complimented his ambassador on his performance, complaining that "the compulsion in Washington to inflict changes in government upon Greece was . . . self-defeating." At the same time, the president suggested that Tasca inform the Greeks that their "staunch friend" would welcome some liberalization to reduce his domestic political problems.[35]

While the president seemed quite satisfied with his policy, Tasca continued to nurture doubts. Prior to his Washington visit, the ambassador expressed concern about the difficulties of defending the policy. After meeting with Nixon, Tasca sought to get a better sense of the president's objectives from Kissinger, noting that the junta was unlikely to grant any form of "liberalization" as a quid pro quo for the further endorsement it would receive from a planned visit from Vice President Agnew. Kissinger explained that the United States had no intention of pressing the Greek junta for democratic reform, lessening pressure on the ambassador to achieve the sort of dramatic improvements he was incapable of securing.[36]

Liberalization was further away than ever. Papadopoulos was busily consolidating his personal power at the expense of rivals within the junta. One of his admirers commented that the Greek prime minister lived, ate, and breathed power. Thus he had little interest in granting U.S. requests for actions that would lead to his removal and the restoration of democracy. Greece's nonelected leader was incensed by the House hearings and angry about Tasca's sudden decision to increase official U.S. links with the opposition. When the ambassador relayed Nixon's request, Papadopoulos responded that he was making no concessions and that he was canceling plans to lift martial law as a response to the House hearings. U.S. aid to Greece, the prime minister continued, was not a matter of friendship, but the fulfillment of its obligations and in America's best interests.[37]

A continuing flow of high Nixon administration officials to Greece countered whatever comfort congressional hearings gave to junta opponents. The visit of Spiro Agnew to Greece (October 16–18, 1971) increased the benefits the junta extracted from its powerful ally without corresponding concessions. The Greek opposition protested vigorously as Agnew toured Greece in the company of junta officials, met twice with Papadopoulos, and had talks with other senior military officers. Privately, Agnew pressed the junta for a return to civilian government, playing on the damage Greek intransigence was doing to the NATO alliance. Although Papadopoulos treated Agnew respectfully, his laconic response was that "principle" required keeping the "revolution" on its authoritarian course.[38]

Having failed to nudge the junta toward reform, Tasca expanded his ties to the opposition. A late September meeting with Karamanlis produced little, except to anger the junta. Karamanlis had little use for Tasca. He was convinced that the United States could oust the junta, that such a move was in its best interests, and correspondingly was annoyed that the Nixon administration was seeking neither his advice nor cooperation. Tasca also met with former foreign minister Evangelos Averoff to discuss plans for a peaceful transition to democracy. Papadopoulos's successes against more radical junta opponents and his willingness to talk with Averoff created momentary optimism at the U.S. embassy. Dutch ambassador Barkman, who did not grasp at straws, noted that the regime was still dominated by determined opponents of parliamentary government.[39]

The United States continued to bestow favors on the junta during 1972, while the Colonels carried out policies that damaged U.S. interests in the region. In February, Nixon approved a U.S. Navy plan to "homeport" an aircraft carrier, six destroyers, and support ships in Athens. Homeporting, the brainchild of Admiral Elmo Zumwalt, was designed to increase enlistments and maintain more ships on station by transferring both the units and the sailors' families into the Mediterranean. The political implications of homeporting were secondary to Zumwalt, who ignored objections from the State Department. Kissinger warned Nixon that the plan "could have significant political liabilities," including a loss of leverage over the junta and deepening discontent among U.S. allies. Homeporting increased U.S. identification with the junta and achieved some of the benefits Zumwalt sought. While happy to have a few U.S. ships in Athens as a display of American backing, the junta, always prickly on issues of national sovereignty, resisted the full deployment of a carrier group, causing the navy to delay implementation of the planned next phases of the program.[40]

The junta also displayed how dangerous it was to U.S. interests by provoking a major crisis with the government of Cyprus. After a junta-backed assassination attempt against the archbishop-president failed, Makarios decided to improve the combat readiness of his personal militia. The Cypriot National Guard, officered by Greeks, was in the hands of his most relentless enemies, the Papadopoulos junta. Moreover, the Greek government was busily seeking an accommodation with Turkey that would lead to Makarios's removal and presumably a partition of the island. Tasca endorsed the junta's plan, arguing it was in the U.S interest. However, the Greeks were unable to meet Turkish demands while Makarios outmaneuvered them as well as their allies inside the Orthodox Church of Cyprus during a February–March 1972 confrontation.[41] (See chapter 8.)

Ruthless efforts to oust Makarios were another in a series of warning signs that junta foreign policy was inherently dangerous to U.S. regional interests. The junta's internal instability was underlined in April when Papadopoulos ousted the regent, General Zoitakis, and appointed himself as successor. Tasca commented that Papadopoulos's further consolidation of personal power could be the prelude to long-promised reforms or to the creation of one-man rule. A month later, the U.S. ambassador warned that Papadopoulos's position was increasingly shaky although the regime was strong. Papadopoulos had no plans for implementing the 1968 constitution and appeared to be aiming at absolute power. The dictator had deceived "us" Tasca concluded, while the growing corruption of the regime and his inability to reorganize the Greek state had badly weakened the prime minister. Faced with these realities, the U.S. ambassador suggested increasing contacts with the opposition. By September 1972, Tasca estimated that Papadopoulos's survival was at best a "fifty-fifty" proposition.[42]

A hypersensitive junta continued to confront the United States on issues small and large. In addition to obstructing the implementation of the second phase of homeporting, the Greek military demanded and got an apology from the Joint Chiefs of Staff for some mildly critical comments about the dictatorship made during an off-the-record military briefing for visiting Greek officers. The junta continued to arrest political opponents who tried to exercise the right of free speech. It refused minimal cooperation with representatives of U.S. congressional committees. When Secretary of State Rogers visited Athens on July 5, Papadopoulos listened in stony silence to the secretary's plea for him to improve relations with Greece's NATO allies. Tasca credited the regime's touchiness on almost every issue to its internal instability.[43]

PAPADOPOULOCRACY

By mid-1973, both Papadopoulos and Nixon faced serious challenges to their continued rule. The American president was losing control of the cover-up of the Watergate break-in. Fighting for his political life, Nixon lost focus, began to drink heavily, and largely abandoned his lifelong concentration on foreign affairs. As Nixon's political career collapsed under press and congressional investigations, Henry Kissinger emerged as the sole director of U.S. foreign policy, a position solidified in September 1973 when Nixon nominated him as secretary of state. Greek policy developed into an intermittent dialogue between the two Henrys, Kissinger and Tasca.

Papadopoulos, meanwhile, faced renewed challenges to his rule and responded by taking unexpected risks. Greek students were openly flaunting the regime's regimentation. Unrest within the military services increased, particularly in the Hellenic Navy. Opposition leaders became bolder in their criticisms of the junta. In March, Walter Silva, chief of the State Department's Office of Greek Affairs, visited Athens. Long a frustrated critic of Tasca, Silva found reinforcement from his talk with one Greek professor who remarked that Greek students believed as "dogma" that the United States was propping up Papadopoulos and predicted: "You are going to be in a lot of trouble in Greece."[44]

In late April, Karamanlis, sensing the dissolution of Papadopoulos's regime and aware that his American protector was in deep political trouble, broke a long public silence to issue a strong denunciation of the regime and to call for the restoration of democracy. The following month officers on a Greek warship revolted. While the threat was easily contained by government security services, it revealed the degree to which military discipline had crumbled. Tasca warned that the incident called into question the "effective contribution of Greece to NATO," the rationale for supporting the regime. Papadopoulos's position further eroded as military police chief Ioannides openly suggested a change of leadership.[45]

The navy revolt aimed at restoring the king. Papadopoulos seized the opportunity to restore his personal credit with radicals inside the army by calling a plebiscite to abolish the monarchy and replace it with a "presidential republic." The vote would solidify his personal position and simultaneously distance him from direct responsibility for the day-to-day operations of a corrupt state. Karamanlis, intent on asserting his leadership of postjunta politics, urged Greeks to boycott the vote. Other opposition leaders issued similar statements. Tasca acidly commented that his former ally had "failed essentially as a political leader." In fact, Papadopoulos remained a skillful operator. On June 6, the soon-to-be president of Greece opened talks with Spyridon Markezinis aimed at creating a government that would carry out elections for a new parliament. Papadopoulos's objective was to preside over a governmental structure that would be backed both by the military and the old political class. Markezinis, who was looking for a way to restore parliamentary government while marginalizing radicals like Andreas Papandreou, opened talks with opposition leaders designed to provide a base of support for his government and simultaneously to secure Papadopoulos's personal position. He faced an uphill battle. Few opposition leaders wanted anything to do with "Papadopoulocracy." However, he was sure of one source of backing. The possibility of free elections under a Markezinis government reawakened Tasca's dream of carrying Greece back to democratic government through the mediation of Papadopoulos.[46]

The certainty of a rigged plebiscite and the evident disarray of the Greek military led to cautious efforts within the American government to raise the question of modifying U.S. policy. Tasca countered that despite the "uncertainties" in Athens, the United States should continue following its current policy, "a guiding light to the Greek people," while Kissinger, when approached by NSC aides, insisted that any criticism of the Greek regime be done in the "least offensive way."[47]

In lieu of a change of policy, Tasca suggested a private meeting with Papadopoulos to express U.S. frustration with the repressive nature of the regime. Tasca's boss, Assistant Secretary of State Joseph Sisco, who nurtured his own doubts about U.S. policy, persuaded an equally concerned Secretary of State Rogers to approach Nixon and secure presidential approval for a démarche to secure a fair plebiscite and push for democratic reforms. Nixon agreed, and on July 16 Tasca met with the prime minister for the first time in three months. Ignoring Tasca's presentation, Papadopoulos launched into a long recital of his grievances with the United States.[48]

Tasca's sense of frustration, expressed most openly to his fellow diplomat Barkman, was also growing in Washington. After years of careful public neutrality, Archbishop Iakovos, the cautious head of the Orthodox Church in the Americas, and a Karamanlis ally, defined the regime as "tyranny" in a private letter to Rogers. Karamanlis kept up his public attacks on the plebiscite, ironically resurrecting the rhetoric of George Papandreou to denounce the regime for the use of "force and fraud." The embassy warned that Papadopoulos's problems were mounting with the Greek public and his military colleagues. INR predicted that the Greek dictator would shortly fall. On July 28, with criticism in Congress mounting, Rogers advised Nixon to disengage from the Greek junta, suspending the second phase of the homeporting scheme as the initial step. The president ignored the suggestion.[49]

The August 1973 referendum that ousted the monarchy and simultaneously made Papadopoulos president brought the large majority he wanted through use of rigged voting. The new president had no more legitimacy than the old prime minister, relying on military power to govern. Shortly after his presidential inauguration, Papadopoulos, turned to the elite he had overthrown for that legitimacy, appointing Markezinis and a civilian cabinet. The new prime minister announced he would hold free and fair elections as the initial step toward a restoration of constitutional rule. Tasca, as always, reacted positively to any hint of reform, ignored the rigged nature of the vote, and returned to his pro-Papadopoulos positions. Pappas supported the ambassador's proposal that Nixon visit Greece to bolster its president. Kissinger took a more cautious view of events, including Nixon's declining political prospects, and advised against the plan. The internal Greek political opposition, recognizing the weakness of both Papadopoulos and Nixon, refused to support Markezinis. Still, the new government and its pledges left the opposition in a difficult position. They did not want to legitimize the president's rule, throwing Papadopoulos a lifeline through cooperation, but elections under Markezinis offered the best path to escaping military rule. Moreover, if the Markezinis experiment failed, Greece faced the prospect of a more reactionary military government.[50]

Tasca, as always, was preoccupied with the possibility that the failure of the Papadopoulos experiment would lead to a coup by a "Greek Nasser." As a result, the United States offered no public complaints when Markezinis, acting on direct orders from Papadopoulos, denied the use of its airspace to supply Israel during the October 1973 Middle East (Yom Kippur) War. While the Greek president expressed negative sentiments about the United States in "gutter language," Tasca embraced Markezinis with the same fervor as he had earlier backed Papadopoulos. Their widely reported extended latenight meetings led the British ambassador to observe: "On internal affairs, my rather volatile colleague seems to have gone entirely overboard for the Markezinis venture."[51]

The first signs of loosened government control invited university students to test their new freedoms. Protest meetings at the Polytechnic Institute of Athens, located in the city center, led to a confrontation with police. The opposition gave its full support to the protestors. The crisis escalated, and on November 17, 1973, the military violently suppressed the student uprising. Tasca claimed that the extremists of left and right had destroyed Papadopoulos's reform efforts. Recognizing that the government's harsh repression doomed both Papadopoulos and Markezinis, he suggested that the time was right for Karamanlis's return to Greece, without explaining how to win military consent to this idea. Tasca heatedly protested against the Athens visit of a U.S. admiral just days after the repression, explaining, with no evident sense of irony, that such visits increased the public identification of the United States with the regime and anti-American feeling.[52]

NONDISENGAGEMENT

On November 25, 1973, Brigadier Ioannides and a small group of officers overthrew Papadopoulos. Tasca and Pappas immediately recommended that the United States disengage as quickly as possible from its previous support of the military government and take a strong public position favoring the immediate restoration of constitutional government and backing Karamanlis. Sisco endorsed the first part of the recommendation. Kissinger, however, had other ideas, instructing Tasca: "All elements of the mission should stay out of the domestic maneuvering now going on in Greece. The mission should monitor developments, not participate in them."[53]

It was probably too late to repair America's tattered image in Greece. Shortly after his ouster, Markezinis remarked that the only path now left to the military rulers was an intense internal struggle that would end in the collapse of the regime. Anti-Americanism would increase, and Andreas Papandreou was in the wings, he added gloomily. The British ambassador agreed, warning that what remained of the combat effectiveness of Greece's army was collapsing as the officer corps became ever more involved in political maneuvers designed to protect their individual careers. Karamanlis and other moderate junta opponents reacted slowly to Papadopoulos's fall, while Andreas Papandreou boldly exploited the coup to bolster his claims that only the radical anti-American policies he offered could restore Greece's self-respect and independence.[54]

As the new regime settled in and began to display a near total incompetence, its Greek opponents took heart: the dictatorship's collapse was near. Tasca, too, believed that the Colonels had little time left and, supported by Pappas, desperately tried to win Kissinger's backing for using American power to restore democracy. The ambassador informed Washington that Greece's new rulers were fanning rumors of CIA involvement in the November coup to create an image of U.S. support. The State Department warned the Defense Department of the dangers of further senior military contacts with the Greeks, while INR attempted to awaken the secretary to the precariousness of Ioannides's rule. Kissinger was unmoved: "I have no intention of intervening publicly or otherwise in Greece's internal political evolution."[55]

Tasca refused to accept Kissinger's instructions as final. Hoping to force a policy change, he reported the evident dissolution of the Greek military and stressed the lack of cooperation between the Ioannides junta and the United States on critical matters, such as counterterrorism. Tasca accepted an invitation to testify before closed-door congressional hearings on Greece and refused to see Ioannides when the Greek strongman set "absurd" conditions to keep their discussion secret. The ambassador unsuccessfully requested a private meeting with his besieged patron, Nixon, to secure a change in policy.[56]

On March 20, 1974, Tasca meet with Kissinger and senior State Department officials in Washington to thrash out a policy for Greece. Underlining the extremely limited base of military support the junta possessed and the conflicts between Ioannides and senior Greek officers, he tried to convince Kissinger that the only way to protect U.S. security interests was to push democratization. The ambassador, however, cut a poor figure, veering into near incoherence as his presentation continued. Professor Kissinger subjected him to a withering oral examination. Sisco tried to provide Tasca some support, but Kissinger trivialized his arguments. Tasca raised the possibility that Ioannides's "primitive foreign policy approach" could "easily lead" to a conflict with the Turks. Kissinger dismissed this as a "foreign policy problem" unrelated to the issue of a public confrontation with the junta on democracy for Greece. As the discussion wound down, the secretary of state remained unmoved: "With all respect, this issue is being put in a hopelessly abstract manner because the issue isn't between democracy and non-democracy." The man who helped topple the government of Chile added: "We conduct foreign policy here, not domestic policy. We don't muck around with other countries. Now before we change course, I want to hear overpowering reasons why we should." Kissinger concluded: "We work with whoever is in power as long as they are not anti-American." The U.S. would not confront Ioannides. Instead, Kissinger in June 1974 supported additional arms sales to the junta. A few weeks later Ioannides, in an unusual personal message, informed Tasca that he intended to take a hard line with both the Turks and Makarios, signaling a radical shift in Greek policy.[57] Kissinger soon had ample reasons to regret his decision to continue U.S. support for the Greek dictatorship.

8

A PERFECT STORM : CYPRUS, 1967–1974

> The stakes are high: the overall strategic interests of the US (and the Alliance), the facilities for the Sixth Fleet, the risk of Greek-Turkish conflict.
> — Ambassador Carl Barkman, 1974

> In failing to finalize an agreement on the basis of the results of the 1967–1974 negotiations . . . we Greek [Cypriots]s were our worst enemies.
> — Glaufkos Klerides, 1990

In a 1957 letter to Egyptian president Gamal Abdel Nasser, Greek prime minister Constantine Karamanlis claimed that Cyprus was not the only or necessarily the most important element in Greece's foreign policy. Improving relations with its communist Balkan neighbors, entry into the European Economic Community, achieving national security through membership in the Atlantic alliance, protection of diaspora communities abroad, and dealing with a complex set of problems posed by its powerful Anatolian neighbor, Turkey, were among the critical issues facing the Greek state. Nevertheless, from 1955 onward, Cyprus was the center of Greece's foreign policy, and this issue complicated efforts to achieve most of its other critical international objectives. In concentrating on the Cyprus issue, Greece's political leaders lost a good deal of control over their national foreign policy to the Cypriot ethnarch, Makarios III. By signing the London-Zurich agreements, Karamanlis reasserted Greece's control over its foreign policy. However, the prize of immediate enosis was too tantalizing for his successors. In his frantic efforts to secure enosis in the summer of 1964, George Papandreou handed a large measure of control over Greek policy back to Makarios. Papandreou and his successor, Stephanos Stephanopoulos, who both insisted Athens must direct a combined Greek-Greek Cypriot strategy, tried to regain leverage by sending a large force of Greek soldiers to the island and by placing all Greek and Greek Cypriot forces under the command of George Grivas. In doing so, they created another, quite unpredictable independent power center on the island. Grivas's principal objectives were to unseat Makarios and to force the

Turkish Cypriot community to accept Greek Cypriot dominance by whatever means necessary. Not surprisingly, Makarios's reaction was to treat Athens as a threat. Mutual mistrust between Makarios and the government in Athens meant that Greek policy in Cyprus frequently was in total conflict with that of the Greek Cypriot leader. The two sides spent as much time manipulating each other as making common cause against Turkey. Grivas constituted a wild card, operating largely outside of anyone's control at the head of joint military forces. All three sides claimed to speak for the united will of Hellenism.[1]

The Colonels inherited a dysfunctional Cyprus policy and made it worse. Makarios initially seemed to believe he would be able to work out a modus vivendi with the ultranationalists who had seized power in Athens. He was quickly disabused of this notion. Like their predecessors, the Colonels were committed to securing enosis as quickly as possible and were alarmed at the archbishop's success in maintaining Cypriot independence. Within six months of seizing power, and less than a month after Papadopoulos pledged to work with Makarios's government, the Colonels held a summit meeting with Turkey in an effort to resolve the Cyprus issue without reference to the archbishop.[2] The summit failed embarrassingly. The Turks rejected Greek offers to return to the Acheson proposals as the basis of a settlement. Their territorial and political demands were far greater than in 1964. Rebuffed in its initial diplomatic efforts, the junta would continue to follow a dual-track policy mapped out by the Papandreou and Stephanopoulos governments: seek a modus vivendi with Turkey that would permit enosis, even at the cost of territorial concessions, and simultaneously undermine Makarios. The difference was in the methods Athens was ready to use to achieve enosis. Unrestrained by democratic institutions like parliament, and manipulating an already aroused public opinion through the press, the Colonels did not shrink from using force to eliminate Makarios. Ultimately, the junta's attack on another Hellenic state destroyed remaining Greek Cypriot support for enosis and consolidated Cypriot independence.

OUR S.O.B.

As the Colonels embarked on their effort to destroy Makarios, U.S. policy was completing its conversion to grudging acceptance of Makarios as the leader of an independent state. After the failure of the Acheson mediation, American officials decided to take a back seat and give discreet private support to continued Greek-Turkish talks over a deal permitting enosis. Whenever the two sides appeared to make progress, however, Makarios exercised his veto over Greek diplomacy. From the U.S. perspective, a negotiated settlement ending in enosis was highly unlikely. Makarios's flirtation with the Soviet Union, which actively supported independence for Cyprus and ardently opposed enosis, reinforced his already strong position. Warned by the Acheson experience, the United States had no interest in using its diplomatic capital to openly back a highly improbable Greek-Turkish deal that would drive the Cypriot leader into greater dependence on the Soviets.[3]

The November–December 1967 Greek-Turkish crisis over Cyprus took the United States a long step further toward accepting an independent Cyprus as the solution that best favored its interests. Not surprisingly, the crisis was the work of Grivas. The chief of Greek and Greek Cypriot forces utilized a minor incident to attack the Turkish village enclaves at St. Hillarion and Kophinou as part of his program of slicing away the Turkish Cypriots' already limited power and autonomy. Grivas's attacks provoked Turkey to seek a showdown with the junta. The United States, whose key regional interest was keeping both Greece and Turkey inside the NATO camp, intervened with a high-level mediation team led by presidential envoy Cyrus Vance. The Vance mission initially concentrated on working out a deal between Athens and Ankara that involved a military stand-down by Turkey in exchange for Greece making a humiliating withdrawal of most of its Cyprus military force and recalling Grivas. Once this essential preliminary agreement was out of the way, Vance headed for Nicosia to try to win Makarios's cooperation. The Cypriot president was quite pleased with an agreement that would remove both Grivas and the threat posed by the large concentration of Greek troops on the island, but he wanted more: the complete withdrawal of both the Greek and Turkish contingents created under the London-Zurich agreements. The Cypriot president was bidding for a diplomatic trifecta: getting rid of the junta's forces, driving the Turks off the island, and breaching the London-Zurich accords. After repeated efforts to craft a compromise failed, Vance won Makarios's agreement not to interfere with the Greek-Turkish settlement and to shelve the issue of non-Cypriot forces on the island pending the U.N. secretary-general's effort to expand the role of U.N. peacekeepers on Cyprus (UNFICYP) to include their disarmament.[4]

Both the tone and tactics adopted by the United States during and after the crisis showed that Washington understood the importance of bringing Makarios fully into the arrangements. In part, this desire to work directly with Makarios was a reaction to the inability of Athens to control the archbishop. It also reflected a U.S. belief that Turkey would attack Cyprus if Makarios continued to operate without restraints. Above all, the United States understood that it lacked leverage: "[The] problem all along with Makarios has been that [the] U.S. does not have much of a handle on him. We have no economic or military aid program, and communications facilities, for which we are to pay rent, are distinctly to our advantage." Moreover, after four years of U.S. actions to prevent Turkish invasions, Makarios was convinced that he could always rely on American intervention to protect him. He breezily told the U.S. envoy that he "had slept while Vance worked in Ankara, confident that nothing would happen." Disabusing Makarios of this confidence proved extremely difficult.[5]

The United States, of course, had certain advantages. It stopped cold Makarios's efforts to obtain weapons from the Soviet Union, most notably in March 1965. Both Greek Cypriot and American leaders knew that the Soviet support for Cyprus was hedged by Russian eagerness to conclude a special arrangement with Turkey. Moreover, U.S. intelligence enjoyed a complex but special relationship with Makarios's government. The Cypriot president, who was as addicted as most Greeks to a conspiratorial worldview, looked the other way as the CIA ran various intelligence operations from the British sovereign base areas and the National Security Agency conducted its eavesdropping activities. His interior minister, the ultranationalist Polykarpos Georkadjis, cooperated intensely with long-standing U.S. efforts to create anticommunist Cypriot political parties. Makarios sought credit with Washington to solidify his government against challenges from both Athens and Ankara.[6]

Dealing with the archbishop was frustrating. His beliefs closely reflected those of his countrymen. In December 1966 outgoing British high commissioner Sir David Hunt commented that "Cypriots regard their island as if it were the center of a pre-Copernican universe," were outright contemptuous of Greeks, and "enjoy the spectacle of their president putting his foot on the neck of the Greek government."[7] Three years later, Hunt's departing successor, C. E. Costar, used his valedictory telegram to warn that renewed violence on the island would likely provoke a disaster: "The people of Cyprus are charming, intelligent, and hospitable. But they are too narrowly concerned about their own political problem whose solution is not made easier by their love of hard bargaining for its own sake and their tendency to reach firmly held convictions on inadequate and unverified premises often emotional in genesis." Makarios "has one guiding principle: to ensure a Greek Cyprus in which the Turks, if they survive at all, shall be reduced to the position of a politically powerless minority." An economy that, against all odds, flourished in the midst of civil war impeded the "deflation of the [Greek] Cypriots' idea of their own importance." In the end, Costar predicted, they would pay a high price for their hubris and the skillful but self-defeating maneuvering of their leader.[8]

Makarios's chief negotiator and sometime political ally, Glaufkos Klerides, agreed with this analysis. While Makarios stubbornly insisted on reducing the political status of the Turkish Cypriots, the internal unity of the Greek Cypriot community dissolved over the issue of enosis as the junta stepped up its efforts to widen this breach and isolate or eliminate the archbishop.[9]

From Washington's viewpoint, divisions between Greek Cypriots seemed much less important than the fact that the Greek and Turkish Cypriot communities began direct negotiations. Greece's foreign minister, Panagiotis Pipinelis, laid the groundwork for direct talks immediately after the Vance mediation. Pipinelis, who wanted to improve strained relations with Ankara, proposed joint sponsorship of intercommunal talks to a receptive Turkish government. Pipinelis's plan offered both nations the opportunity to strengthen control over their respective Cypriot ethnic communities and laid groundwork for their agreement to a final settlement on Cyprus that the Greeks assumed would be enosis. Overcoming Makarios's resistance was difficult. The proposed deal would require concessions to both the Greek government and Turkish Cypriots and simultaneously would lay the basis for the Cypriot president's ultimate replacement by a Greek provincial administrator. Nevertheless, talks eventually began in Lebanon in June 1968. American officials recognized that a wide gap separated the positions of the two ethnic communities but were relieved that intercommunal negotiations finally were under way.[10]

Whatever slim chances existed that the talks would promote greater cooperation between Athens and Nicosia evaporated in August 1968, when Alexander Panagoulis, an antijunta Greek, attempted to assassinate Papadopoulos. Subsequent Greek investigations established incriminating connections between the would-be assassin, Cypriot interior minister Georkadjis, and Makarios's personal physician, political ally, and militia chief, Vassos Lyssarides. More embarrassingly, the attempt took place on the day that Klerides was in Athens outlining the Greek Cypriot views on intercommunal talks to Pipinelis. Makarios, who appears to have known nothing of the plot, made a hasty trip to Athens to smooth over the incident. The archbishop seized the opportunity to dismiss the dangerous Georkadjis, but the price was a humiliating retreat before a Greek government's demands. Greek Cypriot involvement in the assassination attempt was an open invitation for the regime in Athens to respond in kind. Restraint was not one of the hallmarks of the junta.[11]

In January 1969, the Nixon administration inherited a complex situation. On the one hand, the intercommunal talks were going forward, creating optimism about an ultimate solution. Greece and Turkey also were discussing terms for a solution to Cyprus rather than confronting each other over the island. Makarios's decision both to seek a renewal of his own mandate and elect a new parliament, while angering Turkish Cypriots, gave a major impetus to a long-term U.S. objective: the creation of anticommunist political parties, including a coalition led by Georkadjis, Klerides, and former EOKA fighter Tassos Papadopoulos (the Unified Party). On the other hand, deteriorating relations between Athens and Nicosia meant that Greece had even less influence over the archbishop's strategic decisions regarding the intercommunal talks and that it encouraged Greek Cypriot extremists' efforts to create anti-Makarios paramilitary bands. A January 1970 INR memorandum warned that Greek Cypriot terrorism against Makarios's government was turning Nicosia into a Cypriot version of the wild west.[12]

Nixon and Kissinger regarded Makarios as the primary guarantee of overall regional stability. His replacement, especially if achieved by violence, would likely bring about a conflict between Greece and Turkey and open the door to Soviet involvement on the island. In order to prevent war between NATO allies and to contain Soviet influence in the region, the United States began to court Makarios. While an embittered George Ball publicly labeled Makarios an "s.o.b" (1969), the practical Kissinger felt that the United States had to rely on this particular s.o.b. to keep the lid on the eastern Mediterranean. "For all his faults—and they are many—only he commands the overwhelming popular support that is a stabilizing factor within the Greek Cypriot community and a base from which compromise and flexibility are at least possible."[13]

In line with this pragmatic, if scarcely enthusiastic, appraisal of Makarios, the United States sent a highly capable diplomat, David Popper, to Nicosia in 1969 to replace the veteran Cyprus hand and Makarios advocate Taylor Belcher. The new ambassador, who carried a great deal more weight in Washington than his predecessor, cracked down on the CIA, ultimately removing its anti-Makarios station chief, Eric Neff, as a signal to the archbishop of Nixon administration backing. The CIA was carefully monitoring its old ally, Georgkadjis, and discovered that the former interior minister was actively plotting with Greek intelligence to eliminate the archbishop. Armed with a continuing flow of intelligence from the CIA, Popper forwarded information on the plot to a traveling Makarios.[14]

This cooperation reached its apogee in October 1970, when Makarios made his second White House visit. Nixon opened the conversation by assuring Makarios: "We understand your foreign policy of technical neutrality." Taking his clue from this display of sophistication, Makarios assured his host that nonaligned Cyprus was, in fact, pro-Western. He promised that the Orthodox island would not fall under the control of AKEL. Nixon picked up on this to piously insist that religion constituted the principle bulwark against the communist menace. After telling the U.S. president that he would continue to keep communists away from the levers of power, Makarios modestly explained: "I don't rely on the army or the police, my strength is my goodness . . . and the fact I don't particularly want to continue as president makes me stronger." Nixon insisted that he wanted "very close relations," and these two disciples of Machiavelli closed their love fest with a final volley of compliments.[15]

Makarios left Washington without winning any support for his position on the intercommunal talks. Washington, London, and Athens shared a common desire to see the talks wrapped up as quickly as possible, though for different reasons. Makarios, on the other hand, continued to oppose concessions to the Turkish Cypriots above all on local government, in spite of the other side's willingness to find a compromise. By stringing out the talks, the archbishop frustrated Athens's primary objective: laying the basis for enosis by cooperation with the Turks. Throughout 1971 the archbishop resisted advice from all three states as well as from the United Nations and his own chief negotiator to abandon his rigid position on municipal government and settle with the Turkish Cypriots. Athens' patience snapped in August 1971, and the junta decided to apply a hot poker to Makarios in the form of Grivas. The ex-EOKA chief was permitted to leave Greece secretly and return to his homeland. For months, the old guerrilla leader lay low, reorganizing his followers into a new secret army, EOKA-B. Makarios cooperatively ignored Grivas's presence on the island and even opened up a line of communication. Still, the mere presence of Grivas cranked up tensions among Greek Cypriots. Thomas Boyatt, the State Department's Cyprus desk officer warned: "Ten years of experience with the Cyprus problem demonstrates one constant: when the parties to the dispute are not negotiating, the probability of violence increases exponentially." A few months later the British high commissioner alerted the Foreign Office that the intercommunal talks had run "into the sand," which was encouraging the Turkish Cypriots to seek a confrontation and simultaneously providing the Greeks, Turks, and Grivas with an excuse to take a more active role in the next stage of the island's drama.[16] Makarios was losing control.

DUELING

During the winter of 1972, the Papadopoulos junta maneuvered to replace Makarios. Greek Cypriot popular support for enosis had largely evaporated. But the junta could count on the cooperation of a "disloyal opposition," now concentrated around Grivas. This minority included not only political extremists, many from EOKA, but also the three metropolitan bishops of the island, who had turned on the archbishop. This group was ready to use any means to overthrow the archbishop president and lead Cyprus into union with Greece. Junta plans called for utilizing these fanatics to liquidate Makarios and then to neutralize Grivas as part of a final deal with Turkey that would deliver enosis against the will of the Greek Cypriot majority.[17]

Makarios provided a case for action against his government by secretly importing Czech arms for his militias. The Greek Cypriot National Guard was firmly in the hands of its Greek officers, whose loyalty was to Athens. Grivas was armed and ready to act. Makarios, not unnaturally, wished to defend both his government and his life, and again sought weapons from the Soviet bloc. In doing so, he provided the junta with a plausible justification for action. Intervention, Papadopoulos explained to NATO allies, would head off a communist-dominated Cypriot government. Tasca dutifully chimed in to support the junta's demand for action to restrain Makarios. Kissinger was tempted by a policy of nonintervention that would leave Athens with a free hand.[18]

Popper, however, had other ideas, as did the professional staff of the National Security Council. Both warned that any policy that encouraged or tolerated enosis, even in the form of a Greek-Turkish agreement to divide the island, would work against U.S. interests. Makarios remained key to regional stability. Moreover, accepting a junta move against the Cypriot leader was very risky. It could provoke a civil war and offer the Soviet Union the chance to intervene. "It is perfectly legitimate to look at the Cyprus problem in balance of power terms, but we had better be sure we have thought through the risks of a Greek power play directed against Makarios."[19]

As in past crises, Makarios played the U.S. card. On February 14, 1972, he instructed Klerides to approach Popper and inform the American ambassador that a Greek-inspired coup would commence within hours. The Cypriot president counted on the United States to call off the Colonels. Washington delivered. Tasca warned Papadopoulos against military intervention. Meanwhile, the embassy in Nicosia pounded home to senior American officials the dangers to U.S. interests of any move against Makarios. "Round one" went to the archbishop, Popper commented, although the situation remained very unstable. Both sides needed to step back, a maneuver that would force the archbishop to make concessions.[20]

Under pressure from the major regional powers, the United Nations, the United Kingdom, and the United States, Makarios backed down. He surrendered the Czech arms to U.N. control and met one of the junta's minimal demands by firing his foreign minister, Spyros Kyprianou. He rejected the demands of the internal opposition, refusing calls from Grivas and the bishops for his resignation as head of state. The Greek Cypriot position in the intercommunal talks was weakened. Both the Turkish Cypriots and Turkish government pushed harder for concessions, including recognition of the legal equality of the Turkish community. The junta meanwhile repeated the experience of earlier Greek governments. Having sent Grivas back to do its bidding, it lost control of the EOKA chief, who extended his personal power over other proenosis extremists. The low level but increasingly bloody civil war continued between the extremists and the vast majority of Cypriots who supported Makarios. The Cypriot government's effort to repress EOKA-B was hampered by a lack of arms. Neither the British nor the Americans were willing to provide Makarios with the type of support he craved. The archbishop's refusal to recognize or abide by the London-Zurich agreements meant that Britain would not supply him. The United States, like Britain, was not eager to see Makarios fall but also wanted to maintain close ties with both Athens and Ankara. Kissinger instructed his subordinates that all matters concerned with Cyprus be cleared with him. U.S. policy was mired in contradiction: it wanted to arrive at a solution that would be acceptable to both Cypriot communities as well as Athens and Ankara, a practical impossibility as long as Makarios maintained his objectives.[21]

Makarios needed to show those tactical skills he had displayed so often in the past but uncharacteristically dug in. The archbishop was quite capable of fending off the challenge to his position mounted by rebel bishops but refused to offer the compromises on the intercommunal talks that would hold the Greek and Turkish governments at bay. Makarios's inner circle appears to have reinforced his refusal to compromise. Nikos Kranidiotis, a Makarios loyalist and Cypriot ambassador to Athens, recalled that when intercommunal talks started the Greek side controlled 95 percent of the island's territory and 50 percent of the Turkish Cypriot population. Holding this strong hand, Makarios saw little reason to offer concessions that would only strengthen his opponent's position. The Cypriot president, faithfully mirroring majority Greek opinion, was interested in cutting away the remaining independence of Turkish Cypriots, not rewarding their tenacity. Compromise was not a part of the postindependence Cypriot political tradition. Facing a dangerous challenge from a group of Greek Cypriots who aimed to destroy him both politically and physically, the Cypriot president took no moves that might undercut his popular support. Feeling the need to reaffirm his legitimacy, Makarios rejected advice from Klerides and called presidential elections in 1973, recognizing that this action would further alienate the besieged Turkish population and solidify Rauf Denktash's "provisional" administration. Intransigence, ironically, accelerated the seepage of Makarios's personal authority among both Cypriots and foreign governments. His enemies in both Athens and Ankara were emboldened, as were his Cypriot opponents.[22]

As long as Papadopoulos remained in power and had to negotiate his own difficult path through the challenges of his more extremist colleagues, Makarios could fend off the most dangerous external threat. The Greek dictator's move toward the restoration of parliamentary-style government prompted Makarios to fly to Athens to test the waters. He discovered that the new government was as committed as its predecessors to achieving enosis by means of a deal with Turkey. Papadopoulos's fall, nonetheless, created widespread uneasiness among Greek Cypriots. The devil they knew was gone, and a much more dangerous group now controlled the Greek Cypriot National Guard. Makarios's internal enemies rejoiced and stepped up their preparations for a final confrontation.[23]

THE PERFECT STORM

In less than a year the new Greek dictatorship and its allies on Cyprus would create a disaster for the Greek Cypriot community. The real issue is how much assistance they received from other actors, to wit: Makarios, Turkey, the United States, and the United Kingdom. The question is clouded by a lack of archival materials for Greece, Cyprus, and Turkey and by the proliferation of conspiracy theories that attempt to explain and excuse the actions of some of the principal actors, above all Greek Cypriot.

The tragedy of 1974 commenced with the simultaneous unraveling of the governments of Cyprus, Greece, and the United States. With Ioannides in power, Greece had only the façade of a public administration. The formal government was without power, the bureaucracy was dissolving, and the military was divided among various factions. Ioannides ruled largely in isolation. The situation was Kafkaesque and intensely frustrating to foreign diplomats trying to deal with Greece's phantom authority. Makarios, while formally head of state, was under siege from the Greek Cypriot National Guard, the Greek military mission, EOKA-B, and an extremist press, all under control of the one part of the Greek government that continued to function effectively: its intelligence service. Richard Nixon's isolation in power accelerated during the fall of 1973, after he fired the special prosecutor charged with investigating the break-in at opposition Democratic Party headquarters and public outrage forced the embattled president to appoint another prosecutor. During the winter and spring of 1973–74, ever more information of Nixon's improprieties leaked out. The U.S. Congress carefully set in motion the archaic mechanisms of impeachment to force the president from power. Nixon lost control of the government, and his health crumbled. Despite repetitious official claims that its mechanisms were working smoothly, the Nixon administration was paralyzed. Meanwhile, Britain's newly elected Labour government lacked authority. Foreign Secretary James Callaghan continued a fifteen-year-old British policy of attempting to distance his nation from involvement with Cyprus while maneuvering to replace a largely discredited prime minister, Harold Wilson.[24]

Cyprus's internal problems elicited little concern from U.S. officials. The Nixon administration's Cyprus policy was centered on the promotion of intercommunal talks to prevent violence between Greeks and Turks. Senior U.S. officials consistently downplayed or ignored the threat to stability created by tensions between Greek Cypriot factions. In March 1974, the Soviet Union raised the issue with the United States, suggesting talks on the issue. Kissinger asked his senior deputy for the region, Rodger Davies, if there was "any truth" to Soviet claims. "No," Davies replied, and dismissed reports of plots against Makarios as a Soviet "ploy." Kissinger decided not to follow up on the issue. At exactly this time the archbishop was laying the groundwork for a confrontation with the junta over its support for his internal opponents.[25]

U.S. attention was briefly focused on the Greek-Turkish clash over petroleum exploration rights in the Aegean but faded as the crisis lessened. Nor did U.S. officials react to a growing body of intelligence that showed that Ioannides was preparing to move against Makarios. By late June the U.S. embassies in Athens and Nicosia were signaling that trouble was likely. Tasca, an insistent critic of the new Greek regime, warned that Ioannides detested Makarios and lacked the sophistication to realize that replacing Makarios with a proenosis Cypriot would trigger Turkish intervention. Both the Greek and Cypriot desks at the State Department suggested a vigorous and direct approach to the Greek dictator to head off trouble. Tasca, however, detested Ioannides and preferred to meet with the powerless civilian leaders of Greece, with the figurehead president, General Phaedon Gizikis, and with the archbishop of Athens, Seraphim, rather than pass the message directly to the "policeman" who ran the country. Kissinger and his chief lieutenants acquiesced in this decision.[26]

Kissinger's lack of attention largely derived from his domestic political problems. In March 1974 a federal grand jury named Nixon an "unindicted coconspirator" in the Watergate plot. The secret jury bill of indictment quickly leaked to the press. In April the president began a tug-of-war over the release of his tape-recorded conversations with both Congress and the courts. Kissinger escaped Washington for a grueling month of shuttle diplomacy in the Middle East during May. He returned to the U.S. capital in early June to accompany Nixon on two long trips abroad. During the first, on June 10, the secretary of state threatened to resign in response to press inquiries into his involvement in a legally dubious and morally indefensible wiretapping of his own staff and reporters. Nixon returned to Washington on June 21 and checked into Walter Reed army hospital with a potentially life-threatening case of phlebitis. On July 9 the House Impeachment Committee released its damming transcriptions of Nixon's taped conversations. Three days later it followed up with the release of over three hundred pages of evidence implicating the president in an illegal cover-up. Nixon was finished, and only the moment of his departure remained in question. Kissinger's career was hanging by a string. In addition to wiretapping, Kissinger's involvement in the coup in Chile remained highly controversial. His Vietnam diplomacy was under attack from both left and right, as was détente with the Soviet Union, the centerpiece of Nixon-Kissinger foreign policy. Both the secretary of defense and the CIA director were sniping at their politically wounded colleague. The newly installed vice president, Gerald Ford, might find it politically advantageous to dismiss the secretary of state as soon as he assumed power from Nixon. Kissinger tried to underline his continued "indispensability" in power by successfully guiding Nixon toward resignation.[27]

Cyprus was scarcely the top item on Kissinger's crowded foreign policy agenda. Makarios's behavior in retrospect is more puzzling than Kissinger's. "Makarios," one U.S. diplomat observed, "being a man of cunning and reason himself, assumed too much reason and too little ethnocentricity on the part of the junta.... He taunted their smallness" and then challenged them. The archbishop told the Israeli ambassador that he had no fear of cornering the rulers in Athens. They would act rationally because "they are weak." The Cypriot president, as usual, was staking his future on the American card. He was sailing toward a confrontation with Greece that was likely to prompt intervention by Turkey. The U.S. role, restraining both states, was, as always, critical to Makarios's calculations and success. Yet, the diplomatic credibility of the American state stood at a historic low. After a series of highly controversial Nixon administration activities in Latin America and Africa, the U.S. congress finally summoned up its courage and began to impose restraints on Kissinger's ability to conduct foreign policy. Much of the world was watching in amazement as the United States prepared to unceremoniously oust its national leader. Apparently neither Makarios nor his advisers were included among them. Clearly the archbishop failed to draw the evident logical inference that a crisis of the magnitude of Watergate would severely curtail American power and attention. The Greek Cypriot leadership was a prisoner to its ethnocentricity. On July 2, 1974, Makarios met with his cabinet and outlined the text of an explosive letter he planned to send the following day to Greek president Gizikis. In his communication, Makarios accused the Athens government of trying to kill him and demanded the removal of its officers from the island. The Cypriot leader had thrown down the gauntlet and few doubted the reaction from Athens would be furious and immediate.[28]

In spite of their quite precise reading of Ioannides, Greek Cypriot leaders from Makarios down acted as though nothing would occur. They too ignored numerous intelligence warnings during the next two weeks. Meanwhile, the "official" government of Greece continued to act in complete ignorance of what Ioannides was planning. Greece's ambassador to Cyprus, Efstathios Lagakos, returned to Athens to meet with the Greek prime minister and foreign minister on July 12. The ambassador pleaded for cutting off aid to the EOKA-B in order to calm the situation on the island. His superiors insisted that no aid was being given to the anti-Makarios extremists. They could find no mention of support in the printed national budget. The prime minister concluded the meeting with the suggestion that they talk again after the weekend.[29]

TILTING TO GREECE

Official inertia in Athens, Nicosia, and Washington, the product of severe political crises in all three capitals, opened the way to action for two men who were prepared to exploit this weakness: Ioannides and Turkish Prime Minister Bulent Ecevit.

Ioannides acted first. On the morning of July 15, 1974, Makarios returned to Nicosia from a weekend in the Troodos Mountains. Ironically, his car passed by the barracks of a Greek National Guard as troops were loading weapons to overthrow him. His enemies missed an excellent chance to kill the archbishop. An hour or so later tanks and infantry began moving on the presidential palace. Makarios, cool in a crisis, escaped while his bodyguard delayed the attackers and, flagging down a car, fled to the British sovereign base area. The following day, the British airlifted him off the island and on to London.

Displaying a lack of sophistication that rivaled their boldness, Ioannides's agents tapped Nikos Samson, an extremist journalist, former EOKA killer, and enosis enthusiast as Cyprus's president. The Greek-led national guard speedily gained military control of the island, but with Makarios alive the coup makers lacked legitimacy on Cyprus and abroad. Samson's installation as president was a red flag to Ankara. "The Greeks committed an unbelievably stupid move," a Turkish diplomat explained, "giving us the opportunity to solve our problems once and for all. Unlike 1964 and 1967, the United States' leverage on us was minimal. We could not be scared off by threats of the Soviet bogeyman."[30]

With the coup botched, all eyes turned to Washington. In spite of Watergate, the United States possessed the tools necessary ultimately to resolve the Cyprus crisis: influence with all the major players, a powerful military force close at hand, and major interests in seeing that the situation was settled without damage to its most important alliance. What it lacked was a statesman with a sense of his nation's real interests and an ability to lead. Over the next month Henry Kissinger compounded the errors that had plagued U.S. policy toward Greece from the beginning of the Nixon administration. His misplaced focus on the Soviet "threat" further damaged U.S. interests on the island. Incompetence, not malice, characterized his maneuvers.

When Kissinger arrived at his desk on the morning of July 15, he faced a crisis he neither needed nor wanted. Information was confused and inaccurate. Initial reports indicated that Makarios was dead. The Greeks were sending out signals of cooperation in a frantic attempt to fend off a Turkish invasion. The attention of Kissinger and his staff immediately focused on the Soviet reaction to the coup. Greek control of the island set up the possibility that a formerly nonaligned state long friendly to Russia soon could host NATO bases.[31]

Kissinger responded to warnings from the U.S. embassy in Ankara and tried to head off enosis in a message to the Greek government that declared support for an independent Cyprus. Hoping to avoid earlier mistakes, the secretary of state instructed Tasca to personally deliver this message to

Ioannides. He ignored Tasca's advice to exploit the occasion to publicly condemn Makarios's overthrow and demand the restoration of democracy in Greece.[32]

At 5:30 p.m. Kissinger began discussions with Soviet Ambassador Anatoly Dobrynin designed to find a Cyprus modus vivendi between the two great powers. Kissinger asked for confirmation of reports that the Soviet Union was offering to send its forces into Cyprus to restore "order." Dobrynin discounted the story. Kissinger insisted on being consulted before the Soviets acted, warning that the United States "would not look on it with favor" and suggesting that both sides wait until the situation in Cyprus was clearer before making any major decisions. An hour later Dobrynin called back to report that Makarios might be alive. Kissinger commented that if true, this "puts a new complexion on the situation," and he offered to coordinate action with the Soviets, assuring the Russian diplomat that the United States supported "the existing constitution" and had no intention of unilateral action. In a telephone conversation the following morning, Kissinger assured Dobrynin that neither Turkey nor Great Britain would act alone.[33]

A few minutes later, in a discussion with British Foreign Secretary Callaghan, Kissinger started to lay out his thinking about Cyprus. The U.S. secretary of state began by telling his British counterpart that he intended to continue to recognize the "existing government," apparently a reference to Makarios. "Hold on," Callaghan responded. He informed Kissinger that Makarios was leaving the island and would most likely head to New York to address the U.N. Security Council. The West should "go slow" in legitimizing Makarios. Kissinger agreed: "We won't want to have him leading an outside movement and asking for Soviet help." Callaghan then offered some advice to Kissinger: the U.S. embassy in Athens should lean on the Greek junta to remove its officers from the island. Kissinger wanted to wait: "Once there is a clear outcome, fine. But if there is a civil war, we would be getting involved." Kissinger added that "my main concern is to keep outside powers out of this." He tried to reduce the distance between U.S. and British positions by promising to push the Greeks on the officers issue, noting that the United States had insisted on a Greek declaration of its intentions, had stated its opposition to enosis to Athens, and was working with Turkey to avoid intervention.[34]

The conversation with Callaghan revealed key elements of Kissinger's strategy: keep the negotiations and final decision on the island's fate within a tight circle, the Guarantor Powers and the United States, cooperate closely with the British to achieve this aim, restrain the junta and the Turks. In the meantime, the United States would play for time and frustrate Makarios's efforts, as well as those of the Soviets, to involve the Security Council or, as one senior NSC official explained to Nixon, carry out "a U.S. holding action while events sort themselves out." The British and Europeans, Kissinger complained, agreed on strategy but lacking means to carry it out, demanded that the United States act for them. He would not play along.[35]

Kissinger continued his stalling tactic throughout July 17. Late that afternoon he called Nixon, who was holed up at San Clemente, California, to seek approval for the policy that was already evolving. [Kissinger] "The problem is [that] the Europeans have taken a united position that Makarios ought to be brought back and they want us to bring pressure on the Greeks. My worry is that Makarios now has to lean on the communists [AKEL] and Eastern Bloc. All our evidence is that the opposition is in total control of the island. My recommendation is that . . . we work for a compromise in which neither Makarios [n]or the other guy [Samson] takes over. They want us to rake the Greeks but if they get overthrown then that will jeopardize our position." The secretary of state wanted to slow down progress toward a Makarios solution and prevent the fall of the junta in Greece. Replacing Ioannides with another group of military men would drag Greece toward the communist bloc, meaning that the Cyprus "coup will have shifted the balance to the left." To head off these threats, Kissinger decided to dispatch an envoy to Europe to delay action and round up support. Nixon approved the reasoning and the policy.[36]

Meanwhile, evidence was mounting that Greece and Turkey were on a collision course. The U.S. embassy in Athens warned that the Greeks might seek to infiltrate more troops into Cyprus and the following day added that the junta would not reduce its officer corps on the island. About 11 P.M. July 16, another message from Athens provided a dramatic glimpse of Ioannides, his objectives, and his lack of realism. The CIA station chief read the Greek dictator a U.S. message calling for restraint: "The general literally blew up, jumped up, backed up, knocked over a table and uttered a strong obscenity. He continued that one day Kissinger makes public statements regarding noninterference in Greek internal affairs and a few weeks later . . . threatens interference." The (Greek Cypriot) majority, Ioannides continued, would make the final decision on the island's future. The coup of July 15 had been the work of Cypriot nationalists, and Turkey would not oppose their will. Removing the "deviate" [sic] Makarios opened the way for a final settlement on Cyprus. However, "if Makarios succeeded in kicking [the] Greeks out of Cyprus, what could keep him [from] thinking he could not kick the junta out of Greece?" Makarios was "still alive, but who cares?" The archbishop was a powerless fugitive. Without international support he would remain one. Ioannides expected to get the Turks' assent to the fait accompli on Cyprus by offering talks on the full range of Greek-Turkish issues and sharing exploration of the Aegean seabed. He added that he planned to induce Ankara to evacuate the Turkish Cypriots (presumably to Turkey) after a year.[37]

Word from Turkey was equally disturbing. Ankara judged that unless immediately reversed the Cyprus coup was a success that would set the stage for enosis and the inevitable deterioration of the position of an already besieged Turkish Cypriot community. Turkey would intervene unless a "constitutional government" with or without Makarios took control, Greek officers left the island, and the Turkish Cypriots were given control of a corridor to the sea.[38]

Joseph Sisco, Kissinger's special envoy, had to head off a Turkish invasion and preserve the Greek dictatorship with virtually nothing effective to offer Ankara. Moreover, Kissinger's insistence that Makarios was compromised as well as Ioannides's refusal to consider restoring the archbishop to power meant that the United States needed to find a "third guy" acceptable to both Greece and Turkey. For the next forty-eight hours, the U.S. officials pursued the "Klerides alternative," presenting the ambitious president of the Cypriot house of representatives as the constitutionally sanctioned interim successor to Makarios. If, as was likely, the Greeks failed to cooperate, the United States was prepared to abandon them and tilt toward Turkey, standing by as Ankara used military force to oust Samson and accept the ultimate outcome: double enosis, partition, or an intercommunal solution imposed by Turkey.[39]

As chief of U.S. diplomacy, Henry Kissinger preferred loyal subordinates to independent-minded collaborators. His senior lieutenants, whatever their individual competence, were above all yes-men who carried out policy with a minimum of dissent. Professor Kissinger kept them in line with crude psychological ploys: subjecting them to his sarcasm, playing one off another, belittling them to others. In the first days of the Cyprus crisis, the weaknesses of this management style became evident. In Athens, Henry Tasca displayed a sulky unwillingness to carry out his instructions. He continued to dodge direct contact with Ioannides, presumably as a means of undermining the regime Kissinger was trying to save. In Nicosia, rookie ambassador Rodger Davies, a loyal Kissinger associate, was totally at sea, recommending that Washington recognize Samson while Kissinger bent all efforts to convince both foreign governments and the Democrats in Congress that he would never back the coup leader. Sisco, meanwhile, was clearly uncomfortable with the mediation mission that he believed was doomed to fail. Only Kissinger's repeated direct orders prevented his own emissary from returning. At home the State Department's professional diplomats were showing signs of deep discontent with a policy that appeared to cut the United States off from its allies, impede a peaceful settlement, and bind Washington to repressive regimes in Athens and Nicosia. This dissent would widen and deepen as the crisis continued.[40]

The revolt was engendered by Kissinger's concentration on short-term goals. Rather than consider the longer-term interest of the United States in securing the restoration of democracy in Greece and Cyprus, Kissinger pursued a policy of frustrating presumed Soviet objectives. By vetoing the restoration of Makarios, Kissinger, who fancied himself the "kingmaker" for Cyprus, overturned the Nixon administration's previous policy of backing the archbishop as a bulwark against both internal and foreign communism.[41]

TILTING TOWARD TURKEY

July 19, 1974, was decisive for the future of Cyprus. At the United Nations, Makarios and the junta's representative dramatically clashed in front of the world. The Turks put the final touches on their invasion plans. And Henry Kissinger decided to abandon the junta, accepting a Turkish invasion of Cyprus as the least damaging outcome to the crisis.

By the morning of July 19, Kissinger, visiting Nixon at San Clemente, faced ample evidence that Turkey had tired of his delaying effort. Without major concessions from the Greeks an invasion was certain. Sisco, who had spent the morning in a fruitless attempt to extract a dramatic offer from the Greeks, was in the air headed for Ankara, carrying a new proposal that did not meet the Turks' basic demands. "I have the distinct impression that no matter what is done ... the Turks [will] see it as ideal to achiev[ing] by military intervention a long-standing objective, namely double enosis." Kissinger instructed Sisco to offer a package of U.S. pledges to reinforce Athens's meager offer and to urge Ecevit to avoid action until diplomacy had run its course. The secretary of state promised in return that he would not "let them down on this issue."[42]

Kissinger, in fact, was increasingly isolated. Opposition with the State Department was intense, and embarrassing press leaks continued throughout the day. Senate majority leader Mike Mansfield (D-Mont.) told Kissinger that the use of U.S. forces was not a policy option under any conditions, further reducing the secretary's margins for maneuver. The British were fed up with his efforts to stall discussions at the United Nations. The Greek junta rejected his suggestions for a radical change of course—abandoning Samson for Klerides and accepting Makarios's ultimate restoration—as a last opportunity to save their regime. At 7:30 P.M. July 19 (Washington time), press spokesman Robert McCloskey informed the secretary that the Turks would move that evening. Kissinger ordered the weary Sisco to Athens to persuade the Greeks not to fight back. McCloskey suggested turning to the U.N. "No, no, God no!" the secretary responded. The U.S. would concentrate on restraining the Greek junta. Talking with Nixon a few minutes later, Kissinger confirmed that an invasion was under way but confidently assured the besieged president that his diplomatic moves had neutralized "liberal" opposition by aligning the United States with Turkey.[43] The secretary of state's political sensors had failed him. Congressional opposition to Greece was directed against the junta. As it collapsed, the U.S. Greek Orthodox Church, aided by Greek American congressmen, academics, and many political liberals, rallied around the cause of Greece and the Greek Cypriots against the Turkish "invaders."

Throughout the crisis, Kissinger tended to take Turkish assurances on face value. In accepting the invasion, he relied on Ankara's guarantees that its forces would stabilize the situation and that the Turkish government was prepared for a return to the status quo. He expected a rapid Turkish withdrawal. Naively he trusted Turkish assurances that the invasion would take place without the use of force and was briefly taken aback when the Turkish army shot its way ashore, using aerial close support against suspected Greek positions. At 9:35 P.M. (Washington time), CIA director William Colby dashed Kissinger's hopes for a bloodless occupation, informing him that both Greek army and Cypriot national guard units would resist and adding that major combat was likely on the Greek-Turkish border in Thrace unless the junta could be restrained. McCloskey prepared instructions for Sisco to lean on Athens to avoid war. Kissinger and his press deputy then discussed a public statement blaming the junta for the Cyprus disaster. The tilt toward Turkey was complete.[44]

By the early morning of July 20, Kissinger's State Department was fully engaged in cutting short a war in the eastern Mediterranean. However, the U.S. secretary of state had lost the initiative to the Turks. Ecevit was calling the tune and would continue to do so until Ankara achieved its objectives. Kissinger ordered Sisco to prevent the junta from going to war by any means necessary and to inform the Greeks that they must pay the price for a Cyprus settlement, including changes in the territorial status quo. In a coordinated message to Gizikis, Nixon pressed the point that only Greece could avoid war with Turkey.[45]

Ioannides responded negatively, telling Tasca that he would "declare enosis and declare war on Turkey" unless his terms were met: a ceasefire and the immediate withdrawal of Ankara's forces. However, within hours the junta pulled the rug out from under itself with a hasty and badly botched mobilization that revealed the demoralized state of the armed forces. Greece was as much at the mercy of Turkey as was Greek Cyprus. Astute Greek diplomats began working with their European counterparts to prepare for a quick transition of political power to Karamanlis, while senior Greek military officials began laying plans for removing Ioannides.[46]

While the junta dissolved, Kissinger pressed the Turks to declare a cease-fire. Throughout the day Ankara stonewalled. Ecevit cleverly defended his refusal by telling Callaghan that the junta could not be trusted and that by continuing its military offensive Turkey could bring democracy back to Greece. Meanwhile, the deeply humiliated and angry Greeks kept changing course, offering a cease-fire, then backing off. Eventually, Greek leaders recognized that they had to sign on to an immediate cease-fire. Athens had no options. It could not reinforce its forces on Cyprus and could not defend its northern borders in case of a Turkish attack. Ecevit continued to evade U.S. pressure, at one point telling Kissinger that the Greeks were "duping" him and had sent reinforcements to Cyprus. Turkish forces meanwhile advanced toward their objectives in the face of stiff and largely unexpected Greek and Greek Cypriot resistance. Once the Turks achieved their essential military objectives (July 22), Ankara agreed to a cease-fire and the immediate convocation of talks in Geneva.[47]

ABANDONING THE GREEKS

The cease-fire was, as is usual, extremely tenuous, especially in its first days. The Turks continued to probe, seeking to expand the area under their control. The junta collapsed. On July 23 the Greek military, in a confession of total bankruptcy, summoned the moderate and conservative political leaders it had turned out seven years earlier and asked them to save the nation from disaster. Kanellopoulos made an effort to reclaim leadership before Averoff guided assembled politicians to agreement on a Karamanlis government. The new prime minister made a dramatic return to Athens in the early hours of July 24. Later that day he appealed to Nixon for support in rebuilding Greek democracy and in resolving the Cyprus crisis.[48]

Whatever Nixon's views on the issue of Greek democracy, they had little weight in the calculations of the man making the decisions. Henry Kissinger's worldview was Spenglerian. He was hoping to stave off the inevitable collapse of the West. Kissinger's diplomacy was always about securing breathing space for the United States by carefully delineating spheres of influence with the Soviets. Tactical advantage, not careful consideration of longer range U.S. interest, were the staple of Nixon administration foreign policy. Kissinger accepted any sort of regime, no matter how odious, as long as it was willing to provide assistance in the effort to rein in Soviet power. In the case of Cyprus, this policy meant supporting Makarios as long as he appeared to be immune to Soviet control and trying to deal him out of a solution when, in Kissinger's judgment, the archbishop could no longer operate independently. By July 23, with Klerides installed as interim president of Cyprus, Kissinger was confident that Makarios had "had it." In the case of Greece, the policy successively was close ties with Papadopoulos, tolerating Ioannides, and casting adrift Karamanlis. In his first talk with Greece's democratic opposition leaders (July 22), Kissinger promised U.S. support for Greece's new government. That support largely consisted in persuading Ecevit to allow Karamanlis to assemble a foreign policy team before making further demands on Greece ("You are causing a lot of trouble," Kissinger admonished the Turkish prime minister.) The secretary of state's immediate objective was to get the two nations to sit down in Geneva under British mediation and work out a settlement to the Cyprus issue. Kissinger assumed that the deal would be based on major Greek concessions: Ioannides had initiated the crisis, and Turkey held the military upper hand. Democratic Greece would have to pay for the junta's mistakes.[49]

This approach aroused the opposition of Henry Tasca. The ambassador's late but sincere conversion to the cause of Greek democracy and his strong support for Karamanlis brought about a serious clash with his boss. Kissinger, for the moment, was stuck with his restive emissary in Athens. Nixon was a great admirer of Tasca and even in the midst of his own troubles had paid a glowing tribute to his man in Greece during a July 19 conversation with Kissinger. On July 24, Tasca urged Kissinger to strong-arm Turkey on Cyprus, thus providing Karamanlis's fledgling government with needed support against the threat of another Ioannides-led coup. The military police chief remained in his office, enjoyed support from a faction of younger officers, and was waiting for further setbacks in Cyprus to discredit Karamanlis and Greece's restored democracy. Kissinger's July 25 response was a bath of Cold War "realism." Greece, despite its weakness, had the responsibility of repairing the damage it had done to NATO during the previous ten days by restoring its relationship with Turkey through a "viable" Cyprus solution that froze out the Soviet influence. Tasca was to tell Karamanlis that the

United States would not offer its own plan and would back either Makarios or Klerides as Cypriot leader as long as they understood that its "support was not just a free ride."[50]

While Kissinger was laying down his policy line, Karamanlis was attempting to salvage something from the disaster created by Ioannides. He was navigating in extremely difficult waters. In the first place, Karamanlis had to save the honor of the Greek army. Humiliated by its inability to defend Greece's interests and with its officer corps divided along political and demographic lines and many of its members skeptical about democratic government, the Greek army constituted the prime minister's major preoccupation. In a July 25 address to the nation, Karamanlis stressed the need to reconcile the army and the Greek people. He appealed for national unity. Somehow, the new government had to purge the army of political radicals without further damaging its shaky morale. With Turkish troops holding part of Cyprus, Greece needed a credible military to give it leverage in the Geneva talks. Success in the talks, in turn, appeared critical to Karamanlis's overriding objective: keeping the military in its barracks as he reestablished a democratic regime in Greece.[51]

From Karamanlis's perspective, two states could play a central role in democratic stabilization: Turkey and the United States. On July 24, Ecevit established direct contacts with the Greek leader. Subsequently, Ankara offered cooperation on Cyprus but not the withdrawal of its forces, which Karamanlis believed was the key to consolidating Greek democracy. The Greek leader was counting on the United States to leverage Turkish forces off the island. From his first days in office, Karamanlis complained about Washington's lack of support. In his initial conversation with Kissinger, the prime minister pleaded for U.S. pressure on Turkey. Kissinger limited himself to a pledge to do what he could but focused on securing a complete cease-fire. The same day, however, he rejected Tasca's pleas to aid Karamanlis (and do something for the U.S. public image) by intervening to stop Turkish violations of the cease-fire, denouncing Ioannides's misgovernment, and warning the Greek army that a move against its new government would mean a total and immediate shutdown of military supplies. Kissinger ordered the ambassador to cease supporting Greek demands and to tell the Greeks to exercise "patience and restraint" since they "must bear some responsibility for the course the Turks [are] now embarked upon." The secretary issued a stern personal rebuke to Tasca for his efforts to promote Greece's cause. Unable to immediately remove the ambassador, Kissinger fell back on a standard Nixon administration ploy. He chose Monteagle Stearns as Tasca's new deputy and instructed him to report directly to Washington, isolating the U.S. ambassador. Stearns refused to cooperate, but Kissinger appointed him anyway, providing the U.S. mission with expertise on Greek affairs and Washington politics.[52]

Kissinger's refusal to support Greece's nascent democracy, a bow toward the strategic importance of Turkey, won him no credit in Ankara. Ecevit was convinced that the secretary of state was "openly against us" and, under intense pressure from his own military, refused to consider Greek demands for the withdrawal of his forces. In his talks with Kissinger, Ecevit laid down his bottom line: Turkey would not withdraw its forces "Not unless, not until a state for Turks is established on the island." A few days later, Turkish officials advised American diplomats that they wanted a swift agreement on Cyprus and that existing Greek Cypriot proposals were "too late."[53]

Nor was U.S. policy on Cyprus yielding benefits. Makarios was isolated and increasingly a bystander. However, with the Greek Cypriot community deeply divided, Klerides was too weak to offer the difficult compromises needed to achieve a deal. The Klerides and Karamanlis governments could not coordinate their strategies, in part because of their differing views on the future of Makarios. Kissinger's grand design for a quick settlement was being undercut by his unwillingness to provide support to the shaky democratic governments in Nicosia and Athens. Their evident weakness and America's domestic political agony emboldened Turkey's political leadership.[54]

Greek and the Greek Cypriot errors competed with Kissinger's maladroit diplomacy in laying the groundwork for the disaster that followed. Karamanlis played his part by taking a hard line toward Ankara. In an August 3 meeting with the Greek chiefs of staff, he got his military to admit that they could not defend Cyprus or Greece. Later that day, Arthur Hartman, Kissinger's special representative, met with the Greek prime minister for a dialogue of the deaf. After reiterating American support for Klerides, Hartman reminded the Greek leader that the junta's actions and Nicosia's treatment of its Turkish Cypriot minority had triggered Ankara's action. Karamanlis was having none of this. The Colonels were responsible, and the Turks were exploiting their actions, he replied, and if the United States wanted to prevent Soviet exploitation of the Cyprus situation it had to restrain Turkey. Nor would Karamanlis provide any political cover to Klerides. The interim president, whose interest in holding on to power coincided with a real need to avoid civil war, complained that the Greeks wanted him to take full responsibility for any compromises while continuing to publicly support the restoration of Makarios. The archbishop, in turn, was demanding that Greece back his refusal to make any concessions.[55]

Karamanlis had decided to sacrifice Cyprus to retain his domestic position. Greek public opinion did not hold its government responsible for the situation in Cyprus. It was focused on American responsibility for all of Greece's ills. Klerides was unlikely to remain in power in Nicosia, and given both Makarios's intransigent views and likely return to power, Greece's long-term interests were better served by avoiding any commitment to the existing Cypriot government. After sounding out the Soviet Union, and discovering that the Russians had no interest in supporting either Greece or Greek Cypriots, and assured once again by the military chiefs that their nation faced annihilation on the battlefield, Karamanlis and his cabinet decided to avoid compromising and await events.[56]

In a relaxed moment early in the Cyprus crisis, Kissinger told a friend: "There is no nation of maniacs that I don't get involved in [sic]." Among the various players involved in the crisis, none outdid Bulent Ecevit in his apparent irrationality. Under extreme pressure, the Turkish prime minister repeatedly gave vent to his stronger (and doubtless sincere) feelings in conversations with the U.S. secretary of state. His anger was intense. So was the Turkish leader's determination to forge a final solution to Cyprus that would favor his nation's interests. Hartman got a taste of Turkish determination when he visited Ankara on August 5. After disingenuously claiming that Washington's political crisis was not affecting America's ability to act decisively, Hartman appealed to Ecevit to show victor's moderation. Ecevit and his ministers told him that they would carve out a Turkish Cypriot zone on the island and then negotiate a final settlement. They would not again sacrifice Turkish interests to Greece or the United States. The Soviets, Ecevit added, had no problems with Turkish plans. Washington's job was to sell Ankara's plan to Athens.[57]

By the time Hartman filed his report on Turkey's "hard line," Washington was totally fixated with its own problems. On July 24, 1974, the U.S. Supreme Court ordered Richard Nixon to surrender further key tape recordings to both the Watergate special prosecutor and the House Impeachment Committee. One of these tape recordings, made June 23, 1972, was the smoking gun demonstrating that the president had organized a cover-up of his involvement in the break-in at Democratic National Committee headquarters. Nixon faced two unpalatable alternatives: quick resignation or sure impeachment. As Cyprus talks formally opened at Geneva, Kissinger was spending much time trying to nudge a highly emotional president toward resignation. Finally, on August 8, Nixon faced reality and told a national television audience that he would resign. He handed over power the following day. Gerald Ford assumed control. On August 10, Kissinger warned Ford that trouble was brewing in Cyprus. He counted on Greek agreement to create "two or three" Turkish Cypriot communes to head off further military action. Karamanlis, however, would not abandon his position, and in messages to the new U.S. leadership he insisted that Washington restrain Turkey without offering any Greek concessions. Kissinger, "playing for time," tried to get Ecevit to engage on a plan for a limited "temporary" partition. On August 12, the Turks unveiled their demands for 34 percent of the island and a continuing military occupation. Ankara gave the Greeks and Greek Cypriots twenty-four hours to agree to their basic demands and offered to work out the details at "leisure." Ecevit twisted the knife further by telling Kissinger to inform the Greeks that Turkey would not accept any "delaying tactic." Later that afternoon, he signaled imminent military action by accusing the Greek Cypriots of "imprisoning our units." Greece and the Cypriot government tried to play for time, but Ankara was not cooperating. Klerides appealed without success for Greek military aid. On August 14, the Turks unleashed a second military offensive that quickly established control over the northern part of the island. Ankara contrived a massive forced exchange of populations. Advancing Turkish and Turkish Cypriot forces drove northern Greek Cypriots from their villages at gunpoint while Turkish radio, denouncing Greek atrocities against Muslims, urged Turkish Cypriots to flee north to the security of the newly expanding Turkish enclave. Exploiting diplomatic miscalculations and political upheaval in Athens, Nicosia, and Washington, Turkey "settled" the Cyprus question to its specifications.[58]

EPILOGUE THE ANDREAS ERA

> Greece's century-and-a-half old habits as a client state of larger powers and the congenital propensity of Greeks to reject what does not serve their sense of personal and ethnic self-esteem, require foreign scapegoats on occasions such as this: the CIA, Dr Kissinger, and the U.S. Sixth Fleet qualified.
> — Foreign and Colonial Office, November 1974

On August 5, 1974, Henry Kissinger addressed a meeting of disgruntled State Department officials and defended his handling of the Cyprus crisis. Dismissing "learned reports from the bowels of the Department" as inadequate to the task of warning him of the likelihood of an invasion, Kissinger insisted that his management of the Cyprus issue had defined "objectives that would retain United States control" and had adopted "tactics in which the United States would have maximum flexibility as the crisis developed." These actions, Kissinger continued, had weakened the junta and created "maximum obstacles" to Turkish intervention. While "nothing could have stopped the Turks" from exploiting Greek "stupidity," his diplomacy had secured the best of possible results: Karamanlis was in control in Athens, Greece and Turkey had avoided a general war, and a solution on Cyprus acceptable to all was possible. Kissinger concluded this triumphal recounting of his policy successes by assuring his listeners that "the test is going to be in negotiations that are starting next week."[1]

The events of August 13–15 left Kissinger's diplomacy in tatters but not his self-confidence. Failure to preserve peace and stability in the eastern Mediterranean, the secretary of state was soon explaining, was the responsibility of everyone except himself. He rewarded those junior State Department officials who had warned him of the dangers that his actions were creating with a systematic effort to destroy their careers. The secretary refused to provide Congress with the complete accounting of his actions and pointed the finger of blame for the Cyprus mess at the Democratic majorities in the House and Senate, which, after years of supinely accepting Nixon administration policies, finally nerved themselves to take back part of their constitutional role in the management of foreign affairs. Kissinger complained loudly about growing congressional "micromanagement" of U.S. relations with Greece, Cyprus, and Turkey and many other parts of the world. He overlooked the role his fumbling played in leaving the Congress without alternatives. Other objects of Kissinger's ire were the Greek, Cypriot, and Turkish leaders, particularly Karamanlis, Makarios, and Ecevit. In retirement, the former secretary of state expressed his pique initially in the second part of his memoirs and then in a long, selectively documented, chapter of the final volume. Weakness at home, engendered by the Watergate crisis, "congressional meddling," ethnic hatred, and obstinacy abroad, Kissinger explained, had undercut his peacemaking efforts.[2]

Many of Kissinger's critics have insisted that the secretary's actions were motivated by a clear design to harm the Greek Cypriot community and particularly his nemesis, Makarios. They give him too much credit. While Kissinger's obsession with anti-Soviet grand strategy certainly played a role in his maneuverings, incompetence not malevolence was the persistent hallmark of his eastern Mediterranean policy. Whatever the level of his personal pique against Makarios (and it seems to have grown over the course of the crisis), Kissinger was much less interested in the archbishop's fate, or that of his island, than in avoiding a situation in which he presented his new boss, Gerald Ford, with a major foreign policy disaster during the first days of his presidency. With Nixon ensnared in a legal process, with the Democratic majority in the Congress restless over the costs and consequences of Kissinger's foreign policy, with both the 1972 Vietnam settlement and the Middle East peace process threatening to unravel, with a revolution in progress in Portugal, Spain's dictatorship on its last legs, and Italy's Communist Party apparently closing in on a power-sharing arrangement, a crisis in another part of the world, especially the Mediterranean, could be fatal to his own ambitions to remain at the center of U.S. foreign policy.[3]

When the Greek dictatorship unilaterally attacked Cyprus, the objective of Kissinger's crisis management was putting the issue on ice until Nixon was replaced and Ford could assert his authority. Kissinger's initial decision to back Dimitrios Ioannides and his later decision to shift U.S. support from the Greek junta to the Turkish government, as well as his efforts to keep the quick-witted Makarios off the island, were designed to secure a cease-fire. In a moment of self-revelation, Kissinger admitted to Monteagle Stearns, the newly appointed deputy chief of mission to Tasca, that he did not understand the issues and that he lacked control over his own diplomats. In the midst of the July phase of the crisis, British foreign secretary Callaghan reported to his cabinet colleagues on Kissinger's confusion: obsessed with Soviet-American regional geopolitics, the "Americans had been slow to appreciate the importance of the situation in Cyprus." Far from having a strategy for exploiting the crisis, Kissinger temporized. Bulent Ecevit, not Henry Kissinger, was the only player who had a clear set of objectives and the capacity and determination to impose them.[4]

The 1974 Cyprus fiasco was the denouement of a policy toward the eastern Mediterranean that Kissinger and Nixon constructed in the first weeks of an ill-fated presidency. Greek-American relations went sour during the 1964 Cyprus crisis. Although Lyndon Johnson's administration played no role in the 1967 coup, its subsequent failure to confront the junta and its quick adoption of an engagement policy laid the groundwork for Kissinger-Nixon realpolitik.[5] Determined to have Greece's "10 divisions" on its side in the event of a showdown with the Soviet bloc, the Nixon-Kissinger team swallowed every affront from the ultranationalist junta. George Papadopoulos, not Andreas Papandreou, was the first Greek leader consistently to "stand up" to American power in the name of Greek nationalism. He regularly ignored appeals and advice from Washington, snubbed its diplomats, and told off the Americans in the name of Greek national sovereignty. Ironically, the Nixon administration accepted this battering from the junta and gained nothing. Despite renewed U.S. arms assistance, Greek fighting capacity declined rapidly under the junta. By July 1974 the Greek army was too politicized and, as a result, too disorganized to mount a homeland defense against Turkey much less confront the Warsaw Pact. U.S. support for the junta degraded the defense capacity it was supposed to protect.[6]

The Cyprus crisis was the apogee of Kissinger's blundering. Placing his own determination to hold on to power ahead of U.S. national interest, he blustered, temporized, misused his department, and in the end had nothing to show but the creation of an enormous reservoir of ill will in the United States and in the eastern Mediterranean. By the time of the second Turkish offensive (August 1974), Kissinger and the United States had alienated Greece, Turkey, and both communities in Cyprus. By supporting the junta in the first days of the crisis and then turning his back on Karamanlis, Kissinger finalized the alienation between the United States and Greece that had developed since the early 1960s and opened the door for the clever and demagogic exploitation of Greek feelings by the politician American officials most mistrusted, Andreas Papandreou. Greek Cypriots, of course, insisted that Kissinger had engineered the whole crisis, overlooking the central role of their own leaders in conjuring up the catastrophe. Kissinger's cavalier treatment of Ecevit during the crisis undermined U.S. credibility with Turkey even before a congressional arms embargo infuriated Ankara. The secretary of state's determined efforts to repeal the embargo got little appreciation from the Turks, who recognized Kissinger's growing political weakness and that of the Ford administration. Moreover, ignoring Turkish aggression, however justified by larger strategic considerations, outraged not only Greeks, but also Greek Americans and large sectors of American liberal and congressional opinion, creating an instant credibility problem for the Ford administration.[7]

Great powers frequently walk away from their mistakes with limited damage, and in the long run, both Greece and Cyprus were cases in point. During the later part of the 1970s, the United States unloaded the Cyprus issue onto international forums, principally the United Nations, rebuilt its relationship with Greece, Turkey, and the Greek Cypriot administration in Nicosia, and accepted the long-term division of the island as the least harmful of many unpalatable alternatives. Greek anger eventually died down, and subsequent Greek governments found that camouflaged cooperation with Washington was in the national interest. The Greek Cypriots, too, recognized their need to get along and shaped their policies to cooperate rather than confront Washington. Turkey repeatedly found that its key interests were best served by a close relationship with the United States. Washington, in turn, was ready to support international efforts to resolve the crisis but ruled out any role as sole or even principal mediator. It lost any lingering taste for imposing a solution, much to the irritation of outraged nationalists on both sides of the dispute. Ultimately, the role of deal maker passed to the European Union (EU) paired with the U.N. secretary-general, weak reeds (even when backed by Washington) but the best options available.

As Washington withdrew from the leading role in Cyprus, it concentrated on maintaining the NATO alliance. While the eastern Mediterranean part of that alliance retained its traditional role of weak link, the United States, Greece, and Turkey could congratulate themselves on having conjured up a semblance of unity within NATO's Potemkin village and could maintain something of a common front toward the Soviet Union until 1991 and then throughout the Balkan wars of the 1990s. The benefits of NATO membership helped restrain Greece and Turkey during periods of confrontation. In the late 1990s, the two states found that they had a set of mutually rewarding objectives, and a still-fragile but hopeful dialogue began. Turkey's desire to join the EU and Greek recognition that a careful management of the process of Turkish membership could aid it in securing its critical national objectives, including a final solution of Cyprus, encouraged both sides to cooperate.[8]

The Kissinger-Nixon years were the turning point in Greek-American relations. Between 1950 and 1967 American policy makers had achieved some notable successes. American aid in the civil war meant that Greece avoided falling into the Soviet sphere with its high costs in terms of human freedom and economic backwardness and its considerable damage to Western strategic situation in the eastern Mediterranean. After the war, further U.S. assistance fostered both reconstruction and modernization. The United States nudged the Greek establishment toward greater democratization and respect for human rights. NATO provided Greece with security against both the Soviet bloc and its Turkish neighbor.

Few Greeks saw it that way, and the number steadily diminished as a result of the national humiliations that followed: the collapse of parliamentary democracy, the military dictatorship, and the ongoing frustration over Cyprus. These issues were closely interlocked, and the setbacks largely were the result of the errors of Greek political leaders. By 1952 the Greeks were quite free to chart their own course in both domestic politics and foreign policy. They chose the wrong course on both. The Greek political right insisted on keeping its society in a police straitjacket long after the threat of communist insurrection disappeared. Anticommunist repression justified the right's continued hold on power and allowed the monarchy and military to operate largely outside legal control. Simultaneously, Greece's politicians, bidding for power and national expansion, worked with Greek Cypriot nationalists to undermine British colonial rule and demanded the annexation of Cyprus, ignoring the interests of the Turkish Cypriot minority and, more dangerously, of Ankara. By consistently raising the ante in Cyprus, Greek leaders completely misjudged their own ability to deliver, misled Greek public opinion on the possibility of enosis, and placed themselves in the always-embarrassing position of depending on the great powers, thereby exposing Greek weakness to their own people. Neither the Soviet Union nor the United States had any reason to meet Greek demands. For the Soviets, Greek acquisition of Cyprus would simply expand NATO. For the United States, support for Greek demands would alienate two more important allies. The Americans, at least, tried to fashion a compromise solution. These efforts met with rejection from a Greek nation whose emotional belief in its self-evident right to Cyprus blinded it to the concrete interests that other peoples and other nations had in the terms of a Cyprus solution. Greek insistence on its "right" to Cyprus triggered an equally intransigent Turkish response. Greek determination to have this "right" led George Papandreou, Papadopoulus, and Ioannides to plot military action against the elected head of the Greek Cypriot community.

Greek politicians as a group underestimated the skill and objectives of Makarios III. "The priest," as George Papandreou ruefully admitted, outmaneuvered them all. Makarios's goal, a Cyprus under complete Greek Cypriot control, was unrealizable. Neither enosis nor independence offered a path to this objective. Makarios came to prefer independence. It was the best means of securing his personal position. Everything the Greek leadership did after 1960 reinforced Makarios's preference for going it alone. Greek Cypriot public opinion moved in the same direction. The Greek-directed overthrow of Makarios solidified a consensus on Cyprus that enosis was not desirable and two "national centers" of Hellenism were.

In their efforts to achieve enosis against the interests of Makarios, the United States, the Soviet Union, and Turkey, Greek politicians could rely on nearly unanimous popular support at home. Vox populi, however, is not consistently right. Karamanlis recognized the dangers in a heedless pursuit of enosis, although during the early 1960s he expected to achieve union with Cyprus on a slow timetable.

Meanwhile, Greece's political institutions were breaking down under the accumulated weight of the Cyprus issue and of the country's rapid economic modernization. The political right fostered growth but refused to adapt Greece's political, economic, and social systems to the effects of rapid urbanization. The moderate center publicly challenged the system's legitimacy while working within it. The Cyprus issue became a key tool in the assault of the center on the right. Mixing demands for greater openness, pledges of economic redistribution, and appeals to Greek nationalism, George and Andreas Papandreou, two of the most ambitious and reckless Greek politicians, polarized the nation, drove their moderate opponents into more extreme positions, and gave the far right an opportunity to "solve" the issue in its own manner.

For over a decade, Greek politicians of the center had relentlessly tried to draw the United States into supporting their position. Sofokles Venizelos had been the most tireless manipulator of the American factor. George Papandreou picked up the practice. Andreas Papandreou took the practice one step further by trying to blackmail the United States into backing his father with his anti-American behavior. Violating every maxim of common sense, the Papandreous came to rely on the same Americans they daily attacked to provide them with a guarantee against the crown, the military, and the conservative establishment. To their evident surprise, the tactic failed. The Papandreous' hubris cleared the ground for a military coup. As the Papandreous challenged the legitimacy of the crown and the opposition, agitated for dramatic action on Cyprus, and alienated the Americans, they offered a group of military extremists the ammunition with which they could neutralize their superiors' concerns over unconstitutional actions and then mount a military coup in the name of but without the authorization of the crown and army high command.[9]

While conservative political and military elites rapidly regained their senses after April 21 and began cooperating in efforts to oust the junta, they had no effective tools and discovered that both the Johnson and Nixon administrations were ready, reluctantly in the first case, enthusiastically in the second, to work with men who used Greece's NATO membership as a shield against foreign intervention. Greeks drove their political system over an embankment; the Americans did nothing to help get it out of the ditch.

When the junta finally collapsed, U.S.-Greek diplomatic relations entered into a profound crisis that ultimately proved therapeutic. The dramaturge was Andreas Papandreou. Once the junta was gone, Kissinger realized that something had to be done about the tattered state of U.S. relations with Greece. The first response was removing his antagonist, Henry Tasca, from Athens. Although a critic of the Ioannides regime, no one was more tarred by past U.S. support of the Greek dictatorship than Tasca. Removing the ambassador and replacing him with Jack Kubisch, a senior diplomat skilled at resuscitating dialogue in difficult circumstances, was Kissinger's best move in nearly six years of managing Greek affairs. The secretary of state sent over a veteran Greek hand, Stearns, to manage the transition from Tasca to Kubisch and to stay as the number-two man at the embassy. Stearns's close personal relationship with Andreas Papandreou was a plus. Over the next decade and a half, Washington carefully selected its senior diplomats with an eye to doing no further harm and if possible to expanding the dialogue with an increasingly dominant and resentful Greek left. Stearns returned as ambassador in 1981, and another diplomat of markedly pro-Papandreou views, Robert Keeley, succeeded him in 1985. This arrangement permitted Andreas to maintain a high profile anti-American stance and quietly cooperated on a series of mutually beneficial programs.

Behind-the-scenes cooperation did not heal the wounds created by Cyprus and the junta. The Greek political establishment and Greek public opinion were united on one issue, blaming their errors on the United States. For the next two decades, the United States served as a national piñata, trooped out by left and right, on every possible occasion, to assuage national feelings of humiliation and to avoid a national debate over the real causes of both the rise of the Colonels and the Cyprus disaster.

Greeks drew one clear conclusion from the colonels' regime. They needed to reduce overdependence on Washington. Karamanlis, who returned from his eleven years of exile with a different vision of what democracy in Greece ought to be, offered the most articulated solution. While Washington remained the key to Greek national security, membership in the European Community would permit Greece to place some of the burden on other shoulders and, more importantly, would give Greeks an alternative model for democratic development that was untarnished by the real and alleged sins of the United States. Greece's political and economic modernization became easier when dressed as a "return" to Europe.[10] European investment in Greece provided a powerful aid to building essential infrastructure. In the immediate aftermath of the Cyprus disaster, Karamanlis drew on the example of that "anti-American ally" par excellence, France, to retain Greece's American tie while apparently rejecting it. Following Charles de Gaulle's 1966 actions, Karamanlis ostentatiously withdrew from NATO's military wing while retaining a Greek political and military presence at the alliance's headquarters in Brussels. Withdrawal permitted Karamanlis to assert national dignity and, not incidentally, to unload some of his personal anger on Kissinger. A few years later, Karamanlis's successor, George Ralles, led Greece back into NATO's military wing at the cost of some politically embarrassing concessions to Turkey.

Karamanlis's greatest contribution to his homeland consisted in the way in which he guided Greece toward a mature democratic system. The Greek populace and political class were sobered by the experience of seven years of military rule. "Either Karamanlis or the tanks," summarized public opinion in the first uneasy years after the fall of the dictatorship. The prime minister utilized the maneuvering room created by public fears of another coup to reshape political life in his homeland. He gradually brought a restive military under civilian control. The senior junta leaders were tried and sentenced. Avoiding a repeat of the costly mistakes of 1922, Karamanlis voided death sentences for Papadopoulos, Pattakos, and Makarezos. In 1962, then prime minister Karamanlis had proposed revisions of the constitution. After the junta's collapse, Karamanlis shaped a new set of rules in the constitution of 1975 that would guide Greek democracy. Recognizing, though never admitting, that his own management of the politics in the 1950s and early 1960s had laid the groundwork for the collapse of "crown democracy," Karamanlis rid Greece of its monarchy and introduced a style of politics that recognized the rotation in power between political parties as the best means of stabilizing democracy. In the five years he served as prime minister, Karamanlis built a party (New Democracy or ND) that was a bit less personal than his previous ERE and that prepared for its and his replacement by the opposition, which by the late 1970s meant Andreas Papandreou. By giving the presidency fairly wide powers and assuming that position in 1980, Karamanlis provided guarantees for those on the right, including elements of the Greek military, still worried about Andreas's ultimate aims.[11]

In October 1981, Andreas Papandreou won an overwhelming victory for *alagé* (change), the suitably amorphous slogan that captured the Greek majority's view that whatever Karamanlis had done to liberalize state and society was not enough. Real change, for most Greeks, meant a new political leadership drawing its legitimacy from opposition to the junta and its "master," the United States. Campaigning against foreign domination and in favor of Greek self-assertion, Andreas pledged to close U.S. bases, to pull Greece out of NATO and the EC, to create a truly independent Greek foreign policy, and to impose Greek socialism on his still economically underdeveloped nation. Predictably, and wisely, Papandreou reneged on his promises to withdraw from either NATO or the EC, winning some concessions from both and inflating these into national triumphs. He negotiated a reduction in the number of U.S. bases but left the Americans with the prize, Souda Bay, Crete. Greece's more independent, high-decibel foreign policy alienated most of its traditional allies and led it into another dangerous confrontation with Turkey over Cyprus. Papandreou wisely retreated behind a smoke screen of nationalist verbiage. His essay at economic nationalism (Greek socialism) turned out to be a return to policies of financing economic expansion by building national debt. The policy, which focused on job creation in the public sector, kept his Panhellenic Socialist Movement (PASOK) in power while the country dropped further behind other Western democracies in terms of real growth. The great irony of Andreas's career was that such a brilliant politician and academic economist was such a terrible manager of the national economy. Scandals involved with the creation and expansion of a vast web of political patronage eventually drove Andreas from power in 1988–89.[12]

Andreas's legacy, however, was not limited to bad economic policy and increasingly stale rhetoric. His first two terms in office were a period of real liberalization in Greek society. Labor unions became stronger, and workers' rights expanded. The Karamanlis and Papandreou governments placed effective restraints on internal security forces and repealed legislation that permitted their previous excesses. Women's issues moved to the fore. PASOK tackled questions of church-state relations, albeit with limited success. A long-delayed, symbolic national reconciliation between the forces that had fought the Greek civil war took place under Papandreou. Despite a fixation on its own national interests that irritated other EC members, Greece began to play a small role in broader European affairs. A sense of greater national independence and psychological self-worth was certainly reinforced by Andreas's ability to say no to the Americans, publicly.

In 1993 an aged Andreas returned to power with a new set of objectives. Sobered by the failure of Greek "socialism" and by resistance to his past economic mismanagement within his own party, recognizing that he could not continue to demagogue issues relating to the Balkans without harm to Greek interests, Papandreou embraced more cautious policies designed to close the gap between Greece and the rest of the European Union (EU). Never abandoning his nationalist stance, he sought a public reconciliation with the United States, arguing that having chastened the Americans, he could now work with them in building an improved post–Cold War environment. The Clinton administration responded, and in 1994, as his health and hold on power declined, Papandreou achieved a long-held personal goal, a formal White House visit at which an American president lauded him as a valuable ally. The prodigal son basked in a last triumph, happily arranged by a fellow American who shared some of his particular political talents.[13] The following year Andreas was gone. His successors, led by Costas Simitis, were pragmatic in both foreign and domestic policy. They responded to the prevailing Greek public desire for a more efficient and less-isolated Greece by increasing its involvement in EU affairs and through greater cooperation with the United States. As Washington and Athens engaged in a discrete but wide-ranging cooperation on major international issues, anti-U.S. rhetoric survived mostly on the pages of the national press, and until the advent of George W. Bush, anti-Americanism was a form of extreme nationalist, anarchist, or communist-inspired street theater. Bill Clinton became the first U.S. president to visit Athens since Dwight Eisenhower and, to the embarrassment of his official hosts and probably a majority of Greeks, was greeted with a display of old-fashioned, anti-American street rioting in Athens. Greeks, like most Europeans, soon regretted Clinton's retirement.

In the late 1990s, a public opinion poll asked Greeks to rank their national leaders in terms of greatness. Venizelos emerged as number one, followed by Karamanlis and then Andreas Papandreou. Andreas's positioning in this pantheon was a tribute to his careful management of the legacy of Greece's tumultuous past. Few leaders have ever exploited myth and symbols as successfully. Essentially, Andreas wrote a version of the history of his times that so successfully coincided with deeply held Greek beliefs that other political leaders felt compelled to accept its broad terms and to compete with Papandreou on the playing field he constructed. History became a bridge to his ultimate ambition of leading Greece. Fortunately for Greece, Papandreou was dispassionate enough to avoid being captured by his own myths. He created and exploited them selectively, retaining the margins of maneuver to avoid personal or national disaster. It was the essence of his political genius.[14]

NOTES

Abbreviations Used in Notes

ADST	Oral History Project, Association for Diplomatic Studies and Training
BA	Benaki Archives, Athens, Greece
CAB	British Cabinet Papers
CIA RDP	Central Intelligence Agency Records Declassification Project
CO	British Colonial Office
DBFP	*Documents on British Foreign Policy*
DDF	*Documents Diplomatiques Français*
DDI	*Documenti Diplomatici Italiani*
DSCF	Department of State Central Files
FCO	British Foreign and Colonial Office
FO	British Foreign Office
FRUS	*Foreign Relations of the United States*
GLA	Gennadius Library Archives, Athens, Greece
HHSA	Haus-, Hof- und Staatsarchiv, Vienna, Austria
INR	State Department Bureau of Intelligence and Research
JFKL	John F. Kennedy Presidential Library, Boston, Massachusetts
MAE	Archives, Ministère des Affaires étrangères, Paris, France
MERF	Middle East Regional File
NA	National Archives, Washington, D.C.
NEA/GRK	Office of Greek Affairs, Department of State
NPM	Nixon Presidential Materials
NSF	National Security File
PREM	Prime Minster's Files (United Kingdom)
PRO	Public Record Office/National Archives, London
RG	Record Group

Preface

1. Gilman, *Mandarins of the Future*.

2. De Grazia, *Irresistible Empire*, is extremely stimulating if not entirely convincing. Pells, *Not Like Us*, on the degree to which Europe has mastered and modified American cultural products.

3. Not surprisingly, the clash of cultural exceptionalism and American imports has produced some quite telling studies, above all regarding France. My views have been significantly influenced by the pleasures of two summers in France and by Roger, *L'ennemi américain*, and Kuisel, *Seducing the French*.

4. Lieven, *America Right or Wrong*. On the background, Stephanson, *Manifest Destiny*.

5. McNeill, *Greek Dilemma* and *Metamorphosis of Greece since World War II*; Smothers, McNeill, and McNeill, *Report on the Greeks*. Pirounakis, *Greek Economy*, asks the right questions about the relation of social organization and economic choice.

6. For example, Herodotus, Ιστορία [History], 1:135, 1:195–97, 1:214–16. Myers, *Herodotus*, discusses the approach.

Introduction

1. Roger, *L'ennemi américain*, 100–138, on French efforts to partition the United States.

2. Bailyn, *Ideological Origins*, 19–20, on the growth of exceptionalism; Fields, *America and the Mediterranean World*, 3–26, on the development of an American "mission" abroad; Link, *Woodrow Wilson and a Revolutionary World*, 146–74, on Wilson's codification of this mission; and Steel, "Missionary," on the persistence of the Wilsonian tradition.

3. *FRUS 1868*, 2:142.

4. British actions also responded to its reading of national interest. See the June 1829 assessment by the philhellene George Finlay in Hussy, *Journals and Letters*, 1:4. On Ottoman resistance and Greek reliance on great-power aid, comments of Panagiotis Svntzo, n.d., Berichte Varia, 1826–27, Türkei VI, Staatenabteilungen, HHSA.

5. Thouvenel, *Grèce du Roi Othon*, 79. On the intellectual background of the megali idea, Zakythinos, *Making of Modern Greece*, 157–79.

6. *FRUS 1866*, 2:48–49.

7. Raymond, *Grèce de Gobineau*, 355–58; Finlay in Hussy, *Journals and Letters*, 2:726–28. Anderson, *Eastern Question*, on great-power diplomacy.

8. French diplomatic reporting from Constantinople is particularly informative on the reasoning behind this judgment. See reports filed in 1710, 1730, 1769–76, and 1822 by the French representative, Turquie, tomes 7 and 19, Mémoires et Documents, MAE. Karsh and Karsh, *Empires of the Sand*, on Ottoman diplomacy. See also Thouvenel, *Grèce du Roi Othon*, 110–11.

9. British embassy in Constantinople to the Foreign Office, April 2, 1854, FO 286/168, PRO; British legation to Foreign Office, February 4, 1878, FO 286/310, PRO; Koliopoulos, "Ληστεία"; British note to the Greek government, January 24, 1886, box 7, series 2, Stefanos Dragoumis Papers, GLA.

10. Pentzopoulos, *Balkan Exchange of Minorities*. On Greek claims, Venizelos to Lord Curzon, August 5, 1920, FO 286/746, PRO.

11. Petropulos, *Politics and Statecraft*, 23–28, 41–60, for a detailed treatment of the class divisions and conflicts among Greek revolutionaries. In "Considerations on the State of Greece," n.d., but late 1826, the Austrian representative commented: "Con-

siderable sums which the philhellene community has poured into the treasury of the Greek government have been entirely exhausted by those charged with administering them. . . . Discord reigns now, more than ever, among the Greek captains. . . . Orders issued by the government are not followed." Berichte Varia, 1826–1827, Türkei VI, Staatenabteilungen, HHSA.

12. *FRUS 1870*, 439–43, for the analysis. For an overview of banditry, Koliopoulos, "Ληστεία." Jenkins, *Dilessi Murders*, on the relationship of crime and politics. On the initial popular response to Othon, British legation to Foreign Office, March 25, 1832, FO 286/24, PRO.

13. Kapodistrias, "Notes de la Grèce 1831," folder 1826–31, and letters from Marshal Maison to Kapodistrias, March 16 and July 28, 1829, Correspondence Marshal Maison, both Kapodistrias Papers, BA; Petropulos, *Politics and Statecraft*, 166–67, 373, 376–81, 441–42; Koliopoulos, "Ληστεία"; Veremis, *Military in Greek Politics*, 20–21, 26. On the constitutional problems, dispatch 16 to the Foreign Office, March 26, 1833, FO 286/31, PRO, and dispatch 78 to the Foreign Office, July 10, 1843, FO 286/92, PRO. On the monarchy's efforts to build ties with the military, British legation to Foreign Office, October 4, 1912, FO 286/550, PRO; Finlay in Hussy, *Journal and Letters*, 1:5.

14. Raymond, *Grèce de Gobineau*, 149.

15. Telegram 87 to the Foreign Office, June 18, 1909, FO 286/251, PRO.

16. *FRUS 1872*, 1:229–30.

17. *FRUS 1875*, 1:658–62; Thouvenel, *Grèce du Roi Othon*, 272; Raymond, *Grèce de Gobineau*, 244–45, 417; British legation to Foreign Office, January 24, 1878, FO 286/310, August 5, 1897, FO 286/442, and June 11, 1909, FO 286/521, all PRO; Dakin, *Unification of Greece*, 99–100, 186. The parallels with pre-1967 Greece are evident. See the assessments of "Athenian" [Rouphos], *Inside the Colonels' Greece*, 61–70, and Legg, *Politics in Modern Greece*, 127, 165–66, 172.

18. Markopoulos, "King George I"; Raymond, *Grèce de Gobineau*, 303–5; *DDI*, 2nd ser., 13:485–86.

19. On the causes of the revolt, see the comments of Prince Nicholas of Greece to Foreign Office, October 7, 1909, FO 286/522, PRO. Counsel in Pireaus to legation in Greece, June 11, 1909, FO 286/521, PRO, discussed sources of military discontent. British legation to Foreign Office, August 30, 1909, FO 286/522, PRO, analyzed the revolt. On the origins, course and consequences of the 1909 revolt, Papacosma, *Military in Greek Politics*. On Venizelos's use of parties, Mavrogordatos, *Stillborn Republic*, 114–15, 312.

20. Macmillan, *Peacemakers*, 358. Compare the comments of the philhellene British historian, Dakin, *Unification of Greece*, 183–85, 221.

21. *FRUS 1916 Supplement*, 83–84; *FRUS 1917 Supplement* 1:47–49; *FRUS 1920*, 2:708–9; *FRUS 1921*, 2:139–45; Visvizi-Dontas, "Communauté européenne et la diplomatie venizelienne"; Veremis, *Military in Greek Politics*, 69, 72–73. King Con-

stantine, while opposed to Venizelos on the question of alliance with the Entente, shared his ambition to exploit the war to seize more of the Ottoman state. British legation to Foreign Office, September 1, 1916, FO 286/586, PRO. Smith, *Ionian Vision*, on the causes and course of the 1919–23 disaster in Asia Minor.

22. Jenkins, *Dilessi Murders*, 109–29. On the writing of ethnocentric history, Koliopoulos, "Unwanted Ally." On Greek ethnocentricity, Thouvenel, *Grèce du Roi Othon*, 95–96. Alexis Phylactopoulos, director of the College Year in Athens program, provided an interesting reading of the ongoing problems of comprehension between Greeks and Americans in the fall 2005 edition of the *Owl*, the program's newsletter. Legg and Roberts, *Modern Greece*, 57, 64.

23. On the efforts of Kapodistrias to exploit these feelings in the context of a sophisticated set of strategic arguments, see untitled aide memorandum in folder 1819–1825 and undated aide memorandum in folder 1826–31, both Kapodistrias Papers, BA. On the rationale for Greek entry into the EEC, see Commission of the European Community, *Opinion on Greece's Application*; on the initial effects, Kazakos and Ioakimidis, *Greece and EC Membership Evaluated*.

24. Storace, *Dinner with Persephone*; Dakin, *Unification of Greece*, 7–8, 254; "Εισαγωγή," [Introduction] in Veremis, *Εθνική Ταυτότητα*, 11–26.

25. Twain, *Innocents Abroad*, 262–63.

26. A Greek version of Theotokas's "Free Spirit" is in Farmakides, *Diamonio*. See also Doulis, *George Theotokas*. On Henry Miller, Keeley, *Inventing Paradise*.

27. Makrides, "Science and the Orthodox Church in the 18th and early 19th Centuries"; Kitromilides, "'Νεορές κοινότητες'"; Finlay, *History*, 8–11. See also John Gennadius to archbishop of Athens, September 15, 1929, series 1, box 3, "Church," Gennadius Papers, GLA.

28. Kitromilides, "'Νεορές κοινότητες,'" 54; Serwo, "Die ersten staatlichen Kirchengesetze in Griechenland 1833"; McGrew, *Land and Revolution*, 140–41, 148–49.

29. *FRUS 1883*, 539–40; Petropulos, *Politics and Statecraft*, 192, 484.

30. *FRUS 1872* 1:246–47; Iatrides, *Ambassador MacVeagh Reports*, 143–48; dispatch 43 to the Foreign Office, April 18, 1959, FO 371/144579/RG1782/4, PRO.

31. Kitromilides, "'Νεορές κοινότητες.'" On the use of persuasion and coercion to create national identity, Karakasidou, *Fields of Wheat*, has raised the hackles of Greek nationalists. McCarthy, *Death and Exile*, is a controversial but well-argued study of the impact of the ethnic cleansing of Muslims in the Balkans and other parts of the Ottoman world. On the degree to which Greek actions against the Muslim population of Turkey contributed to the 1922 cataclysm in Asia Minor, *DDF 1920*, 1:359–60; *DBFP*, 1st series, 4:654–58, 683, 733; *FRUS 1919*, 2:841. On Greek commitment to ethnic cleansing as a solution to Balkan problems, Angelopoulos, "Population Distribution of Greece Today," explains that by driving "Moslem, Slav and Jewish intruders" out of Macedonia, Greece achieved "a country with practically ideal ethnic, linguistic and religious homogeneity and unity."

32. Panayotopoulos, "Great Idea and the Vision of an Eastern Federation"; Nicolopoulos, "From Agathangelos to the Megali Idea"; Finlay, *History*, 1–2, 7.

33. Zakythinos, *Making of Modern Greece*, 193–98; Petropulos, *Politics and Statecraft*, 507–8; Dakin, *Unification of Greece*, 144–45; Petsalides-Diomides, *Greece at the Paris Peace Conference*, 67. On postwar public opinion in Greece, the British minister reported: "I do not think there is now a single paper which does not claim Constantinople for Greece, and most of them write as if possession were not only a future certainty but a very imminent one." Legation to Foreign Office, July 30, 1920, FO 286/746, PRO.

34. Kitromelides, "'Νεορές κοινότητες'"; Dakin, *Unification of Greece*, 163, 176–77; Kofos, "Εθνική κληρονομία," "Dilemmas and Orientations of Greek Policy in Macedonia, 1876–1886," and "Patriarch Joachim III (1878–1884) and the Irredentist Policy of the Greek State."

35. On the effects on this sense of national mission, Berktay, "National Memories," and Kanellopoulos, "Η Πατρα," in *Δοκίμια και Αλλα Κείμενα*, 117–23.

36. Zakythinos, *Making of Modern Greece*, 115–39, 150–57; Karathanassis, "Contribution à la connaissance de la vie et de l'oeuvre de deux Grecs de la diaspora"; Petropulos, *Politics and Statecraft*, 44.

37. While piling such loaded adjectives as "feeble," "brutal," "cowardly," and "superstitious" on the Byzantines, Gibbon did recognize the courage of their final defense of Constantinople. Gibbon, *Decline and Fall of the Roman Empire*, 3:745–75.

38. Petropulos, *Politics and Statecraft*, 38–42.

39. *FRUS 1875*, 1:666.

40. Dragonas and Frangoudaki, "Introduction"; Avdela, "Teaching of History." Compare Mackridge and Yannakakis, *Ourselves and Others*, 33, 42; and Clogg, *Greece, 1981–89*, ix, 2–5, 13–15. The struggle over the content of history textbooks rages on; see *Athens News*, March 23, 2007.

41. Athens: OEBD (1992), 7, 13, 35. Compare comments of Papacosma, *Military in Greek Politics*, 13, and Petropulos, *Politics and Statecraft*, 28. On the collaboration between Greek and Ottoman elites, untitled memoir on Turkey, ca. 1807, "Turcica 1755–88," Türkei I, and the psychological analysis of subject Greeks in an untitled 1770 memoir, "Collectanan Konskript Türk," Türkei V, both Staatenabteilungen, HHSA; Doumanis, *Myth and Memory*, 13.

42. "History," in Vassilikos, *And Dreams Are Dreams*, 48–111; Couloumbis, Petropulos, and Psomiades, *Foreign Interference*. Compare Avdela, "Teaching of History." According to the *Athens News*, November 5, 2000, 38 percent of Greeks polled admitted to xenophobic feelings as compared to 4 percent of Spaniards. Mackridge and Yannakakis, *Ourselves and Others*, 46.

43. Mouzelis, *Modern Greece*, 29, 152–54.

44. Thouvenel, *Grèce du Roi Othon*, 17–20, 129–45; Raymond, *Grèce de Gobineau*, 319–22; Kapodistrias, "Notes de la Grèce en 1831," folder 1826–31, Kapodistrias

Papers, BA; Koliopoulos, "Greek Foreign Policy and Strategy, 1939–1941"; Petropulos, *Politics and Statecraft*, 6–7, 12–13, 44, 48, 122; Vatikiotis, *Popular Autocracy*, 111; Legg, *Politics in Modern Greece*, 76.

45. Deane, *I Should Have Died*, 59, 113–14. The memorandum of conversation, June 11, 1964, is in *FRUS 1964–68*, 16:125–29. U.S. State Department memoranda are subject to careful vetting when a presidential discussion is involved, but they are very reliable in terms of representing the tone of a meeting. Johnson's impatience shows through, but so does his effort to win Greek support. He had some reason for these feelings. The previous week he had stopped a Turkish invasion of Cyprus and having done the Greeks and Greek Cypriots a major favor was searching for some aid from Athens to restrain Ankara. Gigantès's memorandum to Department of State, October 20, 1964, Pol 15-1 Royal Family, NEA/GRK, RG 59, NA. On Gigantès's career, Killick to Dodson, April 18, 1963, Sykes to Dodson, July 13, 1964, and minute by Dodson, April 22, 1964, all FO 371/174806/CE1011/38, PRO. For an example of the diffusion of Deane's story, see the summary of John Tomkinson, "Athens under the Americans 2."

46. *FRUS 1946*, 7:91–92, 97–98, 230–32. Iatrides, *Ambassador MacVeagh Reports*, contains the best U.S. reporting on Greece over more than a decade while Smothers, McNeill, and McNeill, *Report on the Greeks*, 13, 33–34, 50, 97, 113, 146, is an equally sobering look at the internal situation prepared just as the U.S. decision for intervention was being taken.

47. Jones, *Fifteen Weeks*, 147. Bailyn, *Ideological Origins*, 26, provides another key to reading the U.S. attitude toward Greece. Americans, even in the nineteenth century, were among the least philhellene of Westerners. American attitudes toward the classics and the ancient world were different from those of Europeans. While the classics might provide examples, the Founding Fathers did not use antiquity as a model for future political development. Doumanis, *Myth and Memory*, 11–12.

48. *FRUS 1946*, 7:170, 238–39, 241; *FRUS 1948*, 4:3; *FRUS 1949*, 6:242, for examples of this view. Embassy in Greece to ministry, February 15, 18, and 26, 1952, vol. 95, Greece, MAE; Coufoudakis, "United States, the United Nations, and the Greek Question, 1946–1952"; Wittner, "American Policy toward Greece, 1944–49," 233; Briam, *Will to Win*, 182. Among Greek memoirs, Markezinis, Σύγχρονη Πολιτική Ιστορία, 3:6–7; Ralles, Πολιτικές Εκμυστηρεύσεις, 21.

49. On the damaging extremism of the Greek right, see *FRUS 1946*, 7–241. Porter's memorandum is in *FRUS 1947*, 5:17–22. See also Tsoucalas, "Ideological Impact of the Cold War," and Fatouros, "Building Formal Structures of Penetration."

50. *FRUS 1948*, 4:26–27, 180 (Grady quote).

Chapter 1

1. And not only in these two states; see "La Leçon de Politique du Cinéma Italien," *Le Monde* (Internet edition), March 8, 2004.

2. In a December 11, 1956, report, the French ambassador commented that because of past American aid, U.S. effectiveness far outpaced its real power. Vol. 206, Greece, MAE. On the negative effects of U.S. dominance and elite collaboration, particularly on Greek public opinion, Iatrides, "United States, Greece, and the Balkans."

3. Norbert L. Anschuetz, Daniel Brewster, and Benjamin Dixon oral histories, ADST. Grady commented on his problems with Van Fleet in telegram 246 from Teheran, July 28, 1950, 781.00/7-2850, DSCF, RG 59, NA. On the Grady-Van Fleet duel, Briam, *Will to Win*, 164, 168, 186–88, 202.

4. *FRUS 1949*, 6:233–35, 240, 309–11, 318. On U.S. efforts to discourage a dictatorship, Norton to Bateman, December 12, 1948, FO 371/78346/R57G, PRO, and embassy in Greece to Foreign Office, January 6, 1949, FO 371/78346/R190G, PRO. Peurifoy's initial reports on discussions with the king and queen are indicative of his problems understanding Greek political culture. See telegram 1465 from Athens, November 1, 1950, 871.00/11-150, DSCF, RG 59, NA. The ambassador had been briefed about the difficulties that the "hard working but politically dangerous couple" posed to U.S. objectives. Dispatch 509 from Athens, September 28, 1950, 781.00/9-2850, DSCF, RG 59, NA. See also Yost, *History and Memory*, 228.

5. CIA reports September 22, 1947, August 5, 1948, February 17, 1949, CIA RDP 82-00457, NA. These documents, placed on CD-ROMs as part of an ongoing CIA public relations effort, constitute a very problematic resource for historians because their actual provenance is unknown. Many of the identifying document numbers are blacked out, and most disturbingly, the CDs lack documentation dealing with policy making or with the activities of CIA stations.

6. Peurifoy passed this story along to his British colleague. Ambassador in Greece to the Foreign Office, September 19, 1951, FO 371/95118/RG 10114/45, PRO. See also Chatzeantoniou, Νικόλαος Πλαστήρας, 199–201.

7. Telegrams 514 from Athens, March 9, 1950, 781.00/3-950, and 71 from Athens, January 10, 1950, 781.00/1-1050, both DSCF, RG 59, NA; CIA Intelligence Report, February 27, 1947, CIA RDP 82-000457, NA. On Papagos's stature and control of national defense issues, Karamanlis, Αρχείο 1:129–30.

8. On Papagos's career, Papagiannopoulos, Στρατάρχης Αλεξάνδρος Παπάγος.

9. Airgram 332 from Athens, March 2, 1950, 781.00/3-2250, DSCF, RG 59, NA. On press harassment of the U.S. embassy, memorandum of conversation between Ambassador Peake and Venizelos, August 26, 1952, FO 371/101808/WG1052/5, PRO. Papagos, while sympathetic to embassy problems, commented that a "good deal of feeling . . . [was] aroused at the thought that Greece's future might be decided by a third power." Memorandum of conversation between Peake and Papagos, August 26, 1952, FO 371/101808/WG1052/5, PRO. See also Legg, *Politics in Modern Greece*, 112–13.

10. Dispatch 1 from Athens, January 3, 1950, 781.00/1-350, DSCF, RG 59, NA; *FRUS 1948*, 4:176–77; *FRUS 1949*, 6:465–66. In June 1947, MacVeagh, the U.S. official most experienced at working with the Greek political class, vented his frustra-

tions over the "childish and petulant inaccuracies concerning alleged foreign 'intervention' in Greek affairs" by then prime minister Tsaldaris. *FRUS 1947*, 5:203. For press efforts to provoke American intervention, embassy in Greece to ministry, September 1, 1951, vol. 95, Greece, MAE.

11. *FRUS 1949*, 6:256–57; memorandum of conversation with Diomedes, January 12, 1950, 781.00/1-1850, DSCF, RG 59, NA; embassy in the United States to the Foreign Office, June 26, 1950, FO 371/87787/RG1945/1, PRO.

12. Acheson to Marshall, March 6, 1950, 781.00/3-650, telegrams 499 from Athens, March 8, 1950, 781.00/3-850, and 513 from Athens, March 9, 1950, 781.00/3-950, all DSCF, RG 59, NA; *FRUS 1950*, 5:345–47; Daphnes, Σοφοκλής Ελευθερίου Βενιζέλος, 454–55, 457.

13. *FRUS 1950*, 5:347–48, 351–52; telegram 642 from Athens, March 24, 1950, 781.00/3-2450, DSCF, RG 59, NA.

14. Telegrams 657 from Athens, March 25, 1950 (quote), and 694 from Athens, March 30, 1950, both DSCF, RG 59, NA; *FRUS 1950*, 5:354–55.

15. *FRUS 1950*, 5:356–57.

16. Letter from Grady to Venizelos, March 31, 1951, 781.00/3-3150, DSCF, RG 59, NA; *FRUS 1950*, 5:359–61, 364–65. "Greece: Annual Review for 1950," January 9, 1951, treated Grady and his efforts with considerable sympathy, concluding that Greek political maneuvers made 1950 the "year of hope deferred." FO 371/95016/RG1011/1, PRO. See also Daphnes, Σοφοκλής Ελευθερίου Βενιζέλος, 464–69. McGhee sought to patch up relations with Venizelos in a message thanking the former prime minister for his "understanding." McGhee to Venizelos, May 19, 1950, Genika, Box 21, Sofokles Venizelos Papers, BA.

17. Telegram 104 from Athens, April 3, 1950, DSCF, RG 59, NA.

18. Iatrides, *Ambassador MacVeagh Reports*, 474.

19. Legg, *Politics in Modern Greece*, 74. In November 1952, after his party suffered a crushing defeat, Venizelos told the Athens daily *Eleftheria* that he would not engage in intrigues versus Greece "by involving the U.S. embassy." Dispatch 624 from Athens, November 24, 1952, 781.00/11-2652, DSCF, RG 59, NA. In marginalia, one U.S. official wrote: "The broken record." On Venizelos's cultivation of the embassy, *FRUS 1950*, 5:418–22. The king was equally ready to take offense at U.S. "interventions" that did not favor his views. Ambassador to the Foreign Office, February 2 and 6, 1952, FO 371/101799/WG 1017/2 and 3, PRO.

20. NSC 109: "The Position of the United States with Respect to Turkey" [May 1951], *FRUS 1951*, 5:1151. Compare with National Intelligence Estimate 9, February 26, 1951, *FRUS 1951*, 5:1119–20.

21. *FRUS 1951*, 3:501–6, 508–15, 520–22, 568–73, 592–95, 613–15; *FRUS 1952–54*, 5:271–72. Athanassopoulou, *Turkey*, on accession to NATO.

22. *FRUS 1948*, 4:210–12; *FRUS 1949*, 6:440–42; *FRUS 1950*, 5:335–38, 363 (quote).

23. *FRUS, Conference at Potsdam, 1945*, 2:670–77, 1048–57; *FRUS 1946*, 7:226–30; *FRUS 1949*, 6:427–28; *FRUS 1950*, 5:387–90. On the question of minorities, Karakasidou, *Fields of Wheat*; Mackridge and Yannakakis, *Ourselves and Others*; Clogg, *Minorities in Greece*.

24. *FRUS 1949*, 6:245–48.

25. *FRUS 1950*, 5:406.

26. Quote from the "First Progress Report on NSC 42/1, March 6, 1950, in *FRUS 1950*, 5:432–44. On efforts to curb Greek violations of prisoners' human rights, *FRUS 1947*, 5:203; *FRUS 1948*, 4:58; *FRUS 1949*, 6:259–60, 465–66. See also airgram 974 from Athens, June 21, 1950, 781.00/6-2150, DSCF, RG 59, NA. For European pressures, folder 1950, box 2, Plastiras Papers, BA. On the horrors of the civil war, Mazower, *Inside Hitler's Greece*. On U.S. policy and wartime Greek judicial practice, Wittner, *American Intervention in Greece*. On prisoners, Voglis, *Becoming a Subject*.

27. *FRUS 1950*, 5:386–87.

28. Iatrides, *Ambassador MacVeagh Reports*, 23–24. For investor's complaints, "Le Krach de Myli-Kalamata Responsabilité du Gouvernement Hellénique" (1891), Stefanos Dragoumis Papers, series 2, box 53, Railroads: Folder 2, GLA; Mazower, *Greece and the Interwar Economic Crisis*. On patronage and postwar economic policy, Pirounakis, *Greek Economy*, chap. 3.

29. Memorandum of conversation between Grady and Economou-Gouras, Washington, June 7, 1950, 781.00/6-750, DSCF, RG 59, NA. See also Chatzeantoniou, Νικόλαος Πλαστήρας, 205–7, 213–18.

30. The control process can be followed in great detail in the exchanges between the U.S. Mission (ERP) and Sofokles Venizelos, Exoterika, box 21, Sofokles Venizelos Papers, BA. On U.S. efforts to prod Greek action, Polites to Venizelos, July 15, 1950, Greek embassies, box 21, and minutes of meetings of Greek and U.S. representatives, September 15 and November 24, 1950, Ekonomia, box 29, both Sofokles Venizelos Papers, BA. On the consequences of the Greek economic takeoff, Peurifoy to Venizelos, August 30, 1953, Sofokles Venizelos Papers, BA.

31. *FRUS 1950*, 5:371, 375–76; telegrams 928 from Athens, June 9, 1950, 781.00/6-950, 1440 from Athens, June 17, 1950, 781.00/6-1750, and 44 from Athens, July 5, 1950, 781.00/7-550, all DSCF, RG 59, NA. Quotations from a memorandum of conversation between Minor and Metaxas, July 5, in dispatch 94 from Athens, July 17, 1950, 781.00/7-1750, DSCF, RG 59, NA. On George Papandreou's role in the maneuverings, see Stephanides, "Γεώργιος Παπανδρέου και οι Κυβερνήσεις του Κέντρου."

32. *FRUS 1950*, 5:380, 386–87, 395–96, 399–400; dispatch 150 from Athens, July 26, 1950, 781.00/7-2650, DSCF, RG 59, NA.

33. Telegram 209 from Athens, July 18, 1950, 781.00/7-1850, DSCF, RG 59, NA.

34. *FRUS 1950*, 5:401–2. Minor's position was endorsed by McGhee and incoming ambassador Peurifoy in telegram 453 to Teheran (Grady), August 25, 1950, 781.00/8-2350, DSCF, RG 59, NA.

35. U.S. involvement can be traced in *FRUS 1950*, 5:405–7, 410–22, 425–26. Quote from telegram 878 from Athens, September 14, 1950, 781.00/9-1450, DSCF, RG 59, NA.

36. Dispatch 800 from Athens: "The High Cost of Crisis in Greek Governments," November 2, 1950, 781.00/11-250, DSCF, RG 59, NA. Ambassador to the Foreign Office, January 31, 1951, FO 371/95116/RG10114/2, PRO, on U.S. thinking.

37. *FRUS 1950*, 5:432–34.

38. Dispatches 1008 from Athens, January 4, 1951, 781.00/1-451, and 1075 from Athens, January 11, 1950, 781.00/1-1151, both DSCF, RG 59, NA; CIA Intelligence Report April 30, 1951, CIA RDP 82-00457, NA; *FRUS 1951*, 5:474.

39. The incident is covered in *FRUS 1951*, 5:475–83. The quote is from telegram 5141 to Athens, June 25, 1951, 781.00/6-2551, DSCF, RG 59, NA. British reporting downplayed the officers "revolt" as "very minor incidents." Telegram 123, June 1, 1951, and dispatch 110, June 4, 1951, both to the Foreign Office, FO 371/95143/RG 1195/2 and 7, PRO. See also Stavrou, *Allied Politics and Military Interventions*, 153. In the mid-1920s, Venizelos, beneficiary of military interventions in 1909 and 1916–17 and future participant in a 1930s coup, warned his lieutenants that the military was out of control. Venizelos to "Friends," June 27, 1926, folder 1916–36, Emmanuele Tsouderos Papers, BA.

40. Papahelas, *Βιασμός*, 26–29.

41. Telegram 4673 from Athens, June 28, 1951, 781.00/6-2851, DSCF, RG 59, NA. Quote from *FRUS 1951*, 5:492–93.

42. *FRUS 1951*, 5:498–505. Embassy in Greece to ministry, September 15, 1951, vol. 95, Greece, MAE.

43. Karamanlis, *Αρχείο*, 1:145; embassy in Greece to ministry, January 13, 1952, vol. 95, Greece, MAE. On elections, British ambassador to the Foreign Office, August 15 and 16, 1951, telegrams 227, September 14, 1951, and 101, November 8, 1951, both to the Foreign Office, and minute by Cheetham, August 27, 1951, all FO 371/95118/RG 10114/29, 30, 33, 41, and 63, PRO.

44. Basic documentation on the Plastiras government is in Athanasiades-Novas, *Πεπραγμένα της Κυβερνήσεως Πλαστηρα-Βενιζέλου*. Dispatch 1188 from Athens, April 1, 1952, reported that Plastiras had done everything he could to avoid the Beloyiannis execution while publicly endorsing it. 781.00/4-152, DSCF, RG 59, NA. The United States had no role in the judicial process or subsequent appeals and execution. American propaganda tried to capitalize on revelations of "Cominform . . . subversion and interference [in] internal affairs" of Greece as a "common danger to all Western nations." *FRUS 1952–54*, 5:270. Minute, June 16, 1952, FO 371/101798/WG1016/44, PRO, on communist infiltration in Greece.

45. French analyses of Greek internal politics, September 9, November 20, December 27, 1951, and February 18 and 22, 1952, vol. 95, Greece, MAE. Comments of exiled

KKE leaders reported in telegram 121 from embassy in Hungary to the ministry, vol. 96, Greece, MAE. See also Chatzeantoniou, Νικόλαος Πλαστήρας, 229–32.

46. *FRUS 1952–54*, 8:782, 784–85, 801–2. On U.S. frustrations, telegram 53 to the Foreign Office, February 9, 1952, FO 371/101799/WG1017/7, PRO.

47. Embassy in Greece to ministry, February 18, 1952, and "Greece at the Beginning of 1952," February 15, 1952, both vol. 95, Greece, MAE.

48. *FRUS 1952–54*, 8:789–90; *New York Times*, March 15, 1952 (quote); embassy in Greece to ministry, vol. 94, Greece, MAE.

49. Peurifoy to Roundtree, March 31, 1952, 781.00/3-3152, and telegram 4151 from Athens, March 17, 1952, 781.00/3-1752, both DSCF, RG 59, NA; memorandum of conversation between Strange and King Paul, February 28, 1952, FO 371/101808/WG 1052/1, PRO. On Greek anger over U.S. actions, see reports in FO 371/101799/WG1017/11-13, PRO.

50. *New York Times*, March 16 and August 21, 1952.

51. On Papandreou's maneuvers, telegrams 5123 from Athens, May 29, 1952, 781.00/5-2952, and 383 from Athens, July 31, 781.00/7-3152, both DSCF, RG 59, NA. On currency reform, *FRUS 1952–54*, 8:799–800, 802–6. On the royal couple, embassy to Greece to ministry, August 3, 1952, vol. 96, Greece, MAE.

52. *FRUS 1952–54*, 8:806–9; embassy in the United States to ministry, October 15, 1952, vol. 96, Greece, MAE.

53. *FRUS 1952–54*, 8:817–30. On activism of Papagos's government, "Annual Report on Greece, 1953," February 3, 1954, FO371/112830/WG1011/1, PRO, and embassy in Greece to ministry, June 19, 1953, vol. 96, Greece, MAE. Papagos underlined his intention to pursue his goals without U.S. restraints in a talk with Peake, November 27, 1952, FO 371/101808/WG 1052/9, PRO. On Papagos's relationship with royal family and initial problems with the Eisenhower administration, Markezinis, Σύγχρονη Πολιτική Ιστορία, 3:16–18, 37–38.

54. *FRUS 1952–54*, 8:834–40; Peake to Foreign Office, June 4, 1953, FO 371/107495/WG 10345/1, PRO.

55. *FRUS 1952–54*, 8:810–11, 813–17; dispatches 1340 from Athens, May 20, 1953, 781.1/5-2053, and 1167 from Athens, April 15, 1953, 781.14/4-1553, both DSCF, RG 59, NA; memorandum by Foreign Office, October 30, 1952, FO 371/101798/WG1016/52, PRO.

56. Dispatch 1288 from Athens, May 9, 1953, 781.00/5-853, and Peurifoy to Porter, June 2, 1953, 781.00/6-2353, both DSCF, RG 59, NA. On center's problems, comments of Karamanlis in Genevoix, *Greece of Karamanlis*, 120–21.

57. Telegram 1760 from Athens, December 2, 1952, 781.00/12-252, and Peurifoy to Baxter, June 30, 1953, 781.11/6-2053, both DSCF, RG 59, NA; *FRUS 1952–54*, 8:841–42.

58. *FRUS 1952–54*, 8:842–46, 859–64.

59. Memorandum of conversation between Eden and Papagos, April 4, 1954, FO

371/1074449/WG 1052/3, PRO. The Churchill-Frederika correspondence, March 23 and April 7, 1954, with comments by the prime minister's aides, PREM 11/682, PRO.

60. *FRUS 1955–57*, 24:527–28 (quote), 530–31.

Chapter 2

1. Telegram 2 to Colonial Office, July 28, 1878, CO 67/2, PRO; high commissioner to Colonial Office, September 25 and December 19, 1878, CO 67/1, PRO. On infrastructure improvements, Grivas, *Memoirs*, 16.

2. Markides, *Rise and Fall*, 514, on central role of the church. Quataert, *Ottoman Empire, 1700–1922*, esp. 62–68, on impact of the equalization of rights.

3. Statement by the high commissioner, February 17, 1897, CO 67/104/4448, PRO. On legal code and police force, Wolseley to Salisbury, September 25 and December 19, 1878, both CO 67/1, PRO. See also Klerides, *Cyprus*, 1:109–12.

4. High commissioner to Colonial Office, April 9, 1913, CO 6/169/13153, PRO. On the judicial issue, see Minute, "Judicial Organization," April 4, 1882, CO 67/2/3146, PRO; Venezis, *Makarios: Faith and Power*, 33, 69. On communal tensions, Bahcheli, *Greek-Turkish Relations*.

5. Minutes, n.d., and June 30, 1915, with attached extract from legislative council debates, April 21, 1915, CO 67/177/29877, PRO.

6. The notion that Britain practiced divide and rule is deeply ingrained in Greek and Greek Cypriot analyses of the region. Georghallides, "Turkish and British Reactions to the Emigration of Cypriot Turks to Anatolia." The most recent archives-based study, Holland, *Britain and the Revolt in Cyprus*, 67, refutes that idea. Venezis, *Makarios: Faith and Power*, 69, agrees. McHenry, *Uneasy Partnership*, 26–27, on British efforts to assist Turkish Cypriots.

7. Embassy in Greece, "Memorandum on Confidential Paper 'South Eastern Europe and the Balkans,'" February 2, 1919, FO 286/702, PRO.

8. Comments of British administrators to Colonial Office, February 6 and 28, 1929, CO 67/228/5, PRO, and Storrs to Colonial Office, April 17, 1931, CO 67/237/10, PRO. On the KKK/AKEL's complex problems, Adams, *AKEL*, 10–25.

9. Dispatch 245 from the embassy to the Foreign Office, May 7, 1930, CO 67/234/1, PRO; memorandum: "The Cypriot Question from the Greek Angle," n.d., but October 1932, CO 67/244/9, PRO. Gennadius to the archbishop of Cyprus, December 18, 1929, series 5, box 13, Cyprus 1898–1932, John Gennadius Papers, GLA, and E. Venizelos to Tsouderos, February 7, 1933, Emmanuele Tsouderos Papers, folder 1916–36, BA, for Venizelos's views.

10. Nicholson to Colonial Office, February 6, 1929, CO 67/228/5, PRO; minute, August 12, 1931, CO 67/237/11, PRO.

11. Storrs to Colonial Office, October 27, 1931, CO 67/240/10, PRO; Sir John Simon to Colonial Office, January 30, 1934, CO 67/254/1, PRO.

12. Telegram 112, November, 8, 1931, CO 67/240/10, PRO; Palmer to Colonial Office, June 17, 1937, CO 67/272/16, PRO. On the growth of a Turkish Cypriot identification, Palmer to Colonial Office, April 10 and May 3, 1935, both CO 67/262/2, PRO; McHenry, *Uneasy Partnership*, 33.

13. Memorandum of conversation with Mr. Henniker-Heaton, December 31, 1931, CO 67/241/4, PRO. On Storrs's "weakness," minutes, CO 67/24/4, PRO. Text of Cyprus Law 21 (1931), December 21, 1931, CO 67/240/12, PRO. See also Palmer to Colonial Office, January 17, 1934, CO 67/253/10, PRO.

14. Palmer to Colonial Office, June 24, 1934, CO 67/254/3, and June 4, 1938, CO 67/291/3, both PRO. On August 19, 1938, the Colonial Office approved Palmer's specific proposals. CO 67/291/3, PRO. Palmer to Colonial Office, March 3, 1939, CO 67/293/3, PRO, on efforts to choke off covert church funding of the enosis movement. In December, the colonial government stopped impeding an archiepiscopal election since the "present state of the Church, both from a spiritual and temporal point of view is a scandal and it is just possible that with an able man as Archbishop the thoughts of his flock will be occupied for some years as much with reform . . . as with its political mission." Battershill to Colonial Office, December 9, 1939, CO 67/297/4, PRO. On British efforts to undermine the church, Venezis, *Makarios: Faith and Power*, 70, and McHenry, *Uneasy Partnership*, 105–6.

15. Palmer to Colonial Office, November 19, 1934, CO 67/253/10, PRO, and January 6, 1939, CO 67/301/3, PRO. The press and the Church of England remained headaches for the British government throughout the Cyprus crisis. Macmillan, *Riding the Storm*, 225.

16. Minutes of January 4, 1942 (Acheson), and April 4, 1943 (illegible), CO 67/314/12, PRO.

17. Battershill to Colonial Office, December 13, 1940, CO 67/307/8, and January 7, 1941, CO 67/314/10, both PRO; minute by Luke, January 30, 1945, CO 67/327/16, PRO; Foot, *Start in Freedom*, 146.

18. Holland, *Britain and the Revolt in Cyprus*, 13–32; Mayes, *Cyprus and Makarios*, 18–20, 274; *FRUS 1952–54*, 8:743–45; Bitsios, *Cyprus*, 42; Averoff-Tossizza, *Lost Opportunities*, 9–13, 16, 24–27; Alexandrakis, Theodoropoulos, and Lagakos, *Κυπριακό*, 16–17; Vlachou, *Δέκα Χρόνια Κυπριακού*, 47–49, on the growth of Greek public concern about Cyprus. British reporting clarifies the gradual buildup of public discontent. See minutes by Fisher February 1, 1947, March 2, 1949, August 3, 1950, CO 67/342/2 and CO 67/368/7 and 8, PRO; consulate in Thessaloniki to the Foreign Office, September 20, 1950, FO 371/87724/RG1081/134, PRO; telegrams 25 and 81 to the Foreign Office, FO 371/95133/RG 1081/36 and 47, PRO. See also Bahcheli, *Greek-Turkish Relations*, 29–33.

19. *FRUS 1952–54*, 8:674–75. Dulles summarized the policy: "We sympathize with the aspirations of those wanting self-determination. We appeal to Greece to keep this matter within reasonable bounds." *FRUS 1952–54*, 8:271–72.

20. Greece faced opposition from other U.S. ethnic groups to its claims. Memorandum of the Macedonian Political Association of the United States, 1957, Greek American Organizations, NEA/GRK, RG 59, NA, for criticism of Greece's record with minorities.

21. U.S. diplomats were skeptical about British claims concerning the AKEL threat. Courtney to Wood, April 26, 1957, Official Informal Correspondence (Nicosia), NEA/GRK, RG 59, NA. On divisions among British officials, minute October 22, 1945, CO 67/327/15, PRO; minutes by Luke, January 30, 1951, and Burton, October 4, 1945, both CO 67/327/16, PRO.

22. On Britain's strategic position, *FRUS 1951*, 5:259, 403; *FRUS 1955–57*, 24:282–84. On signals intelligence, Raymond Courtney oral history, ADST. McHenry, *Uneasy Partnership*, 19, 32, 65–71, on prewar Cyprus strategic debate. On U.S. assessment, Nicolet, *United States Policy towards Cyprus*, 99–100; minute by Barnes, April 23, 1952, FO 371/101810/WG1081/16, PRO.

23. At their March 21, 1957, meeting, "The Prime Minister and President agreed that the military importance of Cyprus today has become rather less, although it was still useful to have a base there." *FRUS 1955–57*, 24:465. Compare their Mediterranean *tour de horizon* on March 20, *FRUS 1955–57*, 24:464.

24. *FRUS 1955–57*, 24:351, 465–66.

25. *FRUS 1958–60*, 10:575–78.

26. Telegram 29 to the Foreign Office, January 25, 1950, FO 371/87716/RG1081/145, PRO; memorandum of conversation between Assistant Secretary of State Burton Berry and Erkin, July 26, 1951, Cyprus 1950–54, and memorandum by Ali Nur Bey, August 29, 1955, Cyprus January–August 1955, both Turkish Desk Files, RG 59, NA. On Turkish government responsibility, see the CIA report dated September 12, 1955, printed without attribution to the agency, *FRUS 1955–57*, 24:284. Turkish popular opinion remained seized of the issue. Miner to Jones, April 11, 1957, Official Informal Correspondence (Athens), NEA/GRK, RG 59, NA; Daniel Newberry oral history, ADST. On the Turkish decision to enter into the Cyprus morass, Bahcheli, *Greek-Turkish Relations*, 36–39, and Michalopoulos, Ελλάδα και Τουρκία, 69–74.

27. Memorandum from Davis to Snyder, November 7, 1955, Relations with Greece, 1950–55, Turkish Desk Files, RG 59, NA; Menderes to Eisenhower, January 18, 1958, *FRUS 1958–60*, 10:577–78.

28. *FRUS 1955–57*, 24:378–79. Menderes backed away from the war threat but clearly achieved his objective of demonstrating Turkish intensity to an "amazed" Nixon.

29. Holland, *Britain and the Revolt in Cyprus*, 51–52, 58, 64; Averoff-Tossizza, *Lost Opportunities*, 45–49.

30. *FRUS 1955–57*, 24:332–26. On the character, motivations, and aims of Grivas, the best source is his *Memoirs*. The Greek government publicly questioned Grivas's mental stability in 1959. Telegram 385 to the Foreign Office, September 22, 1959, FO

371/144519/RG 1015/27, PRO. For British embassy comments on the issue, dispatch 90 to the Foreign Office, September 23, 1959, FO 371/144519/RG 1015/28, PRO. On links and support provided by the church as well as the tense relations with Makarios, Grivas, *Memoirs*, 17–21, 29, 40; Nicolet, *United States Policy towards Cyprus*, 97; Bitsios, *Cyprus*, 43–45, 63. On the British error in arresting the archbishop, Peake to Ward, April 9, 1956, FO 371/123884/RG1081/769, PRO.

31. *FRUS 1955–57*, 24:319.

32. Averoff-Tossizza, *Lost Opportunities*, 63–64; Karamanlis, Αρχείο, 2:18, 23. On Makarios's mistrust of Greek objectives, Vlachos, Δέκα Χρόνια Κυπριακού, 104–6; Kranidiotis, Δύσκολα Χρόνια, 137–40, 148. Trying to peer into Makarios's mind is difficult. The archbishop kept his own counsel. However, a number of U.S. officials, who had generally positive views of Makarios, reached this conclusion. Courtney oral history, ADST. In 1969, a group of U.S. diplomats involved in mediating the 1967 Cyprus crisis came to similar conclusions. Their consensus was that Makarios wanted the right to enosis as part of a strategy designed to break the Turkish Cypriots' insistence on being treated as a coequal community and to reduce them to the status of a minority. He wanted the enosis option but had no intention of carrying out union unless he was sure that he would emerge as a Cypriot "Venizelos" dominating Greek politics. Transcript of discussion, September 1969, 19–21, Eastern Mediterranean Project at Arlie House, Cyprus Crisis Files 1967, RG 59, NA. Makarios himself outlined a quite similar position during a question-and-answer session at the National Press Club in Washington, D.C., on September 24, 1957. A transcript of the meeting is in Visits: Makarios, NEA/GRK, RG 59, NA. For years Greek Cypriots were loath to admit the ambivalence; see Venezis, *Makarios: Faith and Power*, 104–5, and Makarios's comments quoted therein, 134. After the 1974 Cyprus coup, Venezis claimed that Makarios had decided to pursue an independent Cyprus in 1967. Venezis, *Makarios: Pragmatism v Idealism*, 172. On Makarios's negotiating style, Foot, *Start in Freedom*, 182.

33. *FRUS 1955–57*, 24:496. Compare Eden to Eisenhower, June 7, 1956, *FRUS 1955–57*, 24:354–65.

34. *FRUS 1955–57*, 24:347–48, 356–57, 471. On the Greek view, Karamanlis, Αρχείο, 2:309–10.

35. In late 1956 the United States sent Julius Holmes on a secret mission to Europe to sound out the views of the three involved states. The British politely but firmly discouraged Holmes's efforts, and the Americans immediately abandoned any idea of mediation. Documentation in *FRUS 1955–57*, 24:387–421; minute to the prime minister, October 10, 1956, FO 371/123937/RG 1081/G2047, PRO. For details, Nicolet, *United States Policy towards Cyprus*, 85–90.

36. On the "plan" to create a democratic "empire," crystallized in the Northwest Ordinance, Wood, *American Revolution*. The influence of race and of nativism in the formation of U.S. foreign policy can be traced in Hietala, *Manifest Design*, and Borstel-

mann, *Cold War and the Color Line*. On nativism and migration, Higham, *Strangers in the Land*. On the marriage of racist and nativist ideas and the creation of American "empire," Zimmerman, *First Great Triumph*. Eisenhower came from a generation brought up with a "scientific" racist view of the world but presided over the first steps in a major reorientation of U.S. domestic and foreign policy regarding race.

37. Peurifoy's comment, *FRUS 1951*, 5:529–31; Dulles's, *FRUS 1955–57*, 24:446–48. See also Alexandrakis, Theodoropoulos, and Lagakos, Κυπριακό, 128–29.

38. *FRUS 1950*, 5:260, and *FRUS 1951*, 5:259.

39. NSC 5708/2: "State of U.S. Policy in Turkey," June 29, 1957, *FRUS 1955–57*, 24:720–30. On efforts to convince the Turks to take a softer line, *FRUS 1955–57*, 24:277–79; the two quoted passages are in memoranda from Baxter to Allen, August 22, 1955, Cyprus, January–August 1955, and Woods to Holmes, April 30, 1957, Partition, NEA/GRK, both Turkish Desk Files, RG 59, NA. On U.S. attitudes toward Turkey, and *enosis*, Archer Blood oral history, ADST; Michalopoulos, Ελλάδα και Τουρκία, 34–35.

40. *FRUS 1955–57*, 24:311–13, 583–84.

41. On ties between Greece and the insurrection, Grivas, *Memoirs*, 17–19, 29, 63, 115–18, 130–31, 152; Averoff-Tossizza, *Lost Opportunities*, 37–38, 43–44, 150–55. The U.S. perspective, *FRUS 1950*, 5:378–79; *FRUS 1952–54*, 8:676–7, 740. On Makarios's efforts to win Greek political support, telegrams 4079 from Athens, May 24, 1951, 781.00/5-2451, and 1089 from Athens, March 23, 1953, 781.00/3-2353, both DSCF, RG 59, NA. On Papagos and Cyprus, Markezinis, Σύγχρονη Πολιτική Ιστορία 3:42. On British reaction to Greek-backed EOKA terrorism, Bitsios, *Cyprus*, 24; Holland, *Britain and the Revolt in Cyprus*, 32–33. On the church's anti-U.S. role, Averoff-Tossizza, *Lost Opportunities*, 51. On Cyprus's effect on Greek internal politics, Karamanlis, Αρχείο, 1:278–80; 2:23.

42. Karamanlis's statement, Αρχείο, 1:256–57; 2:24, 201–2. See also Αρχείο, 2:18–20, 41–47, 63–73, 454; Genevoix, *Greece of Karamanlis*, 135; *FRUS 1955–57*, 24:322–25.

43. On the policy and internal criticism, *FRUS 1955–57*, 24:269–71, 281–82, 288–89, 299–302. On blocking Greece at the United Nations, Karamanlis, Αρχείο, 1:180–81. On the psychological impact of mob violence and the Turkish government's role, see the comments of Patriarch Athenagoras, September 12, 1955, memorandum of conversation with U.S. ambassador Warren, Cyprus, September 1955, Turkish Desk Files, RG 59, NA. See also Michalopoulos, Ελλάδα και Τουρκία, 84; and Averoff-Tossizza, *Lost Opportunities*, 51.

44. For the prime minister's public and private statements, Karamanlis, Αρχείο, 1:278–80, 292–94, 311, 322, 325–29; 2:18–20, 41–47, 443; *FRUS 1955–57*, 24:417–18. On the relationship of domestic developments and Cyprus policy, Michalopoulos, Ελλάδα και Τουρκία, 89–90.

45. Karamanlis's approaches to the United States, *FRUS 1955–57*, 24:547–49,

FRUS 1958–60, 10:315–16, 322–25, 394–96, 430–32, 561–63; Dulles's views, *FRUS 1958–60*, 10:446–48, 457; the September 17, 1959, Eisenhower-Dulles conversation, *FRUS 1958–60*, 10:506. Bistios, *Cyprus*, 43–44, 75, admits that his government decided to stop EOKA violence in late 1957 when Grivas's actions against fellow Greek Cypriots had become a major propaganda problem. A June 1957 analysis suggested that the Cyprus issue would not lead to the overthrow of Karamanlis. CIA, National Estimates Memorandum 33-57: "Outlook for Cyprus, June 13, 1957," CIA RDP 79T00937, NA; Karamanlis, Αρχείο, 2:151.

46. *FRUS 1955–57*, 24:385–88; Wood to Belcher, August 9, 1957, Official Informal Correspondence (Nicosia), NEA/GRK, RG 59, NA; Karamanlis, Αρχείο, 2:195–99, and 3:205–8; Nicolet, *United States Policy towards Cyprus*, 119–20.

47. *FRUS 1958–60*, 10:591–92; Nicolet, *United States Policy towards Cyprus*, 92–93; Kranidiotis, Δύσκολα Χρόνια, 291.

48. Courtney oral history, ADST; *FRUS 1955–57*, 24:319–20.

49. *FRUS 1955–57*, 24:310–11, 316–18, 374–75, 436–37, 467–68; Karamanlis, Αρχείο, 2:309–10. On the first of Macmillan's maneuvers, memorandum from the Greek embassy to the Department of State, December 26, 1956, Radcliffe Proposals, NEA/GRK, RG 59, NA. Compare Holland, *Britain and the Revolt in Cyprus*, 48, 137–38, 169–70, 246–47; minutes on Greece and Cyprus, September 1956, FO 371/123850, PRO.

50. *FRUS 1955–57*, 24:488–50, 460–64. Averoff-Tossizza, *Lost Opportunities*, 108, 140–42, 183; Karamanlis, Αρχείο, 2:344–45; Murat Williams oral history, ADST.

51. *FRUS 1955–57*, 24:464–65, 467; Michalopoulos, Ελλάδα και Τουρκία, 119, on the U.S. role in pushing Macmillan to release Makarios and Karamanlis's prodding of the Americans.

52. NSC memorandum of August 5, 1957, *FRUS 1955–57*, 24:493–94.

53. Karamanlis, Αρχείο, 2:137–38, 223–26, 262–64; 3:57–58, 187–93; Averoff-Tossizza, *Lost Opportunities*, 232, 237–38, 240.

54. Karamanlis, Αρχείο, 2:297–309, 3:226–28; Alexandrakis, Theodoropoulos, and Lagakos, Κυπριακό, 26–27; Averoff-Tossizza, *Lost Opportunities*, 132, 237–38, 240–41, 254, 267–68; "Greece: Annual Review for 1958," January 16, 1959, FO 371/144516/RG1011/1, PRO.

55. *FRUS 1958–60*, 10:793–94; Karamanlis, Αρχείο, 3:307–20, 395–96, 399, 403–4; Averoff-Tossizza, *Lost Opportunities*, 340–41.

56. Holland, *Britain and the Revolt in Cyprus*, 290, 311.

57. Grivas, *Memoirs*, 187, 191–93; Venezis, *Makarios: Pragmatism v. Idealism*, 114.

58. On the evolution of the Greek negotiating strategy and position, Karamanlis, Αρχείο, 3:408, 4:21; Averoff-Tossizza, *Lost Opportunities*, 363–64, 369, 387; Bitsios, *Cyprus*, 38, 42–45, 63, 72–75, 83–85. See also Woodhouse, *Karamanlis*, 87, 123. Karamanlis's comments to Eisenhower, *FRUS 1955–57*, 24:523–24, and *FRUS 1958–60*, 10:575–76. On skilled Greek diplomacy, "Annual Review of Developments in Greece in 1959," January 13, 1960, FO 371/152961/RG1011/1, PRO.

59. Lee, *Athenian Adventure*, 107. Compare Penfield, memorandum of conversation with Myrianthis, May 23, 1957, Independence, NEA/GRK, RG 59, NA. See also Michalopoulos, *Ελλάδα και Τουρκία*, 131–33.

60. USIA Greek Public Opinion Study, October 2, 1957, Communism, NEA/GRK, RG 59, NA. The characterization of Greek opinion is from Lee, *Athenian Adventure*, 119.

Chapter 3

1. John Owens and W. Tapley Bennett oral histories, ADST. French documentation paints the same picture; see especially the reports in vol. 206, Greece, MAE.

2. On Dulles's views, see chapter 2. Kennedy's and Rusk's views, *FRUS 1961–1963*, 16:658–61, 675, 679–80. On maintaining distance from Karamanlis, Baker to Allen and Jernegan, April 20, 1955, 781.00/4-2055, DSCF, RG 59, NA.

3. Note by the ministry, April 21, 1953, vol. 96, Greece, MAE. In his analysis of the effects of the Papagos victory, Peurifoy delphically commented: "In the present circumstances, the embassy is likely to be the most effective part of the opposition." Peurifoy to Porter, June 2, 1953, 781.00/6-2353, DSCF, RG 59, NA. King Paul's comments, July 23, 1957, in dispatch 102 from Athens, August 6, 1954, 781.00/8-654, DSCF, RG 59, NA. On the increased public role of IDEA and its threat to civil control, *FRUS 1955–57*, 24:540–41; and Lambert to Young, Athens, July 9, 1954, FO 371/112832/WG10112/9, PRO. The CIA analysis of the impact of Papagos's death is in *FRUS 1955–57*, 24:547.

4. On the maneuverings prior to Papagos's death, including the king's approach to the CIA, *FRUS 1955–57*, 24:541–46; Karamanlis, *Αρχείο*, 1:259–62; Averoff-Tossizza, *Lost Opportunities*, 54. On Washington's appreciation of Karamanlis, Papahelas, *Βιασμός*, 46–54.

5. On Karamanlis's political style, *Αρχείο*, 1:89, 165, 170, 174–76, 213–114, 225–27, 236–37, 250. On factors aiding Karamanlis to hold power, "Greece: Annual Review 1956," March 7, 1957, FO 371/130012/RG1011/1, PRO; telegram 73 to the Foreign Office, April 11, 1956, FO 371/123847/RG 1017/32, PRO, together with the recollections of Markezinis, *Σύγχρονη Πολιτική Ιστορία*, 3:66–71, and of Ralles, *Πολιτικές Εκμυστηρεύσεις*, 33–37. Karamanlis's self-appraisal of his role as a modernizer is in letter to Rusk, July 22, 1961, Karamanlis, *Αρχείο*, 5:121–22, and Genevoix, *Greece of Karamanlis*, 132. A contemporary appraisal of Karamanlis is "Athenian" [Roufas], *Inside the Colonels' Greece*, 36–37.

6. *FRUS 1958–60*, 10:652–55. Karamanlis earlier outlined his objectives during a November 1956 official visit to the United States. *FRUS 1955–57*, 24:573–78. On his views of the United States, Karamanlis, *Αρχείο*, 1:130, 146. On the transformation of postwar Greek society, McNeill, *Metamorphosis of Greece*. On Karamanlis's ties to the royal family, "Greece: Annual Review 1956," March 7, 1956, FO 371/130012/RG1011/1, PRO.

7. For example, *FRUS 1955–57*, 24:568–69, 572–73; *FRUS 1958–60*, 10:671–73; minute by Gallsworthy, March 8, 1957, FO 371/120023/RG410345/1, PRO.

8. NSC 5718/1, August 5, 1957, *FRUS 1955–57*, 24:585–92. Compare with embassy in the United States to ministry, February 10, 1956, vol. 206, Greece, MAE. While the comparative size of the U.S. aid package was drastically reduced, Greece still retained a leading position among recipients: between 1953 and 1961 it garnered $1.2 billion in U.S. aid, making it the fourth largest recipient of American aid in Europe. Calvo-Gonzales, "Neither a Carrot nor a Stick."

9. Draft memorandum and letter to Karamanlis, ca. August 9, 1957, Economic Aid, NEA/GRK, RG 59, NA. The letter was signed by Eisenhower on August 14. Telegram 1993 from Athens, December 1, 1956, 781.00/12-156, DSCF, RG 59, NA, contains the embassy analysis of Karamanlis's position. See also NIE 32–56, "Outlook for Greece," June 26, 1956, *FRUS 1955–57*, 24:566–67. For overall policy judgment of keeping some distance from Karamanlis, Operations Coordination Board Report on Greece, December 11, 1957, *FRUS 1955–57*, 24:603–7. In a December 13, 1956, report on Greek politics, Ambassador George Allen stressed the desire of both the opposition and the Palace for a U.S. policy that avoided too close an embrace of the prime minister. *FRUS 1955–57*, 24:580–81. A month earlier Allen had noted that Karamanlis's unexpected criticism of a speech the ambassador made showed the prime minister wanted to avoid being tagged as a U.S. "stooge." Allen to Woods, November 11, 1956, 781.00/11-1656, DSCF, RG 59, NA.

10. *FRUS 1955–57*, 24:553–57. See also NSC 5718/1, August 5, 1957, *FRUS 1955–57*, 24:585–92.

11. *FRUS 1955–57*, 24:538–40, 557–60, 570–71; *FRUS 1958–60*, 10:709–12; Karamanlis, Αρχείο, 1:296–97.

12. Briggs quote, *FRUS 1958–60*, 10:726. The bond issue impasse is covered in *FRUS 1958–60*, 10:602–3, 664–65, 682–84, 650–52, 673–75, 697–99, 705–7; *FRUS 1961–63*, 16:604–8, where Karamanlis laid out his views during his April 1961 visit to Washington; and *FRUS 1961–63*, 16:616.

13. Karamanlis, Αρχείο, 4:145.

14. *FRUS 1958–60*, 10:611–12; Karamanlis, Αρχείο, 4:465–66.

15. "The Influence of Emotion on Greek Policy," dispatch 124 from Athens, August 25, 1956, 781.00/8-2556, DSCF, RG 59, NA; Birgfeld to Wood, September 11, 1957, Official Informal (Athens), NEA/GRK, RG 59, NA; *FRUS 1955–57*, 24:562–63, 594–96; *FRUS 1958–60*, 10:604, 685–87, 703–4; *FRUS 1961–63*, 16:655–57. Compare "First Impressions of Greece," September 26, 1957, FO 371/130014/RG1015/13, PRO, and dispatch 331 to the Foreign Office, March 7, 1958, FO 371/136220/RG1015/6, PRO. See the comments on Karamanlis in minute by Goodall, March 11, 1958, FO 371/136220/RG1015/6, PRO. On the impact of the Armour report, embassy in Greece to the ministry, March 7, 1957, vol. 206, Greece, MAE; and Karamanlis, Αρχείο, 2:288–92. On the 1958 elections, Averoff-Tossizza, *Lost Opportunities*, 222.

16. *FRUS 1955–57*, 24:600–602. The quote is from Laingen to Belcher, October 1, 1957, Official Informal Correspondence (Nicosia) 1957, NEA/GRK, RG 59, NA. On the cooperative high-level relationship, rooted in a common analysis of the threat posed by the USSR, *FRUS 1958–60*, 10:688–94; *FRUS 1961–63*, 16:608–12; Karamanlis, Αρχείο, 4:84–90, 145–46, 222–26, 283–85, 298–300; Averoff-Tossizza, *Lost Opportunities*, 223. On the 1955 riots, see chapter 2.

17. *FRUS 1952–54*, 8:741–42; *FRUS 1958–60*, 10:632–33, 661–64, 696–71, 700–702, 718–20, 735–36; *FRUS 1961–63*, 16:612–14, 616–19, 622, 625–31, 637–44, 646, 653–61; Averoff-Tossizza, *Lost Opportunities*, 219. On publicity problems, Karamanlis, Αρχείο, 3:246–48, 378–79; 4:163–66, 222–26; 5:369–71, 421–22; embassy in Greece to ministry, January 8, 1960, and May 19, 1960, both vol. 206, Greece, MAE; Peake to Foreign Office, December 7, 1955, FO 371/117686/RG11345/3, PRO.

18. Telegram 3319 from Athens, May 26, 1958, reported Karamanlis's views. 781.00/5-2658, DSCF, RG 59, NA. On Karamanlis's campaign, telegram 3320 from Athens, May 27, 1958, 781.00/5-2758, DSCF, RG 59, NA. On the causes of EDA's triumph, dispatch 476 from Athens, January 2, 1958, 781.11/1-258, DSCF, RG 59, NA. Dulles's comments, May 14 meeting of the Operations Coordination Board, *FRUS 1958–60*, 10:613–14. The embassy's quoted comment is in telegram 3258 from Athens, May 21, 1958, 781.00/5-2158, RG 59, NA. See also Genevoix, *Greece of Karamanlis*, 140; Karamanlis, Αρχείο, 3:42–43.

19. Brewster oral history, ADST.

20. On intelligence operations in Greece as well as the special relationships between the royal family and the agency, Brewster, Owens, Anschuetz, and Dixon oral histories, ADST; dispatch 226 from Athens, September 22, 1958, 781.00/9-2258, RG 59, NA. On the value of CIA intelligence, Owens commented that the "only difference between us [CIA and embassy] was that we didn't pay for our information."

21. These operations bring out political paranoia, as a speedy Google search testifies. Documentation is extremely limited. What is available, including some apparent forgeries, is to be found at www.isn.ethz.ch/php. State Department efforts to get the "official" (U.S.) version of the story out can be sampled at www.usinfo.state.gov/media/archive. The debate largely centers on whether the "stay behind" operation in Italy ("Gladio") became a center for antidemocratic action. The Greek left seized on this to suggest that its country's 1950s' stay-behind (variously reported as "Sheepskin" or "LOK") was connected in some way to events of 1967.

22. Daniel Zachery oral history, ADST.

23. The program was outlined in telegram 3895 from Athens, 1967, partially printed, with deletions, in *FRUS 1964–68*, 16:541–42. A fuller text of the first page of the document, which includes information on the covert-funding program, was printed in Papahelas, Βιασμός, 279–80. By the late 1950s, the CIA specialized in these sorts of operations. On the evolution of the program see Miller, "Taking Off the Gloves" and "Roughhouse Diplomacy." In comparison with the Italian project, CIA

activities in Greece were rather limited. Covert funding in Greece was restricted to the election cycle. In Italy the CIA carried out a five-year "civic action" program that aimed to build democracy at every level of Italian society. See Colby, *Honorable Men*, 108–40, for a description of the program. Richardson, *My Father the Spy*, 122–23, claims that the CIA mounted a major effort in support of Karamanlis's 1958 election campaign. Richardson was a five-year-old child at the time, rendering his telling of events in Greece a bit suspect, particularly on issues of timing. Moreover, while the CIA may have been less obsessive about security in the 1950s, it strains credulity that secret operations were a subject of family discussion.

24. The OCB report for Greece, December 17, 1958, is censored at precisely the point at which political action was indicated. It differs markedly in phrasing from the two previous and uncensored OCB reports published in the volume of the *FRUS* series dealing with Greece: *FRUS 1955–57*, 24:566–67, 603–7; *FRUS 1958–60*, 10:643–49. NIE 32-58, September 23, 1958, in *FRUS 1958–60*, 10:634–35; see also dispatches 629 from Athens, February 4, 1959, 781.00/2-459, and 455 from Athens, December 28, 1958, 781.00/12-2858, and telegram 1798 from Athens, February 9, 1959, 781.00/2-959, all DSCF, RG 59, NA. For the U.S. analysis of the outcome of the 1959 elections, see telegrams 2273 from Athens, April 6, 1959, 781.00/4-659, and 2851 from Athens, June 15, 1959, 781.00/6-1559, both DSCF, RG 59, NA. See also dispatch 63 to the Foreign Office, June 20, 1959, FO 371/144518/RG1015/13, PRO.

25. The embassy's reasoning was outlined in dispatch 226 from Athens, September 22, 1958, 781.00/9-2258, DSCF, RG 59, NA. See also Holden, *Greece without Columns*, 189. In 1961 Karamanlis, "speaking with fervor, went on to say that the electoral law had been planned by him with a view to assisting the buildup of an intelligent, loyal opposition, which he feels the country needs." Memorandum of conversation with Karamanlis, July 24, 1961, 781.00/7-2461, DSCF, RG 59, NA. "Annual Report for 1960 (Greece)," December 30, 1960, FO 371/160191/RG1011/1, PRO.

26. Memorandum of conversation with Karamanlis, July 24, 1961, 781.00/7-2461, DSCF, RG 59, NA; Zachary and Brewster oral histories, ADST. Brewster recalled that he and Stearns spent months trying to educate Ellis Briggs that someday Karamanlis would go and Papandreou would be in power. Ralles, *Πολιτικές Εκμυστηρεύσεις*, 57–60; *FRUS 1958–60*, 10:676–77. Karamanlis, *Αρχείο*, 4:347–48, for comments of Greek officials on political situation provoked by elections.

27. Papandreou quoted in memorandum of conversation, September 6, 1961, 781.00/9-1561, DSCF, RG 59, NA. On U.S. concerns about Venizelos and analysis of Papandreou, dispatches 189 from Athens, June 19, 1959, 781.00/6-1959, and 18 from Athens, August 23, 1960, 781.00/8-2360, both DSCF, RG 59, NA.

28. Dispatch 18 from Athens, DSCF, RG 59, NA. The evolution of the center-left opposition is outlined in reports by the British embassy in Greece, February 28, 1957, FO 371/130014/RG 1015/2, March 7, 1957, FO 371/130014/RG 1015/5, April 17, 1959, FO 371/144518/RG 1015/8, and May 5, 1959, FO 371/144518/RG1015/9, all PRO.

29. Dispatches 617 from Athens, January 19, 1961, 781.00/1-1961, and 211 from Athens, September 21, 1961, 781.00/9-2161, both DSCF, RG 59, NA. See also Karamanlis, *Αρχείο*, 4:368-69.

30. Telegram 599 from Athens, November 6, 1961, 781.00/11-661, DSCF, RG 59, NA; NSC briefing paper, September 28, 1960, CIA RDP 79R00890, NA.

31. Daphnes, *Σοφοκλής Ελευθερίου Βενιζέλος*, 561-62; Markezinis, *Σύγχρονη Πολιτική Ιστορία* 3:96-98; Karamanlis, *Αρχείο*, 5:75-82; Holden, *Greece without Columns*, 225.

32. Karamanlis, *Αρχείο*, 5:206-7, 214, 224-26, 234-38, 269, for a summary of charges and counter charges and Karamanlis's comments. "Annual Review for 1961: Greece," January 1, 1962, FO 371/163442/CE1011/1, PRO, and Symon to Jameson, Athens, March 30, 1962, FO 371/163433/CE1015/11, PRO, analyze the validity of the charges. One of Papandreou's critics, Holden, *Greece without Columns*, 190-91, admitted some level of fraud.

33. Brewster oral history, ADST.

34. *FRUS 1961-63*, 16:623. Brewster oral history, ADST. The text of the Briggs statement and the French embassy report on the incident, December 28, 1961, are in vol. 238, Greece-US, MAE.

35. Owens oral history, ADST. Rouphos believed that the fraud was too limited to produce Karamanlis's victory. See "Athenian" [Rouphos], *Inside the Colonels' Greece*, 42.

36. *FRUS 1961-63*, 16:632-33, for the U.S. embassy's analysis; "Annual Review for 1961: Greece," January 1, 1962, FO 371/163442/CE1011/1, PRO, for the British take. On military involvement in earlier elections, see Lambert to Young, Athens, March 16, 1956, FO 371/123847/RG 1017/29, PRO. Ralles, *Πολιτικές Εκμυστηρεύσεις*, 61-71, admits to irregularities but charges that Papandreou exaggerated them. Genevoix, *Greece of Karamanlis*, 154, for Karamanlis's defense.

37. Memorandum of conversation with Papandreou, September 7, 1962, attachment to airgram A-209 from Athens, September 10, 1962, 781.00/9-1062, DSCF, RG 59, NA.

38. Dispatch 111 from Athens, April 6, 1962, 781.00/4-662, DSCF, RG 59, NA. The entire covert program, particularly its long continuance, owed a great deal to what one critic has called the "cult of intelligence." As German political parties showed with great effect, the creation of open "foundations" to support democratic parties allowed foreign political groups to fund democratic movements without the stigma of intervention and without breaking the host nation's laws. The United States continued to employ covert funding until the 1970s, largely because the CIA insisted that it had the "trade craft" skills to carry out these actions in secret. In fact, almost every agency funding operation had its "cover" blown at some point. After cooperating with the German "stiftungs" in Portugal during the 1970s, the U.S. government recognized the benefits of open funding of political parties and set up publicly financed "endowments" to support democratic political development.

39. Memorandum of conversation between Papandreou and Labouisse, June 1, 1962, in dispatch 796 from Athens, June 4, 1962, 781.00/6-462, DSCF, RG 59, NA. See also dispatch 49 to the Foreign Office, April 4, 1962, FO 371/163483/CE1941/6, PRO; Currie to Jameson, August 30, 1962, FO 371/163444/CE1015/24, PRO; telegram 771/83 to the ministry, September 4, 1962, vol. 238, Greece-US, MAE; Karamanlis, Αρχείο, 5:320-21.

40. Memorandum of conversation, November 14, 1962, transmitted in airgram A-396 from Athens, November 14, 781.00/11-1462, DSCF, RG 59, NA. Missing from the discussion and from the documentation I examined was any indication of an ongoing CIA program of covert funding for the Greek parties. It seems likely that the program adopted in 1958-59 would have continued into 1961, but neither Labouisse nor his Greek visitors made any reference to it. For comments on the effectiveness of Papandreou's strategy, Curle to Tomkins, Athens, January 31, 1962, and Murray to foreign secretary, September 19, 1962, FO 371/163443/CE 1015/1 and 24, PRO; Saunders to Komer, May 7, 1962, with attached report by Lagoudakis, Greece, White House memorandums, Komer Files, NSF, JFKL. For a sample of the parliamentary debate, see Karamanlis, Αρχείο, 5:347-53.

41. Papandreou quoted in airgram A-127 from Athens, August 8, 1962, 781.00/8-862, DSCF, RG 59, NA. Zachary, Owens, and Brewster oral histories, ADST; Karamanlis, Αρχείο, 5:302-3.

42. See airgram A-577 from Athens, January 8, 1963, 781.00/1-863, and *FRUS 1961-63*, 16:661, for U.S. analysis of the Palace's shift toward the EK. "Greece: Annual Review 1962," January 22, 1963, FO 371/169054/CE1011/1, PRO, on the effect of Papandreou's attacks. Blakeway to Alexander, Athens, January 15, 1963, FO 371/169055/CE1015/3, PRO, on the divisions among EK leaders over approaching the king. Embassy in Greece to ministry, January 30, 1963, vol. 193, Greece, MAE, for the French analysis.

43. Vice president's report to the president, September 10, 1962, Vice President's Visit 1962, NEA/GRK, RG 59, NA. A summary of Johnson's discussions is in *FRUS 1961-63*, 16:647-51. See also Karamanlis, Αρχείο, 5:453; telegram 773 from embassy in Greece to the ministry, August 30, 1962, vol. 238, Greece-US, MAE.

44. *FRUS 1958-60*, 10:610-11 for Ambassador Riddleberger's initial positive view of royal couple. Dispatch 216 from Athens, "The Condition of the Greek Crown," September 11, 1959, 781.00/9-1159, DSCF, RG 59, NA, paints a more pessimistic scenario. The quoted passage is from dispatch G-227 from Athens, January 17, 1960, 781.00/1-1760, DSCF, RG 59, NA.

45. Anschuetz oral history, ADST. The queen discussed her courtship of U.S. Officials in *A Measure of Understanding*. The quote from Briggs is in dispatch 351 from Athens, November 13, 1961, 711.11/11-1461, DSCF, RG 59, NA.

46. Dispatch 352 from Athens, November 13, 1961, 781.11/11-1361, DSCF, RG 59, NA. The analysis was authored by Brewster, head of the political section of the embassy.

47. Dispatch 351 from Athens, November 13, 1961, 711.11/11-1461, DSCF, RG 59, NA.

48. *FRUS 1961-63*, 16:662-63. Successive agency chiefs of station enjoyed the privilege of such discussions with the queen. On the prime minister's awareness of royal plotting, see Karamanlis, *Αρχείο*, 5:469-74, 477-78, 535-36. Woodhouse, *Karamanlis*, 148, on the prime minister's problems with the royal family. British comments in FO 371/130064/RG1942/1, PRO, and French views in telegram 912 to the ministry, vol. 23, Greece, MAE.

49. *FRUS 1961-63*, 16:664-68. The documents in question were heavily and haphazardly censored by the CIA for reasons that escaped me as editor of the volume. There was no CIA involvement in the plot. On Karamanlis and the plot, Woodhouse, *Karamanlis*, 148-49. Labouisse also tipped off George Papandreou. According to Andreas Papandreou, *Democracy at Gunpoint*, 121, the ambassador informed his father of the plot in early 1964. While Andreas's dating is possible, it appears more likely that Labouisse would have informed the elder Papandreou earlier, when the issue was still live, as part of his effort to fulfill his pledge to work with the center-left. Andreas's description of the plot is very similar to that outlined in U.S. documents and indicates that Labouisse was talking about an ongoing activity. Bouloukos, *Υπόθεση ΑΣΠΙΔΑ*, 158, claims that the CIA station was aware of plotting by "the Colonels" as early as 1963 and warned the royal family. This appears to track with the plot described in *FRUS*, even if the Colonels simply participated in the coup-plotting group.

50. For an outline of events and text of the Papandreou letter, Karamanlis, *Αρχείο*, 5:582-94. On maneuverings surrounding the celebration, Blakeway to Wood, April 3, 1963, with attached memorandum of conversation between Ambassador Murray and Pipinelis, FO 371/169055/CE1015/7, PRO. The French embassy reported on these events on April 5, 1963, vol. 238, Greece-US, MAE.

51. Telegrams 742, May 28, 1963, and 915, June 20, 1963, to the ministry commented on the implications of the murder and subsequent crisis: vol. 193, Greece, MAE. Karamanlis, *Αρχείο*, 5:646-57; 6:16-17, 20, 30, for documentation on these events and Karamanlis's comments. See also Ralles, *Πολιτικές Εκμυστηρεύσεις*, 82; Woodhouse, *Karamanlis*, 147-48.

52. Karamanlis, *Αρχείο*, 6:26-28, 33, 38, 60, 67-69. Telegrams 974 and 989 to the ministry, July 4 and 6, 1963, vol. 193, Greece, MAE, on Karamanlis's plans. Minute by Jamieson, June 13, 1963, FO 371/169055/CE1015/16, surveys the early maneuvering. Woodhouse, *Karamanlis*, 159-60, on the collaboration of crown and Papandreou. See also "Current Foreign Relations," August 7, 1963, Greece, Komer Files, NSF, JFKL; Tzeremias, *Karamanlis*, 80-82.

53. *FRUS 1961-63*, 16:676-77, and 684-85 (queen quoted).

54. *FRUS 1961-63*, 16:685-88.

Chapter 4

1. See *Hostage to History* and its precursor, *Cyprus*. Stern, *Wrong Horse*, represents a much more nuanced, if very pro–Greek Cypriot reading of events from 1965 to 1974 that also places blame on the United States for the tragedy.

2. O'Malley and Craig, *Cyprus Conspiracy*, vii–viii.

3. The complexities of this Cyprus policy have been carefully explored in Nicolet, *United States Policy towards Cyprus*. On partition, see page 283 and the comments of Alexandrakis, Theodoropoulos, and Lagakos, *Κυπριακό*, 13, on the shared responsibility of all parties. On the effects of political change in Athens in late 1963, Michalopoulos, *Ελλάδα και Τουρκία*, 200–202, and Papademetriou, *Αναλαμπή*, 11–13.

4. On Makarios's position and political actions, see Averoff's comments to U.S. officials in *FRUS 1958–60*, 10:776–79, 787–79. On Makarios's management of the United States, *FRUS 1958–60*, 10:806–7. On the problems created by the London-Zurich arrangements, minute by Ward-Gery, June 13, 1960, FO 371/152883/RC 1015/16, PRO, and high commissioner to the Foreign Office, June 9, 1960, FO 371/152834/RC 1015/35, PRO. See also Klerides, *Cyprus*, 1:81–82. Kranidiotis, *Δύσκολα Χρόνια*, 70, notes that Western obstruction of efforts to include independence on the U.N. General Assembly's debate calendar fed neutralist sentiment.

5. Woodhouse, *Karamanlis*, 123, 125; Klerides, *Cyprus*, 1:81–82; Karamanlis, *Αρχείο*, 3:418–20; 4:15. Compare the comments in the Charles McCaskill oral history, ADST, with those of Alexandrakis, Theodoropoulos, and Lagakos, *Κυπριακό*, 73–75, and Makarios's lieutenant, Kranidiotis, *Ανοχύρωτη Πολιτεία*, 1:47, 73–79. See also Averoff-Tossizza, *Lost Opportunities*, 183, 373–75.

6. On policy, *FRUS 1958–60*, 10:772, and 819–28. See also Wilbur Chase oral history, ADST.

7. *FRUS 1958–60*, 10:783, 786, 792–93, 803–4, 808–10. See also Raymond Hare oral history, ADST.

8. Crawshaw, *Cyprus Revolt*, 356–61; Nicolet, *United States Policy towards Cyprus*, 197, 230–31.

9. *FRUS 1958–60*, 10:772–73, 779–80, 795–99, 829–30, 837–41. O'Malley and Craig's claim, *Cyprus Conspiracy*, 82–83, that the United States did not clear its continued intelligence operations after independence is incorrect.

10. *FRUS 1961–63*, 16:514, for NSAM 71; the Department of State's September 7 response is on page 515. NSAM 93 of September 25, 1961, is in *FRUS 1961–63*, 16:516. See also Komer to Bundy, August 21, 1961, Cyprus 1961, NSF, Cyprus, JFKL; briefing paper on Cyprus, n.d., but spring 1961, Karamanlis Briefing Book, NSF, Greece, JFKL; Nicolet, *United States Policy towards Cyprus*, 166. On the use of economic aid to moderate Cyprus politics and back the Guarantor Powers, telegram 3397 from the embassy in the United States to the Foreign Office, December 14, 1961, FO 371/160379/CC103145/2/G, PRO.

11. *FRUS 1961–63*, 16:512–14, 516–18.

12. *FRUS 1961–63*, 16:520–21.

13. See the analysis in *FRUS 1961–63*, 16:530–32, and the comments of Nicolet, *United States Policy towards Cyprus*, 169–72. Kranidiotis, Ανοχύρωτη Πολιτεία, 1:39–41, on Cypriot views of talks.

14. *FRUS 1961–63*, 16:532–36; background paper: "International Political Strategy and Tactics of the Greek Cypriot Leadership," May 26, 1962, Visit of the President, NSF, Cyprus, JFKL; Komer to Kennedy, June 1, 1962, White House Memos, 1961–1963, Cyprus, Komer Files, NSF, JFKL.

15. Reports of the high commissioner (Clark), November 11, 1960, and February 21, 1961, FO 371/160184/RC1015/1 and 4, PRO. McCaskill oral history, ADST, for comment of the Cypriot colors as a "flag of nuisance."

16. Klerides, *Cyprus*, 1:18, 22–24, 86, 198; Klerides's conclusions about Turkish Cypriot reactions, based on documents captured at the time of the outbreak of communal violence, are reprinted on pages 198 and 207. See also Kranidiotis, Ανοχύρωτη Πολιτεία, 1:43–36. Denktash, *Rauf Denktash at the United Nations*, 127, for Turkish Cypriot reading of Makarios.

17. The text of the London-Zurich accords is at http://www.cyprus-conflict.net/Treaties%20-1959-60.html.

18. On AKEL, see British embassy in Turkey to Foreign Office, January 11, 1962, FO 371/163385/C103145/4, PRO, and Makarios's comments in *FRUS 1961–63*, 16:538–39. On the anti-Turkish motivation of Makarios's nonaligned policy, Klerides, *Cyprus* 1:114–26. On Greek-Turkish collaboration and Turkish flexibility on Cyprus and other issues, Averoff-Tossizza, *Lost Opportunities*, 395–97, 413, 415; and discussions with Karamanlis and Averoff reported in *FRUS 1958–60*, 10:676–77, 781–82, as well as in embassy in Turkey to Foreign Office, February 3, 1961, FO 371/160186/RC10314/1, and memorandum of conversation between Macmillan and Karamanlis, February 15, 1961, PREM 11/3383, both PRO. On Makarios's visit to Athens, Karamanlis, Αρχείο, 5:465–68. Averoff outlined Greek policy for French foreign minister Couve de Mourville during a March 6, 1963, meeting in Paris: *DDF 1963*, 1:258–59. The Greek foreign minister contrasted Greek stability under Karamanlis with the continuing problems, including government instability, which a rebuilt Turkish democracy faced in the wake of its 1960 coup and added: "We follow a policy of rapprochement with our neighbor that is again sick." Alexandrakis, Theodoropoulos, and Lagakos, Κυπριακό, 29–31.

19. *FRUS 1961–63*, 16:539–41, 543, 545–48, 550, 553–54.

20. *FRUS 1961–63*, 16:542, 548–49, 551–52, 555–60. For the text of the Averoff letter, Averoff-Tossizza, *Lost Opportunities*, 427–30. See also Klerides, *Cyprus*, 1:151–54.

21. Klerides, *Cyprus*, 1:149–50, 164–65; Averoff-Tossizza, *Lost Opportunities*, 424; *FRUS 1961–63*, 16:561–67.

22. *FRUS 1961–63*, 16:568–77. Memorandum of conversation between Komer and Wilkins, July 24, 1963, White House memorandums, Cyprus, Komer Files, NSF,

JFKL. Sanders to Komer, July 7 and 24, 1963, and Komer to Kennedy, October 18, 1963, both White House memorandums, Cyprus, Komer Files, NSF, JFKL.

23. *FRUS 1961–63*, 16:577–84, 592–93; Klerides, *Cyprus*, 1:166–70.

24. *FRUS 1961–63*, 16:685–90. Karamanlis, *Αρχείο*, 6:108, reprints portions of Papandreou's and Venizelos's initial statements on Makarios's Thirteen Points. Averoff-Tossizza, *Lost Opportunities*, 422, 425–26, 430, notes that Makarios did not consult with Papandreou before offering and publishing the Thirteen Points. See also Alexandrakis, Theodoropoulos, and Lagakos, *Κυπριακό*, 44–45, 81–82. Kranidiotis, *Ανοχύρωτη Πολιτεία*, 1:81–82, 89–95, for the impact of Papandreou on Greek Cypriot calculations. On the development of tensions between Athens and Nicosia, Vlachou, *Δέκα Χρόνια Κυπριακού*, 281–82, 285–88. On George Papandreou's Cyprus positions, Krateros, "Γεώργιος Παπανδρέου και οι Συμφωνίες Ζυρίχης Λονδίνου για την Κύπρο."

25. Averoff-Tossizza, *Lost Opportunities*, 425–26; Klerides, *Cyprus*, 1:207–12, 219, 221 (text of the Akritas Plan, 212–19). See also *FRUS 1961–63*, 16:594–98. On Makarios's moves and his paper, see the recollections of Lagakos in Alexandrakis, Theodoropoulos, and Lagakos, *Κυπριακό*, 32–33, 45–46.

26. Averoff-Tossizza, *Lost Opportunities*, 430. For some admiring evaluations of Makarios by U.S. officials who dealt with him see Victor Stier, McCaskill, and Carleton Coon oral histories, ADST. On Makarios's haste to act, Alexandrakis, Theodoropoulos, and Lagakos, *Κυπριακό*, 34, 51. Klerides, *Cyprus*, 2:47–48; 3:365–67, lists every opportunity for compromise that Makarios rejected between 1963 and the 1974 disaster. On Makarios's conflicts with Greek government leaders and on the effects of their split, Klerides, *Cyprus*, 1:329 and 2:175–78.

27. Memorandum by the prime minister, January 2, 1964, CAB 129/116/2, PRO. See also Klerides, *Cyprus*, 1:237–38, 257–62, 323, and 2:17; *FRUS 1964–68*, 33:945–50, 961–62.

28. *FRUS 1964–68*, 16:2–3.

29. *FRUS 1964–68*, 16:4–9; Garoufalias, *Ελλάς και Κύπρος*, 142.

30. Raymond Hare, oral history interview (1969), 35, JFKL.

31. *FRUS 1964–68*, 33:952–53, 965–66, 984–85 for Komer's views and 987–91 for Ball's. See also *FRUS 1964–68*, 16:42–44; Ball, *Past*, 342–46.

32. *DDF 1964*, 1:179–80; *FRUS 1964–68*, 16:9–17; *FRUS 1964–68*, 33:971–75, 978–80.

33. *FRUS 1964–68*, 16:22–24 and 33:980–82, for the two quotes. Kranidiotis, *Ανοχύρωτη Πολιτεία*, 1:122, for Greek Cypriot version of talks.

34. *FRUS 1964–68*, 16:17–37; 33:984–87.

35. *FRUS 1964–68*, 16:37–39.

36. Klerides, *Cyprus*, 2:85–94. Kranidiotis, *Ανοχύρωτη Πολιτεία*, 1:165–71, for Greek internal politics. "Current Security Situation of Greece," May 1963, and untitled paper by Vasiliis Damalas for the king and senior officials of the Greek govern-

ment, January 18, 1964, both box 30, Sofokles Venizelos Papers, BA, on trading for U.S. concessions.

37. Alexandrakis, Theodoropoulos, and Lagakos, Κυπριακό, 35–36, 39, 42–43, 47–50, for an analysis of the relationship from the Greek perspective. Kranidiotis, Ανοχύρωτη Πολιτεία, 1:97–98, 131–40, 155–64, and Vlachou, Δέκα Χρόνια Κυπριακού, 285–88, for Greek Cypriot views.

38. FRUS 1964–68, 16:39–41, 47–53, 237–38.

39. FRUS 1964–68, 16:58–60.

40. FRUS 1964–68, 16:62–65. Kretikos, Ρήξη, 57–73, contains an expanded version of Andreas Papandreou's recollections of these events. The paper was prepared during Andreas's exile in Canada, at about the same time as the manuscript of Democracy at Gunpoint, 128–41, and may represent an earlier draft of the story he tells in the published memoir. The paper, particularly in earlier sections, is a good deal less polemical and more detailed. Compare Garoufalias, Ελλάς και Κύπρος, 51–55, 94–105, on Greek involvement. Kranidiotis, Ανοχύρωτη Πολιτεία, 1:177–78, 185–86, on discussion with Greeks and the impact of Grivas's return.

41. FRUS 1964–68, 16:68–71; Klerides, Cyprus, 2:112–14. The Papandreou paper in Kretikos, Ρήξη, claims twenty thousand men. Alexandrakis, Theodoropoulos, and Lagakos, Κυπριακό, 101–3, discuss the decision and state that the number involved was ten thousand. Garoufalias, Ελλάς και Κύπρος, 124–26, 131, says the number rose to eight thousand and that George Papandreou was unaware of the force size. Garoufalias adds that the force was exposed for lack of support aircraft. See also Kranidiotis, Ανοχύρωτη Πολιτεία, 1:248–49.

42. FRUS 1964–68, 16:73–76, 78–88; Ball quotes, May 10, 86–88. Papandreou paper in Kretikos, Ρήξη. See also Papagiorgiou, Κρίσιμα Ντοκουμέντα του Κυπριακού, 2:7.

43. Embassy in Greece to ministry, May 8, 1964, vol. 238, Greece-US, MAE, on Fulbright's Athens visit. New York Herald Tribune, May 9, 1964, for his problems in Ankara. The press in both nations, while well informed on evolving U.S. thinking, badly misread the intent of the Fulbright probe.

44. FRUS 1964–68, 16:86–88.

45. Compare the analysis of Labouisse, May 18, 1964, FRUS 1964–68, 16:92–94 (quote), with the scalding May 27 critique of Papandreou by Karamanlis in Αρχείο, 6:135–36. On the increasingly out-of-control situation, see FRUS 1964–68, 16:90–92, 94–99.

46. Ball, Past, 350–53, on genesis and nature of the note as well as quotes. The text is in FRUS 1964–68, 16:107–10; documentation on the genesis of note and its impact, 103–7, 111.

47. FRUS 1964–68, 16:114–16. The U.S. embassy analysis in FRUS 1964–68, 16:105–6. George Papandreou to Johnson, June 9, in FRUS 1964–68, 16:122–23. Compare the analysis of the visit by Ball, FRUS 1964–68, 16:132–34, and Past, 352–53,

with its disparaging comments about the elder Papandreou, and by Andreas Papandreou in Kretikos, *Ρήξη*. Both describe the meeting as an exercise in political hardball.

48. *FRUS 1964–68*, 16:118–22.

49. *FRUS 1964–68*, 16:125–29, and volume introduction, 26–27.

50. From the U.S. perspective, *FRUS 1964–68*, 16:137–41, 143–45, 151–66. Andreas Papandreou revisited the discussions in *Democracy at Gunpoint*, 133–36. His paper in Kretikos, *Ρήξη*, provides little additional detail. Nicolet, *United States Policy towards Cyprus*, 251–56, is the best narrative of the meeting. An excellent summary of the meetings as well as American perspectives and objectives, Wright to Dodson, Washington, July 6, 1964, FO 371/174756/C103145/19, PRO. Papagiorgiou, *Κρίσιμα Ντοκουμέντα του Κυπριακού*, 2:44–67, reprints a Greek memorandum of conversation, which has no significant differences with the U.S. version of the meeting. George Papandreou's July 3 report on the meeting to the Boule is reprinted in Kranidiotis, *Ανοχύρωτη Πολιτεία*, 1:201–5. On October 28, 1940, Greek prime minister John Metaxas refused an ultimatum from Mussolini with a simple "no" (*oxi*). This refusal, which drew Greece into World War II, is celebrated with a national holiday.

51. On Ball's views and Papandreou's French visit, *DDF 1964*, 1:664–66, 676–78. The French wanted to widen the talks to permit their participation. *FRUS 1964–68*, 16:170–73, 174–79 (Ball quoted). Andreas Papandreou briefly mentions the Paris visit in both *Democracy at Gunpoint* and Kretikos, *Ρήξη*. Papagiorgiou, *Κρίσιμα Ντοκουμέντα του Κυπριακού*, 2:15–20, 69–71, 82–83, for Greek documentation. Kranidiotis, *Ανοχύρωτη Πολιτεία*, 1:254–56, on the Greek Cypriot reading.

52. Nicolet carefully reconstructs the Acheson mediation in *United States Policy towards Cyprus*, 256–97. Documentation is in *FRUS 1964–68*, 16:167–309. Note for prime minister: "Visit of Mr. Papandreou," July 17, 1964, and memorandum of conversations July 20 and 21, 1964, all PREM 11/4841, PRO. It is doubtful that George Papandreou advanced his case very much by telling whoppers, such as that the Americans had ordered Grivas to Cyprus over his objections or that the increase in Greek troop strength consisted of "volunteers, students, and deserters" who had arrived without the support or knowledge of the Greek government. Andreas Papandreou suggested that a U.N. arms embargo be "imposed on Greece" to permit the government to cut its aid to Makarios. Memorandum of conversation with Butler, July 21, PREM 11/4841, PRO. Andreas Papandreou's paper briefly covers the meetings, noting that they were less confrontational than those in Washington but no more fruitful. In Kretikos, *Ρήξη*. On Greek views of the mediation, letters from the Greek representative in Geneva, Nicolareizes, to Papandreou, in Klerides, *Cyprus*, 2:126–30, 134. Greek documentation in Papagiorgiou, *Κρίσιμα Ντοκουμέντα του Κυπριακού* 2:220–22, 225–30.

53. *FRUS 1964–68*, 16:193–204, 206–8; Klerides, *Cyprus* 2:122; Garoufalias, *Ελλάς και Κύπρος*, 181–83; Papagiorgiou, *Κρίσιμα Ντοκουμέντα του Κυπριακού* 2:79, 99–101,

and 231–32, on Makarios's July 30 statement. Kranidiotis, *Ανοχύρωτη Πολιτεία*, 1:219–20, 230, on Makarios in Athens.

54. *FRUS 1964–68*, 16:209, 211–14, 216–27, 231–36. Regrettably, at this point the Andreas Papandreou paper, in Kretikos, *Ρήξη*, becomes unreliable, mixing hyperbole with simple (and easily identified) misstatements of fact. The actions of George Papandreou after his offer of instant enosis were not something that the self-proclaimed champion of the Cypriot cause wanted to discuss frankly. Nicolet, *United States Policy towards Cyprus*, 255, judges Andreas Papandreou's version of events as self-serving and inaccurate. See also Kranidiotis, *Ανοχύρωτη Πολιτεία*, 1:218–19.

55. *FRUS 1964–68*, 16:236–39, 242–43, 246–47, 249–54; Papagiorgiou, *Κρίσιμα Ντοκουμέντα του Κυπριακού*, 2:102–4, 121–25, 131–33, 254–55; Garoufalias, *Ελλάς και Κύπρος*, 168.

56. *FRUS 1964–68*, 16:254–64, for Belcher's analysis. Alexandrakis, Theodoropoulos, and Lagakos, *Κυπριακό*, 37–40, 48, 50–51; Garoufalias, *Ελλάς και Κύπρος*, 185–86; and documentation on exchanges between Greeks and Greek Cypriots in Papagiorgiou, *Κρίσιμα Ντοκουμέντα του Κυπριακού*, 2:206–17, 323–35. Klerides, *Cyprus*, 2: 85–94, 149–51; Vlachou, *Δέκα Χρόνια Κυπριακού*, 296–310; and Kranidiotis, *Ανοχύρωτη Πολιτεία*, 1:224–26, for Cypriot perspectives.

57. On the collapse of the mediation effort and the recriminations among Greek and American participants, *FRUS 1964–68*, 16:265–69, 273–76, 282–95. Garoufalias, *Ελλάς και Κύπρος*, 189–209, on decision to drop efforts at enosis. Klerides, *Cyprus*, 2:142–48, reprints the written exchanges between Acheson and George Papandreou. Andreas discussed the utilization of the United States as a fall guy for the failure of his father's policy in his paper, in Kretikos, *Ρήξη*. On the exploitation of the "American factor" to disguise Greek failures, embassy in Greece to the ministry, October 16, 1964, vol. 238, Greece-US, MAE.

58. *FRUS 1964–68*, 16:298–302, 308–9, 497; CIA telegram, June 24, 1966, CIA RDP 79T00826A, NA. Papagiorgiou, *Κρίσιμα Ντοκουμέντα του Κυπριακού*, 2:345–46, for Grivas's determination to eliminate the archbishop. Kranidiotis, *Ανοχύρωτη Πολιτεία*, 1:249–52, on effects of Khrushchev's fall.

59. On U.S. policy after the failure of the Acheson mediation, *FRUS 1964–68*, 16:304–6, 312–14, 365–62, 372–76, 383–85, 390–92, 464–66. On the first Papandreou approach, GTI roundup, February 10–16, 1965, Briefing Papers 1965, NEA/GRK, RG 59, NA. On Greek discussions with Turkey, *FRUS 1964–68*, 16:521–23, 527–28; Klerides, *Cyprus*, 2:190; and Alexandrakis, Theodoropoulos, and Lagakos, *Κυπριακό*, 39–40, 42–43, 52–57, 88–90. On changing U.S. policy, Wright to Dodson, Washington, October 22, 1964, FO 371/174756/C103145/28, PRO. See also Hart, *Two NATO Allies*, 12–13, 18, 24–25.

60. Barrington King oral history, ADST.

61. Draft of a joint Foreign Office–Commonwealth Office report, June 29–30, 1967, FCO 9/70, PRO. Compare the conclusions regarding Makarios's strategy in

dispatch 9 from Nicosia to the Foreign and Commonwealth Office, August 30, 1967, FCO 9/70, PRO.

62. *FRUS 1964–68*, 16:320–23; report of the high commissioner (Hunt), July 7, 1965, FO 371/179973/CC1015/41, PRO; Alexandrakis, Theodoropoulos, and Lagakos, *Κυπριακό*, 12, 95–101, 119–22.

63. *FRUS 1964–68*, 16:310–11, 337–39; Hart, *Two NATO Allies*, 55; Kranidiotis, *Ανοχύρωτη Πολιτεία*, 1:294–96. Andreas capitalized certain terms such as Palace, Junta, Establishment in his autobiography in order to focus the reader's attention on the power of his (malevolent) opponents. During my service with the State Department, I noted that the U.S. government and most other states heavily capitalized in their public statements and diplomatic exchanges to draw the reader's attention to their power. (For example, in U.S. usage it is always the U.S. Government, the President, the Department, etc.) Semantics are part of the equation in shaping power and history.

64. On the attention paid to Makarios during Vance's mediation, Hart, *Two NATO Allies*, 92–93, and *FRUS 1964–68*, 16:320–23, 332–36, 346–48. On the changing approach toward Makarios, Stern, *Wrong Horse*, 91, 106–7, and King oral history, ADST.

65. Report of the high commissioner (Hunt), July 7, 1965, FO 371/179973/CC1015/41, PRO.

66. Alexandrakis, Theodoropoulos, and Lagakos, *Κυπριακό*, 85–86, 88–90; Klerides, *Cyprus*, 2:85–94, 175–78. Costopoulos quoted in *FRUS 1964–68*, 16:88–89.

67. *FRUS 1964–68*, 16:312–14, 364–66, 386–89, 405–7. Trust was scarcely increased after the United States discovered that Papandreou was facilitating the shipment of Soviet bloc arms to Makarios via Egypt. *FRUS 1964–68*, 16:368–82, and documentation in Cyprus 1965, NEA/GRK, P Subject Files, RG 59, NA.

68. The king expressed his determination to oust Papandreou in a September 4 meeting with Labouisse. *FRUS 1964–68*, 16:303–4. Labouisse, who suspected that the monarch was fishing for support, was noncommittal. On U.S. appreciation of Constantine's moderation, *FRUS 1964–68*, 16:288–89, 295–96.

Chapter 5

1. Memoir from the French embassy to the ministry, June 28, 1963, vol. 238, Greece-US, MAE.

2. On the political atmosphere and King Paul's support for George Papandreou, M. Papandreou, *Nightmare in Athens*, 66–67, and Karamanlis, *Αρχείο*, 6:68–69. For the king's position, Sulzberger, *Last of the Giants*, 1009–10; Kanellopoulos, *Ζωή Μου*, 159–60. On George Papandreou's campaign, Moberly to Wood, November 8, 1963, FO 371/169058/CE1015/64, PRO. On Karamanlis's strategy, *Αρχείο*, 6:99–100. EDA won 14.3 percent of the vote, giving the center and left approximately 56 percent of the total vote.

3. French views (quoted) in telegram 1542 to the ministry, December 12, 1963, vol. 193, Greece, MAE. French embassy report, November 21, 1963, vol. 193, Greece, MAE. An outline of the situation together with comments and judgments by ERE and EK leaders is in Karamanlis, *Αρχείο*, 6:99, 101, 103, 119, 280–81. British analysis of Papandreou's moves, motivations, and their consequences, Blakeway to Brown, Athens, December 10, 1963, FO 371/169058/CE1015/80, Sykes to Brown, Athens, January 3, 1964, FO 371/174808/CE1015/2, and "Greece: Annual Review for 1963," January 10, 1964, FO 371/174806/CE1011/1, all PRO.

4. On U.S. hands-off policy, Wright to Wood, June 18, 1963 (quote), FO 371/169006/CE103145/2, and embassy in Washington to Foreign Office, July 3, 1963, FO 371/169056/CE1015/36, both PRO. The evaluation of likely EK foreign policy: Current Intelligence Digest, November 4, 1963, NSF, JFKL. Labouisse's assessment of Karamanlis and Papandreou, October 2, 1963, in Sulzberger, *Last of the Giants*, 1008–9. John Owens oral history, ADST. George Papandreou's comments: airgram A-509 from Athens, November 8, 1963, Pol 2-1 Greece, DSCF, RG 59, NA. For Bennett's meetings with Andreas Papandreou, memoranda of conversations, November 13 and December 9, 1963, airgrams A-536, Pol 2 Greece, and A-667, Pol 12 Greece, both DSCF, RG 59, NA.

5. Schott to Bracken, February 19, 1964, Memoranda NEA-GTI, NEA/GRK, RG 59, NA. The favorable embassy view of the incoming Papandreou government, telegram 1261 from Athens, February 19, 1964, Pol 15-1 Greece, DSCF, RG 59, NA.

6. On the impact of the deaths of the king and Venizelos, "Annual Report for Greece 1964," January 5, 1965, FO 371/180004/E1001/1, PRO; Labouisse to Schott, January 14, 1964, Pol 7 Visits (Royal Family), NEA/GRK, RG 59, NA; Owens and Brewster oral histories, ADST. See also *FRUS 1961–63*, 16:662, 684–85; and the analysis of the royal family in an October 6, 1964, paper, Briefings (Mr. Ball) 1964, NEA/GRK, RG 59, NA. On Constantine's upbringing and the queen's politics as seen by an intimate of the Greek royal family, Sulzberger, *Last of the Giants*, 658, 780–85. On the queen's mindset, Frederika, *Measure of Understanding*. Karamanlis's views of the royal couple, *Αρχείο*, 6:116.

7. On Karamanlis's hold on the party and the problems it created for Kanellopoulos, Belios, *Καραμανλής*, 8, 48–51; Holden, *Greece without Columns*, 227. On internal dynamics of the ERE, Karamanlis, *Αρχείο*, 6:135–36, 285–89, 301–3.

8. "The Papandreou Style," airgram A-1247 from Athens, May 20, 1964 (quote), Pol 15 Greece, DSCF, RG 59, NA. On the cabinet, minute by Brown, February 19, 1964, FO 371/174808/CE1015/11, and telegram 315 to the Foreign Office, February 20, 1964 (quote), FO 371/174808/CE1015/12, both PRO. On the grooming of Andreas, airgram 1300 from Athens, June 9, 1964, Pol 15-1, DSCF, RG 59, NA; and consul general in Thessaloniki to embassy, March 5, 1964, FO 371/174807/CE1013/1, PRO.

9. "Democracy in Greece: A Reassessment," telegram 52 to the Foreign Office, July 30, 1964, FO 371/174806/CE1011/41, PRO; airgram A-1346 from Athens, March 4,

1964, Pol Greece-US, DSCF, RG 59, NA; Karamanlis, *Αρχείο*, 6:294-95. On Papandreou and the press, Garoufalias, *Ελλάς και Κύπρος*, 145; Alexandrakis, Theodoropoulos, and Lagakos, *Κυπριακό*, 86-87.

10. Karamanlis, *Αρχείο*, 6:290-91, 300-301, 307-8. *FRUS 1964-68*, 16:204-5, on ERE extremists. "The Progress of Communism in Greece under the Papandreou Government," dispatch 81 to the Foreign Office, November 11, 1964, FO 371/174809/CE1015/50, PRO, with minuted comments, is evenhanded and good on the political fallout.

11. Consul general in Thessaloniki to embassy, May 5, 1964, FO 371/174807/CE1013/1, PRO; telegram 34 to the Foreign Office, October 2, 1964, FO 371/174806/CE1011/49, PRO; Brewster to Bracken, November 13, 1964, Pol 1 Greece 1964, NEA/GRK, RG 59, NA.

12. For opposition analyses and concerns, Karamanlis, *Αρχείο*, 6:198, 296-300, 309-14; Woodhouse, *Karamanlis*, 174-75. On Papandreou's successful utilization of scandals in lieu of a parliamentary program, "Athenian" [Rouphos], *Inside the Colonels' Greece*, 44-46; Legg, *Politics in Greece*, 157; and Blakeway to Parsons, Athens, May 15, 1965, FO 371/180005/CE1015/16, PRO. On the Papandreous' efforts to take control of the intelligence and security services, Stern, *Wrong Horse*, 24. The British embassy's "Annual Report for Greece 1964," January 5, 1965, FO 371/180004/E1001/1, PRO, is a useful summary and analysis of the political maneuvering. George Papandreou's comments to Labouisse were reported in airgram A-1103 from Athens, January 21, 1965, Pol Greece-US, DSCF, RG 59, NA. Other issues are in Fish to Murray, March 9, 1965, telegram 10 to the Foreign Office, January 7, 1965, and Blakeway to Parsons, January 11, 1965, all FO 371/180005/CE1015/4, 6, and 12, PRO; and GTI roundup, January 6-12, 1965, Briefing Papers 1965, NEA/GRK, RG 59, NA.

13. Garoufalias, *Ελλάς και Κύπρος*, 107-9; Kranidiotis, *Ανοχύρωτη Πολιτεία*, 1:331-35.

14. Karamanlis, *Αρχείο*, 6:194-95, and Kanellopoulos, *Ζωή Μου*, 168. On Papandreou's problems with the army, Garoufalias, *Ελλάς και Κύπρος*, 20-22, 25-28, 31-32; Ralles, *Πολιτικές Εκμυστηρεύσεις*, 84; Markezinis, *Σύγχρονη Πολιτική Ιστορία*, 3:115-17.

15. Bouloukos, *Υπόθεση ΑΣΠΙΔΑ*, 140-41, 146-49; Kollias, *Βασιλεύς και Επανάστασις*, 18-19; Holden, *Greece without Columns*, 219; Owens oral history, ADST. Decades later, ASPIDA remains something of a mystery. Citing contradictions between Andreas's 1966 testimony and his memoirs, Bouloukos, *Υπόθεση ΑΣΠΙΔΑ*, 176-80, claims that the younger Papandreou had close ties with the organization and shared its objectives of placing "pro-democracy" officers in key positions within the Greek armed forces. He also states that the organization believed it had to establish ties with the EK and was frustrated by the lack of interest shown by its leaders. Compare Katris, *Eyewitness in Greece*, 146. Pattakos, *Το Απόρρητο Ημερολόγιο*, 15, 17, on the reaction of ultrarightist officers to ASPIDA.

16. *FRUS 1964–68*, 16:351–54. Ralles, Πολιτικές Εκμυστηρεύσεις, 85–86, believed that the case was overblown and prompted dangerous reactions from both Papandreou and the king.

17. Couloumbis, *Greek Political Reaction*, 166–67. Karamanlis, Αρχείο, 6:93, on the repeated use of this strategy by the royal household.

18. George to Andreas Papandreou, September 26, 1960, in Paraskevopoulos, Ανδρέας Παπανδρέου, 14–15. Both A. Papandreou, *Democracy at Gunpoint*, 99–113, and M. Papandreou, *Nightmare in Athens*, 21–25, give Andreas a wider role in Greek-US relations prior to 1964 than is supported by U.S. documentation. See also A. Papandreou, *Strategy for Greek Economic Development*, 5, 14–15, 29–31. In the preface Andreas thanked the U.S. government for supporting the center. M. Papandreou, *Nightmare in Athens*, 22, claims that the United States offered a "humiliating no" in response to Andreas's request for funding.

19. On Andreas's passage to the Ministry of Economic Coordination, M. Papandreou, *Nightmare in Athens*, 72, and telegram 17 to the Foreign Office, June 1, 1964, FO 371/174808/CE1015/30, PRO. Andreas's Trotskyite past and ERE's attack are treated in Kaklamanake, Ανδρέας Παπανδρέου, 24–25, and Blakeway to Brown, Athens, June 16, 1964, FO 371/174806/CE1011/33, PRO. On Andreas's years in the United States and his disinclination to return to Greece, Kaklamanake, Ανδρέας Παπανδρέου, 30–31, 37–40. On the nature of the scandal, see the detailed report from the British embassy, November 13, 1964, FO 371/174809/CE1015/54, PRO. The U.S. embassy was less well informed. Compare airgram A-859 from Athens, November 16, 1964, Pol 15-1 Greece, DSCF, RG 59, NA. In a rare lapse from the common story line, Margaret Papandreou admitted that the issue was financial scandal, not Cyprus. *Nightmare in Athens*, 78. See also Tsoucalas, *Greek Tragedy*, 185.

20. Paraskevopoulos, Ανδρέας Παπανδρέου, 7–10, 17; Holden, *Greece without Columns*, 226; Rousseas, *Death of a Democracy*, 16; "Athenian" [Rouphos], *Inside the Colonels' Greece*, 46–47; and Kargakos, *Ecce Homo*, 9, 12, deal with Andreas's early missteps. Airgram A-1300 from Athens, June 9, 1964, Pol 51-1 Greece, DSCF, RG 59, NA, for U.S. embassy analysis of Andreas Papandreou's political problems. Daphnes, Σοφοκλής Ελευθερίου Βενιζέλος, 562–64, characterized the EK's leadership as a group of "Rasputins," opportunists ready to pounce on its leader and move the party to right or left.

21. Paraskevopoulos, Ανδρέας Παπανδρέου, 28–30, 365–39, on the Papandreous' many misjudgments, including their expectations of U.S. aid. Rousseas, *Death of a Democracy*, 18, argues that because Andreas's views were mainstream American liberalism, Greek conservatives were right to fear him in a way they never did his father, whose loyalty to the existing system was proven.

22. M. Papandreou, *Nightmare in Athens*, 68–69; Paraskevopoulos, Ανδρέας Παπανδρέου, 30–31. Comments by Andreas in airgram A-458 from Athens, December 29, 1965, Pol 12 Greece, DCSF, RG 59, NA. See also Talbot to James Spain, Febru-

ary 10, 1966, Pol 15-1 Andreas Papandreou, NEA/GRK, RG 59, NA; Sykes to Drace-Francis, Athens, February 15, 1966, FO 371/185656/CE1016/1, PRO; note on the Greek crisis, August 16, 1965, vol. 195, Greece, MAE.

23. M. Papandreou, *Nightmare in Athens*, 61, for details of the 1961 visit. Curle to Jamison, Athens, February 16, 1962, FO 371/163443/CE1015/7, PRO, for Andreas's pursuit of Ted Kennedy. Karamanlis, *Αρχείο*, 5:285, for Andreas's denial of his actions. Unsigned and undated, "Memorandum on the Present Greek Government," Greece 1961, NSF, JFKL, presents a laundry list of charges against Karamanlis, refers to "our" [U.S.] interests, and presents the EK position.

24. A. Papandreou, *Democracy at Gunpoint*, 137–38; M. Papandreou, *Nightmare in Athens*, 76; *FRUS 1964–68*, 16:323–25. According to Margaret Papandreou, *Nightmare in Athens*, 71, Joyce had threatened to withdraw U.S. economic support if Andreas attempted to cut off free airtime for U.S. cultural broadcasts. Aside from the improbability that a cultural attaché would threaten to withdraw support over which he had no control, Joyce, in a private communication to Braham, remarked that he had never had any confrontation with Andreas and, in fact, had returned to Washington on what he believed were good terms with the prime minister's son. Joyce to Barham, June 16, 1966, Pol 15-1 Andreas Papandreou, NEA/GRK, RG 59, NA. Joyce's colleague, Victor Stier, stated that U.S. officials suspected that the real reason for the Greek request that Joyce not return to Athens was unfavorable publicity about his wife's Turkish birth in the context of the Cyprus crisis. Stier oral history, ADST. See also Owens and Brewster oral histories, ADST. Andreas exploited this event to burnish his credentials as a staunch defender of Greek interests. See the testy exchange between Andreas and Anschuetz, December 16, 1964, airgram A-928 from Athens, May 20, 1965, Pol 12 Greece, DSCF, RG 59, NA.

25. *FRUS 1964–68*, 16:330–32. Compare A. Papandreou, *Democracy at Gunpoint*, 137–38.

26. *FRUS 1964–68*, 16:330–32; telegram 859 from Athens, November 16, 1964, Pol 15-1 Greece, DSCF, RG 59, NA; Brewster to Kay Bracken, November 13, 1964, Pol 1 Greece 1964, NEA/GRK, RG 59, NA. On Andreas's subsequent efforts to patch up this relationship, airgram A-928 from Athens, May 12, 1965, Pol 12 Greece, DSCF, RG 59, NA.

27. Owens oral history, ADST.

28. Compare Sykes to Dodson, Athens, March 22, 1965, FO 371/180005/CE1015/13, PRO, with airgram A-773 from Athens, March 23, 1965, Pol 15-1 Greece, DSCF, RG 59, NA; and GTI roundup, April 28–May 4, 1965, Briefing Papers 1965, NEA/GRK, RG 59, NA.

29. Kollias, *Βασιλεύς και Επανάστασις*, 34. The king's version is in Sulzberger, *Age of Mediocrity*, 201–2.

30. Telegram 1862 from Athens, June 18, 1965, Pol 15 Greece, DSCF, RG 59, NA, for the embassy analysis. On Papandreou's baiting of his opponents, "Athenian"

[Rouphos], *Inside the Colonel's Greece*, 45–46; Woodhouse, *Karamanlis*, 174–75; and Holden, *Greece without Columns*, 219. On its effects on the EK, telegram 527 to the Foreign Office, July 5, 1965, FO 371/180005/CE1015/25, PRO.

31. Telegram 1862 from Athens, June 18, 1965, Pol 15 Greece, DSCF, RG 59, NA.

32. The elder Papandreou's strategy outlined in A. Papandreou, *Democracy at Gunpoint*, 153–73, and in his discussion with Barham, June 27, 1965, memoranda of conversation June 27, 1965, NEA/GRK, RG 59, NA. See also embassy in Greece to the ministry, July 16, 1965, vol. 195, Greece, MAE.

33. Embassy in the United States to the ministry, July 21, 1965, vol. 195, Greece, MAE. Memoranda of the three Barham conversations are in memoranda of conversation 1965, NEA/GRK, RG 59, NA. Barham had a previous discussion with Mitsotakis. No record of this conversation was found. Compare Kanellopoulos, *Ζωή Μου*, 168.

34. On the choreography of the crisis, embassy in Greece to the ministry, July 16, 1965, vol. 195, Greece, MAE.

35. *FRUS 1964–68*, 16:416–18.

36. *FRUS 1964–68*, 16:418–20. George Papandreou's decision to dismiss Gennimatas added to the confrontation with the Palace. The chief of staff, whose appointment the prime minister had approved, reputedly was involved in electoral fraud in 1961. Papandreou was aware of these charges at the time of the appointment. For an analysis of the complex factors motivating the confrontation, see *FRUS 1964–68*, 16:412–15. Ambassador Labouisse left Greece on May 8, 1965. His successor, Philips Talbot, appointed in September, presented his credentials on October 10, 1965.

37. Undated, handwritten note, Pol 15 Govt, NEA/GRK, RG 59, NA. The U.S. maintained informal contact with the king through Lt. Col. Lepczyk, a military attaché, who became a tennis partner of the monarch.

38. Portions of the exchange between the king and the prime minister were printed in A. Papandreou, *Democracy at Gunpoint*, 157–73, and in M. Papandreou, *Nightmare in Athens*, 82–85. A complete English-language set of the letters is an attachment to airgram A-71 from Athens, July 26, 1965, Pol 15-1 Greece, DSCF, RG 59, NA. The Greek originals are in Kasinates, *Γεώργιος Παπανδρέου*, 341–54. A memorandum of the Anschuetz-Papandreou conversation was an attachment to airgram A-48 from Athens, July 17, 1965. See also Brewster to Barham, July 27, 1965, Pol 15 Internal Political Crisis, NEA/GRK, RG 59, NA. U.S. officials' efforts to stay out of the contest failed. The French embassy, taking its cue from the Greek press, was convinced that the Americans were taking sides: report to the ministry, July 26, 1965, vol. 195, Greece, MAE.

39. Mitsotakis's comments are in telegram 825 to the ministry, vol. 195, Greece, MAE. The crisis can be followed in the GTI roundup reports of July 14–20, August 4–10, and 12–17, 1965, all Briefing Papers 1965, NEA/GRK, RG 59, NA. French analyses of the crisis are in embassy reports of July 16 and 23, 1965, and telegram 522 to the ministry, July 19, all vol. 195, Greece, MAE. On the letters-to-Washington

effort of Margaret Papandreou, see French embassy comments, July 29, 1965, vol. 238 Greece-US, MAE, and telegram 13 to the Foreign Office, July 24, 1965, FO 371/180006/CE1015/37, PRO. On the king's version of events, Sulzberger, *Age of Mediocrity*, 201–5. For further details and some interesting comments on the bungling royal strategy, Kanellopoulos, *Ζωή Μου*, 171, 175–76, and a compilation of quotes from various sources in Papaionnou, *15 Ιουλιου 1965*, 75–85, 91. Markezinis, *Σύγχρονη Πολιτική Ιστορία*, 3:127–33, for a biting analysis of the amateurism of the royalists. A royalist perspective is Byzantinos, *Αλήθεια*, 7–10; a left-wing critique is Blantas, *Ανδρέας Παπανδρέου*, 50, 59; a foreign one is Holden, *Greece without Columns*, 227.

40. Foreign secretary's cabinet review of the Greek crisis, July 22, 1965, CAB 128/39/40, and dispatch 58 to the Foreign Office, September 2, 1965, FO 371/180006/CE1015/49, both PRO; Note on Greek Political Crisis, July 19, 1965, vol. 195, Greece, MAE; memorandum for files by Barham, July 22, 1965, Pol 15 Greek Internal Political Crisis, and Read to Humphrey, July 31, 1965, Memoranda-White House, both NEA/GRK, RG 59, NA; telegram 279 from Athens, August 20, 1965, Pol 15 Greece, DSCF, RG 59, NA; GTI roundup, September 1–7, 1965, and September 8–14, 1956, both in Briefing Papers 1965, NEA/GRK, RG 59, NA. Markezinis, *Σύγχρονη Πολιτική Ιστορία* 3:134–35, on the crown council meeting that he places in mid-September rather than at the beginning of the month. According to Markezinis, George Papandreou's refusal to compromise led several deputies and leaders to support Stephanopoulos's bid. On the Papandreou campaign for U.S. intervention, M. Papandreou, *Nightmare in Athens*, 84–91; Kanellopoulos, *Ζωή Μου*, 93, 172–73; and the analysis of Kanellopoulos's handling of the entire crisis in Ralles, *Πολιτικές Εκμυστηρεύσεις*, 86–87, 89–90.

41. On the buying of deputies by Papandreou's opponents, Owens to Barham, n.d., Pol 15-1 Andreas Papandreou 1966, NEA/GRK, RG 59, NA. See also Papahelas, *Βιασμός*, 211–15. Papahelas amplified on the event and provided further details in an article in *Βήμα*, March 12, 2000. M. Papandreou, *Nightmare in Athens*, 80–87, 94–98, directly accused the U.S. government of buying votes. "Athenian" [Rouphos], *Inside the Colonels' Greece*, 53–54, and Couloumbis, Petropulos, and Psomiades, *Foreign Interference in Greek Politics*, 134–35, recycled these charges. Katris, *Eyewitness*, 172–73, 178–81, provides a dramatic rendering of the royal vote-buying operation, but its accuracy is as questionable as much of the rest of his story. The alleged American intervention in 1965 was one of the "issues" that the "17 November" terrorists used to justify their attacks on U.S. officials and property. Kassimeris, *Europe's Last Red Terrorists*, 110, 116. Markezinis, *Σύγχρονη Πολιτική Ιστορία* 3:133, believed the United States and the Greek KYP supported the Tsirimokos effort, a highly unlikely suggestion given the prime minister designate's past ties to the left. Philips Talbot, the assistant secretary of state responsible for Greece in 1965 and subsequent U.S. ambassador to Greece, discussed U.S. actions in an interview with Alexis Papahelas, *Βήμα*, April 22, 2001.

42. Airgram A-333 from Athens, November 13, 1965, Pol 1 GR, DSCF, RG 59, NA; "Athenian" [Rouphos], *Inside the Colonel's Greece*, 56–57.

43. M. Papandreou, *Nightmare in Athens*, 102.

44. Pantazopoulos, *"Για το Λαό και το Εθνος,"* 109–12, 114–117. Andreas's penchant for risk was quite similar to that of Bill Clinton. Wills, "Tragedy of Bill Clinton." On the rise of Andreas, Hitch to Drace-Francis, Athens, March 13 and April 5, 1966, FO 371/185654/CE1016/11 and 66, PRO.

45. Bracken to Brewster, November 16, 1966, Pol 15-1 Andreas Papandreou, NEA/GRK, RG 59, NA. On the reformist nature of Andreas's program, Cohen to Barham, February 24, 1966, Correspondence from the Embassy 1966, NEA/GRK, RG 59, NA. Andreas outlined his program for U.S. officials and appealed for understanding at a November 23, 1965, meeting. The memorandum of the conversation is in airgram A-369 from Athens, November 30, 1965, Pol 2 Greece, DSCF, RG 59, NA. For a sample of Andreas's rhetorical powers and ideas see Kretikos, *Ρήξη*, 103–10, 112–30, 193–96, 201–14, 217–31, 259–66, 269–81, 291–95. See also Pantazopoulos, *"Για το Λαό και το Εθνος,"* 89–91.

46. Airgram A-321 from Athens, November 8, 1965, Pol 2 Greece, DSCF, RG 59, NA. According to Woodhouse, *Karamanlis*, 179–80, in September 1965 the king signaled a willingness to support a "deviation" from the constitution if Karamanlis agreed to return to Greece and form a government with "extraordinary" powers. On the attitudes of Greek officials, see Owens and Brewster oral histories, ADST.

47. On the king's approach, Talbot to Bracken, December 14, 1965, KB/Talbot 1965, NEA/GRK, RG 59, NA.

48. Memoranda of conversations, November 23 and December 14, 1965, in airgrams A-369, November 30, 1965, Pol 2 Greece, and A-458, December 29, 1965, Pol 12 Greece, both DSCF, RG 59, NA. On the impact of Andreas's rhetoric, see Holden, *Greece without Columns*, 224; Paraskevopoulos, *Ανδρέας Παπανδρέου*, 36–37; and Kargakos, *Ecce Homo*, 44–47.

49. Telegram 535 from Athens, September 30, 1965, Pol 2 Greece, airgram A-572 from Athens, February 8, 1966, and telegram 713 from Athens, August 11, 1966, Pol 15 Greece, all DSCF, RG 59, NA.

50. Talbot to James Spain, February 10, 1966, Pol 15-1 Andreas Papandreou, NEA/GRK, RG 59, NA.

51. Barham to Howison, March 1, 1966, Briefing Papers, General, NEA/GRK, RG 59, NA.

52. Talbot to Bracken, February 28 and April 15, 1965, KB/Talbot, NEA/GRK, RG 59, NA.

53. On U.S. thinking, airgrams A-941, July 1, 1966, Pol 2 Greece, and 129 from Athens, September 9, 1966, Pol 1 Greece, both DSCF, RG 59, NA; Bracken to Brewster, August 22, 1966, Correspondence from Embassy 1966, NEA/GRK, RG 59, NA; and the analysis of the French embassy, September 26, 1966, vol. 238, Greece-US,

MAE. On the king's approach, Karamanlis, *Αρχείο*, 6:243–44. On Papandreou's concerns, Kanellopoulos, *Δοκίμια και Άλλα Κείμενα*, 332–41.

54. Talbot to Brewster, October 1, 1966, From Ambassador Talbot 1966, NEA/GRK, RG 59, NA. The king expressed a willingness to deal with Papandreou during an October 1, 1966, talk with Sulzberger. *Age of Mediocrity*, 282–84.

55. Talbot to Brewster, October 1, 1966, From Ambassador Talbot 1966, NEA/GRK, RG 59, NA, reveals the degree to which the embassy had been left out of royal confidence. In addition to his concern about being "used" by the king, Talbot commented that his "dialogue" with Constantine "had now progressed" to a stage where he would feel freer to report back to Washington.

56. Airgram A-196 from Athens, October 8, 1966, Pol 2 Greece, DSCF, RG 59, NA. A. Papandreou, *Democracy at Gunpoint*, 194, ignores this meeting, implying that he had not been in contact with the embassy since early summer. M. Papandreou, *Nightmare*, 113–114, provides a detailed account of the summer meeting with Anschuetz and complains that the younger Papandreous were deliberately snubbed by the embassy during the second half of 1966.

57. Weekly Status report, October 4, 1966, Briefing Papers (Under Secretary), NEA/GRK RG 59, NA.

58. Memorandum of conversation, October 18, 1966, Per 4 Ambassador Talbot Visit 1966, NEA/GRK RG 59, NA.

59. Memorandum of conversation, October 20, 1966, NEA/GRK RG 59, NA; Karamanlis, *Αρχείο*, 6:198–99, 225–26, 234–41, 251, 317–20, 323. Ralles, *Πολιτικές Εκμυστηρεύσεις*, 91, stresses Kanellopoulos's concerns about the deterioration of Greek democracy as the prime motivation for seeking a deal with Papandreou.

60. Bracken to Talbot, "Wednesday" (Nov. 2), Per 4 Ambassador Talbot Visit 1966, NEA/GRK, RG 59, NA; airgram A-229 from Athens, October 26, 1966, Pol 15 Greece, DSCF, RG 59, NA; Maury, "Greek Coup."

61. Brewster to Rockwell, October 19, 1966, Pol 12 Center Union; Brewster to Talbot, October 25, 1966, Pol 15-1 Andreas Papandreou; and Bracken to Brewster, November 16, 1966, all DSCF, RG 59, NA; Kanellopoulos, *Ζωή Μου*, 178–79. The Palace's view as relayed to Karamanlis is in *Αρχείο* 6:250. Markezinis's version of the origins of the government, *Σύγχρονη Πολιτική Ιστορία*, 3:136–45. On Kanellopoulos's objectives, see the French embassy analysis, February 3, 1967, vol. 199, Greece, MAE.

62. Talbot to Brewster, December 30, 1966, From Ambassador Talbot 1966, NEA/GRK, RG 59, NA; Karamanlis, *Αρχείο*, 6:248, 251–52, 323–25, 328–29; embassy in Greece to ministry, January 5, 1967, vol. 199, Greece, MAE. A. Papandreou, *Democracy at Gunpoint*, 195–203, and M. Papandreou, *Nightmare in Athens*, 102, 117–127, stress Andreas's surprise at his exclusion from the deal and his opposition. On the effects of Andreas's stand, Paraskevopoulos, *Ανδρέας Παπανδρέου*, 38–39; Blantas, *Ανδρέας Παπανδρέου*, 61–62. For Andreas's public response, Kretikos, *Ρήξη*, 291–95.

63. *FRUS 1964–68*, 16:528–30 (quote), 555–57. Karamanlis, *Αρχείο*, 6:329–30, on the fragility of the deal. Telegram 229 to the Foreign Office, April 6, 1967, FCO 9/120, PRO, for the Palace's views. A very pessimistic French embassy analysis of the prospects for Greece placed equal blame on Andreas and the Palace February 23, 1967, vol. 199, Greece, MAE.

64. *FRUS 1964–68*, 16:541–42; Papahelas, *Βιασμός*, 278–81; Owens, Anschuetz, and Brewster oral histories, ADST. Maury discussed the program in "Greek Coup."

65. *FRUS 1964–68*, 16:552–55. Maury, "Greek Coup," for further details of the meeting. The final part of Rusk's comment is intriguing. It seems to imply that the CIA was in contact with some Greek Americans who shared its concerns about Andreas and may have been suggesting them as a conduit for U.S. funding. In 1948 the CIA turned to Italian Americans during its first successful covert-election operation. Miller, "Taking Off the Gloves." A source summarized the 303 Committee meetings for journalist Marquis Childs shortly after the coup. Childs published a confused recounting of the discussions in the *Washington Post* (May 15, 1967) that seemed to suggest that the U.S. decision to follow a policy of nonintervention opened the way to the coup of April 21. See Rostow's comments in a memorandum to President Johnson, May 15, 1967, *FRUS 1964–68*, 16:611–12. Tsoucalas, in *Greek Tragedy*, 203, basing himself on the Childs article, conjures up a meeting in which representatives of the Greek army and the Palace conspired with U.S. officials to plan the coup.

66. Memorandum of conversation, March 17, 1967, Pol 12-6 Greece, DSCF, RG 59, NA. For the Papandreou version, M. Papandreou, *Nightmare in Athens*, 128–32. Full Greek texts of both speeches are in Kretikos, *Ρήξη*, 311–24, 329–38. The French embassy, in a March 3, 1967, report, judged the March 1 speech a "violent" attack and reported the anger it aroused among American diplomats in Athens. Vol. 238, Greece-US, MAE. Monteagle Stearns, who knew Papandreou well, remarked that Andreas always had a problem differentiating between his former role as a U.S. citizen and political activist and his post-1964 role as a foreign leader. Author's notes of telephone conversation with Monteagle Stearns, May 11, 2001.

67. *FRUS 1964–68*, 16:560–62. On intelligence reporting and the conservatives' political situation, *FRUS 1964–68*, 16:259, 329–30, 333–37; Belios, *Καραμανλής*, 8, 48–51. On the king's views, Hitch to Everett, Athens, March 23, 1967, FCO 9/123, PRO.

68. Kanellopoulos, *Ζωή Μου*, 184; Karamanlis, *Αρχείο*, 6:333–34; Ralles, *Πολιτικές Εκμυστηρεύσεις*, 95.

69. Telegram 4573 from Athens, April 8, 1967, Pol 15 Greece, DSCF, RG 59, NA. Compare the equally negative judgment of Karamanlis, *Αρχείο*, 6:266–68, and the comments of Markezinis, *Σύγχρονη Πολιτική Ιστορία*, 3:150–51, on Kanellopoulos's political judgment. Kanellopoulos's views of the situation are in *Ζωή Μου*, 187, and *Κείμενα, 1967–1974*, 45–48. The importance of amnesty for Andreas as a deal breaker is underlined in M. Papandreou, *Nightmare in Athens*, 124.

70. In addition to materials cited in other parts of this chapter, for discussions of the possibility of a coup, see "Annual Review for Greece for 1965," January 17, 1966, FO 371/185653/E1011/1, Murray to Hollar, Athens, July 4, 1966, FO 371/185654/CE1015/66, and dispatch 31 from the embassy in Greece to the Foreign Office, July 28, 1966, FO 371/185654/CE1015/22, all PRO; telegram 1918 from Washington to the Ministry of Foreign Affairs, April 15, 1967, vol. 238, Greece-US, MAE; Karamanlis, Αρχείο, 6:321–23; Bracken to Talbot, n.d., but November 1966, Per 4 Phillips Talbot Visit, NEA/GRK, RG 59, NA, and Bracken to Brewster, November 22, 1966, Correspondence AmEmbAthens, 1966, both NEA/GRK, RG 59, NA; airgram A-229, October 26, 1966, Pol 15 Greece, DSCF, RG 59, NA. According to CIA chief of station Maury, "Greek Coup," the CIA's sole contact with the "Colonels" was not one of the regular ("paid") sources, and the contacts were "casual." Among memoirs treating talk of a coup, M. Papandreou, *Nightmare in Athens*, 136, 138–39; Rousseas, *Death of a Democracy*, 53. On U.S. precoup information about the "Colonels" see Stern, *Wrong Horse*, 42. Compare the observations of Veremis, *Military in Greek Politics*, 154, 158. The British were aware of the existence of Papadopoulos's group and failed to recognize the threat. Telegram 275 to the Foreign Office, April 21, 1967, FCO 9/124, PRO. On the failure of Greek senior officers to correctly estimate the threat, see their comments, reported in Couloumbis, *'71–'74: Σημειωσεις*, 124–25, and Sulzberger, *Age of Mediocrity*, 574–76. During my work in State Department archives, I discovered an unclassified list of CIA reports entitled "Conspiratorial Group," which listed fourteen separate reports concerning their activities, the earliest dating from October 1964 through December 1966. These reports were: (TD) CSDBs 312/00855–64, 312/00748–66; 312/03383–66; 311/13966–66; 315/03041–66; 315/03301–66; 315/03206–66; 314/00405–64; 311/06926–65; 311/10327–65; 315/02609–65; 311/05301–65; and DCS-D-315/03206–66.

71. Pattakos, *Απόρρητο Ημερολόγιο*, 15, 30–32, 36, 52, 57–64, 73, 79–82.

72. Telegram 4574 from Athens, April 9, 1967, Pol 15 Greece, DSCF, RG 59, NA.

73. Kretikos, *Ρήξη* 285–89; M. Papandreou, *Nightmare in Athens*, 132–39; Rousseas, *Death of a Democracy*, 54; Blantas, *Ανδρέας Παπανδρέου*, 55, 67–69.

74. *FRUS 1964–68*, 16:572–77. Similar British and French analyses are in embassy in Greece to Foreign Office, January 31, 1967, FCO 9/120, PRO; French consul general in Thessaloniki to embassy, February 15, 1867, and embassy in Greece to ministry, March 9, 1967, both vol. 199, Greece, Europe, MAE. Maury, "Greek Coup," states that on April 20, senior Greek officers held a meeting at which the authorization for a coup was deferred. Pattakos, *Απόρρητο Ημερολόγιο*, 102–25, recalled that the reluctance of senior officers to move was one factor that provoked his group to finally act.

75 Telegram 179151 to Athens, April 20, 1967, Pol 15 Greece, DSCF, RG 59, NA.

76. One of the canards that arises in every discussion of the coup is the idea that the United States, and specifically the CIA, in some manner encouraged or supported the Colonels. The discussion is complicated by the Central Intelligence Agency's not-

very-intelligent decision to suppress much of the documentation relating to its activities in Greece. The agency appears to believe that denying the existence of a station in Greece somehow enhances its "cover." CIA stonewalling does increase confusion over its role and, as a result, Greek paranoia about both CIA and U.S. involvement in their nation's internal affairs. The agency hamstrung the efforts of State Department historians to provide an accurate record of events that largely clarifies U.S. policy. Thanks in good part to the detective work of Laurence Stern and Alexis Papahelas, we know that the CIA had some contacts with the middle-level military conspiracy that would eventually overthrow the Kanellopoulos government. Having failed to secure a U.S. blessing, the plotters cut off contact by February 1967. The agency was well informed through its own agents and military attachés (often one in the same) of the existence of high-level plotting. Stern, *Wrong Horse*, 35–46; Papahelas, *Βιασμός*, 255–57, 270–76, 279–82, 292–93, 313. Compare Pattakos, *Απόρρητο Ημερολόγιο*, 30–32, 57–64, 73, 79–82. Former general Solon Ghikas confirmed this to Sulzberger in 1969. *Age of Mediocrity*, 574–76. Based on a careful reading of the trial records for the junta leaders, Woodhouse, *Rise and Fall of the Greek Colonels*, 7. 19–20, dismisses the idea that the coup was the work either of foreign actors or the Greek high command. Maury, "Greek Coup," notes that both U.S. military and intelligence officers were ordered to stay away from any officers promoting a coup as part of an effort to discourage Greeks from assuming that such a move would have U.S. blessing. This, he adds, meant that the United States lacked access to exactly the people who would ultimately topple the government. The best explanation for the Colonels' ability to keep both U.S. and Greek senior officials ignorant of their plans has been provided in Robert Keeley oral history, ADST. On the confusing effects of CIA stonewalling, Klarevas, "Were the Eagle and the Phoenix Birds of a Feather?"

77. This analysis recognizes another factor: the rapid modernization of Greece's society and economy played a major role in laying the groundwork for the coup. In 1967, *Balkan Studies* published an intriguing series of analyses of the effects of modernization prepared prior to the coup. See, in particular, McNeill, "Dilemmas of Modernization in Greece," and Saunders, "Greek Society in Transition." Keeley, May 30, 1974, in Couloumbis, *'71–'74: Σημειώσεις*, 316–23, stressed the shared responsibility of the entire Greek political class for the coup.

78. Embassy in Greece to the ministry, February 17, 1967, vol. 238, Greece, MAE.

79. On Washington's strategy, Brewster and Keeley oral histories, ADST.

80. *FRUS 1964–68*, 16:586–87, 624–26, and telegram 365 from Athens, March 27, 1968, Pol 1 Greece-US, DSCF, RG 59, NA.

Chapter 6

1. Herodotus, *Ιστορία*, 1:60.
2. On Andreas's limited influence, Rousseas, *Death of a Democracy*, 150–51, 154,

158–59; Kaklamanake, Ανδρέας Παπανδρέου, 118–19; Paraskevopoulos, Ανδρέας Παπανδρέου, 44–45; Mandelaras, Μια Πολιτική Μαρτυρία, 35–37. The junta considered him washed-up. Comments of Pattakos in Sulzberger, *Age of Mediocrity*, 458. On his problems with other exiles, report of the Greek representative to the Socialist International, April 23, 1968, details center-left opposition to Papandreou, FCO 9/143, PRO. One prominent socialist, British foreign secretary George Brown, commented that he "would not touch the case of Andreas Papandreou with a barge pole." Telegram 5046 to the British mission to the United Nations, September 22, 1967, FCO 9/128 PRO. On Andreas's exaggerated claims to leadership of the Greek resistance, *Daily Mail*, August 17, 1968. On the effects his efforts to work with the EDA in-exile produced, *New York Times*, August 23, 1968; and Bridges to Macrae, August 23, 1968, FCO 9/143, PRO. Andreas abandoned his claim to leadership of the EK in-exile a year after his departure from Greece. He put the best face on his setback in an open letter to the EK membership, January 24, 1969, reprinted in Voultepses, Πολιτική Διαθήκη του Γεωργίου Παπανδρέου, 110–12. In "Letter to EK in-Exile," February 3, 1969, he continued to style himself as the EK's "Representative in the Exterior." Voultepses, Πολιτική Διαθήκη του Γεωργίου Παπανδρέου, 113. On George Papandreou's views, see A. Papandreou, *Democracy at Gunpoint*, 24–25. The elder Papandreou purportedly told the king, "My son is the biggest curse that ever happened to me." Letter to Maitland, May 28, 1968, FCO 9/143, PRO.

3. An example of this sense of betrayal is to be found in two volumes by the Greek American historian Jon Kofas. In *Intervention and Underdevelopment*, 2–4, 169–80, Kofas adopts the Papandreou version of events and portrays Andreas as dedicated to saving his people from the effects of American imperialism. A decade later, in *Under the Eagle's Claw*, 181–228, Kofas portrays his erstwhile hero as a man who talked like a leftist but betrayed Greeks by governing from the right. Compare Kariotis, *Greek Socialist Experiment*, esp. 1–126; Clogg, *Greece, 1981–1989*, 26–64, 113–30; Kurth and Petras, *Mediterranean Paradoxes*, 160–215; Blantas, Ανδρέας Παπανδρέου; Paraskevopoulos, Ανδρέας Παπανδρέου; and from the far right, Kargakos, *Ecce Homo*.

4. Perhaps best summarized in A. Papandreou, *Paternalistic Capitalism*, 133. The "canonical" texts on which the "Andreas Version" is based are A. Papandreou, *Democracy at Gunpoint*, and M. Papandreou, *Nightmare in Athens*. Other important titles include Rousseas, *Death of a Democracy*; Katris, *Eyewitness in Greece*; Deane, *I Should Have Died*; and Tsoucalas, *Greek Tragedy*. Testimony of Margaret Papandreou, July 14, 1971, in U.S. Congress, *Greece, Spain, and the Southern NATO Strategy*, 169–181. Papandreou's press secretary, Yiannis Roubatis's *Tangled Webs* is a widely cited reiteration of Andreas Papandreou's version of events. A number of foreign journalists, most notably Eric Rouleau, a longtime fixture at *Le Monde*, also spread the gospel. French-Canadian sociologist Jean Meynaud, *Rapport sur l'abolition de la démocratie en Grèce*, adopts the basic Papandreou line and is a standard work of reference despite its near total reliance on pro-EK press reporting. A good introduction to the debate at its ori-

gins is Xydis, "Coups and Countercoups." An interesting example of the speed with which the Andreas version took hold is provided by the papers and exchanges in Couloumbis and Hicks, *U.S. Foreign Policy toward Greece and Cyprus*. Stern, *Wrong Horse*, a brilliantly written and well-researched piece of journalism, remains the most influential statement of this thesis. The Papandreou version's staying power is demonstrated in Murtagh, *Rape of Greece* (1994), which recycles the versions of events offered in the early 1970s without any effort to verify their validity, and in Greek in Papaioannou, *15 Ιουλοον 1965* (1995), which sets remarkable standards for getting basic facts wrong. Among more scholarly works, the same tendency is visible. See, for example, Danopoulos, *Warriors and Politicians in Modern Greece*; Goldbloom, "United States Policy," 234–41; and the slightly modified exegesis of Couloumbis in Couloumbis, Petropulos, and Psomiades, *Foreign Interference in Greek Politics*, 135–36. A Greek reading that finds the "dark hand" of the CIA behind all of Greece's post-1959 troubles and links this to U.S. intervention in the Cyprus issue is Psyroukes, *Ιστορία της Σύγχρονης Ελλάδα*, vols. 3 and 4. The "Andreas version" has not gone unchallenged in Greece. Mouzelis, *Modern Greece*, 128, 131, while sharing many analytical and ideological starting points, makes a fairly convincing argument against U.S. involvement with the Colonels, relying on common sense rather than a documentary base. A polemical but careful deconstruction of Andreas's memoirs from the left, Blantas, *Ανδρέας Παπανδρέου*, 53, places the blame for the coup in Athens squarely on the shoulders of the Papandreous. From the right, Theodoracopoulos, *Greek Upheaval*, esp., 133–34, similarly targets Andreas's responsibility. Veremis expresses skepticism in *Military in Greek Politics*, 155–56. Perrakes, "Εξωτερική Πολιτική της Ενωσεως Κέντρου," ignores Andreas's charges.

5. In addition to the memoirs, see A. Papandreou, *Man's Freedom* and *Paternalistic Capitalism*, two well-crafted appeals for support from U.S. elites. On the influence of conspiracy theory, especially on the Greek left's views of events of 1950s and 1960s, see comments of Stavrou, *Allied Politics and Military Interventions*, 130. On the junta's manipulation of the public belief in American support, Goldbloom, "United States Policy," 240. Holden, *Greece without Columns*, 244, 248–49, provides an outline of the factors that led most Greeks to cling firmly to the belief in U.S. manipulation of the events of 1965–67. An important reason for Greek acceptance of the Papandreou version was the collective need of the postjunta political leadership, from Karamanlis to Papandreou, to cover their mistakes. The utility of a foreign scapegoat is evident.

6. On her role, see M. Papandreou, *Nightmare in Athens*, 162–63, 191–94, 210–12, 215. A. Papandreou, *Democracy at Gunpoint*, 36, expressed his appreciation of her efforts. Probably the best telling of Margaret's battle to save Andreas is N. Papandreou, *Father Dancing*, which, despite its subtitle, *An Invented Memoir*, is the most incisive and reliable account of the Papandreou family story during the 1960s and early 1970s.

7. *FRUS 1964–68*, 16:581–82, on Talbot's initial efforts. M. Papandreou backhandedly acknowledges embassy efforts in *Nightmare in Athens*, 145, 152–55. Walter Heller, a Papandreou family friend, commented favorably on embassy efforts to secure good treatment and ultimate release for Andreas. "Report on Athens Trip, July 22–25, 1967," FCO 9/128, PRO. Shortly after Andreas's release, a U.S. official confirmed to the British his government's readiness to grant Andreas a visa for a return to the United States, admitting that though they feared "the embarrassment which his public appearances may cause them, the thought of rejecting his admission had not even entered their heads." Smart to Macrae, February 16, 1968, FCO 9/143, PRO. Lucius Battle and Brewster oral histories, ADST.

8. Embassy in Greece to ministry, June 9, 1967, vol. 238, Greece-US, MAE; M. Papandreou, *Nightmare in Athens*, 243.

9. Karamanlis, *Αρχείο*, 7:37–38, and telegram 4955 from the Foreign Office, September 20, 1967, FCO 9/128, PRO, on Andreas's approaches to Karamanlis and the king. The king's views on Andreas were reported in letter to Maitland, London, May 28, 1968, FCO 9/143, PRO. M. Papandreou, *Nightmare in Athens*, 228, 241–42; *FRUS 1964–68*, 16:603, on the health issue.

10. Voultepses, *Πολιτική Διαθήκη του Γεωργίου Παπανδρέου*, 35; M. Papandreou, *Nightmare in Athens*, 339–41. On the state of Greek public opinion in the months after the coup, *FRUS 1964–68*, 16:609–11; ambassador to Foreign Office, October 19, 1967, FCO 9/120, and minute by Davidson, December 1, 1967, FCO 9/123, both PRO. Compare the ironic comments of the French embassy, January 10, 1968, vol. 199, Greece, MAE; of Smith, *Athens*, 40; and of publisher Eleni Vlachou in Sulzberger, *Age of Mediocrity*, 334.

11. Pattakos taped his talk with Papandreou and published it in *Ημέραι και Έργα*. A. Papandreou, *Democracy at Gunpoint*, 293–94, and M. Papandreou, *Nightmare in Athens*, 368–69, for the meeting with Talbot and their objectives. The U.S. record is in *FRUS 1964–68* 16:721–25.

12. Telegram 3613 from Athens, February 19, 1968, Pol 29 Greece, and airgram A-383 from Athens, January 22, 1968, Pol Greece-2, both DSCF, RG 59, NA; Karamanlis, *Αρχείο*, 7:66, 76, 249–50. On Kaysen's views, Rousseas, *Death of a Democracy*, 104–8; Foley, Notes on Meeting with Andreas Papandreou, July 24, 1968, FCO 9/143, PRO. George Papandreou's comments are from a letter reprinted in Voultepses, *Πολιτική Διαθήκη του Γεωργίου Παπανδρέου*, 11–16.

13. Voultepses, *Πολιτική Διαθήκη του Γεωργίου Παπανδρέου*, 106–7, 120–22, 135–37, 153–54, reprints a number of Andreas's public and private letters. His approaches toward Karamanlis are documented in *Αρχείο*, 7:111–12, 164, 258–61.

14. Andreas's plans can be followed in A. Papandreou, *Από το ΠΑΚ στο ΠΑΣΟΚ*, 12–14, 20–24, 27–33, 35–39, 41–56, 61–74. Compare his letter of October 10, 1971, reprinted in Paraskevopoulos, *Ανδρέας Παπανδρέου*, 47–49, and the report and comments of Couloumbis in Karamanlis, *Αρχείο*, 7:344–45. On efforts to build a North

American base for Andreas, Mercouri, *I Was Born Greek*, 232–33, and on this and Andreas's search for his Greek roots, N. Papandreou, *Father Dancing*.

15. Rousseas, *Death of a Democracy*, 13–14, 18 (Andreas as American idealist), 31–32 (CIA and Defense Department machinations), 39 (U.S. responsibility), 97, 101–2 (embassy opposition to the Papandreous), 153, 163 (forecast of likely civil war). Margaret Papandreou endorses the book in *Nightmare in Athens*, 113.

16. Katris, *Eyewitness*, 95–96, 137, 305–6. George Papandreou died in 1968.

17. Katris, *Eyewitness*, 45–47 (1961 CIA approach and Pappas's claims to be a CIA agent), 293–95 (Marquis Childs column), and 305–6 (only the United States can topple junta). On the mosaic technique, see M. Papandreou, *Nightmare in Athens*, 185–86. Compare Holden, *Greece without Columns*, 248–49.

18. M. Papandreou, *Nightmare in Athens*, 144–45 and 254 (failure of Greeks to resist), 279–71 (Andreas as cause of coup), 161, 236, 275 (comments on Greek journalists and on national character), 92–94 (outburst against Sulzberger).

19. Blantas, *Ανδρέας Παπανδρέο*, 18–19, 39–44, 73. Many of Andreas's claims regarding his relation with the U.S. embassy either cannot be confirmed (despite the richness of the U.S. record) or are contradicted by the contemporary record.

20. Between 1971 and 1974, Ted Couloumbis of American University (Washington, D.C.) made a series of trips to Greece, taking the pulse of elite opinion. Couloumbis, *'71–'74: Σημειώσεις*, 77, 79 (cited) 182, 186, 189–91, 199–205, 217, documents the ever more negative view of the United States.

21. Papandreou, *Democracy at Gunpoint*, viii–ix, 7, 10–11, 26, 97–98, 103, 223–24, 229–30, 250, 261, 330–34, 339.

22. Papandreou, *Democracy at Gunpoint*, 52–54, 61–62, 64–65, 67–75, 81–82, 86–88, 91 (United States extends control), 93–94 (Karamanlis), 112, 119 (Kennedy), 136–37 (Cyprus), 152–55 (ASPIDA), 99, 186, 196–98, 202, 298 (battle for George Papandreou's soul). Among the accounts of the Greek Civil War that cast the United States in Greece in a negative role, Kolko, *Politics of War*, 172–77, 190, and Kolko and Kolko, *Limits of Power*, 218–20, 224, 231–32, 411–12. On Andreas's claims to the political heritage of George Papandreou, M. Papandreou, *Nightmare in Athens*, 370, and Lucarelli, *Socialismo mediterraneo*, 45–46.

23. Papandreou, *Democracy at Gunpoint*, 341–42, 354. On his early view, Kritikos, *Ρήξη*, 33–40, 45–55, and A. Papandreou, *Strategy for Greek Economic Development*, 14–15, 29–31, 102–4. On his changed views, Kritikos, *Ρήξη*, 311–38, and A. Papandreou, *Political Element in Economic Development*, 16–19. For his criticism of the Western democratic model, A. Papandreou, *Paternalistic Capitalism*, esp. 121–43, and *Man's Freedom*, 12–13, 24–25, 46–47, 52–54, 63, 65, and Andreas's comments in Lucarelli, *Socialismo mediterraneo*, 16–28, 34–36, 49–54. On the melding of socialist and Greek national ideas with anti-American themes, see the programmatic statement of PASOK, September 3, 1974, in A. Papandreou, *Από το ΠΑΚ στο ΠΑΣΟΚ*, 78–84. On the development of Papandreou's ideology, Pantazopoulos, "*Για το Λαό και το Έθνος*,"

33–34, 91–105, 111. Andreas would continue to bid for American public support even after his attacks on government policy; see his 1971 speech at Amherst College in Papandreou, "Greece: An American Problem."

24. Brewster oral history, ADST; *FRUS 1964–68*, 16:580; dispatch 18 from Athens, May 20, 1967, FCO 9/126, PRO; Sulzberger, *Age of Mediocrity*, 335; Stern, *Wrong Horse*, 47; Keeley oral history, ADST.

25. *FRUS 1964–68*, 16:580, 582–83.

26. *FRUS 1964–68*, 16:583–86.

27. *FRUS 1964–68*, 16:584–87. See also U.S. Department of State *Bulletin*, May 15, 1967. On policy making in Washington, oral history of Lucius Battle, Oral History Collection, LBJL.

28. Brewster oral history, ADST; *FRUS 1964–68*, 16:587–90, 604–6. The British too judged the junta to be in "full and unchangeable control." Telegram 332 to the Foreign Office, April 23, 1967, FCO 9/124, PRO. Stern, *Wrong Horse*, 12, was convinced that neither the embassy nor the CIA station was involved in the coup.

29. Stern, *Wrong Horse*, 48; Keeley oral history, ADST; Sulzberger, *Age of Mediocrity*, 324–44, 463; *FRUS 1964–68*, 16:594–97.

30. One of the critics of the handling of the Colonels was Jack Maury, the CIA station chief, who later argued ("Greek Coup") that by taking a firm stance (without threatening military action), the United States would have served its own best interests.

31. Keeley oral history, ADST.

32. Pattakos's character is best revealed in Ημέραι και Εργα. See also his statements to Sulzberger, *Age of Mediocrity*, 324–27. The French characterization is in embassy in Greece to ministry, June 9, 1967, vol. 206, Greece, MAE.

33. Keeley oral history, ADST. Sulzberger, *Age of Mediocrity*, 327–28, 459–61, on the character of Papadopoulos.

34. Papahelas, Βιασμός, 181, 237–42, 256–57, 270–76; *FRUS 1961–63*, 16:64–68; *FRUS 1964–68*, 16:474–76, 519–20. Speculation about links between CIA Greek-American employees and the coup planners is downplayed in Stern, *Wrong Horse*, 44, and in Keeley oral history, ADST. Nevertheless, speculation continues: Klarevas, "Were the Eagle and the Phoenix Birds of a Feather?"

35. *FRUS 1964–68*, 16:597–602. Telegram 1461 to the Foreign Office, May 2, 1967, FCO 9/125, PRO, on U.S. policy and memorandum of conversation between Foreign Minister Brown and Ambassador Murray, London, May 3, 1967, FCO 9/126, PRO, on the king's weakness and the determination of the junta leadership. Murray, while admiring the king's courage, thought him a risky bet. Embassy in Greece to ministry, May 5, 1967, vol. 206, Greece, MAE. Constantine discussed his plans for the coup with Sulzberger on May 3: *Age of Mediocrity*, 336–44. Karamanlis's comments, *Age of Mediocrity*, 339, 567. See also Karamanlis, Αρχείο, 7:26–28, 59.

36. *FRUS 1964–68*, 16:607–9, 613–18, 628–30; Stern, *Wrong Horse*, 50; comments of Markezinis, Σύγχρονη Πολιτική Ιστορία 3:155–57.

37. *FRUS 1964-68*, 16:632-35, for U.S. positions and record of the talks. A Greek version, prepared by Archbishop Iakovos, on the basis of his subsequent discussions with King Constantine, is in Karamanlis, *Αρχείο*, 7:34-36.

38. *FRUS 1964-68*, 16:599-612, 624-28, 641-42. Telegrams 477, May 19, 1967, and 4525, September 12, 1967, from the embassy in Greece to the ministry, and a report from the embassy, July 12, 1967, all vol. 238, Greece-US, MAE. See also Stewart to Holder, September 27, 1967, FCO 9/120, PRO. On the regime's staying power, Stewart to Holder, October 12, 1967, FCO 9/120, PRO. Stern, *Wrong Horse*, 59, for the effects of the arms embargo.

39. Karamanlis's pessimism and his nuanced but nevertheless poor advice to Constantine can be traced in his November 19, 1967, interview with Eric Rouleau in Genevoix, *Greece of Karamanlis*, 182-92; in his comments to Sulzberger, *Age of Mediocrity*, 323; and in his letter to King Constantine, November 9, 1967, *Αρχείο*, 7:42-44. On the open nature of the king's coup planning, see telegram 364 from the embassy in Sweden to the ministry, November 30, 1967, and Note for the Minister, December 1, 1967, both vol. 206, Greece, MAE. *FRUS 1964-68*, 16:700-702, for the situation in late November. An excellent analysis of the reasons for the countercoup's failure is Consul General, Thessaloniki to Ministry of Foreign Affairs, December 15, 1967, vol. 206, Greece, MAE.

40. U.S. isolation and indecision during dramatic hours of the failed royal coup is documented in *FRUS 1964-68*, 16:703-13. Maury, "Greek Coup," provides some details of the drama. Compare also British and French reporting in telegram 3935 to the Foreign Office, December 13, 1967, FCO 9/140, PRO, and telegram 6532 to the ministry, December 13, 1967, vol. 206, Greece, MAE. Keeley oral history, ADST, on embassy response to the coup and the contrast between the king's more or less public plotting and the methods of the Colonels. Stern, *Wrong Horse*, 57, on Talbot's position after the coup.

41. *FRUS 1964-68*, 16:713-15. For similarly pessimistic analyses of the situation see telegram 118 to the ministry, December 14, 1967, vol. 206, Greece, MAE, and "Greece: Annual Report 1967," January 9, 1968, FCO 9/118, PRO.

42. *FRUS 1964-68*, 16:719-21.

43. *FRUS 1964-68*, 16:730-31, 741-43, 751-55 (Talbot quoted). Greek ambassador Palamas's views are in Karamanlis *Αρχείο*, 7:68-69. See also Stern, *Wrong Horse*, 49.

44. The U.S. retreat can be traced in *FRUS 1964-68*, 16:756-57, 765-67; telegram 1809 to the Foreign Office, June 6, 1968, and letter from Bendall to Beith, August 1, 1968, both FCO 9/174, PRO. British policy conclusions were not greatly different from those of the United States. Smith to the Foreign Office, May 7, 1968, and memorandum by the Central Department, n.d., both FCO 9/121, PRO. Sulzberger's comments, *New York Times*, October 4, 1968. See also Couloumbis, *'71-'74: Σημειώσεις*, 19-20.

45. *FRUS 1964–68*, 16:776–77. Rockwell's comments reported in Stewart to Beith, Athens, May 13, 1968, FCO 9/174, PRO.

Chapter 7

1. "Greece: Implications for U.S.-Greek Relations of the Junta's Continuation," March 16, 1971, Pol 15 Greece, DSCF, RG 59, NA.

2. On the junta the best study is Woodhouse, *Rise and Fall of the Greek Colonels*. Xydis, "Coups and Countercoups," is a useful summary of the junta years. Two multi-volume publications published shortly after the fall of the junta provide a wealth of material: Rodakis, *Δίκες της Χούντας* and Gregoriades, *Ιστορία της Δικτατορίας*. Other valuable contemporary studies include Clogg and Yannopoulos, *Greece under Military Rule*; "Athenian" [Rouphos], *Inside the Colonels' Greece*; and Holden, *Greece without Columns*. Veremis, *Military in Greek Politics*, is a useful overview of the military's involvement in politics. In terms of U.S. policy, the best study is Stern, *Wrong Horse*. The number two man in the dictatorship until 1973, Stylianos Pattakos, defends the record of the junta in his *Ημέραι και Εργα*. Couloumbis and Hicks, *U.S. Foreign Policy towards Greece and Cyprus*, although not terribly informative, underlines the passion that surrounded these issues. See also Kissinger, *White House Years*, 1188–92, and *Years of Renewal*, 192–237. Carl Barkman's *Ambassador in Athens* is a devastating appraisal of U.S. performance by a foreign diplomat who was largely sympathetic to the difficulties faced by American officials.

3. "Greece: Annual Review for 1968," January 14, 1969, FCO 9/838, PRO; embassy in Greece to ministry, November 11, 1968, vol. 206, Greece, MAE.

4. For an example of Pipinelis's skillful presentation of the junta's positions, *FRUS 1964–68*, 16:726–28. Karamanlis, *Αρχείο*, 7:63–64, 70–72, 87, 97, 251–52, on opposition divisions and confusion.

5. *FRUS 1964–68*, 16:715–16; Couloumbis, *'71–'74: Σημειώσεις*, 18–19. Comments of Kanellopoulos in Sulzberger, *Age of Mediocrity*, 573. See also Karamanlis, *Αρχείο*, 7:255.

6. Embassy in Greece to ministry, April 16, 1969, vol. 206, Greece, MAE; Andreas Papandreou to Harold Wilson, February 11, 1969, FCO 9/836, PRO; Karamanlis, *Αρχείο*, 7:132, 256–57.

7. Memorandum of conversation between Ambassador Palamas and Acting Secretary of State Eliot Richardson, March 1, 1969, Greece, vol. 1, MERF, NSF, NPM, NA.

8. Stuart Rockwell and Robert Keeley oral histories ADST. Alexander Butterfield to Henry Kissinger, March 24, 1969, Greece, vol. 1, MERF, NSF, NPM, NA. The best source of information on the Nixon visit, ironically, is in embassy in Greece to ministry, June 23, 1967, vol. 238, Greece-US, MAE. See also Couloumbis, *'71–'74: Σημειώσεις*, 323; Pattakos, *Ημέραι και Εργα*, 56.

9. "Chronology of the Greek Embroglio [sic]," n.d., Greece, vol. 1, MERF, NSF, NPM, NA; Walsh to Kissinger, n.d., Eisenhower Funeral-Cables, VIP Visits, MERF,

NSF, NPM, NA; memorandum on King Constantine, n.d., Appointments with Foreign Dignitaries, Eisenhower Funeral-Cables, VIP Visits, MERF, NSF, NPM, NA.

10. Entry of March 31, 1969, President's Daily Diary, NPM, NA; memorandum of conversation between Nixon and Pattakos, March 31, 1969, Pol 7 Greece, DSCF, RG 59, NA; memorandum of conversation between Pipinelis and Kissinger, April 1, 1969, Greece, vol. 1, MERF, NSF, NPM, NA.

11. Memorandum of conversation between King Constantine and Agnew, April 1, 1969, Pol 7 Greece, DSCF, RG 59, NA. When Agnew met Pattakos the same day, the U.S. vice president underlined the need for a return to democracy. The memorandum of the conversation is also in Pol 7 Greece, DSCF, RG 59, NA. This message was notably missing during Nixon's meeting with Pattakos. In subsequent meetings with Secretary of State Rogers and Secretary of Defense Melvin Laird, on April 1 and 2, respectively, Pattakos pressed for the resumption of arms shipments. Telegram 51211 to Athens, April 3, 1969, Pol 7 Greece, DSCF, RG 59, NA.

12. James Webel to Kissinger, April 23, 1969, with attachments, Greece, vol. 1; memorandum of conversation between Webel and Harold Saunders, NSC staff, May 6, 1969; Saunders to Kissinger, May 6, 1969; John Walsh to Kissinger, May 7, 1969, all MERF, NSF, NPM, NA. Given Andreas Papandreou's history of anti-American diatribes, a decision to avoid contact was comprehensible. Karamanlis, however, had been a close collaborator with the Eisenhower and Kennedy administrations and was widely regarded as Greece's preeminent statesman. See Karamanlis to Iakovos, February 21, 1970, in Belios, *Καραμανλής*, 170, 230–33.

13. Saunders to Kissinger, April 8, 1969, and Rose Mary Woods to Kissinger, n.d., both Greece, vol. 1, MERF, NSF, NPM, NA; memorandum of conversation between Angelis and Agnew, April 11, 1969, Pol Greece-US, DSCF, RG 59, NA.

14. Haig to Kissinger, June 13, 1969, with attachment, Greece, vol. 1, MERF, NSF, NPM, NA; INR Research Note: "NATO and Greece," October 14, 1969, Pol 23-9, DSCF, RG 59, NA.

15. In an October 7 memorandum to the president, the NSC staff commented that the issue of military supply was political, not military, as it would signal U.S. support for one side in Greece's internal politics. Greece, vol. 1, MERF, NSF, NPM, NA. On the junta's preoccupation with the issue, Saunders to Kissinger, June 6, 1969, and Agnew to Kissinger, July 1, 1969, both Greece, vol. 1, MERF, NSF, NPM, NA. On the opposition's insistence that continued suspension of aid would move the junta, T. W. Evans to Nixon, August 7, 1969, Greece, vol. 1, MERF, NSF, NPM, NA, and memorandum of conversation between Constantine Mitsotakis and Vigderman, November 17, 1969, Pol Greece, DSCF, RG 59, NA. On the administration's assurances to NATO allies that military aid needed to resume, telegram Unsec 28 from London, November 8, 1969, and INR Intelligence Note 737, October 14, 1969, both Pol 23-9 Greece, DSCF, RG 59, NA. The administration's determination to provide military aid found strong support from the embassy in Greece, where chargé Roswell McClelland wrote: "I continue

to believe rather strongly that our best course would be to de-link military assistance from the question of internal political progress." McClelland to Rockwell, September 25, 1969, Pol Greece-US, DSCF, RG 59, NA. McClelland coupled his recommendation with an emphasis on the need to make a strong expression of opposition to the antidemocratic nature of the junta.

16. On Tasca's Italian adventures, Harper, *America and the Reconstruction of Italy*, 11, 34; Brewster, Blood, King, and Rockwell oral histories and Stuart Kennedy memoir, ADST; McClelland to Vigderman, April 30, 1970, Pol 15 Greece, DSCF, RG 59, NA.

17. NSDM 34, November 14, 1969, Greece, vol.1, MERF, NSF, NPM, NA; memorandum of conversation between Nixon and Vitsaxis, November 18, 1969, Pol 17 Greece-US, DSCF, RG 59, NA. Word of the administration's intentions was quickly picked up. The Greek press reported Nixon's support for the junta. Telegram 5224 from Athens, November 25, 1969, Pol 1 Greece-US, DSCF, RG 59, NA. During 1971 House Foreign Affairs Committee hearings, Congressman Benjamin Rosenthal (D-N.Y.) focused on the chronology of the arms-supply decision while questioning Tasca. The ambassador refused to confirm that the decision occurred before his arrival in Athens. U.S. Congress, *Greece, Spain, and the Southern NATO Strategy*, 306–8.

18. Memo from Watt to Kissinger, January 27, 1970, with attached copy of telegram 323 from Athens, January 26, Greece, vol.1, MERF, NSF, NPM, NA.

19. President's Weekly Briefing, January 27, 1970, Greece, vol. 1, MERF, NSF, NPM, NA. A copy of telegram 324 from Athens, January 26 (Tasca's report on the meeting), was attached.

20. Telegram 743 from Athens, February 18, 1970, Pol 29 Greece, DSCF, RG 59, NA; Barkman, *Ambassador in Athens*, 18–20. Human rights issues were rarely discussed in senior-level reviews of the Greek situation, and embassy reporting was limited, even before Tasca's arrival. Under Tasca, the embassy soft-peddled violations of human rights and free speech. Telegram 1613 from Athens, April 1, 1970, Greece, vol. 1, MERF, NSF, NPM, NA, and airgram A-301, July 31, 1970, Pol 29 Greece, DSCF, RG 59, NA. Tasca dodged a meeting requested by Jean-Jacques Servan-Schreiber, the French editor, to address the junta's use of torture. Telegram 1899 from Athens, April 17, 1970, Pol 29 Greece, DSCF, RG 59, NA. David Fritzlan, head of the consular section in Athens, stated that the CIA covered up the use of torture. Fritzlan oral history, ADST. Ignoring the junta's use of torture figured into a policy of seeking to lessen points of tension with the Greek dictatorship. Press reports of torture were widespread, and the Council of Europe was involved in a full-scale investigation. Corry, "Greece: The Death of Liberty."

21. Telegram 970 from Athens, March 2, 1970, Greece, vol. 1, MERF, NSF, NPM, NA.

22. Memorandum to the president, May 21, 1970, with attached report by Tasca, MERF, NSF, NPM, NA. In his report, Tasca essayed a historical analysis of twentieth-

century Greece that stressed dictatorship as a normal feature of public life and underlined the infighting within the junta but concluded that the U.S. ambassador had created sufficiently good ties with the regime to help guide it toward democratic reform (and presumably self-dissolution). This analysis does not square with Tasca's March 2 musings.

23. Telegram 63344 to Athens, April 28, 1970, Greece, vol. 1, MERF, NSF, NPM, NA.

24. U.S. Department of State *Bulletin*, October 12, 1970.

25. Smith, "Waiting for the Army," *Spectator*, November 8, 1969; "Greece: Annual Review for 1969," January 5, 1970, FCO 9/1192, PRO; Barkman, *Ambassador in Athens*, 14; Karamanlis, Αρχείο 7:102–11 (analysis of Kanellopoulos), 272 (Ralles quoted), 276–77. Compare Karamanlis's comments to Kranidiotis, Ανοχύρωτη Πολιτεία, 1:525. See Sulzberger, *Age of Mediocrity*, 601–2, on king's views. See also Fritzland, King, and Blood oral histories, ADST. On British and French analysis and policy, see summary of meeting at FCO, July 3, 1969, FCO 9/886, PRO, and embassy in Greece to ministry, May 27, 1970, vol. 206, Greece, MAE. In comments echoing those coming from Washington, the British concluded that although the objective of reaching a democratic solution in Greece had not succeeded, the policy was "nonetheless right."

26. Note by prime minister on meeting with Nixon, January 28, 1970, FCO 9/120, PRO; papers WSG 1/15, November 19 and December 3, 1969, FCO 9/837, PRO, for internal situation in Greece. See also telegram 5224 from Athens, November 25, 1969, Pol 1 Greece-US, DSCF, RG 59, NA; INR Intelligence Note, October 19, 1970, with Haig annotations, Greece, vol. 1, MERF, NSF, NPM, NA.

27. Beckman, *Ambassador in Athens*, 37; conversations between Nixon and H. R. Haldeman, March 2, 1973, and Nixon and Rose Mary Woods, May 23, 1973, in Kuttler, *Abuse of Power*, 218–19 and 549. Pappas's influence was particularly high at this point. He had, apparently unknowingly, provided cash to buy the silence of the Watergate burglars. Kuttler, *Abuse of Power*, 217, 497.

28. Telegrams 2403 from Athens, May 13, 1970, 2596 and 2597 from Athens, both May 25, 1970, 3034 from Athens, June 12, 1970, 3414 from Athens, June 29, 1970, and 3586 from Athens, July 6, 1970, all in Greece, vol. 1, MERF, NSF, NPM, NA, provide a representative sampling of Tasca's reporting on these issues. Kissinger to Nixon, n.d., but ca. June 17, 1970, comments on the ambassador's lobbying for a public announcement on arms shipments. Greece, vol. 1, MERF, NSF, NPM, NA. In seeking to explain the regime's refusal to reform, Tasca put the best face on his own efforts and Papadopoulos's leadership in a July 22 report: "I am satisfied that we have been doing as well as can be expected under the circumstances, but I want to emphasize that if we attempt to force Papadopoulos to accelerate his time table to the point that he can no longer carry along his colleagues we may well undermine his political position. He then might be obliged to slow down the pace towards full constitutional government;

he might even be replaced." Tasca added that the Greek prime minister was in the minority, the majority of the junta being "reluctant" to adopt democracy. Telegram 3994 from Athens, Greece, vol. 1, MERF, NSF, NPM, NA This type of reporting litters U.S. files through November 1973. Even without the benefit of hindsight, a number of State Department officials were cognizant of the incongruity of the case Tasca was making. INR: "Greece: Implications for US-Greek Relations of Junta's Continuation," Greece, vol. 1, MERF, NSF, NPM, NA. On Tasca's efforts to promote reform, Kennedy memoir, ADST.

29. Telegram 5210 from Athens, September 18, 1970, Greece, vol. 1, MERF, NSF, NPM, NA; telegrams 1522 to Athens, January 6, 1971 (meeting the king), Pol 30 Greece, and 184173 to Athens, November 9, 1970, and 6856 from Athens, December 23, 1970 (political prisoners), both Pol 29 Greece, all DSCF, RG 59, NA; telegram 2313 from Athens, May 11, 1970 (Karamanlis and the state of the military), Greece, vol. 1, MERF, NSF, NPM, NA. Tickell to Cullen, London, September 29, 1972, FCO 9/1530, PRO, for a summary of the problems of a deterioration of the Greek army. Tasca urged the release of political prisoners as part of his effort to improve the regime's image. He was correct about the prospects for a post-Papadopoulos regime. Deputy Foreign Minister Palamas told Barkman that a "victory of Papadopoulos' opponents would result in a radical change of policy." Barkman, *Ambassador in Athens*, 30.

30. Telegrams 516, 540, and 542 from Athens, all February 2, 1971, telegram 597 from Athens, February 5, 1971, telegram 643 from Athens, February 9, 1971, all Greece, vol. 2, MERF, NSF, NPM, NA, provide a running commentary on the controversy. The staff aids, Richard Moose and James Lowenstein, discussed their feelings with Barkman, *Ambassador in Athens*, 44–46.

31. Memorandum from Saunders to Haig, February 3, 1971, and telegram 646 from Athens, February 10, 1971, both Greece, vol. 2, MERF, NSF, NPM, NA; NSC Interdepartmental Group for Near East and South Asia, Response to NSSM 116, March 8, 1971 (the king), esp. annex III, CF 498, Conference Files, DSCF, RG 59, NA; telegrams 43474 to Athens, March 16, 1971, Pol 23-9 Greece, and 1240 from Athens, March 17, 1971, Pol 15-3 Greece, both DSCF, RG 59, NA. Reviewing the policy, Assistant Secretary of State Joseph Sisco commented: "Our present, essentially passive policy, has assured access to facilities in Greece but has not proved effective in either satisfying our critics or in moving the Greek regime." Memorandum to the under secretary, March 19, 1971, Pol 1 Greece-US, DSCF, RG 59, NA. Barkman, *Ambassador in Athens*, 46, on the negative reaction of junta leaders to the U.S. policy statement.

32. Saunders to Haig, April 9, 1971, Greece, vol. 2, MERF, NSF, NPM, NA. The president's comments, made to Senator Hugh Scott (R-Pa.), the Senate minority leader, were relayed to the banquet.

33. The text of the protest is in Kanellopoulos, Κείμενα, 1967–1974, 89–95. On Stans's visit, Pattakos, Ημέραι και Εργα, 148. Saunders to Haig, June 25, 1971, Greece,

vol. 2, MERF, NSF, NPM, NA. Haig approved the request since "Tasca can take care of himself."

34. Telegrams 3086 from Athens, June 21, 1971, Greece, vol. 2, MERF, NSF, NPM, NA, and 3470 from Athens, July 11, 1971, Pol Greece, DSCF, RG 59, NA. Tasca reported on his meeting with the king in telegram 3469 from Athens, July 11, Greece, vol. 2, MERF, NSF, NPM, NA. Seeking to improve his ties with the United States, the king supported the resumption of arms aid but underlined his irritation at the treatment he received during the Eisenhower funeral. On the mutual dislike between Tasca and the opposition, Sulzberger, *Age of Mediocrity*, 770–73. On junta disdain for Tasca's initiative, telegram 3367 from Athens, July 6, 1971, Greece, vol. 2, MERF, NSF, NPM, NA.

35. U.S. Congress, *Greece, Spain, and the Southern NATO Strategy*, 1–24 (Couloumbis), 64–110 (Demetracopoulos), and 169–81 (M. Papandreou). See also memorandum of conversation, August 4, 1971, Greece, vol. 2, MERF, NSF, NPM, NA. On Tasca's view of Demetracopoulos, telegram 3136 from Athens, June 13, 1971, Pol 15 Greece, DSCF, RG 59, NA.

36. Saunders to Kissinger, July 2, August 5, September 8, 1971, Greece, vol. 2, MERF, NSF, NPM, NA. The Washington visit marked the first indication of NSC staff discontent with Tasca's performance. Saunders's July 2 memorandum reported Tasca's concern about defending the policy and suggestion that he cancel his congressional presentation. Kissinger's deputy, Alexander Haig, annotated: "HAK—Tasca is loosing his cool and guts."

37. Telegram 4368 from Athens, August 21, 1971, Greece, vol. 2, MERF, NSF, NPM, NA; "Greece: Annual Review for 1971," December 31, 1971, FCO 9/1514, PRO; Couloumbis, *'71–'74: Σημειώσεις*, 116–17; and Sulzberger, *Age of Mediocrity*, 771–72, for analyses of Papadopoulos.

38. Telegram Vipto 36, October 18, 1971, Greece, vol. 2, MERF, NSF, NPM, NA. The text of the protest in Kanellopoulos, *Κείμενα, 1967–1974*, 98. See also Couloumbis, *'71–'74: Σημειώσεις*, 126–28.

39. Telegram 16553 from Paris, October 10, 1971, Pol 1 Greece-US, DSCF, RG 59, NA, reported on the meeting with Karamanlis. See also Saunders to Kissinger, November 29, 1971, Greece, vol. 2, MERF, NSF, NPM, NA; Barkman, *Ambassador in Athens*, 54, 58; Karamanlis, *Αρχείο*, 7:131–32, 141–43, 291; Couloumbis, *'71–'74: Σημειώσεις*, 140–47.

40. Kissinger to Nixon, February 8, 1972, Greece, vol. 2, MERF, NSF, NPM, NA. Nixon approved homeporting on February 17. Kissinger to secretaries of State and Defense, February 17, 1973, Greece, vol. 2, MERF, NSF, NPM, NA. In a report on the progress of the plan, Harold Saunders of the NSC commented that the U.S. Navy was "not in the mood to take no for an answer." As frequently occurred in the Cold War, foreign policy calculations played a distinctly secondary role when the military rounded up its wide array of jingoist congressional backers. Saunders to Kissin-

ger, April 26, 1972, Greece, vol. 2, MERF, NSF, NPM, NA. Saunders reported on Greek government resistance to homeporting in a May 17, 1972, memo to Kissinger. Greece, vol. 2, MERF, NSF, NPM, NA. Tasca complained to Barkman about Greek foot-dragging on the issue. Barkman, *Ambassador in Athens*, 84. Zumwalt, *On Watch*, 124–36, 353–54, reveals the political myopia of navy leaders as well as their ability to round up congressional support for bad policy.

41. Telegram 793 from Athens, February 11, 1972, Pol 15 Greece, DSCF, RG 59, NA.

42. Telegram 2842 from Athens, May 19, 1972, Greece, vol. 3, MERF, NSF, NPM, NA; telegrams 1937 from Athens, April 6, 1972, Pol Greece, and 5053 from Athens, September 7, 1972, Pol 15-1 Greece, both DSCF, RG 59, NA, for Tasca's analysis. The State Department's Bureau of Intelligence and Research filed an equally pessimistic report: "Papadopoulos—On the Way Out?" November 11, 1972, DSCF, RG 59, NA. On Tasca's increasing disillusionment with Papadopoulos, Barkman, *Ambassador in Athens*, 81–82, 84. The U.S. ambassador told Barkman that the prime minister, supposedly meeting with his ministers, kept him cooling his heels for an hour when he arrived with a message from Nixon. On entering, Tasca found Papadopoulos sitting alone with his head in his hands. When the ambassador asked where the other officials were, the prime minister responded he was having a meeting with the ministers of foreign affairs and defense and the regent. Papadopoulos held all these positions.

43. Davis (NSC) to Eliot (State Department), May 12, 1972, and telegram 3350 from Athens, June 15, 1972, both Greece, vol. 3, MERF, NSF, NPM, NA; telegrams 3416 and 3417 from Athens, both June 19, 1972, Pol 15-1 Greece, DSCF, RG 59, NA; telegram Secto 233 from Athens, July 9, 1972, and Rogers's carefully diplomatic arrival statement at Athens airport, July 4, both CF 499, Conference Files, DSCF, RG 59, NA. For the opposition's comment on the visit and U.S. policy, see Kanellopoulos, Κείμενα, 1967–1974, 112–14. Papadopoulos told Barkman on July 26 that he was pleased with Greece's relationship with the United States and that while he preferred a Nixon reelection victory in November, the junta could deal as well with Democratic Party candidate George McGovern. The United States, he opined, had no policy options. This confidence, coupled with internal political problems, may explain Greek willingness to adopt confrontational policies. Barkman, *Ambassador in Athens*, 81.

44. Kissinger to Nixon, March 7, 1973, Greece, vol. 3, MERF, NSF, NPM, NA; telegram 2394 from Athens, April 20, 1973, Pol 13-2 Greece, and memorandum of conversation, April 13, 1973, Pol 23-9 Greece, both DSCF, RG 59, NA; Markezinis, Σύγχρονη Πολιτική Ιστορία, 3:171–73.

45. Telegram 3282 from Athens, May 29, 1973, Greece, vol. 3, MERF, NSF, NPM, NA; Karamanlis, Αρχείο, 7:169–73, 319; and Barkman, *Ambassador in Athens*, 101. Telegram 4621 from Rome, May 30, 1973, Pol Greece-US, DSCF, RG 59, NA, for the views of the king. On the Greek navy, Woodhouse, *Rise and Fall of the Greek Colonels*, 116–18.

46. Telegram 3593 from Athens, June 4, 1973, Greece, vol. 3, MERF, NSF, NPM, NA; Karamanlis, *Αρχείο* 7:181–82; Markezinis, *Σύγχρονη Πολιτική Ιστορία*, 3:178–80; "Abolition of the Greek Monarchy," June 14, 1973, FCO 9/1713, PRO; Couloumbis, *'71–'74: Σημειώσεις*, 272–74, 276, 285–86.

47. *FRUS 1973–76*, 30:9–18. Sisco to Rush, June 7, 1973, Pol Greece-US, DSCF, RG 59, NA, recommended directly approaching Nixon about a policy review. Telegram 3648 from Athens, June 5, 1973, Pol Greece-US, DSCF, RG 59, NA, contains Tasca's views. See also memorandum from Harold Appelbaum and Saunders to Kissinger, June 2, 1973, Greece, vol. 3, MERF, NSF, NPM, NA; Couloumbis, *'71–'74: Σημειώσεις*, 258–59; Wilberforce to Goodison, October 15, 1973, FCO 9/1725, PRO.

48. Telegram 4124 from Athens, June 23, 1973, Pol 14 Greece, and Sisco to Rogers, June 26, 1973, Pol 15 Greece, both DSCF, RG 59, NA; Rogers to Nixon, June 26, 1973, Greece, vol. 3, MERF, NSF, NPM, NA. Kissinger approved the démarche after being assured that it would do no serious harm to U.S.-Greek relations. Applebaum and Saunders to Kissinger, July 5, 1973, Greece, vol. 3, MERF, NSF, NPM, NA. Tasca reported on his meeting with Papadopoulos in telegram 4831 from Athens, July 16, 1973, Greece, vol. 3, MERF, NSF, NPM, NA. He discussed the meeting with Barkman on July 17. Barkman, *Ambassador in Athens*, 112–13.

49. Barkman, *Ambassador in Athens*, 106–7. See also telegram 5394 from Athens, August 2, 1973, Greece, vol. 3, MERF, NSF, NPM, NA, and Iakovos to Rogers, June 29, 1973, Pol 15 Greece, DSCF, RG 59, NA. The letter was leaked to the press, creating considerable embarrassment for the archbishop. INR report "Greek Plebiscite: The Republic's Inauspicious Beginning," August 1, 1973, *FRUS 1973–76*, 30:18–20; Rogers to Nixon, July 28, 1973, Pol Greece-US, DSCF, RG 59, NA. Nixon apparently felt that the United States had gone as far as it ought in the Tasca démarche. No action was taken on the recommendation. Rogers resigned shortly thereafter, and his successor, Kissinger, opposed any "interference" in Greek internal affairs. Karamanlis, *Αρχείο*, 7:190–93, 325; "The Greek Referendum of 1973," FCO 9/1714, PRO. See the editorials in the *New York Times*, July 5, 1973, and the *Washington Post*, July 28, 1973.

50. Barkman, *Ambassador in Athens*, 117–18, 124; telegram 7035 from Athens, October 10, 1973, Greece, vol. 3, MERF, NSF, NPM, NA; Pappas to Nixon, October 9, 1973, and Kissinger to Nixon, n.d., both Greece, vol. 4, MERF, NSF, NPM, NA; telegrams 7387 from Athens, October 23, 1973, and 7076 from Athens, October 11, 1973, both Greece, vol. 3, MERF, NSF, NPM, NA; Tomykins to Goodison, October 25, 1973, FCO 9/1725, PRO.

51. Hooper to Goodison, October 18, 1973 (quote), and November 15, 1973, and Denson to Goodison, November 8, 1973, all FCO 9/1725, PRO. See also Karamanlis, *Αρχείο*, 7:197; Markezinis, *Σύγχρονη Πολιτική Ιστορία*, 3:185, 211–13. Comments of Hartman and Davies (February 19, 1974) in U.S. Department of State *Bulletin*, March 18, 1974.

52. "I consider it most unfortunate that a full admiral, wearing a U.S. uniform, came to Athens in a period of severe political tension without notification to the ambassador or any consultation." Telegram 8178 from Athens, November 23, 1973, Greece, vol. 4, MERF, NSF, NPM, NA. On the fear of a Greek Nasser, telegram 7610 from Athens, November 1, 1973, Greece, vol. 4, MERF, NSF, NPM, NA. On opposition support for the students, Kanellopoulos, *Κείμενα, 1967–1974*, 218–20. See also memorandum of a telephone conversation between Tasca and Rodger Davies, November 17, 1973, 10 A.M., Pol 13-2 Greece, DSCF, RG 59, NA. On Tasca's views about plots by left and right against Papadopoulos and his call for a Karamanlis solution, *FRUS 1973–76*, 30:20–21, and telegram 8078 from Athens, November 19, 1973, Greece, vol. 4., MERF, NSF, NPM, NA. Congressional discontent with Tasca was fueled by the coincidence that a delegation of five congressmen was in Athens on November 17. With small-arms fire audible from the embassy, the political counselor, Elizabeth Brown, assured the visiting delegation that a small disturbance was taking place over curriculum issues. The congressmen concluded that either the embassy was incompetent or was deliberately attempting to mislead them. Letter from Nedzi to Kissinger, November 27, 1973, Pol 23-9 Greece, DSCF, RG 59, NA. A few days later, Brown met with a Greek observer who bluntly informed her that U.S. efforts to win Greek goodwill had "utterly failed." "You are hated, you know." Memorandum of conversation, November 20, 1973, Pol 23-9 Greece, DSCF, RG 59, NA. See the discussion of the crisis in Markezinis, *Σύγχρονη Πολιτική Ιστορία*, 3:201–8, 211–15.

53. Telegram 8233 from Athens, November 25, 1973, Greece, vol. 4, and Saunders and Appelbaum to Scowcroft, November 26, 1973, both MERF, NSF, NPM, NA. Telegram 231386 to Athens, November 25, 1973, MERF, NSF, NPM, NA, contains Kissinger's instructions. See also Sisco to Kissinger, November 26, 1973, Pol Greece-US, DSCF, RG 59, NA. The recognition of policy failure was palpable in a memorandum of conversation between Rodger Davies and former general and junta opponent Orestis Vidalis, November 30, 1973, Pol 23-9 Greece, DSCF, RG 59, NA.

54. Hooper to Goodison, November 29, 1973, FCO 9/1712, PRO; British embassy in Greece: "Praxicopematics: Or the Fall of Papadopoulos," December 6, 1973, FCO 9/1717, PRO; Karamanlis, *Αρχείο*, 7:202; A. Papandreou, *Από το ΠΑΚ στο ΠΑΣΟΚ*, 61–74.

55. Tasca's views were laid out in telegrams 8445 from Athens, November 30, 1973, and 8473 from Athens, December 3, 1973, both Greece, vol. 4, MERF, NSF, NPM, NA. Kissinger rejected these views in telegram 236011 to Athens, December 1, 1973; see also the comments of Saunders and Appelbaum to Scowcroft, December 10, 1973, both Greece, vol. 4, MERF, NSF, NPM, NA. State Department concerns are reflected in Rush to Clements, December 8, 1973, Pol 1 Greece, and in INR report: "Greece: Precarious Mandate for New Regime," December 11, 1973, Pol 15 Greece, both DSCF, RG 59, NA. Barkman, after meeting the new Greek foreign minister, confided to his diary, he "seems an utter fool." Barkman, *Ambassador in Athens*, 149.

Few Greek civilian conservatives were willing to cooperate with the new military government. Hooper to Goodison, December 13, 1973, FCO 9/1717, PRO. On the opposition's views, Karamanlis, *Αρχείο*, 7:212–13, 333–34, 336–40; and Couloumbis '71–'74: *Σημειώσεις*, 289–93, 295.

56. Telegrams 512 from Athens, January 24, 1974, 1158 from Athens, February 22, 1974, 43153 to Athens, March 4, 1974, all Greece, vol. 4, MERF, NSF, NPM, NA. See also *FRUS 1973–76*, 30:24–29, 46–47. Springsteen to Scowcroft, March 11, 1974, Greece, vol. 4, MERF, NSF, NPM, NA, contains Tasca's request for a meeting with Nixon. By this point, Nixon was too heavily engaged in defending his presidency to have any interest in Greek affairs. Tasca, however, could count on his continued personal support, a factor that allowed him to challenge Kissinger's line with some impunity. Telegram 1539 from Athens, March 13, 1974, MERF, NSF, NPM, NA, outlines Tasca's abortive contact with the reclusive Ioannides and a plan for a public discussion of the return to democracy before the committee. Barkman, *Ambassador in Athens*, 152.

57. Transcript of meeting of March 20, 1974, *FRUS 1973–76*, 30:47–60; Kennedy to Kissinger with annotations, June 1, 1974, Greece, vol. 4, MERF, NSF, NPM, NA; *FRUS 1973–76*, 30:69–70, for Ioannides's statements.

Chapter 8

1. Karamanlis, *Αρχείο*, 2:23, 287 (letter to Nasser); 3:226–28; 4:73–75, 132–36; 6:147–48; Averoff-Tossizza, *Lost Opportunities*, 37–38, 63–64; Alexandrakis, Theodoropoulos, and Lagakos, *Κυπριακό*, 14–16, 42–43, 88–90, 93–95; Kranidiotis, *Ανοχύρωτη Πολιτεία*, 1:100–101, 186–87, 221–23, 292–93, 352, 359; Vlachou, *Δέκα Χρόνια Κυπριακού*, 273. The appraisals of Karamanlis to French officials in *DDF 1961*, 2:63, and *DDF 1963*, 1:497–502. Compare *FRUS 1955–57*, 24:311–13, 561–62. Papagiorgiou, *Κρίσιμα Ντοκουμέντα του Κυπριακού*, 3:10–15, 29–33, 53, 136–39, 170–81, 198–202, 206–8, 297–98, for Greek efforts to control Makarios.

2. Klerides, *Cyprus*, 2:193; Kranidiotis, *Ανοχύρωτη Πολιτεία*, 1:429–41. *FRUS 1964–68*, 16:607, 621–23, 630–32, 636, 638.

3. The evolution of U.S. policy 1964–67 can be traced in *FRUS 1964–68*, 16:316–17, 326–30, 340–43, 355–56, 367–68, 390–94, 400–403, 489–91, 463–64, 480–81, 494–96, 498–99, 507–9, 516–19. See also British discussions with the State Department in FO 371/18562/CC103145/4, 14, and 18, PRO. On Cypriot objectives, Kranidiotis, *Ανοχύρωτη Πολιτεία*, 1:402–7; and Klerides, *Cyprus*, 2:190.

4. *FRUS 1964–68*, 16:643–98. Hart, *Two NATO Allies*, on American crisis diplomacy. From the Cypriot side, Kranidiotis, *Ανοχύρωτη Πολιτεία*, 1:454–79, esp. 472–77. M. Papandreou, *Nightmare in Athens* 343, allowed: "From all reliable information, the killing of Turkish villagers far exceeded the provocation."

5. *FRUS 1964–68*, 16:310–11, 314–16, 378–82 (on Turkey), 332–36, 536–40, 679–80 (on need to deal with Makarios), 682–84 (on sleeping well).

6. Kranidiotis, Ανοχύρωτη Πολιτεία, 1:308–14; FRUS 1961–63, 16:537; FRUS 1964–68, 16:326–30, 346–48, 386–76, 666–67.

7. High commissioner to Commonwealth Office, December 17, 1966, FO 371/185620/CC1015/16, PRO.

8. High commissioner to Commonwealth Office, March 26, 1969, FCO 9/785/1, PRO.

9. Klerides, Cyprus, 2:381–82.

10. FRUS 1964–68, 16:637, 739–45, 759–60, 762–65; Alexandrakis, Theodoropoulos, and Lagakos, Κυπριακό, 53–57.

11. Klerides, Cyprus, 2:259–63; FRUS 1964–68, 16:768–71.

12. Kranidiotis, Ανοχύρωτη Πολιτεία, 1:425, 554–55, 557–63; Alexandrakis, Theodoropoulos, and Lagakos, Κυπριακό, 133, 139–40; Klerides, Cyprus, 2:289–95, 313–16; FRUS 1964–68, 16:732–73, for Kyprianou's assessment of the situation in Cyprus in 1968. Edmonds to Snodgrass, September 26, 1969, FCO 9/792, PRO, reported Turkish views of the relationship with the Greek junta. INR memorandum: "Terrorism in Cyprus," January 19, 1970, Cyprus, vol. 1, MERF, NSF, NPM, NA.

13. Stern, Wrong Horse, 84 (Ball quoted); Kissinger, Years of Renewal, 194, 197–99, 204; Eliot to Kissinger, March 18, 1970 (quote), Cyprus, vol. 1, MERF, NSF, NPM, NA; William Crawford oral history, ADST.

14. Fallaci, Intervista con la storia, 596. Compare Stern, Wrong Horse, 86–87. See also draft memorandum Saunders to Kissinger, March 8, 1970, Cyprus, vol. 1, MERF, NSF, NPM, NA; Alexandrakis, Theodoropoulos, and Lagakos, Κυπριακό, 60–66; Klerides, Cyprus, 2:366–69. On Georgkadjis, Markides, Rise and Fall, 91–93.

15. Memorandum of conversation, October 25, 1970, Cyprus, vol. 1, MERF, NSF, NPM, NA. According to Kranidiotis, Ανοχύρωτη Πολιτεία, 2:55–56, Makarios was disappointed with the lack of concrete concessions from the American president.

16. Alexandrakis, Theodoropoulos, and Lagakos, Κυπριακό, 61; Klerides, Cyprus 2:342–44 and 3:42–43, 70, 75, 82–83, 116; Kranidiotis, Ανοχύρωτη Πολιτεία, 2:66, 84–89, 104, 109–11, 145–46; "Cyprus: Strategy for the Next Steps," August 27, 1971 (Boyatt quoted), Cyprus, vol. 1, MERP, NSF, NPM, NA. On British analyses, "Cyprus: Annual Review for 1970," January 1, 1971, FCO 9/1358, PRO, and "Cyprus: Annual Report for 1971" (quote), January 1, 1972, FCO 9/1494, PRO. Cabinet minutes of January 26, 1971, CAB 128/49/4, and October 28, 1971, CAB 128/49/52, both PRO.

17. Markides, Rise and Fall, 76–77, 80–81; Alexandrakis, Theodoropoulos, and Lagakos, Κυπριακό, 64–65.

18. Kranidiotis, Ανοχύρωτη Πολιτεία, 2:161; Klerides, Cyprus, 3:15–16; telegram 258 from Nicosia, February 7, 1972, and Kissinger annotation to memorandum from Saunders and Neaher, February 10, 1972, both Cyprus, vol. 1, MERF, NSF, NPM, NA.

19. Memorandum to Kissinger, Cyprus, vol. 1, MERF, NSF, NPM, NA; telegrams 226 from Nicosia, February 3, 1972, and 313 from Nicosia, February 13, 1972 (quote), both Cyprus, vol. 1, MERF, NSF, NPM, NA.

20. Klerides, *Cyprus*, 3:131–37, 140–43; Kranidiotis, *Ανοχύρωτη Πολιτεία*, 2:172–73; telegrams 322, 356 (quote), and 389 from Nicosia, February 14, 16, and 18, 1972, all Cyprus, vol. 1, MERF, NSF, NPM, NA.

21. Klerides, *Cyprus*, 3:144–50, 156–59, 250–52; Alexandrakis, Theodoropoulos, and Lagakos, *Κυπριακό*, 62–64, 67. On British policy, Goodison to Oliver, London, October 17, 1973, FCO 9/1683, and undated MS, "Political Situation [Cyprus]," FCO 9/1679, both PRO. On U.S. views, Saunders to Kissinger, May 5, 1973 (with Kissinger annotations), Cyprus, vol. 1, MERF, NSF, NPM, NA, and comments of Boyatt in Couloumbis, '71–'74: *Σημειώσεις*, 271.

22. Kranidiotis, *Ανοχύρωτη Πολιτεία*, 1:515; Averoff-Tossizza, *Lost Opportunities*, 63, 347–51. Klerides, *Cyprus*, 2:381–82; 3:19–22, 205–6, 258–61, 381–82, critiques Makarios's leadership and outlook at this critical point. The British views are in Leland to Davis, Ankara, November 6, 1973, FCO 9/1679, and the comments in FCO 9/1670, both PRO.

23. Markezinis, *Σύγχρονη Πολιτική Ιστορία*, 3:194–97, for his talks with Makarios. Kranidiotis, *Ανοχύρωτη Πολιτεία*, 2:309–13, on Makarios's comments and motivations, and 321–22, on his reaction to the fall of Papadopoulos. Beattie to Davis, Nicosia, December 3, 1973, FCO 9/1680, PRO, on general Cypriot reaction to Papadopoulos's ouster. On the initial and threatening position of the new Greek regime, Tomykins to Beattie, Athens, December 20, 1973, FCO 9/1680, PRO.

24. Thomas Boyatt memoir, ADST; Kissinger, *Years of Upheaval*, 1191–92. On Greek ties to the extremists, telegram 155 from Nicosia to the Foreign Office, June 25, 1974, FCO 9/1950, PRO.

25. Transcript of meeting of March 22, 1974, Kissinger Staff Meeting Transcripts, Staff Secretariat, RG 59, NA. On U.S. concentration on intercommunal talks for stabilizing Cyprus, Eliot to Kissinger, July 30, 1971; Rogers to Nixon, December 17, 1971; telegram 790 from Nicosia, April 24, 1973, all Cyprus, vol. 1, MERF, NSF, NPM, NA. On Makarios's strategic decisions, Kranidiotis, *Ανοχύρωτη Πολιτεία*, 2:335–40; Robert McCloskey and Lindsay Grant oral histories, ADST.

26. Telegrams 3936 from Athens, June 24, 1974, Greece, vol. 4, and 1224 from Nicosia, June 27, 1974, Cyprus, vol. 1, both MRF, NSF, NPM, NA; *FRUS 1973–76*, 30:263–71. On instructions to Tasca, *FRUS 1973–76*, 30:272–73; telegram 4179 from Athens, July 1, 1974, Greece, vol. 4, MERF, NSF, NPM, NA; and Kissinger, *Years of Renewal*, 203–5. The House Select Committee on Intelligence (Pike Committee) outlined the intelligence warnings but then chose to label what followed a "failure of intelligence policy." In fact, the failure was not in the reporting from either Nicosia or Athens, but in a clear lack of concentration on the available information by Kissinger and his senior advisors. The committee's unreleased report, leaked to the *Village Voice*, was published with useful annotations by CIA antagonist Philip Agee as *CIA: The Pike Report*, 158–67.

27. Woodward and Bernstein, *Final Days*, 186; Callaghan, *Time and Chance*, 339.

28. Kranidiotis, *Ανοχύρωτη Πολιτεία*, 2:365, 372–73. On the impact of the letter, Barkman, *Ambassador in Athens*, 174; Kanellopoulos, *Κείμενα, 1967–74*, 236–38; and Averoff in Karamanlis, *Αρχείο*, 7:217–18. See also Boyatt memoir and Grant oral history (quote), ADST; Oliver to Goodison, Nicosia, July 8, 1974 (quoting Makarios), FCO 9/1950, PRO; *FRUS 1973–76*, 30:273–74.

29. Kranidiotis, *Ανοχύρωτη Πολιτεία*, 2:374–75; Alexandrakis, Theodoropoulos, and Lagakos, *Κυπριακό*, 112–13; memorandum of conversation with Urquhart, July 10, 1974, FCO 9/1950, PRO.

30. Crawford and McCloskey oral histories and Boyatt memoir, ADST; Stern, *Wrong Horse*, 117 (quote).

31. *FRUS 1973–76*, 30:275–76.

32. Kissinger, *Years of Renewal*, 202–3; telegrams 5589 from Ankara, July 15, 1974, Turkey, vol. 4, and 4493 from Athens, July 15, 1974, Greece, vol. 5, both MERF, NSF, NPM, NA; *FRUS 1973–76*, 30:277–83.

33. Dobrynin-Kissinger telephone conversations, 5:50 and 6:30 P.M. July 15 and 9:50 A.M. July 16, 1974, Chronological File, Kissinger Telephone Conversations, NPM, NA.

34. Kissinger-Callaghan telephone conversation, 10:15 A.M. July 16, 1974, Chronological File, Kissinger Telephone Conversations, NPM, NA; telegram 5609 from Ankara, July 16, 1974, Turkey, vol. 4, MERF, NSF, NPM, NA. The two men's initial evaluations: Kissinger, *Years of Renewal*, 208–10, and Callaghan, *Time and Change*, 336–37.

35. Kissinger-Waldheim conversation, *FRUS 1973–76*, 30:295–96; Kissinger-Dobrynin telephone conversations, 11:50 A.M. and noon, July 16, 1974, Chronological File, Kissinger Telephone Conversations, NPM, NA; Scowcroft to Nixon, 1 P.M. July 16, 1974, Cyprus, vol. 1, MERF, NSF, NPM, NA; Kissinger, *Years of Renewal*, 216; Callaghan, *Time and Change*, 338–39. The evolution of Kissinger's policy can be traced in his discussions within the Washington Special Action Group, in *FRUS 1973–76*, 30:276–81, 288–94, 304–8, 313–17, 324–29, 340–47, 355–64, 374–82, 432–34.

36. *FRUS 1973–76*, 30:311–12. Kissinger, *Years of Renewal*, 212, defends support for the junta.

37. *FRUS 1973–76*, 30:296–30 (quote); telegrams 4530, July 16, 1974, and 4538, July 17, 1974, Greece, vol. 5, MERF, NSF, NPM, NA.

38. *FRUS 1973–76*, 30:302–4. Callaghan, *Time and Change*, 339–40, on Ecevit's initial demands.

39. Saunders to Kissinger, July 17, 1974, Cyprus, vol. 2, MERF, NSF, NPM, NA; *FRUS 1973–76*, 30:309–11; telephone conversations between Kissinger and Sisco, 12:45 and 5:10 P.M.; Callaghan, 5:04 P.M.; and Dobrynin, 6:50 P.M., July 17, 1974, Chronological File, Kissinger Telephone Conversations, NPM, NA. The policy was conveyed to the involved embassies in telegram State 156312, July 18, 1974, Cyprus, vol. 1, MERF, NSF, NPM, NA. Callaghan, *Time and Change*, 341–42, on his initial

talks with Sisco. Sisco's version of his mission, *FRUS 1973-76*, 30:320-21, 329-30, 339-40, 354.

40. Telegrams 4565 from Athens and State 155400, both July 18, 1974, Greece, vol. 5 (Tasca), telegrams 1446 from Nicosia, July 17, 1974, and 1463 from Nicosia, July 18, 1974 (Davis), all Cyprus, vol. 2, MERF, NSF, NPM, NA; telephone conversations between Kissinger and Fulbright, 12:56 P.M. July 17, 1974, and Kissinger and Vance, 11:45 A.M. July 18, 1974 (the Democrats), and Kissinger and Nixon discussion, 2:48 P.M. July 18, 1974 (resistance to the policy), all Chronological File, Kissinger Telephone Conversations, NPM, NA.

41. These confused priorities were summarized by Kissinger in his telephone conversation with British Ambassador Ramsbotham, 11 A.M. July 18, 1974, Chronological File, Kissinger Telephone Conversations, NPM, NA. Compare the July 18, 1974, comments of Barkman, *Ambassador in Athens*, 180, and Callaghan, *Time and Change*, 342, on differences with the Americans. William Kontos, James Morton, and Robert S. Dillon oral histories, ADST, on Kissinger's leadership problems. McCloskey (oral history, ADST) stated that he warned the secretary that failing to reinstate Makarios or to condemn Samson would be red flags to the Turks. Kissinger quotes are from telephone conversation with McCloskey, July 19, 1974, Chronological File, Kissinger Telephone Conversations, NPM, NA. On Kissinger's belief that he would play the "kingmaker," *FRUS 1973-76*, 30:304-8.

42. Klerides, *Cyprus*, 3:350 (Makarios at UNO); telegram 5693 from Ankara, July 19, 1974, Turkey, vol. 4, MERF, NSF, NPM, NA; Kissinger-Sauvagnarges telephone conversation, 11:45 A.M. (Turkish intentions), July 19, 1974, Chronological File, Kissinger Telephone Conversations, NPM, NA. Sisco's comments are in telegram Polto 20 (quote), July 19, 1974, Greece, vol. 5, MERF, NSF, NPM NA. Kissinger conference calls, 9:30 and 11:50 A.M., and Kissinger-McCloskey telephone conversation (instructions to Sisco), 12:45 P.M., all July 19, 1974, Chronological File, Kissinger Telephone Conversations, NPM, NA. Telegram State 157127, July 19, 1974, Turkey, vol. 4, MERF, NSF, NPM, NA, stated that Kissinger wanted an approach demonstrating "compassion and understanding" for Turkey's position.

43. The tilt toward Turkey can be traced in Kissinger's conversations with Ingersoll, 12:05 P.M., McCloskey, 12:45, 3:40, 4:45 P.M., and 7:30 P.M.(quote), Mansfield, 1:15 P.M., State and NSC officials, 2:30 P.M., and Nixon, 8 P.M., all July 19, 1974, Chronological File, Kissinger Telephone Conversations, NPM, NA.

44. Kissinger conversations with Schlesinger, 8:15 P.M. and 9:10 P.M.; Callaghan, 8:22 P.M.; McCloskey, 8:45 and 9:55 P.M.; Colby, 9:35 P.M., and Nixon, 10:06 P.M., all July 19, 1974, Chronological File, Kissinger Telephone Conversations, NPM, NA. Compare *FRUS 1973-76*, 30:331-33, 336-40.

45. State telegrams 157939 and 157945, both July 20, 1974, Greece, vol. 5, MERF, NSF, NPM, NA. Compare tone with State 157937 (Kissinger to Ecevit) and State 157984 (Nixon to Koruturk), both July 20, 1974, Turkey, vol. 4, MERF, NSF, NPM, NA.

46. Telegram 4664 from Athens (Ioannides quote), July 20, 1974, Greece, vol. 5, MERF, NSF, NPM, NA; Karamanlis, Αρχείο, 7:222-24.

47. State 157969 and telegram 5745 from Ankara, both July 20, and telegram 5763 from Ankara, July 21, 1974, all Turkey, vol. 4, MERF, NSF, NPM, NA; telegrams Polto 42 and 45, telegrams 4716 and 4722 from Athens, and telegrams Topol 63 and 66, all July 21, 1974; telegrams 4812 from Athens and Polto 49 and 50, all July 22, 1974, all in Greece, vol. 5, MERF, NSF, NPM, NA. See also FRUS 1973–76, 30:348–49, 364–65. Kissinger telephone discussions with Ecevit, 10:40 A.M., 1:25 P.M., 5:30 P.M., with Callaghan, 11:15 A.M., with Androutsopoulos, 12:01 P.M., all July 21, 1974, Chronological File, Kissinger Telephone Conversations, NPM, NA; Callaghan's telephone conversation with Ecevit, 4:55 GMT, July 21, 1974, FCO 9/1917, PRO. For Kissinger's evaluation of Ecevit, FRUS 1973–76, 30:379.

48. Markezinis, Σύγχρονη Πολιτική Ιστορία, 3:233–38, and Kanellopoulos, Κείμενα, 1967–74, 244–47, for two memoirs of the military's retreat from power. Karamanlis, Αρχείο, 8:17, and telegram 4962 from Athens, July 24, 1974 (Karamanlis appeal), Greece, vol. 5, MERF, NSF, NPM, NA. See also FRUS 1973–76, 30:391–402.

49. Kissinger telephone conversations with McCloskey and Buffum, 1:45 P.M. July 20, 1974 (Makarios "had it"), with Greek officials and Tasca, 5 P.M. July 22, 1974 (support for Greeks), with Ecevit, 3:30 P.M. July 23, 1974, and 3:05 P.M., July 24, 1974, all Chronological File, Kissinger Telephone Conversations, NPM, NA. See also telegrams State 158230 and 160197, both July 24, 1974 (Greeks to Geneva), Greece, vol. 5, MERF, NSF, NPM, NA; telegram 1681 from Nicosia and State 159994, both July 23, 1974 (Klerides), Cyprus, vol. 2, MERF, NSF, NPM, NA. Kissinger stonewalled Makarios when they met. FRUS 1973–76, 30:410–15; Kranidiotis, Ανοχύρωτη Πολιτεία, 2:431–32. On Kissinger's strategy, Callaghan's observations, July 22, 1974, CAB 128/55/28, PRO; those of the British embassy in Washington, telegram 2518 to the Foreign Office, July 25, 1974, PREM 16/19, PRO; those of Barkman, Ambassador in Athens, 183; and those of Kissinger, Years of Renewal, 220, 223–24.

50. Kissinger telephone conversations with Nixon 10:06 P.M. July 19, 1974 (on Tasca), and with Buffum, 4:18 P.M. July 26, 1974 (weakness of Greeks), Chronological File, Kissinger Telephone Conversations, NPM, NA; telegrams 4967 from Athens, July 24, 1974, and State 161369, July 25, 1974, both Greece, vol. 5, MERF, NSF, NPM, NA. Tasca reiterated his plea for support of Karamanlis in telegram 5048 from Athens, July 26, 1974, MERF, NSF, NPM, NA.

51. Kartakes, Καραμανλής της Μεταπολίτευσης, 13–14. Defense Minister Averoff's plans for dealing with the army, telegram 5135 from Athens, July 28, 1974, Greece, vol. 5, MERF, NSF, NPM, NA. Karamanlis to Wilson, July 28, 1974, FCO 9/1918, PRO, appealed for British intervention in support of Greece.

52. Karamanlis, Αρχείο, 8:20, 38–40; Kissinger telephone conversation with Karamanlis, 1:25 P.M. July 26, 1974, Chronological File, Kissinger Telephone Conversations, NPM, NA; telegrams 4825 from Athens, July 23, 1974, 5046 and 5098 from

Athens and State 162942, all July 26, 1974, and 5109 from Athens, July 27, 1974, all Greece, vol. 5, MERF, NSF, NPM, NA. Memorandum of conversation between Callaghan and Mavros, July 28, 1974, FCO 9/1917, PRO, provides information on Greek strategy. Author's notes of telephone conversation with Monteagle Stearns, May 11, 2001.

53. Karamanlis, *Αρχείο*, 8:40–41. Kissinger telephone conversation with Ecevit, 6:05 P.M. July 29, 1974, Chronological File, Kissinger Telephone Conversations, NPM, NA; telegram 6135 from Ankara, August 2, 1974, Turkey, vol. 4, MERF, NSF, NPM, NA. On the Turkish approach, Callaghan to Wilson, Geneva, July 30, 1974, PREM 16/20, PRO.

54. Karamanlis, *Αρχείο*, 8:38, 51; Kranidiotis, *Ανοχύρωτη Πολιτεία*, 2:438 (Greek strategy and Makarios's isolation); telegrams 1723 from Nicosia, July 24, 1974, 1844 from Nicosia, July 27, 1974, 1932 and 1968 from Nicosia, July 29, 1974, and 2093 from Nicosia, August 2, 1974, all Cyprus, vol. 2, MERF, NSF, NPM, NA; State 102101, July 25, 1974 (Cypriot internal difficulties and problems with Greece), Greece, vol. 5, MERF, NSF, NPM, NA. Klerides's views on Makarios were reported in telegram 592 from Nicosia to the Foreign Office, August 3, 1974, FCO 9/1919, PRO.

55. Karamanlis, *Αρχείο*, 8:51–54, 64; telegram 2176 from Nicosia, August 5, 1974, Cyprus, vol. 2, MERF, NSF, NPM, NA.

56. Barkman, *Ambassador in Athens*, 197 (Greek public opinion); Karamanlis, *Αρχείο*, 8:59–60; Klerides, *Cyprus*, 4:81–82; telegram 1842 from Nicosia, July 27, 1974 (approaches to Soviets and state of Greek military), Cyprus, vol. 2, MERF, NSF, NPM, NA. In a discussion with the British, Denktash commented that only Klerides could make the concessions needed to make a deal but that without Greek backing he simply dared not make them. Memorandum of conversation between Denktash and Callaghan, August 12, 1974, WSC 1/13: "The Geneva Conference on Cyprus," FCO 9/1918, PRO. Klerides confirmed this in discussions with Callaghan and Denktash, August 12, 1974, also WSC 1/13, FCO 9/1918, PRO. Kissinger's hostile assessment of Karamanlis is in *Years of Renewal*, 228–29. On Karamanlis's handling of Cyprus, see the antagonistic but informed Kardianos, *Καραμανλής και Κυπριακόν* and *Καραμανλής και "Φάκελος."*

57. Kissinger telephone conversation with Laird, 5 P.M. July 22, 1974, Chronological File, Kissinger Telephone Conversations, NPM, NA; telegram 6167 from Ankara, August 5, 1974, Turkey, vol. 4, MERF, NSF, NPM, NA; memorandum of conversation between Callaghan and Gunes, August 9, 1974, WSC 1/13: "The Geneva Conference on Cyprus," FCO 9/1918, PRO.

58. *FRUS 1973–76*, 30:419–20 (Ford conversation quoted); Karamanlis, *Αρχείο*, 8:66–67; Klerides, *Cyprus*, 4:61–63, 66–67, 69; Kissinger telephone conversations with Ecevit, 9:35 A.M. and 11:55 A.M. August 11, 1974, and 4:15 P.M. and 5:26 P.M. August 12, 1974, Kissinger Telephone Conversations, U.S. State Department Freedom of Information Electronic Reading Room (www.foia.state.gov); CIA telegram [Athens

Station] to White House [cable number deleted], August 13, 1974, CIA RDP 82-00457, NA. One aspect of this Turkish triumph was the U.S. role in the Geneva conference. Since the conference was called by the British as a signatory of the London-Zurich accords, no direct American involvement was possible. Kissinger tried to influence events from the sidelines, with little success and little apparent enthusiasm. In summarizing preparations for the meetings, Callaghan reported to the cabinet (Aug. 1) that a peaceful and satisfactory solution to Cyprus would be very difficult. The Turks were subverting the cease-fire by continuing their military buildup and were ready to humiliate Greece and renew the war to gain their objectives. Cabinet Paper CC (74), 27th Conclusions, minute 4, August 1, 1974, FCO 9/1917, PRO. Turkish foreign minister Gunes confirmed this appraisal on August 10, telling Callaghan that the only acceptable outcome would be partition. Telegram FCO 800, August 10, 1974, PREM 16/20, WSC 1/13: "The Geneva Conference on Cyprus," FCO 9/1918, PRO. On the same day, Denktash laid out the Turkish Cypriot position with clarity and brutality: the Turkish army was not in Cyprus "to play football," but to ensure the security of Turkish Cypriots. His community demanded regional autonomy based on the geographical separation of the two Cypriot communities. Federalism was a dead issue, and the Greek Cypriots had to accept the victor's demands immediately. U.K. Mission in Geneva to FCO, August 10, 1974, WSC 1/13: "The Geneva Conference on Cyprus," FCO 9/1918, PRO. On August 10 and 11, Callaghan tried to get a more precise sense of what Kissinger would do to stay the Turks. Kissinger's deputy, Arthur Hartman, the U.S. observer at the Geneva talks, reported that his boss would continue to press Ecevit for moderation but confessed that Kissinger had no plan if Turkey used force. A frustrated Callaghan responded that the Turks would surely use force and reminded Hartman that with twelve thousand of its citizens on the island, Britain needed a better sense of U.S. intentions. Memoranda of conversations, August 10 and 11, 1974, both WSC 1/13: "The Geneva Conference on Cyprus," FCO 9/1918, PRO. Callaghan's efforts to talk directly with Kissinger failed, and he was left repeating the same warning to Sisco. Memorandum of telephone conversation, August 11, 1974, WSC 1/13: "The Geneva Conference on Cyprus," FCO 9/1918, PRO. On August 12, Callaghan's talks with Denktash and Gunes resulted in clear signals of imminent military action. Memoranda of conversation with Denktash, 8 P.M., and with Gunes, 10:22 P.M., WSC 1/13: "The Geneva Conference on Cyprus," FCO 9/1918, PRO. Unable to move Kissinger from his refusal to go beyond "pressing" Ecevit, Callaghan effectively threw in the towel at a 10 A.M. August 13 meeting, telling Klerides that the Greek Cypriot side had no options but substantive concessions and added that neither the United States nor the United Kingdom would back the Greek Cypriots with force or diplomacy. The choice facing the Greek side was war or concessions. During a 12:15 A.M. telephone call to Kissinger, both men defined Turkish actions as "intolerable" and agreed to do nothing. WSC 1/13: "The Geneva Conference on Cyprus," FCO 9/1918, PRO. Gunes, meanwhile, laid a take-it-or-leave-it position before the foreign ministers, together with a deadline. The Greek and Greek Cypriot governments refused to make the concessions demanded and tried unsuccessfully to stall for time. Callaghan flew back to London on August 14, informed Wilson that given U.S. unwillingness to intervene and the precariousness of Britain's position on the island, he saw "no prospect for a diplomatic solution at present." Minutes of meeting, 3 P.M. August 14, 1974, WSC 1/13: "The Geneva Conference on Cyprus," FCO 9/1918, PRO. Wilson talked with President Gerald Ford, and on the basis of Callaghan's report, the two men agreed to "let the dust settle." Memorandum of telephone conversation, August 14, 1974, PREM 16/20, PRO.

Epilogue

1. Staff Meeting of August 5, 1974, "Cyprus Critique," Kissinger Staff Meeting Transcripts, 1973-77, RG 59, NA.

2. Kissinger, *Years of Upheaval*, 1191-92, and *Years of Renewal*, 200, 228-30, 234. On the secretary's vindictive efforts to purge his junior-level State Department critics as well as the chaos created by his fumbling efforts to manage the Cyprus crisis, Dillon, William Kontos, and Wells Stabler oral histories and Boyatt memoir, ADST. Kissinger began the blame game early; see his comments to Cyrus Vance, August 21, 1974, Kissinger Telephone Conversations, U.S. State Department FOIA Electronic Reading Room (www.foia.state.gov).

3. On Kissinger's management, see the comments of senior U.S. diplomats to Barkman, *Ambassador in Athens*, 214-17. The belief in Kissinger's subtle manipulation of the Cyprus situation is entrenched in Greek and Greek Cypriot mythology, for example, Nikolinakos, *Widerstand und Opposition*, 305. Kranidiotis, *Ανοχύρωτη Πολιτεία*, 2:30, recognized that Watergate seriously upset U.S. ability to conduct foreign policy but quite illogically insisted that the facts notwithstanding, Kissinger manipulated every aspect of the crisis. The best critique of these conspiracy theories is the documentation on Greece's handling of Cyprus in Kardianos, *Από την Ζυρίχην εις τον Αττίλαν*, 3:283-329. On Kissinger's concern about the effects of Cyprus on the position of the incoming president, *Years of Renewal*, 192.

4. Minutes of cabinet meeting, July 22, 1974 (quote), CAB 128/55/28, PRO; author's notes of telephone conversation with Monteagle Stearns, May 11, 2001.

5. Although the documentary record for this statement was laid out in chapter 5, the comment will no doubt leave skeptical those addicted to conspiracy theory. In 1972, for example, conservative former prime minister Stephanos Stephanopoulos told Couloumbis that American policy was made in the Pentagon and that the State Department simply provided cover for military decisions. Couloumbis, *'71-'74: Σημειώσεις*, 187-89. Andreas Papandreou promoted this idea for his own ends (see chapter 6). Ties between the CIA and the Defense Department in Greece were close, as were those between the U.S. military and intelligence advisors and their Greek counterparts. Thus many Greeks have speculated that "low-level" U.S. person-

nel encouraged or directed or were in some way involved in the coup. Skeptical and careful investigators with no connections to the U.S. side, such as Laurence Stern (*Wrong Horse*) and Alexis Papahelas (*Βιασμός*), found no evidence linking low-level U.S. employees to the coup. The 1975 trials of the junta leaders offered no evidence supporting this idea. Rodakis, *Δίκες της Χούντας*. Stearns, who knew both Greece and the inner workings of the U.S. government, discounted the idea. Jack Maury, the CIA station chief, denied any such plot, and his actions at the time of the coup tend to confirm this denial. Maury, "Greek Coup." Despite wide official access to CIA, White House, State, and Defense department files, I never found a single lead suggesting such a scenario. All things are possible, but forty years after the event, evidence is yet to come forward confirming such a hypothesis.

6. Extract of a meeting between Karamanlis and the Greek chiefs of staff, August 14, 1974, in Klerides, *Cyprus*, 4:82–84, for the Greek army's estimate of its state of readiness to defend Cyprus and Greece. Klerides adds that the meeting was a "for-the-record" exercise by Karamanlis to get the Greek military to admit the effects of its seven-year rule. On the Greek army's politicization and military capability, "The Political Role of the Greek Armed Forces," November 22, 1972, FCO 9/1516, PRO.

7. On the feared rise of Andreas, comments by Silva to Couloumbis, '71–'74: *Σημειώσεις*, 334, and Zachery oral history, ADST. Compare *FRUS 1973–76*, 30:86–90, 117–20. On Greek's sense of betrayal, Barkman, *Ambassador in Athens*, 245. The best commentaries on the problems created by Kissinger's diplomacy are the assessments of his handpicked ambassador, Jack Kubisch, and of Wells Stabler, both oral histories, ADST.

8. Iatrides, "United States, Greece and the Balkans" and "United States and Greece in the Twentieth Century."

9. On the mismanagement of Greek internal politics compare the testimony collected during the trials of the coup leaders, Rodakis, *Δίκες της Χούντας*. On Andreas, the lapidary 1974 comment of Ioannis Zigdis: "Without Andreas there would not have been the coup of 1967." Couloumbis, '71–'74: *Σημειώσεις*, 327.

10. Of course, whether it was a return is an interesting point of speculation. Greece's parallel political evolution since the Roman Empire argued strongly that after 1821 it had been engaged in an initial experiment with Europe rather than a "return," but philhellenism created a set of myths that in stressing the Greek origins of the West has profoundly influenced our treatment of modern Greece. See the introduction.

11. On the delicate situation after Karamanlis's return, *Αρχείο*, 8:67–71.

12. Andreas's ability to modulate the message to the audience can be observed in comparing his public statements in Greece (for example, *Από το ΠΑΚ στο ΠΑΣΟΚ*, 24–27, or his comments reported in Couloumbis, '71–'74: *Σημειώσεις*, 307–13) with those made before American audiences. Transcripts of his appearances on the television programs *Evans-Novak Report*, May 11, 1969, and *Issues and Answers* October

25, 1981, both in author's possession. Compare "Socialism in One Country": Survey of Greece, the *Economist* July 3, 1982.

13. *Public Papers and Addresses of the Presidents of the United States: William J. Clinton*, 1994, 1:755–62.

14. Pantazopoulos, *"Για το Λαό και το Εθνος,"* 120–26, 137–38.

BIBLIOGRAPHY

Primary Sources

ARCHIVAL MATERIALS

Austria
Haus-, Hof-, und Staatsarchiv, Vienna
    Staatenabteilungen
        Ottoman Empire

France
Archives de Ministère des Affaires étrangères, Paris
    Mémoirs et Documents
    Affaires Politique
        Europe: Grèce

Great Britain
Public Record Office–National Archives, Kew
    Cabinet Papers (CAB)
    Colonial Office (CO)
    Foreign Office (FO)
    Foreign and Colonial Office (FCO)
    Prime Minister (PREM)

Greece
Benaki Archives, Athens
    Kapodistrias Papers
    Nikolaos Plastiras Papers
    Emmanuele Tsouderos Papers
    Eleftherios Venizelos Papers
    Sofokles Venizelos Papers
John Gennadius Library Archives, Athens
    Stefanos Dragoumis Papers
    John Gennadius Papers
    Skouloudis Papers

United States
Association for Diplomatic Studies and Training, Washington, D.C.
    Oral History Project
National Archives, Washington, D.C.
    Declassified Central Intelligence Records (CREST)
    General Records of the Department of State
    Presidential Libraries

Lyndon Johnson Presidential Library, Austin, Tex.
   National Security File
   President's Daily Diary
   Oral History Collection
John F. Kennedy Presidential Library, Boston, Mass.
   National Security File
   Robert Komer Papers
   Oral History Collection
Richard Nixon Presidential Materials, Washington, D.C.
   National Security File
   President's Daily Diary

PUBLISHED DIPLOMATIC DOCUMENTS SERIES

France. *Documents Diplomatiques Français.*
Great Britain. *Documents on British Foreign Policy.*
Italy. *Documenti Diplomatici Italiani.*
United States. *Foreign Relations of the United States.*

DOCUMENTARY COLLECTIONS

Agee, Philip, ed. *CIA: The Pike Report.* Nottingham, U.K.: Spokesman Books, 1977.
Athanasiades-Novas, George. *Τα Πεπραγμένα της Κυβερνήσεως Πλαστήρα-Βενιζέλου* [Transactions (Activities) of the Plastiras-Venizelos government]. Athens: n.p., 1952.
Commission of the European Community. *Opinion on Greece's Application.* Brussels: European Commission, 1976.
Denktash, Rauf. *Rauf Denktash at the United Nations.* Edited by M. Moran. Huntington, U.K.: Eothen, 1997.
Fallaci, Oriana. *Interviste con la storia.* Milan: Rizzoli, 1977.
Hussy, Joan M., ed. *The Journals and Letters of George Finlay.* 2 vols. Camberley, U.K.: Porphyrogenitus, 1995.
Iatrides, John, ed. *Ambassador MacVeagh Reports.* Princeton, N.J.: Princeton University Press, 1980.
Kanellopoulos, Panagiotes. *Δοκίμια και Αλλα Κείμενα Σαράντα Πέντε Ετών* [Forty-five years of articles and papers]. Thessaloniki: Egnatia, 1980.
———. *Κείμενα, 1967–1974* [Papers, 1967–74]. Athens: Gialleles, 1987.
Karamanlis, Konstantinos. *Κωνσταντίνος Καραμανλής: Αρχείο* [Konstantine Karamanlis: Archive]. 12 vols. Athens: Karamanlis Foundation, 1992–96.
———. *Ο Πολιτικός Λόγος του Κωνσταντίνου Καραμανλή* [Statements of Konstantine Karamanlis]. Athens: Karamanlis Foundation, 2002.
Kardianos, Dionysios [Spyros Papagiorgiou], ed. *Από την Ζυρίχην εις τον Αττίλαν* [From Zurich to Attila]. 3 vols. Athens: Ladia, 1980–82.

Kartakes, Eleftherios, ed. *Ο Καραμανλής της Μεταπολίτευσης* [Karamanlis in the years of political change]. Athens: Roes, 1993.
Kretikos, Panagiotes, ed. *Η Ρήξη* [Rift/Break]. Athens: Chalandri, 1998.
Kutler, Stanley I., ed. *Abuse of Power: The New Nixon Tapes*. New York: Simon and Schuster, 1998.
Lucarelli, Enrica. *Il socialismo mediterraneo: Andreas Papandreou*. Cosenza, Italy: Lerici, 1977.
Papagiorgiou, Spyros. *Τα Κρίσιμα Ντοκουμέντα του Κυπριακού* [Essential documents relating to the Cyprus question]. 3 vols. Athens: Ladia, 1983.
Papandreou, Andreas. *Από το ΠΑΚ στο ΠΑΣΟΚ* [From PAK to PASOK]. Athens: Ladia, 1976.
———. *Η Ελλάδα στους Έλληνες* [Greece for the Greeks]. Athens: n.p., 1976.
Public Papers and Addresses of the Presidents of the United States. Washington, D.C.: U.S. Government Printing Office, 1946–.
Raymond, Jean François de, ed. *La Grèce de Gobineau*. Paris: Belles Lettres, 1985.
Rodakis, Perikles, ed. *Οι Δίκες της Χούντας* [Trials of the junta]. 3 series, 13 vols. Athens: Demokratikoi Kairoi, 1975–76.
Thouvenel, Louis, ed. *La Grèce du Roi Othon*. Paris: Calmann Levy, 1890.
U.S. Congress. *The Decision to Homeport in Greece: Report of the Subcommittees on Europe and the Middle East of the Committee on Foreign Affairs, House of Representatives*. Washington: U.S. Government Printing Office, 1972.
———. *Greece: February 1971; A Staff Report Prepared for the use of the Committee on Foreign Relations, United State Senate*. Washington: U.S. Government Printing Office, 1971.
———. *Greece, Spain, and the Southern NATO Strategy: Hearings before the Subcommittee on Europe of the Committee on Foreign Affairs, House of Representatives*, 92nd Cong., 1st sess. Washington: U.S. Government Printing Office, 1971.
———. *Political and Strategic Implications of Homeporting in Greece: Joint Hearings before the Subcommittee on Europe and the Subcommittee on the Near East of the Committee on Foreign Affairs, House of Representatives*, 92nd Cong., 2nd sess. Washington: U.S. Government Printing Office, 1972.

DIARIES AND MEMOIRS

Alexandrakis, Menelaos, Byron Theodoropoulos, and Efstathios Lagakos. *Το Κυπριακό* [Cyprus issue]. Athens: Helleniki Euroekdotiki, 1987.
Averoff-Tossizza, Evangelos. *Lost Opportunities*. New Rochelle, N.Y.: Caratzas, 1986.
Ball, George. *The Past Has Another Pattern*. New York: Norton, 1982.
Barkman, Carl. *Ambassador in Athens*. London: Merlin, 1989.
Belios, Alexandros, ed. *Κωνσταντίνος Καραμανλής* [Konstantine Karamanlis]. Athens: Roes, 1995.

Bitsios, Dimitri. *Cyprus*. Thessaloniki: Institute for Balkan Studies, 1975.
Bouloukos, Aris. *Υπόθεση ΑΣΠΙΔΑ* [Aspida case]. Athens: Typos A. E., 1989.
Callaghan, James. *Time and Chance*. London: Collins, 1988.
Colby, William. *Honorable Men*. New York: Simon and Schuster, 1978.
Couloumbis, Theodore. *'71–'74: Σημειώσεις ενός Πανεπιστημιακού* [1971–74: Notebooks of a professor]. Athens: Pateke, 2002.
Deane, Philip. *I Should Have Died*. Don Mills, Canada: Longmans, 1976.
Foot, Hugh. *A Start in Freedom*. New York: Harper, 1964.
Frederika, Queen of the Hellenes. *A Measure of Understanding*. New York: St. Martin's, 1971.
Garoufalias, Petros. *Ελλάς και Κύπρος* [Greece and Cyprus]. Athens: Bergade, 1982.
Grivas George. *The Memoirs of General Grivas*. New York: Praeger, 1965.
Hart, Parker. *Two NATO Allies on the Threshold of War*. Durham, N.C.: Duke University Press, 1990.
Jones, Joseph. *The Fifteen Weeks*. New York: Viking, 1955.
Kanellopoulos, Panagiotes. *Η Ζωή Μου* [My life]. Athens: Gialleles, 1985.
Klerides, Glaufkos. *Cyprus: My Deposition*. 4 vols. Nicosia: Alithia, 1989–92.
Kollias, Konstantinos. *Βασιλεύς και Επανάστασις* [King and revolution]. Athens: n.p., 1984.
Kranidiotis, Nikos. *Ανοχύρωτη Πολιτεία* [Defenseless state]. 2 vols. Athens: Estia, 1985.
———. *Δύσκολα Χρόνια* [Difficult years]. Athens: Estia, 1981.
———. *Δύο Κρίσιμες Φάσεις του Κυπριακού* [Two critical phases of the Cyprus problem]. Athens: Kranidiotis, 1986.
Katris, John. *Eyewitness in Greece*. St. Louis, Mo.: New Critics, 1971.
Kissinger, Henry. *Years of Renewal*. New York: Simon and Schuster, 1999.
———. *Years of Upheaval*. Boston: Little, Brown, 1982.
———. *White House Years*. Boston: Little, Brown, 1979.
Lee, C. P. *Athenian Adventure*. New York: Knopf, 1957.
Lamprias, Takes. *Καραμανλής, ο Φίλος* [Karamanlis, my friend]. Athens: Potamos, 1998.
Leeper, Reginald. *When Greek Meets Greek*. London: Chatto and Windus, 1950.
Leontarites, Giogios. *Τα Παρασκήνια μιάς Εποχής* [Backstage of an era.] Athens: Philippote, 1989.
Macmillan, Harold. *Riding the Storm, 1956–1959*. New York: Harper, 1971.
Mandelaras, Nikos. *Μια Πολιτική Μαρτυρία* [Political testimony]. Athens: Maurides, 1999.
Markezinis, Spyridon. *Σύγχρονη Πολιτική Ιστορία της Ελλάδος* [Modern political history of Greece]. 3 vols. Athens: Papyros, 1994.
Maury, Jack. "The Greek Coup," *Washington Post*, May 1, 1977.
Mercouri, Melina. *I Was Born Greek*. Garden City, N.Y.: Doubleday, 1971.

Papademetriou, Giannes. *Η Αναλαμπή της Αριστεράς* [Lightening from the left]. Athens: Philistor, 2001.
Papandreou, Andreas. *Democracy at Gunpoint*. Garden City, N.Y.: Doubleday, 1970.
Papandreou, Margaret. *Nightmare in Athens*. New York: Prentice-Hall, 1970.
Papandreou, Nick. *Father Dancing: An Invented Memoir*. London: Viking, 1996.
Pattakos, Stylianos. *Ημέραι και Εργα* [Days and labors]. Athens: Ekdosis, 1999.
———. *Το Απόρρητο Ημερολόγιο του Στυλιανού Παττακού* [Secret diary of Stylianos Pattakos]. Athens: Eleftheria hora, 1990.
Ralles, George. *Πολιτικές Εκμυστηρεύσεις* [Political confidences]. Athens: Proskenio, 1990.
Richardson, John. *My Father the Spy*. New York: Harper, 2005.
Storace, Patricia. *Dinner with Persephone*. New York: Pantheon, 1996.
Sulzberger, C. L. *An Age of Mediocrity*. New York: Macmillan, 1973.
———. *The Last of the Giants*. New York: Macmillan, 1970.
———. *A Long Row of Candles*. New York: Macmillan, 1969.
Vlachou, Angelos. *Δέκα Χρόνια Κυπριακού* [Ten years of the Cyprus issue]. Athens: Estia, 1980.
Xanthopoulos-Palamas, Christos. *Διπλωματικό Τρίπτυχο* [Diplomatic tryptic]. Athens: Philon, 1978.
Yost, Charles. *History and Memory*. New York: Norton, 1980.
Zona, Gioula. *Η Ζωή με τον Πρόεδρο* [Life with the president]. Athens: Gialleles, 2001.
Zumwalt, Elmo. *On Watch*. Richmond, Va.: Zumwalt and Associates, 1976.

Secondary Sources

Adams, T. W. *AKEL*. Stanford, Calif.: Hoover Institution Press, 1971.
Ahmad, Feroz. *The Young Turks*. Oxford: Oxford University Press, 1969.
Aktypes, Dionysius, Aristeides Belalides, Maria Kalia, Theodorus Katsoulakos, Giannes Papagregoriau, and Kostas Choreanthes. *Στα Νεότερα Χρονιά* [Modern Greek history]. Athens: Organismos Ekdoseos Didaktikon Biblion, 1992.
Alexandris, Alexis. *The Greek Minority of Istanbul and Greek-Turkish Relations, 1918–1974*. Athens: Center for Asia Minor Studies, 1983.
Anastasiades, Giorgos, and Pavlos Petrides, eds. *Γεώργιος Παπανδρέου* [George Papandreou]. Thessaloniki: University Studio Press, 1994.
Anderson, M. S. *The Eastern Question, 1774–1923*. London: Macmillan, 1966.
Angelopoulos, Athanasios. "Population Distribution of Greece Today according to Language, National Consciousness, and Religion." *Balkan Studies* 20 (1979): 123–32.
Athanassopoulou, Ekavi. *Turkey: Anglo-American Security Interests, 1945–1952*. London: Cass, 1999.

"Athenian" [Rodis Rouphos]. *Inside the Colonels' Greece*. New York: Norton, 1972.
Augustinos, Gerasimos. *Consciousness and History*. New York: Columbia University Press, 1977.
———. *The Greeks of Asia Minor*. Kent, Ohio: Kent State University Press, 1992.
Avdela, Elia. "The Teaching of History in Greece." *Journal of Modern Greek Studies* 18 (2000): 239–49.
Bahcheli, Tozun. *Greek-Turkish Relations since 1955*. Boulder, Colo.: Westview, 1990.
Bailyn, Bernard. *The Ideological Origins of the American Revolution*. Cambridge, Mass.: Harvard University Press, 1967.
Barker, Elizabeth. *Macedonia*. London: Royal Institute of International Affairs, 1950.
Berktay, Halil. "National Memories." Σημειό Αναφοράς [Point of reference], 1997–98.
Blantas, Demetres. Ανδρέας Παπανδρέου [Andreas Papandreou]. Athens: Maufraki, 1978.
Borstelmann, Thomas. *The Cold War and the Color Line*. Cambridge, Mass.: Harvard University Press, 2001.
Bracevich, Andrew. *American Empire*. Cambridge, Mass.: Harvard University Press, 2002.
Briam, Paul. *The Will to Win*. Annapolis, Md.: U.S. Naval Institute Press, 2001.
Byzantinos, Nikos. Η Αλήθεια [Truth]. Athens: Parotzakes, 1978.
Calvo-Gonzales, Oscar. "Neither a Carrot nor a Stick: American Foreign Aid and Economic Policy Making in Spain during the 1950s." *Diplomatic History* 30 (2006): 409–38.
Chateaubriand, François-René de. *Itinéraire de Paris à Jérusalem*. Paris: Flammarion, 1968.
Chatzeantoniou, Kostas. Κύπρος, 1954–1974 [Cyprus, 1954–1974]. Athens: Ithlos, 2007.
———. Νικόλαος Πλαστήρας [Nicholas Plastiras]. Athens: Parousia, 1999.
Clogg, Richard, ed. *Greece, 1981–89*. New York: St. Martin's, 1993.
———. *The Greek Diaspora in the Twentieth Century*. New York: St. Martin's, 1999.
———. *Minorities in Greece*. London: Hurst, 2002.
Clogg, Richard, and George Yannopoulos. *Greece under Military Rule*. New York: Basic Books, 1972.
Corry, John. "Greece: The Death of Liberty." *Harper's*, October 1969, 72–81.
Coufoudakis, Van. "The United States, the United Nations, and the Greek Question, 1946–1952." In *Greece in the 1940s*, edited by John Iatrides, 275–97. Hanover, N.H.: University Press of New England, 1981.
Coufoudakis, Van, Harry Psomiades, and Andre Gerolymatos, eds. *Greece and the New Balkans*. New York: Pella, 1999.
Couloumbis, Theodore. *Greek Political Reaction to American and NATO Influences*. New Haven, Conn.: Yale University Press, 1966.

Couloumbis, Theodore, and Sally Hicks, eds. *U.S. Foreign Policy towards Greece and Cyprus*. Washington, D.C.: Center for Mediterranean Studies, 1976.

Couloumbis, Theodore, and John Iatrides, eds. *Greek-American Relations*. New York: Pella, 1980.

Couloumbis, Theodore, John Anthony Petropulos, and Harry J. Psomiades. *Foreign Interference in Greek Politics: An Historical Perspective*. New York: Pella, 1976.

Crawshaw, Nancy. *The Cyprus Revolt*. London: Allen and Unwin, 1978.

Dakin, Douglas. *The Greek Struggle for Macedonia, 1897–1913*. Thessaloniki: Institute for Balkan Studies, 1966.

———. *The Unification of Greece, 1770–1923*. London: Benn, 1972.

Danopoulos, Constantine. *Warriors and Politicians in Modern Greece*. Chapel Hill, N.C.: Documentary Publications, 1985.

Daphnes, Gregorios. Σοφοκλής Ελευθερίου Βενιζέλος [Sophokles (son of) Eleftherios Venizelos]. Athens: Ikaros, 1970.

de Grazia, Victoria. *Irresistible Empire*. Cambridge, Mass.: Harvard University Press, 2005.

Doulis, Thomas. *George Theotokas*. New York: Twayne, 1974.

Doumanis, Nicholas. *Myth and Memory in the Mediterranean*. New York: St Martin's, 1997.

Dragonas, Thalia, and Anna Frangoudaki. "Introduction" to special issue: "Youth and History," *Journal of Modern Greek Studies* 18 (2000): 223–24.

Drew, Elizabeth. "Democracy on Ice." *Atlantic Monthly*, April 1968, 56–67.

Duchêne, Hervé, ed. *Le Voyage en Grèce*. Paris: Laffont, 2003.

Fatouros, A. A. "Building Formal Structures of Penetration: The United States in Greece, 1947–48." In *Greece in the 1940s*, edited by John Iatrides, 239–58. Hanover, N.H.: University Press of New England, 1981.

Farmakides, Anne. *To daimonio of George Theotokas*. Montreal: McGill University Press, 1975.

Fields, James. *America and the Mediterranean World*. Princeton, N.J.: Princeton University Press, 1969.

Finlay, George. *History of the Greek Revolution and the Reign of King Otto*. London: Zeno, 1971.

Foley, Charles, and W. I. Scobie. *The Struggle for Cyprus*. Stanford, Calif.: Stanford University Press, 1975.

Genevoix, Maurice, *The Greece of Karamanlis*. London: Doric, 1973.

Georghallides, G. S. "Turkish and British Reactions to the Emigration of Cypriot Turks to Anatolia." *Balkan Studies* 18 (1977): 43–52.

Gibbon, Edward. *The Decline and Fall of the Roman Empire*. 3 vols. New York: Modern Library, 1932.

Gilman, Nils. *Mandarins of the Future: Modernization Theory in Cold War America*. Baltimore, Md.: Johns Hopkins University Press, 2003.

Gkines, Giannes. *Ο Άλλος Καραμανλής* [The other Karamanlis]. Athens: Nastos, 1986.

Goldbloom, Maurice. "United States Policy in Post-War Greece." In *Greece under Military Rule*, edited by Richard Clogg and G. Yannopoulos, 228–54. New York: Basic Books, 1972.

Gounaris, Vasiles. *Steam over Macedonia*. Boulder, Colo.: East European Monographs, 1993.

Gourgouris, Stathis. *Dream Nation*. Stanford, Calif.: Stanford University Press, 1996.

Gregoriades, Solon. *Ιστορία της Δικτατορίας* [History of the dictatorship]. 4 vols. Athens: Kapopoulos, 1975.

Grivas, Kleanthes. *Παπανδρεϊσμός* [Papandreism]. Thessaloniki: Thessalonikes, 1989.

Harlaftis, Gelina. *Greek Shipowners and Greece, 1945–1975*. London: Athlone, 1993.

Harper, John. *America and the Reconstruction of Italy*. New York: Cambridge University Press, 1986.

Hastaoglou-Martinisis, Vilma. "City Form and National Identity: Urban Designs in Nineteenth-Century Greece." *Journal of Modern Greek Studies* 13 (1995): 99–110.

Hietala, Thomas R. *Manifest Design: American Exceptionalism and Empire*. Ithaca, N.Y.: Cornell University Press, 2003.

Higham, John. *Strangers in the Land*. New York: Atheneum, 1964.

Hitchens, Christopher. *Cyprus*. London: Quartet, 1984.

———. *Hostage to History: Cyprus from the Ottomans to Kissinger*. London: Verso, 1997.

Holden, David. *Greece without Columns*. Philadelphia: Lippencott, 1972.

Holland, Robert. *Britain and the Revolt in Cyprus, 1954–1959*. Oxford: Oxford University Press, 1998.

Iatrides, John. "The United States and Greece in the Twentieth Century." In *Greece in the Twentieth Century*, edited by Theodore Kariotis and Fotini Bellou, 69–110. London: Frank Cass, 2003.

———. "The United States, Greece, and the Balkans." In *Greece and the New Balkans*, edited by Van Coufoudakis, Harry Psomiades, and Andreas Gerolymatos, 265–94. New York: Pella, 1999.

Iatrides, John, ed. *Greece in the 1940s*. Hanover, N.H.: University Press of New England, 1981.

Iatrides, John, and Linda Wrigley, eds. *Greece at the Crossroads*. College Park: Pennsylvania State University Press, 1995.

Ioannides, Lakes (Theophilos). *Κωνσταντίνος Καραμανλής* [Konstantine Karamanlis]. Thessaloniki, n.p., 1966.

———. *Γιατί Διαλέξαμε τον Κωνσταντίνο Καραμανλή* [Why we chose Karamanlis]. Thessaloniki: n.p., 1976.

Jenkins, Romilly. *The Dilessi Murders*. London: Prion, 1961.
Kaklamanake, Roula. *Ανδρέας Παπανδρέου* [Andreas Papandreou]. Athens: Patake, 2000.
Karakasidou, Anastasia. *Fields of Wheat, Hills of Blood*. Chicago: University of Chicago Press, 1997.
Karathanassis, A. E. "Contribution a la connaissance de la vie et de l'oeuvre de deux Grecs de la *diaspora*: Athanasios Kondoidis et Anthanasios Skiadas." *Balkan Studies* 19 (1978): 159–84.
Kardianos, Dionysios [Spyros Papagiorgiou]. *Καραμανλής και Κυπριακόν* [Karamanlis and the Cyprus issue]. Athens: Nea Thesis, 1988.
———. *Καραμανλής και "Φάκελος."* [Karamanlis and the (Cyprus) "Dossier"] Athens: Nea Thesis, 1987.
Kargakos, Sarantos. *Ecce Homo*. Athens: Gutenburg, 1990.
Karsh, Efraim, and Inari Karsh. *Empires of the Sand*. Cambridge, Mass: Harvard University Press, 1999.
Kartakis, Eleftherios, ed. *Constantine Karamanlis in Thought and Action*. Athens: Roes, n.d.
Kasimates, Pavlos. *Γεώργιος Παπανδρέου* [George Papandreou]. Athens: Nea Synora, 1988.
Kassimeris, George. *Europe's Last Red Terrorists*. London: Hurst, 2001.
Kazakos, Panos, and P. C. Ioakimidis, eds. *Greece and EC Membership Evaluated*. London: St Martin's, 1994.
Keeley, Edmund. *Inventing Paradise*. New York: Farrar, Straus and Giroux, 1999.
Kitromilides, Paschalis. "'Νεορές κοινοτητες' και οι απαρχές του εθνικου ζητήματος στά Βακάνια" ["'Imagined communities' and the origins of nationality in the Balkans"]. In *Εθνική Ταυτότητα και Εθνικισμος στη Νεοτερη Ελλάδα* [National identity and nationalism in modern Greece], edited by Thanos Veremis, 53–131. Athens: MIE, 1997.
Kitromilides, Paschalis, and Marios Evriviades, eds. *Cyprus*. Santa Barbara, Calif.: Clio, 1995.
Klarevas, Louis. "Were the Eagle and the Phoenix Birds of a Feather? The United States and the Greek Coup of 1967." *Diplomatic History* 30 (2006): 471–508.
Kofas, John. *Authoritarianism in Greece*. Boulder, Colo.: East European Monographs, 1983.
———. *Intervention and Underdevelopment*. University Park: Penn State University Press, 1989.
———. *Under the Eagle's Claw*. Westport, Conn.: Praeger, 2003.
Kofos, Evangelos. "Dilemmas and Orientations of Greek Policy in Macedonia, 1876–1886." *Balkan Studies* 21 (1980): 45–55.
———. "Εθνική κληρονομία και έθνικη ταυτότητα στη Μακεδονια του 19ου και του 20ου αιωνα" ["National heritage and national identity in Macedonia in the

nineteenth and twentieth centuries"]. In *Εθνική Ταυτότητα και Εθνικισμός στη Νεοτερη Ελλάδα* [National identity and nationalism in modern Greece], edited by Thanos Veremis, 199–269. Athens: MIE, 1997.

———. *Nationalism and Communism in Macedonia*. Thessaloniki: Institute for Balkan Studies, 1964.

———. "Patriarch Joachim III (1878–1884) and the Irredentist Policy of the Greek State." *Journal of Hellenic Studies* 107 (1986): 105–121.

Koliopoulos, John. "Ληστεία και άλυτρωτισμος στην Ελλάδα του 19ου αιώνα" [Brigandage and irridentism in nineteenth-century Greece]. In *Εθνική Ταυτότητα και Εθνικισμός στη Νεοτερη Ελλάδα* [National identity and nationalism in modern Greece], edited by Thanos Veremis, 133–97. Athens: MIE, 1997.

———. "Greek Foreign Policy and Strategy, 1939–1941." *Balkan Studies* 29 (1988): 89–98.

———. "Unwanted Ally: Greece and the Great Powers, 1939–41." *Balkan Studies* (1982): 7–25.

Kolko, Gabriel. *The Politics of War*. New York: Random House, 1968.

Kolko, Joyce, and Gabriel Kolko. *The Limits of Power*. New York: Harper Row, 1972.

Kolmer, Kostas. *Η Χρεοκοπία της Τρίτης Ελληνικής Δημοκρατίας* [Bankruptcy of the third Greek republic]. Athens: Delos, 1995.

Krateros, Ioannou. "Γεώργιος Παπανδρέου και οι Συμφωνίες Ζυρίχης Λονδίνου για την Κύπρο" [George Papandreou and the Zurich-London agreements on Cyprus]. In *Γεώργιος Παπανδρέου* [George Papandreou], edited by Giorgios Anastasiades and Pavlos Petrides, 479–88. Thessaloniki: University Studio Press, 1994.

Kuisel, Richard F. *Seducing the French: The Dilemma of Americanization*. Berkeley: University of California Press, 1993.

Kurth, James, and James Petras, eds. *Mediterranean Paradoxes*. Oxford: Berg, 1993.

Legg, Keith. *Politics in Modern Greece*. Stanford, Calif.: Stanford University Press, 1969.

Legg, Keith, and John Roberts. *Modern Greece*. Boulder, Colo.: Westview, 1997.

Leontarites, Giorgios. *Ο Παπάγος το Στέμμα και οι Αγγλοι*. [Papagos, the Crown, and the English] Chalandri: Proseniko, 2003.

Lieven, Anatol. *America Right or Wrong: An Anatomy of American Nationalism*. New York: Oxford University Press, 2004.

Link, Arthur, ed. *Woodrow Wilson and a Revolutionary World*. Chapel Hill: University of North Carolina Press, 1982.

Mackridge, Peter, and Eleni Yannakakis, eds. *Ourselves and Others*. New York: Berg, 1997.

Macmillan, Margaret. *The Peacemakers*. London: Murray, 2001.

Makrides, Vasilios. "Science and the Orthodox Church in 18th and Early 19th Centuries: Sociological Considerations." *Balkan Studies* 29 (1988): 265–82.

Markides, Diana. *Cyprus, 1957–1963*. Minneapolis: University of Minnesota Press, 2001.

Markides, Kyriacos. *The Rise and Fall of the Cyprus Republic*. New Haven, Conn.: Yale University Press, 1977.

Markopoulos, George. "King George I and the Expansion of Greece, 1875–1881." *Balkan Studies* 9 (1968): 21–40.

Mavrogordatos, George. *The Stillborn Republic*. Berkeley: University of California Press, 1983.

Mayes, Stanley. *Cyprus and Makarios*. London: Putnam, 1960.

Mazower, Mark. *Greece and the Interwar Economic Crisis*. New York: Oxford, 1991.

———. *Inside Hitler's Greece*. New Haven, Conn.: Yale University Press, 1993.

Mazower, Mark, ed. *After the War Was Over*. Princeton, N.J.: Princeton University Press, 2000.

McCarthy, Justin. *Death and Exile*. Princeton, N.J.: Darwin, 1995.

McGrew, William. *Land and Revolution in Modern Greece, 1800–1881*. Kent, Ohio: Kent State University Press, 1985.

McHenry, James. *The Uneasy Partnership on Cyprus, 1919–1939*. New York: Garland, 1987.

McNeill, William. "The Dilemmas of Modernization in Greece." *Balkan Studies* 8 (1967): 305–16.

———. *The Greek Dilemma*. New York: Lippincott, 1947.

———. *The Metamorphosis of Greece since World War II*. Chicago: University of Chicago Press, 1978.

Meynaud, Jean. *Rapport sur l'abolition de la démocratie en Grèce*. Montreal: n.p., 1970.

Michalopoulos, Demetres. Ελλάδα και Τουρκία [Greece and Turkey]. Athens: Roes, 1989.

Miller, James. "Roughhouse Diplomacy: The United States Confronts Italian Communism." *Storia delle relazione internazionale* 5 (1989): 279–311.

———. "Taking Off the Gloves: The United States and the Italian Election of 1948." *Diplomatic History* 7 (1983): 35–56.

Mouzelis, Nikos. *Modern Greece*. London: Macmillan, 1978.

Murtagh, Peter. *The Rape of Greece*. London: Simon and Schuster, 1994.

Myers, John. *Herodotus*. Chicago: Gateway, 1971.

Nicolet, Claude. *United States Policy towards Cyprus, 1954–1974*. Mannheim, Germany: Bibliopolis, 2001.

Nicolopoulos, John. "From Agathangelos to the Megali Idea: Russia and the Emergence of Modern Greek Nationalism." *Balkan Studies* 28 (1985): 41–56.

Nikolinakos, Marios. *Widerstand und Opposition in Griechenland*. Darmstadt, Germany: Luchterhand, 1974.

O'Malley, Brendan, and Ian Craig. *The Cyprus Conspiracy*. New York: St. Martin's, 2000.

Pantazopoulos, Andreas. *"Για το Λαό και το Εθνος"* ["For the people and the nation"]. Athens: Polis, 2001.

Panayotopoulos, A. U. J. "The Great Idea and the Vision of an Eastern Federation: A propos of the Views of I. Dragoumis and A. Souliotis-Nicolaidis." *Balkan Studies* 21 (1981): 331–65.

Papacosma, S. Victor. *The Military in Greek Politics*. Kent, Ohio: Kent State University Press, 1977.

Papagiannopoulos, Takis. *Ο Στρατάρχης Αλέξανδρος Παπάγος* [Marshal Alexander Papagos]. Athens: n.p., 1987.

Papahelas, Alexis. *Ο Βιασμός της Ελληνικής Δημοκρατίας* [Rape of Greek democracy]. Athens: Hestia, 1997.

Papaioannou, Kostas. *15 Ιουλίου 1965*. Athens: To Pontiki, 1995.

Papandreou, Andreas. "Greece: An American Problem." *Massachusetts Review* 12 (1971): 655–71.

———. *Man's Freedom*. New York: Carnegie Mellon University, 1970.

———. *Paternalistic Capitalism*. Minneapolis: University of Minnesota Press, 1972.

———. *The Political Element in Economic Development*. Stockholm: Almqvist and Wiksell, 1966.

———. *A Strategy for Greek Economic Development*. Athens: Center of Economic Research, 1962.

Papandreou, Andreas, and Uri Zohar. *National Planning and Socioeconomic Priorities*. New York: Praeger, 1974.

Paraskevopoulos, Potes. *Ανδρέας Παπανδρέου* [Andreas Papandreou]. Athens: Synchrone Hellenike Istoria, 1995.

———. *Ο Καραμανλής στα Χρόνια* [Karamanlis in his era]. Athens: Tipos Phytrakes, 1987.

Pells, Richard. *Not Like Us*. New York: Basic Books, 1997.

Pentzopoulos, Dimitri. *The Balkan Exchange of Minorities and Its Impact on Greece*. London: Hurst, 2002.

Perrakes, Stelios. "Η Εξωτερική Πολιτική της Ενώσεως Κέντρου" [Foreign policy of the Center Union]. In *Γεώργιος Παπανδρέου* [George Papandreou], edited by Giorgios Anastasiades and Pavlos Petriades, 523–40. Thessaloniki: University Studio Press, 1994.

Petropulos, John. *Politics and Statecraft in the Kingdom of Greece*. Princeton, N.J.: Princeton University Press, 1968.

Petsalis-Diomidis, N. *Greece at the Paris Peace Conference*. Thessaloniki: Institute for Balkan Studies, 1978.

Pirounakis, Nicholas. *The Greek Economy*. New York: St. Martin's, 1997.

Priortes, Marios. *Μέγιστον Μάθημα* [Big lessons]. Athens: Phytrakes, 1975.

Psomiades, Harry, and Stavros Thomadakis, eds. *Greece, the New Europe, and the Changing International Order*. New York: Pella, 1993.

Psyroukes, Nikos. *Ιστορία της Σύγχρονης Ελλάδα, 1940–1967* [History of modern Greece, 1940-1967]. 4 vols. Athens: Ekdosis Epikairoteta, 1975–83.

Quataert, Donald. *The Ottoman Empire, 1700–1922*. Cambridge: Cambridge University Press, 2002.
Roger, Philippe. *L'ennemi américain*. Paris: Seuil, 2002.
Roubatis, Yiannis. *Tangled Webs*. New York: Pella, 1987.
Rousseas, Stephen. *The Death of a Democracy*. New York: Grove, 1967.
Saunders, Irwin. "Greek Society in Transition." *Balkan Studies* 8 (1967): 317–32.
Serwo, Mathias. "Die ersten staatlichen Kirchengesetze in Griechenland 1833 und ihre politische Herkunft." *Balkan Studies* 11 (1970): 111–122.
Smith, Michael Llewellyn. *Athens*. Northampton, Mass.: Interlink Books, 2004.
———. *Ionian Vision*. London: Hurst, 1998.
Smothers, Frank, William McNeill, and Elizabeth McNeill. *Report on the Greeks*. New York: Twentieth Century Fund, 1948.
Spourdalakis, Michalis. *The Rise of the Greek Socialist Party*. London: Routledge, 1988.
Stavrou, Nikolas. *Allied Politics and Military Interventions: The Political Role of the Greek Military*. Athens: Papazzis, 1976.
Stavrou, Nikolas, ed. *Greece under Socialism*. New Rochelle, N.Y.: Caratzas, 1988.
Steel, Ronald. "The Missionary." *New York Review of Books*, November 20, 2003, 26–28, 35.
Stephanides, Yiannis. "Ο Γεώργιος Παπανδρέου και οι Κυβερνήσεις του Κέντρου, 1950–51" ["George Papandreou and the Center Governments, 1950–51"]. In *Γεώργιος Παπανδρέου* [George Papandreou], edited by Giorgios Anastasiades and Pavlos Petrides, 345–64. Thessaloniki: University Studio Press, 1994.
Stephanson, Anders. *Manifest Destiny*. New York: Hill and Wang, 1995.
Stephens, Robert. *Cyprus*. New York: Praeger, 1966.
Stern, Laurence. *The Wrong Horse*. New York: New York Times Books, 1978.
Theodoracopoulos, Taki. *The Greek Upheaval*. New York: Stacey, 1978.
Tomkinson, John L. "Athens under the Americans 2: The Fake Democracy (1948–1967)" http://www.anagnosis.gr/index.
Tsoucalas, Constantine. *The Greek Tragedy*. Baltimore, Md.: Penguin, 1969.
———. "The Ideological Impact of the Cold War." In *Greece in the 1940s*, edited by John Iatrides, 319–41. Hanover, N.H.: University Press of New England, 1981.
Tsoukalis, Loukas. *The European Community and Its Mediterranean Enlargement*. London: Allen and Unwin, 1981.
Twain, Mark. *The Innocents Abroad*. New York: Signet, 1966.
Tzermias, Pavlos. *Konstantin Karamanlis: Versuch einer Würdigung*. Tübingen: Francke, 1992.
Vassilikos, Vassilis. *And Dreams Are Dreams*. Translated by Mary Kitroeff. New York: Seven Stories, 1996.
Vatikiotis, P. J. *Popular Autocracy in Greece*. London: Cass, 1998.
Venezis, P. N. *Makarios: Faith and Power*. London: Abelard-Schuman, 1971.

———. *Makarios: Pragmatism v. Idealism*. London: Abelard-Schuman, 1974.
Veremis, Thanos. "Εισαγωγή" ["Introduction"]. In *Εθνική Ταυτότητα και Εθνικισμος στη Νεοτερη Ελλάδα* [National identity and nationalism in modern Greece], edited by Thanos Veremis, 11–26. Athens: MIE, 1997.
———. *The Military in Greek Politics*. London: Hurst, 1997.
Veremis, Thanos, ed. *Εθνική Ταυτότητα και Εθνικισμος στη Νεοτερη Ελλάδα* [National identity and nationalism in modern Greece]. Athens: MIE, 1997.
Visvizi-Dontas, Donna. "La communauté européenne et la diplomatie venizelienne." *Balkan Studies* 32 (1991): 271–92.
Vlantas, Demetres. *Ανδρέας Παπανδρέου* [Andreas Papandreou]. Athens: Maufraki, ca. 1978.
Voglis, Polymeris. *Becoming a Subject*. New York: Berghahn, 2002.
Voultepses, Giannis. *Η Πολιτική Διαθήκη του Γεωργίου Παπανδρέου και η Αντίσταση του Ανδρέα* [Political testament of George Papandreou and the resistance of Andreas]. Athens: Isokrates, 1985.
Wills, Garry. "The Tragedy of Bill Clinton." *New York Review of Books*, August 12, 2004, 60–64.
Wittner, Lawrence. *American Intervention in Greece, 1943–1949*. New York: Columbia University Press, 1982.
———. "American Policy toward Greece, 1944–49." In *Greece in the 1940s*, edited by John Iatrides, 229–39. Hanover, N.H.: University Press of New England, 1981.
Wood, Gordon. *The American Revolution*. London: Orion, 2002.
Woodhouse, C. M. *Karamanlis*. Oxford: Oxford University Press, 1982.
———. *The Rise and Fall of the Greek Colonels*. New York: Franklin Watts, 1985.
Woodward, Bob, and Carl Bernstein. *The Final Days*. New York: Simon and Schuster, 1976.
Xydis, Stephen. "Coups and Countercoups in Greece, 1967–1973 (with postscript)." *Political Science Quarterly* 89 (1974): 507–38.
———. *Cyprus: Conflict and Conciliation, 1954–58*. Columbus: Ohio State University Press, 1967.
———. *Cyprus: Reluctant Republic*. The Hague: Mouton, 1973.
Zakythinos, Dionysius A. *The Making of Modern Greece: From Byzantium to Independence*. Oxford: Blackwell, 1976.
Zimmerman, Warren. *The First Great Triumph*. New York: Farrar, Straus and Giroux, 2002.

INDEX

Acheson, Dean, 37–38, 95, 102, 142
Acheson mediation (July–September 1964), 103–5, 177–78
Acheson Plan, 104
Agnew, Spiro, 160; visits Greece, 167–68
Akritas Plan, 94
Alexandrakis, Menelaos, 108
American exceptionalism, ix
Americanization, viii
Angelis, Odysseus, 160, 166
Anschuetz, Norbert, 103; discussions with Andreas Papandreou, 122, 126–27, 135; meeting with George Papandreou (June 1965), 121–22; proposes covert operation, 123
Armour, Norman, 71
Asia Minor Catastrophe (1923), 5, 9
ASPIDA (Officers, Save the Fatherland, Ideals, Democracy), 116–17, 120; impact on Greek politics, 117, 128, 145
Athanassiades-Novas, George, 122
Averoff-Tossizza, Evangelos, 61, 67, 71, 91–92, 115, 195

Balance of power: impact on Greece, 2–3
Ball, George, 95–96; assessment of Cyprus situation, 100; collapse of Acheson mediation, 105–6; on Makarios, 181; mission to Eastern Mediterranean (June 1964), 101
Banditry, 5–6
Barham, Richard, 121, 122
Barkman, Carl, 162, 168
Battle, Lucius, 133
Belcher, Taylor, 60, 87, 99, 104–5, 181

Beloyiannis, Nikos, 23–24, 37
Bennett, W. Tapley, 67, 113
Bitsios, Demetrios, 129
Blair, Tony, 84
Bouloukos, Aris, 116
Boyatt, Thomas, 182
Brandt, Willie, 146
Brewster, Daniel, 73, 122; reports coup to Rusk, 146
Briggs, Ellis, 71, 76–77, 81
Bundy, McGeorge, 92, 123
Bush, George W., ix, 84, 210
Byzantine Empire, 10, 15

Callaghan, James, 186, 190; judgment on Kissinger, 202–3
Cannon, Cavendish, 57–58; discussion with Paul I, 67
Castle, Barbara, 62
"Ceaseless struggle," 76, 78, 124
Central Intelligence Agency (CIA), 23, 25, 43, 68, 77, 80, 143; analyzes London-Zurich agreements, 63; covert operations, 73–74, 77–78; and disinformation, xii; and elections of 1959, 74–75; and elections of 1961, 76–78; role in Cyprus, 179, 181–82; and threat of military coup in Greece, 128–29, 132
Charbonniere, Guy de Girard de, 112
Childs, Marquis, 143
Clinton, Bill, 210
Colby, William, 194
Constantine I (king of Greece), 8–9, 117
Constantine II (king of Greece), 81, 98, 105, 145, 157, 167; confrontation

with George Papandreou, 120–23; exile, 158; and Frederika, 114; meeting with Johnson, 152; meeting with Nixon, 159–60, 164; organizes countercoup, 151–53; reacts to coup, 147; seeks U.S. support, 126, 128, 159; supports Kanellopoulos, 131–32; U.S. evaluations of, 110, 166

Costar, C. E., 179–80

Cyprus: "Basic Structure" (constitution), 90; British occupation, annexation, and administration of, 44–51; and British offer to Greece, 47, 49; communal chambers, 89–90; communal talks, 180, 182–83; communist party (KKK/AKEL), 48, 85–86, 87, 89, 99, 181–82, 191; and Czech arms crisis of 1972, 169, 183–84; disloyal opposition, 183

Davies, Rodger, 186, 192
Deane (Gigantès), Philip, 18–19
Demetracopoulos, Elias, 167
Denktash, Rauf, 89, 109
Dobrynin, Anatoly, 190
Dovas, Constantine, 78, 115
Dulles, Alan, 73, 80
Dulles, John Foster, 40, 80; approach to Cyprus issue, 56–57, 60–61

Ecevit, Bulent: partition of Cyprus, 193–200, 203
Economic Cooperation Administration (ECA), 28. *See also* Marshall Plan
EDA (United Democratic Left), 31, 39, 68, 70, 114, 118, 127, 131
Eden, Anthony, 44, 50, 59–61
Eisenhower, Dwight D., 40, 52, 69–70, 85, 210; death and funeral of, 158–59
EK (Center Union), 76, 77, 113–15, 117, 120, 136; apostates of, 122–23, 131, 133, 145

EOKA (National Union of Cypriot Fighters), 54, 64, 85
EOKA B, 182, 184, 188
ERE (National Radical Union), 71, 82, 93, 113–16, 120, 128, 143
Ethnic cleansing, 13
European Economic Community (EEC), 9, 11, 70

Ford, Gerald, 158, 200, 202
Frederika (queen of Greece), 18, 27, 79–81, 83, 114
Fulbright, J. William, 100

Garoufalias, Petros, 105, 115
Gennimatas, George, 121–22
George I (king of Greece), 6
Georkadjis, Polykarpos, 94; collaborates with United States, 179; dismissal of, 180; forms party, 181; plot against Makarios, 181
Gizikis, Phaedon, 187–88, 194
Grady, Henry, 21, 26, 34; clash with Venizelos, 28; U.S. role in Greece, 21, 25, 27–28, 32–33
Greece: educational system, 7; evaluating postwar foreign policy of, 205–7; language question, 11; national identity, 9–14; political parties, 7; response to United States, x, xi; U.S. evaluation of strategic importance of, 29–30, 67; westernization, 15–16
—army: overthrow of democracy, 128–29, 132, 134; plots military coup (1963), 81; political role, 6, 8
—elections: of 1950, 33; of 1951, 37; of 1952, 39; of 1958, 70, 72–73; of 1961, 76; of 1963, 82–83; of 1964, 96, 112–13
—monarchy: political role, 6–8
—Orthodox Church: and moderniza-

tion, 12–13; role in society, x, 12; support for enosis, 58
Greek Rally party, 37, 39
Grivas, George, 54, 58, 59, 92, 104–5, 109, 176–78, 182; and ASPIDA, 116

Haig, Alexander, 160; suppresses intelligence report, 164–65
Harding, John, 55
Hare Raymond, 95
Hartman, Arthur, 198–99
Herter, Christian, 71
History: conspiratorial writing of, 17–19; Greek writing of, 16–19; political role of, 15, 18–19
Homeporting, 166, 168–69; consequences, 169
Hunt, David, 179

Iakovos (archbishop), 172
IDEA (Sacred Band of Greek Officers), 26, 36–37, 67–68, 70
Inonu, Ismet, 93, 101
Instant enosis, 104–5
Ioannides, Dimitrios, 162, 171, 174, 202, 206; and Cyprus, 185–86, 188–89, 191–92, 195; overthrows Papadopolous, 173
Ipsilanti, Alexander, 15
Istanbul-Izmir Riots (1955), 59, 62, 71

Johnson, Lyndon B., 18–19, 79, 85, 142, 145, 149, 203; correspondence with Inonu and George Papandreou, 96–97; Cyprus strategy, 95–96, 101–2, 106; on Karamanlis, 80; letter to Inonu, 101, 108; meeting with Constantine II, 152; meeting with Makarios, 88–89; meeting with Matsas, 18–19, 102; visits Athens, 79–80; visits Cyprus, 88–89; and weapons suspension, 155

Johnson-Papandreou talks (June 1964), 102
Jones, Joseph, 19
Joyce, Vincent, 119

Kanellopoulos, Panagiotes, 195; and ASPIDA, 128; management of 1967 crisis, 131; offers compromise, 123; and party problems, 114, 131; plans to oust George Papandreou, 121; succeeds Karamanlis, 113, 140; topples Stephanopoulos ministry, 124
Kapodistrias, Ioannis, 6
Karamanlis, Konstantine, 67, 69–72, 113, 143, 145, 210; building democratic opposition, 75; countercoup, 153; Cyprus policy, 58–59, 64, 90–91, 176, 197–99; dealings with the United States, 58–59, 69–72, 160; and economic development, 69; and military junta, 158, 170–73; recalled to leadership, 195; resignation, 81–83, 112; relations with Makarios, 55–56, 59, 176; relations with military, 68, 197; relations with Palace, 68; restoration of democracy, 197, 208–9; strategy as opposition leader, 82–83, 113–14; succeeds Papagos, 58, 68
Karamessinis, Thomas, 23, 25
Kardamakis, Vassilios, 77, 79, 81
Kastellorizon (island), 103
Kastris, John, 143
Kaysen, Carl, 140
Kazantzakis, Nikos, 16
Keeley, Robert, 149, 207
Kennedy, John F., 67, 80, 83, 85, 145; involvement with Cyprus, 87–88, 91–93
Khrushchev, Nikita, 106
King, Barrington, 107
Kissinger, Henry, 157, 160; assumes

control of U.S. policy, 170; Cold War outlook, 195–96; Cyprus policy, 181, 184, 189–92, 196; defends Greek-Cyprus policy, 201–2; diplomacy critiqued, 202–4; policy for Greece, 173–75; and Tasca, 162, 165, 167, 173–75, 189–90, 192, 196–97, 207; tilt to Greece, 189–93; tilt to Turkey, 193–95; repairing U.S.-Greek relationship, 207; talks with Nixon on Cyprus, 191, 193–94
KKE (Greek Communist Party), 24, 70
Klerides, Glaufkos, 89, 180–81, 192, 194, 196, 198
Kohler, Foy, 130
Kokkas, Panos, 115, 121
Kolettis, Ioannis, 3, 7
Kolko, Gabriel, 142
Kollias, Constantine, 147
Komer, Robert, 92, 95
Krag, Jans Otto, 139
Kranidiotis, Nikos, 184
Kubisch, Jack, 207
Kutchuk, Fazil, 89–91, 109
KYP (Central Intelligence Agency, Greece), 41, 116, 150

Labouisse, Henry, 66, 71, 97, 99, 106, 113–14; comments on Andreas Papandreou, 119; meeting with EK leaders, 78–79
Lagakos, Efstathios, 188
Lambrakis, Christos, 115
Lambrakis, Gregory, 82
LeFeber, Walter, 142
London Conference (1964), 95–96
London-Zurich agreements (1959), 62–63, 85, 86, 88–89, 97, 99, 106, 178; detailed, 90; impact, 63–65; and Turkish Cypriots, 62
Lyssarides, Vassos, 180

Macedonian conflict, 14
Macmillan, Harold, 52, 55, 61–62
MacVeagh, Lincoln, 19, 29, 32
Makarezos, Nikolaos, 150, 208
Makarios III (archbishop; Michael Moskos), 50, 109, 166; arrested and deported, 54–56; assassination attempts, 180; character, 55, 94; clashes with Greek government, 62, 86, 90–92, 98, 108, 177, 206; clashes with junta, 169, 183–84; and election, 51; and London-Zurich agreements, 64, 85, 88, 90–93, 178; overthrow, 188–90; postindependence strategy, 85–86, 98, 178, 184–85; relationship with George Papandreou, 106, 176; relationship with Karamanlis, 60, 62–63, 83, 86, 90–91; restoration as president, 192–94; seeks special relationship with United States, 60, 85–87, 178–79, 183–84; Thirteen Points, 92–93, 95; view of enosis, 98, 107–8, 184; visits to Washington, 88, 182
Manifest Destiny, 2
Mansfield, Mike, 193
Markezinis, Spyridon, 35, 40, 113, 129, 133, 171–73
Marshall, George, 27
Marshall Plan (European Recovery Program), vii, 24–25, 31–32
Matsas, Alexander, 18–19, 102
Maury, Jack, 122; on coup, 148; proposes covert action, 130; warns against coup, 129
Mavros, George, 127
McCaskill, Charles, 89
McCloskey, Robert, 194
McGhee, George, 30, 69
McNamara, Robert, 148
McNeill, William, x

Megali idea, 3, 13, 54
Mehmet II (sultan of Ottoman Empire), 3
Menderes, Adnan, 53–54, 57
Metaxas, Ioannis, 102
Metaxas, Petros, 28, 34
Military coup (1967), 132–35; responsibility for, 134–35
Military junta: and Cyprus policy, 177
Miller, Henry, 11
Minor, Harold, 27, 34
Mitsotakis, Constantine, 115, 118, 121–22
Mouzelis, Nikos, 17
Murphy, Robert, 60

Napoleon I, 1
Napoleon III, 2
National Security Agency (NSA), 179
National Security Council (NSC), 31, 54, 69
Neff, Eric, 181
Nixon, Richard, 155, 202; and Cyprus, 54, 181–82, 194; Cyprus discussions with Kissinger, 191, 193–94; policy toward Greece, 155–58, 162, 167, 203; resignation, 199–200; snubs Constantine II, 159; and Tasca, 167, 196; visits Greece, 159
North Atlantic Treaty Organization (NATO), vii, 69, 72, 204

Othon (Otto; king of Greece), 5–6, 15–16
Ottoman Empire, 1, 3–5, 13–18, 45–46
Owens, John, 67

PAK (Pan Hellenic Liberation Movement), 136, 141
Palmer, Richmond, 49–50
Panagoulis, Alexander, 180
Papadopoulos, George, 23, 94, 132, 161–63, 166, 203, 206; challenges to rule of, 170–71; as coup leader, 149–51; creates presidential republic, 171–73; death sentence voided, 208; effect of ouster on Cyprus policy, 185; expands power, 167–69; letter to Johnson, 154; letter to Nixon, 163; overthrown, 173
Papadopoulos, Tassos, 181
Papagos, Alexander, 25–26, 30, 35, 39, 41, 47; Cyprus issue, 42, 50, 58; death, 58, 68; relationship with royal family, 25–26, 30, 33–36, 38–39, 41–42, 67–68
Papaligouras, Panagiotis, 116
Papandreou, Andreas, xi, 18, 23–24, 115, 118, 143, 158, 171, 206; anti-Americanism of, 118–19, 130, 141, 173–74, 203; arrest and imprisonment, 138–40; and ASPIDA, 116–17; crisis of 1965–67, 124–27; dismisses military coup, 133; efforts to influence U.S. policy, 119, 159; exile, 140–42; parliamentary immunity issue, 13; political ideas, 118, 125, 146; political resurrection, 136–37; as prime minister, 209–11; responsibility for coup, 134–35; U.S. evaluations of, 113–14, 119; writing history, x, 137–38, 142–46, 155–56
Papandreou, George, xi, 14, 27, 24, 36, 39, 82, 100–101, 103, 112–13, 145, 205–6; Acheson mediation, 101–5, 107; and ASPIDA, 116, 120; claims United States involved in vote fraud, 77–79; clashes with Andreas Papandreou, 124, 129, 140–41; Cyprus policy, 97–99, 106, 176–77; on EK, 79; election strategy (1964), 113; London meetings, 103–4; and Makarios, 93–94, 97, 99, 103–5;

INDEX   299

meets de Gaulle, 103; political crisis of 1965–67, 124–25, 127–34; rebuilding the center, 75–76; relationship with Paul I, 79, 82–83, 114, 133, 139; relations with military, 115, 120; returns Grivas to Cyprus, 97, 99; seeks U.S. intervention, 127–28, 130; seeks U.S. support, 75–76; sends Greek forces to Cyprus, 99

Papandreou, Margaret, 124, 133, 143; congressional testimony of, 167; memoir, 144; mobilizes aid for Andreas Papandreou, 138–40

Pappas, Tom, 143, 154; helps junta, 159–60, 165, 173

Paraskevopoulos, John, 83, 94, 129, 131

Patriarchate of Constantinople, 12, 14

Pattakos, Stylianos, 149, 163, 208; interview with Andreas Papandreou, 140; role in coup, 132, 150; Washington talks, 159–60

Paul I (king of Greece), 25, 114; death, 98, 113–14; and Papagos, 15, 26–27, 33–36, 39, 67; and Plastiras, 26–34; and U.S. government, 27, 30, 38–39

Peisistratus, 136

"Pericles" plan, 115–16

Peurifoy, John, 23–24, 29, 35, 42, 56, 67

Pipinelis, Panagiotis, 82, 83, 92, 129; and Cyprus, 180; as foreign minister in military junta, 158; Washington visit, 159–60

Plastiras, Nikolaos, 23, 33–34, 37–39, 41; conflict with Paul I, 26–34

Polytechnic Institute of Athens, 173

Popper, David, 181, 183–84

Porter, Paul, 20–21

Progressive Party, 113

Ralles, George, 164, 208

Rockwell, Stuart, 155

Rogers, William, 157; recommends policy changes, 171; visits Athens, 170

Rosenthal, Benjamin, 166

Rossides, Zenon, 88

Rostow, Walt, 130; recommends post-coup policy, 146, 149

Roundtree, William, 38

Rousseas, Stephen, 142–43

Rusk, Dean, 67, 100, 130, 146, 148

Samson, Nikos, 189, 192

Saunders, Harold, 160

Schlesinger, Arthur, Jr., 142

Sellers, Peter, 24

Seraphim (archbishop), 187

Silva, Walter, 170

Sisco, Joseph, 171, 192, 194

Smith, Michael Llewellyn, 163–64

Spandidakis, Gregory, 147

Stearns, Monteagle, 75, 78–79, 197–98, 202, 207

Stephanopoulos, Stefanos, 78, 123, 124; Cyprus policy, 176–77

Storrs, Ronald, 48–49

Suez Crisis, 52, 61, 63

Sulzberger, Cyrus L., 139; on post-coup U.S. policy, 147, 155; talks with Pattakos, 149

Tacitus, vii, xii

Taksim (partition), 90

Talbot, Phillips, 126; analyses of Greek situation, 129–34; on Andreas Papandreou, 127, 133; and Constantine II's countercoup, 153–54; meetings with king, 132–33, 153; reaction to coup, 147–48; securing Andreas Papandreou's safety, 138, 140; suggests accommodation with junta, 152–55

Tasca, Henry, 157, 161–62; congressional appearances, 167, 174; on

Cyprus issue, 9, 184, 186–87, 189–90; meeting with Karamanlis, 168; relations with Greek opposition, 162, 164, 167–68; relationship with Papadopolous, 162, 165, 169, 171–72; removed, 207; reports on Greece, 162–63; role in Greece, 165; support for Karamanlis, 173, 196; urges policy change, 173–75
Theodorakis, Mikis, 23
Theotokas, George, 11, 16
303 Committee, 130, 143
Treaty of Lausanne (1923), 5, 54
Trikoupis, Kharilaos, 7, 14
Truman, Harry, 20–23; concern with Greek human rights, 31; concern with Greek political situation, 32–33, 37
Truman Doctrine, vii, 28, 32
Tsirimokos, Elias, 123
Twain, Mark, 11

United States: anticommunist policy, vii, ix, 19–21, 30, 56–57, 66, 85; Cyprus policy, 51–52, 56–57, 59–62, 177–83, 188–95; economic assistance to Greece, 32–33; effort to internationalize aid to Greece, 39, 72; estimate of George Papandreou, 109–10, 126, 133–34; interventions, ix, 19–21, 24, 33–36, 38–39; "mission," 2, 14–15; nonintervention policy, 67, 78, 112, 126–27, 129–30; policy critiqued, 28–30, 203–5; post-1974 policy, 204, 207; reconstruction of Greek democratic opposition, 72–73; reduction of aid to Greece, 24, 30, 69, 71; rejects covert actions, 123, 130; relationship with Europe, viii–ix; response to coup, 147–49; seeks Andreas Papandreou's release, 138–40, 152; sources of power, vii; support for modernization, vii; support for Papagos and Karamanlis, 36, 66–67, 71–72
U.S. Congress: examines U.S. policy toward Greece, 166
USIA (United States Information Agency), 65

Vance, Cyrus, 130, 178
Vance mediation, 178–80
Van Fleet, James, 25, 30, 34
Venizelos, Eleftherios, 48, 210
Venizelos, Sofokles, 27, 33, 35, 37–38, 75–76, 113, 206; character and career, 4–5, 8; clashes with United States, 28, 34, 76; mediation, 78–79; Washington visit, 83, 93
Vitsaxis, Basil, 161

Watergate, 170, 187; impact on Cyprus policy, 186, 187–88, 199–200, 202
Wilkins, Fraser, 91–92
Williams, William A., 142
Wilson, Harold, 186; meeting with Nixon, 164
Wilson, Woodrow, 2, 47
Wolseley, Lord, 44

Zoitakis, George, 169
Zumwalt, Elmo, 168–69

www.ingramcontent.com/pod-product-compliance
Lightning Source LLC
Chambersburg PA
CBHW030107010526
44116CB00005B/131